THE STORY

OF A

THOUSAND.

Being a history of the Service of the 105th Ohio Volunteer Infantry, in the War for the Union from August 21, 1862 to June 6, 1865.

BY

ALBION W. TOURGÉE, LL. D.

BUFFALO:
S. McGERALD & SON.
1896.

PREFACE.

The Story of a Thousand is intended to be what the name imports, a story of the service of the 105th Regiment of Ohio Volunteer Infantry in the War of Rebellion, dealing with events of a general interest to all its members rather than with mere personal incident. While it is true that personal incident may be of especial interest to the survivors, the general public and even our immediate descendants, are less concerned about such matters than the general character of the service. I have therefore, endeavored to restrict personal incident almost entirely to illustrative events common to the experience of all.

Fortunately perhaps, the regiment whose history I was asked to write was one in which personal adventure cut a remarkably small figure. In its whole history there is hardly an instance of individual contact with an enemy. There are no startling experiences to relate, no deeds of special daring or hair-breadth escapes. Except Captain Wallace's rush after an escaping spy on the 17th of November, 1864, striking him with the hilt of his saber with such force as to break the guard and render his recapture easy, there is hardly a case of individual conflict. One other officer was saved from a personal encounter with a confederate in the charge made at Chickamauga, by a shot from one of the men. But as a rule, while all experienced many pleasant and unpleasant episodes, they were not of a character to be of general interest or importance. As my own individual recollections end with December 1863, I have endeavored, so far as possible, to allow others to give in their own words, the personal element of the subsequent service.

In this, I have been greatly assisted by the journals of Comrades Parker, Warner, Saddler and Captain Mansfield. Also by extracts from the diaries of Captains Cummings and Wilcox and the remarkable series of letters something near a hundred in all, written during the service by Commissary Sergeant Gibson to his wife. Lieutenant Forbis has given me the benefit of his recollections in regard to the experiences of our foragers and the religious element in the life of the regiment. Comrades Griste, Wm. O. Smith, Nesbitt and many others have by correspondence and otherwise rendered material service in the preparation of the work. To all I desire to express my hearty thanks.

To the newspaper history of the regiment prepared by Comrade Chas. K. Radcliffe I am under great obligation for lightening many labors. By some slip of memory the biographical sketch accompanying his portrait alludes to him as having been captured with the forage-train, though he was not one of that detail.

For the preparation of the Roster and Tables giving all the details of the service of each man with an accuracy, fullness and completeness, hardly ever attempted, I am under the greatest obligation to Comrades Parker and Maynard, the two men whose personal knowledge was most extensive, perhaps, of the personnel of the regiment, who kindly gave of their time and labor to carry out the plan devised. I am also, under especial obligation to Comrade Maynard, as Secretary of the Survivors' Association of the regiment.

I beg to acknowledge the great service which the "History of the Seventy-fifth Indiana," so long our brigade-companion, written by Rev. B. Floyd, has been in the preparation of this work.

Acknowledgment is especially due to Senator John P. Jones of Nevada for books and maps without which the accomplishment of the work would have been well-nigh impossible. Also, to the Adjutant-General of Ohio, who kindly placed the records of his office at my disposal and to Mr. Arthur R. Warren who copied the original muster rolls there on file for the correction of the Roster. Also to Major Stoddard Johnston, who was a member of the staff of General Braxton Bragg of the confederate army, for valuable suggestions touching the campaign in Kentucky.

The Itinerary showing the location of the regiment during every day of its service, was made up from the journal of Comrade L. N. Parker, in some instances corrected and made more definite by comparison with the journal of Comrade Joseph R. Warner. Both of these journals are well-worthy of being printed without note or comment, as interesting memorials of experience recorded at the time the events narrated occurred. The Itinerary is believed to be as correct as it can be made.

One difficulty experienced in preparing the history of this regiment, has been a singular lack of reports of its movements and service. No reports are accessible, if they were made, of the part it took in the Tullahoma campaign, the Chickamauga campaign, Missionary Ridge, the Atlanta campaign, the March to the Sea or the campaign in the Carolinas. Major Edwards is confident that he made a report of the Chickamauga engagement and it is beyond question that Col. Tolles must have made a report of Missionary Ridge, but it has been impossible to get sight of either. The former was probably among papers lost by the transfer of General Reynolds from the command of the division to the place of chief of staff to General Thomas. The excellent portrait of General Thomas, was loaned by Messrs. Coates & Co., of Philadelphia, whose large engraving is no doubt the best portrait in existence of our old commander. The illustration "The Bummers" is from that exquisite collection of war pictures entitled "Bullet and Shell" by Major Williams, illustrated by Edwin Forbes and published by Fords, Howard and Hulbert, New York.

PREFACE.

The maps of Perryville and the vicinity of Chattanooga, were re-drawn from the official charts by Mr Leon J Robbins the gifted son of Adjutant Robbins The other illustrations not direct reproductions and the illuminated initials are the gratuitous work of Miss Aimée Tourgée, the author's daughter, who also supervised the reproduction of photographs many of which required to be re-touched before being available

It is possible that some may be surprised at the absence of amusing narratives of personal experience more or less reliable, which so often form a considerable portion of such works In explanation of this fact, I can only say that I carefully treasured up all such incidents reported to me by my comrades and found so large a proportion of them had long since become stock-anecdotes of war literature that they seemed likely to arouse a suspicion of plagiarism The truth is that this mass of war anecdotes has grown so large that it is hard to designate just where the line of proprietorship runs I have, therefore been rather chary of their use, confining myself to some cases of unquestionable originality Survivors will note that one unpleasant incident has been wholly omitted. This was done from a conviction both that no good could result from its consideration and also because the person most affected by it, was in some sense, the victim of a conspiracy not creditable to those concerned in it Moreover as the record shows he subsequently removed the imputation resting upon him by gallant service

It was the purpose of the author to give an account of the District Committee who had charge of recruiting in the XIXth Congressional District of Ohio To secure the necessary data he addressed letters to parties in each of the counties asking them to procure photographs and such information as was available regarding the members of said committee For some reason quite inexplicable to him, there seemed to be but little interest in the matter He was unable to secure anything like a full account of their work and not wishing to publish an imperfect one, the whole matter was omitted The work of these voluntary organizations ought not to be lost sight of in making up the history of that epoch but a defective account would be sure to do injustice to all

The omission of any specific account of those who suffered in the southern prisons is due to two things The writer exerted himself to the utmost in connection with Comrade L Newton Parker to secure from each of the surviving prisoners of Andersonville and other prisons an account of their experience Being himself one of the three officers of the regiment who had such experience he did for a time contemplate writing an account of the same When he came to consider it more fully, however, he concluded that it would savor too much of the personal to be compatible with the general tone of the work To do so would have required him to go into the whole question of the treatment of prisoners, which at this day could be of little interest and no value One thought in connection with it may be ventured, the Union soldier who was held as a prisoner of war for any time has the consolation of knowing that by keeping a confederate of equal rank, out of the service he was, on account of the disparity of numbers doing even greater service to the Union cause than he would probably have done had he remained in his place As to the treatment of Union prisoners he regards the subject as one not profitable to be considered within such limits as could reasonably be allowed it in this work

The printing was done by Messrs S McGerald & Son of Buffalo, N Y under very embarrassing circumstances, in a manner which speaks for itself

The work has been delayed by sickness and the stress of financial conditions which have rendered its manufacture exceedingly difficult The same would have been impossible but for the liberality of Colonel George T. Perkins

The writer undertook the work with diffidence he has spared no pains in its execution, and whatever its defects may be he can only say it is the best that he was able to do

Mayville, N Y, Dec 1, 1895 THE AUTHOR

TABLE OF CONTENTS.

APPENDIX

LIST OF ILLUSTRATIONS.

LIST OF MAPS.

RECORD OF SERVICE.

Perryville, October 8, 1862

Milton, March 20, 1862

Hoover's Gap, June 24, 1863

Chickamauga September 19—20, 1863

Siege of Chattanooga, September 23—November 25, 1863

Missionary Ridge, November 25, 1863

Resaca, May 14—15, 1864

Kenesaw Mountain, June 27, 1864

Siege of Atlanta, July—August 1864

Peach Tree Creek, July 20, 1864

Ezra Church, July 27, 1864

Jonesborough, September 1, 1864

Pursuit of Hood, October 1864

March to the Sea, November—December 1864

Campaign in the Carolinas, February–March 1865

Johnston's Surrender, April 26 1865

THE STORY OF A THOUSAND.

I

THE MUSTER IN.

"The bayonets were a thousand,
And the swords were thirty-seven,
When we took the oath of service,
With our right-hands raised to Heaven."

IT was the twenty-first day of August, 1862, when our story opens. On that day the Thousand became a unit. The scene is a neglected common near the city of Cleveland in the State of Ohio. It is called University Heights now—then, it was officially known as "Camp Taylor." Its surroundings were squalid. Pigs and thistles abounded. A dozen or two long, low buildings, a guard line and a flagstaff constituted the camp. The buildings were one-story affairs, made of rough hemlock; for the most part, they were sixty feet in length and twenty in width. On each side were rows of bunks, six feet long by three and one-half feet wide, with an eight-inch board running along the front to keep the occupants from rolling out. They were quaint-looking troughs, filled with nothing, save air and splinters; but they were new and clean and sweet, those we occupied, at least—with the breath of the forest and the dust of the sawmill about them. The amber of the riven hemlock oozed out and trickled down in sticky streaks as the hot summer sun beat upon the yellow roofs and sides.

It is ten o'clock. The sun glares fiercely down though there is a breeze from the north that keeps the flag upon the high mast, near the entrance of the camp, softly waving its bright benison above its crude surroundings. Oh beautiful banner! what desert doth it not make bright! How many have its gleaming folds lured on to death! How often glazing orbs have turned lovingly up to it their last glance!

The fifes and drums have ceased to sound. The parade is formed—after a fashion. Two straggling, uncertain lines of unarmed blue-clad men stretch across the uneven field; a group of musicians, with a few fifes and drums, are in their places on the right; the men stand at parade rest with hands clasped loosely before them; the sun beats hot on the glowing napes, which the military caps, just donned for the first time, have left unprotected—the sweat-drops creep down hot, flushed faces; many an eye wanders longingly to the blue, sparkling waves of Lake Erie, of which one might catch a distant glimpse.

A man in the uniform of a captain of the United States Army and one in the uniform of a colonel of Volunteers pass along the line, halting here and there while a clerk calls the names of each company and checks the same upon the rolls, which are carried by an orderly. There are frequent discussions, in which the company's officers take part. Men are shifted from one company to another, until finally all are in their proper places. There is about the line that uneasiness and uncertainty of pose which marks the untrained soldier, and that general looseness of formation which is inseparable from a parade without arms.

When the required changes have been made, the man in the uniform of the Regular Army takes his place in front of the center of the line; behind him his clerk and orderly, and beside him the man in a colonel's uniform.

"Attention!"

ALBERT S. HALL.

ALBERT S. HALL, the first and only man commissioned and mustered as colonel of the 105th regiment of Ohio Volunteers, was born in Charleston, Portage county, Ohio, in 1830, of which town his grandfather was one of the first settlers. He was educated in the district schools of that county and at Geauga Seminary, Chester, Ohio, supporting himself by teaching. He studied law and was admitted to the bar in 1853, and located in Jefferson, Ashtabula county. In 1853 he was chosen prosecuting attorney of said county and again in 1857. In 1859 he removed to Minneapolis, Minnesota, but returned to his native State in 1860, and settled in Warren, Trumbull county. Upon the call for volunteers in April, 1861, he began to raise a company, and early in June was mustered in as captain of Company F of the 20th O. V. I. The regiment

The long blue line sways and rustles as the men straighten themselves into a more or less correct position, take touch of elbows, glance right and left to secure a better alignment, and wonderingly gaze to the front to see what will happen next. A group of spectators, among whom are a few ladies, who carry parasols, stand in front of the right wing. They are evidently interested in what is going on. Some of them intercept the mustering officer's view of that part of the line; he orders them back, but the group is a considerable one and do not understand what is wanted of them. An orderly is sent to repeat the command and see that it is obeyed. The crowd fall back willingly but wonderingly. Then the officer explains that, when the command is given, each one whose name has been called—officers and men alike—will take off his cap with the left hand and holding up his right one with the open palm to the front, repeat after him the oath of service. Then came the command:

"Hats off!"

---

left Camp Chase on July 26, 1861. The first engagement was the battle of Cheat Mountain, W. Va. Captain Hall served through that campaign, and on the 20th of December, 1861, was commissioned major. His regiment was transferred to the Army of the Mississippi and was engaged in the battle of Shiloh, April 6 and 7, 1862. Near the close of the second day's fight, being then in command of his regiment, he received a gunshot wound some two inches above the eyebrow. The wound was a severe one, and before he was able to rejoin his regiment again he was promoted to lieutenant-colonel, and on the 12th of June following, appointed colonel of the 105th. After the battle of Perryville he was for eight days in command of the Tenth Division of the Army of Ohio, being the senior officer of the division after that disastrous fight until General C. C. Gilbert was assigned to its command. After that time, he commanded the Thirty-third Brigade until the organization of the Army of the Cumberland, November 30, 1862. After this, he continued in the command of the same brigade then known as the Second Brigade, Fifth Division, 14th Army Corps, until his death. He was in independent command on several raids and at the battle of Milton, Tennessee, where he repulsed the Confederate General John H. Morgan in command of superior numbers, with great loss. He was attacked with typhoid fever, about the 20th of June, 1863, complicated with the effects of his old wound, of which he died on the 10th of July succeeding, at Murfreesborough, Tennessee. His son, the Hon. Charles L. Hall, is at present (1895) a Judge of the District Court of Nebraska. Colonel Hall was an officer of untiring energy, a strict disciplinarian, and had his life been spared would no doubt have achieved very high distinction in the service. The above engraving is from a crayon portrait by Lieutenant Alden F. Brooks, now a distinguished artist of Chicago.

There is a scuffling in the ranks, each one looking to see if his neighbor has obeyed A good many take off the cap with right hand and have to shift it to the left The crowd titters at the many mistakes

"Hands up!"

Some raise the right hand and some the left The officers look around and correct mistakes Near the middle of the line an intensely red head shows nigh a foot above the line of other heads on either side and a red-bearded face looks calmly over the head of the officer whose station is directly in his front

"Steady!" commands the Regular Army officer, running his eye sharply along the wavering ill-dressed line

"Get down!" he says, as his eye reaches the red head that overtops its neighbors The red face turns one way and the other in wondering search of what has awakened the officer's displeasure. All the other faces in the line turn also

"You man in the Fifth Company there, with the red beard get down off that stump!"

A titter runs along the line Everyone knows what has happened A shout goes up from the spectators Some of the officers laugh The Colonel steps forward and says something in an undertone to the mustering officer The officer looks foolish The red-bearded face ducks a few inches nearer the line of heads about it The face is redder than ever. It was not Jerry Whetstone's fault that his comrades only came up to his shoulder Yet many thousand times on the march and in the camp—before he marches up the Avenue, in the grand review, with his unerring rifle all out of line with the pieces of the little squad which are all that remains of the company—will the great good-natured giant be exhorted to "Get off that stump!" And not once will the injunction fail to raise a laugh no matter how weary those may be who hear it

When the merriment has subsided, the officer directs that all repeat with him the oath of service, each giving his own name when the officer should repeat his.

"I, James R. Paxton, —

A wave of confused murmurs rose from the long lines.

"—Do solemnly swear,"—continued the officer.

The response was heavier and more uniform than before.

"—That I will bear true faith and allegiance—"

Firm and full came the thousand-fold echo.

"—To the United States of America—

An exultant shout went up.

"That I will serve them honestly and faithfully—

How earnest the solemn pledge!

"Against all their enemies whomsoever—

How soon was trial of their sincerity to be made!

"That I will obey the orders of the President of the United States—"

What greater privilege could await one!

"And of the officers appointed over me—"

Obedience is a soldier's duty!

"—According to the Rules and Articles of War!"

What did they include? No matter!

There was a brief pause and the mustering officer added—

"So help me God!"

A solemn reverent murmur came in response.

Then the officer said, with that mixture of smartness and dignity with which a well-disciplined man performs an important routine act:

"—By authority vested in me, I, James R. Paxton, Captain of the Fifteenth Infantry and Mustering Officer of the Department of Ohio, do hereby declare the officers and men of the 105th Regiment of Ohio Volunteer Infantry duly mustered into the service of the United States, to serve for the period of three years or during the war, unless sooner discharged!"

Hardly had the words escaped his lips when the drums rolled, the spectators cheered, the flag was dipped upon the mast, the one gun beside the gate fired a clamorous salute, caps were swung in air, and with the oath of service fresh on their lips, and their right hands yet uplifted the newly-constituted regiment cheered—itself! It must have been itself, since there was nothing else for them to cheer. The sun shone on the bared heads, men clasped each other's hands in earnest gratulation, and there was a hint of tears upon many glistening lids!

The colonel, who had hitherto stood beside the mustering officer now took two steps forward, drew his sword from its sheath, brought it smartly to the shoulder and with a voice rarely excelled for smoothness and evenness of tone and perhaps unequalled in the whole army for distinctness and carrying power, commanded:

"Atten—tion! One Hundred and Fifth—*Ohio*!"

Was it admiration for the soldierly figure, so strikingly resembling in form and feature the portraits of the great Napoleon, the thrill of that marvellous voice they were to hear so often when other voices were unable to pierce the din of strife, or the exquisite modulation which even in command complimented those who stood before him on their newly assumed character, that so quickly hushed the turmoil? An hour before they had been merely a thousand men, now they were "The One Hundred and Fifth Regiment of Ohio Volunteer Infantry," and a part of that Grand Army which Liberty threw across the path of secession, slavery and revolt which threatened the nation's life. All this and more, was conveyed by subtle intonation in the colonel's first command. There was an instant's silence, after each man had restored his cap to its place and stiffened himself into the position of the soldier. Then there was another spontaneous outburst. This time it was the colonel who was cheered. He acknowledged it with a salute, and then commanded sharply and sternly:

"Attention—to orders!"

A smart young officer who had stood a little to the rear of the Colonel, stepped briskly around him, advanced to a position midway between him and the lines and drew a package of papers from his belt. At the same time the Colonel commanded "Parade Rest!" The Adjutant read an order, announcing that "Albert S. Hall, having been appointed Colonel of the 105th Regiment Ohio Volunteer Infantry, hereby assumes command of the same." Then he read another order, announcing the field and staff, and the assignment of line officers to the various companies of said regiment.

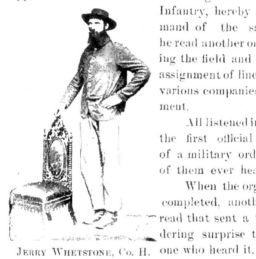

JERRY WHETSTONE, Co. H. Six feet seven inches in height. The tallest man in the army of the Cumberland.

All listened intently to this, the first official promulgation of a military order, that most of them ever heard.

When the organization was completed, another order was read that sent a thrill of wondering surprise through every one who heard it.

It was a telegram from the Governor:

"COLONEL ALBERT S. HALL, 105th O. V. I.

The enemy have invaded Kentucky. You will report with your regiment to Major-General H. G. Wright, commanding Department of Ohio, at Cincinnati, without an instant's delay. Camp and garrison equipage will be forwarded to meet you there.

DAVID TOD, Governor."

It was high noon when the ranks were broken. Sixty minutes afterwards, the regiment was on the march to the depot, and two hours later, was being whirled away to the theater of war.

It takes one's breath away, in these days of peace, when the soldier is recalled only as a pensioner, who is counted a thankless burden to the government to think that men were hurried forward, unarmed, without an hour's instruction in their new duties, to be placed across the path of a victorious enemy But nothing seemed surprising then, and if any were inclined to murmur an instinctive sense of duty overbore their discontent Yet if ever a soldier has a right to complain when once the oath of service has passed his lips, these men surely had It was but eight days since the first of them had left their homes, but forty-six of their number had ever seen an hour's service, hardly half of the companies had had more than three or four hours of drill, and one of them, at least, only one hour! But nothing was strange in those days of miracle and self-forgetfulness! If there was any disposition to complain it was voiced only when they found themselves blamed for lacking the discipline they were given no opportunity to acquire

II.

THE CAUSE OF STRIFE.

"'Tis the motive enfames, not the beggarly prize,
The spirit that lives, the base guerdon that dies."

THE causes from which events result are often of greater consequence than the events themselves. Nations and peoples, like individuals, act always from motives; and collective motives, like personal ones, may be either good or bad. Peoples differ from individuals, however, in one thing,—they are always sincere. They may desire a good thing or a bad one, but there is no question of bad faith in the demand for which men offer their lives upon the field of battle. Words may be false; leaders may seek to deceive; but what a people write in blood upon the page of history, is always true.

It is because of this that the comparative importance of historical events depends very little upon their physical extent, but almost wholly upon the motives of the actors or the sentiment they represent.

Only a few times was the conduct of the Thousand, considered of itself, of any special importance; only once was it pivotal of the issue of a great event. But why

COL. WILLIAM R. TOLLES.

WILLIAM RANSOM TOLLES was born in Watertown, Ct., April 10, 1823. His parents removed to Burton, Geauga County, O., while he was a lad. He came of sturdy New England stock, and after obtaining a common school education, he early engaged in business, and up to the outbreak of the war was active in the promotion of public and private enterprises in the country. He was a merchant in Burton for many years. After the death of his wife, a daughter of Judge Hitchcock, he disposed of his business, being considerably broken in health, and traveled through the South, as the agent of firms doing

these men took the oath of service, what manner of men they were, and what controlling impulse they typified, these things are of deathless import, for on them the destiny of a nation hung and the character of a people's civilization depended

---

business there until just before the beginning of hostilities He was greatly disturbed over the condition of affairs, especially regarding the general idea that the war would be one of short duration He was one of the first to volunteer, and was made captain of Company F, 41st O V I He participated in all the operations of this regiment and often expressed himself peculiarly grateful that his first experience of army life was under so strict and thorough a disciplinarian as its commander, Colonel, afterwards Major-General William B Hazen Promoted to lieutenant-colonel of the 105th he carried to the performance of its duties a painstaking conscientiousness which though at times irksome, contributed not a little to the excellence of drill and discipline for which it was noted throughout its term of service

The command of the regiment was thrown upon him by the command of the Tenth Division being cast on Colonel Hall by the death of his superiors at the battle of Perryville, on the 48th day of the regiment's service and his continuance in command of the brigade thereafter From that time until the middle of June 1863 Colonel Tolles was in command of the regiment and was untiring in promoting its drill and discipline He was unable to serve in the advance from Murfreesborough, but rejoined at Chattanooga, just in time for the battle of Missionary Ridge, which was the fitting climax of his military career No nobler figure is to be found in that most spectacular of battles than this gallant soldier riding his black horse up that flame-swept slope, keeping his eye on his regiment and constantly directing its movements His health constantly grew worse, and on January 29, 1864, the indomitable will was forced to relinquish the hope of farther service, and he resigned After his health was somewhat regained, he removed to Locata, Mich, where he remained for several years, during which time he remarried His health again failing he removed to the San Bernardino Valley Cal, where he continued to reside, highly honored and esteemed until his death, on December —, 1893

As an officer, he was an excellent disciplinarian and a splendid tactician somewhat irritable, somewhat hasty, and as a consequence, not always just there was no one under his command who doubted his unselfish patriotism or his intense desire that the regiment should excel in every soldierly quality and achievement As a man he was exquisitely sensitive, and no doubt often mistook the jests of his men and so failed to appreciate the affection and esteem they had for him

There are those who will recall the fact that the personal relations between Colonel Tolles and Lieutenant Tourgee were not such as would seem consistent with the above estimate of his character No doubt, his ill health had much to do with the prejudices which he entertained, which were in many cases as he afterwards explained to the writer, strengthened by false reports from others While it would be absurd to claim that the wrong is forgotten the writer can truly say that all sense of resentment has passed away and the estimate he gives of the character of Colonel Tolles, is that to which he believes him to have been actually entitled He had his faults but they were subordinate incidents rather than controlling elements of his character

Where a battle is fought and when, who are the opposing commanders, what strategic movements preceded it what tactical methods were employed, how many of the contestants were slain, which army prevailed, and which was put to rout,—all these are in-significant details Whether ten or ten thousand lives were lost is of little consequence. In half a dozen years of growth and bloom, nature will have hidden all trace of the encounter The rain will wash away the blood, the grass will hide the bleached bones, the trees will shadow the graves, the waving grain will obliterate the track of charging squadrons In like manner nature's recuperative power will soon fill up the gaps in the world's life A decade, two decades at the farthest, and the most skillful statistician cannot trace anything of war's havoc in the tables of mortality. But why they fought, why men were mangled and slain, why a thousand or a million men risked their lives in deadly strife, which impulse prevailed and which was forced to yield,—these are questions of the utmost concern, for they may indicate the character of a people, and involve the destiny of unnumbered millions yet unborn History, in the past, has concerned itself with aggregations and events. It has told us how

> "The King of France, with twice ten thousand men,
> Marched up the hill,—and then marched down again"

The history of the future will be more concerned to know why the "twice ten thousand" followed the crowned braggart "up the hill," than in the reasons that inclined them to march "down again,"—it will deal with causes rather than with events.

A year and a half before the time of which we write, one of the most momentous events in history had occurred The great American republic had suddenly fallen asunder. Almost in an instant, eleven states had formally declared the territory of each withdrawn from the control of the Federal union, and their people released from allegiance to the Government of the United States. Almost simultaneously with the act of withdrawal, these states had, with equal formality, banded themselves together and formed what they called "The Confederate States of America" a new government composed of eleven contiguous states, having the same boundaries, the same integral character, and in most cases, the same officials, as when they were constituent parts of the Federal union In a hundred days from the time the first rift appeared, the revolution was complete

A territory nearly equal in extent to all Europe, outside of the Empire of Russia, having a population of twelve million souls, had been cut out of the domain previously claimed and occupied by the United States, and erected into a *de facto* government, complete in all its parts, without the firing of a gun or the shedding of a drop of blood! Only three forts upon its utmost borders still bore the flag of the Union!

Of all the miracles of revolution, there have been none like it for boldness of conception, extent, completeness rapidity of execution, and absolutely bloodless character On the twentieth of December, 1860, South Carolina passed the ordinance of secession On February 4, 1861 forty-five days afterwards, the Provisional Congress met—six states were represented in it On the eighth, a constitution was adopted, on the ninth, a president was chosen, on the fourteenth, another state was added, on the eighteenth, the president was inaugurated. Before the month was ended, the executive departments and an army and navy were organized Thus far, the tide of revolution had met with no resistance from within, and no movement of repression from without

How was such marvel made possible? Volumes have been written in explanation Yet, a few words will suffice to make it clear.

There had grown up within the Union, two peoples They called themselves "the North" and "the South" The one believed that "all men were created equal and

COL. GEORGE T. PERKINS.

GEORGE TOD PERKINS was born near the city of Akron, O., May 5, 1836, on a farm afterwards occupied for some years by John Brown, of Harper's Ferry fame. His parents were Simon and Grace Tod Perkins. His grandfather on the maternal side was the first Chief Justice of Ohio, and father of her great war governor, David Tod. On the paternal side his great-grandfather was a captain in the war of the Revolution, and his grandfather a brigadier-general in the war of 1812. He was educated in the public schools of Akron and at Marietta College. At the outbreak of the war he was engaged in the iron business at Youngstown, O., in company with his uncle, Hon. David Tod, soon afterwards elected governor.

With such an ancestry it was inevitable that he should be among the first to respond to the call to arms, and it is characteristic of the man, the section

endowed with certain inalienable rights among which are life liberty, and the pursuit of happiness.' The other believed that such rights attached only to white men, and that colored men were entitled only to such privileges as the white people of any particular state might see fit to confer upon them. One section was composed of what were termed free-states, the other of what were known as slave-states. Between them, slavery dug a deep, almost impassable gulf. The lines of interstate migration ran chiefly from east to west. The South peopled the new states of the southwest, the North sent its sons and daughters to shape the sentiment of the northwest. Only the poor of the South fled into the free northwest, to escape the blight which slavery put upon the opportunity

---

from which he came, and the spirit of the time, that a young man of independent means and influential connections, such as he possessed, should have enlisted as a private soldier in Company B 19th O. V. I., in the three months' service. The men of his company afterwards elected him its 2d lieutenant. He participated with his regiment in the West Virginia campaigns, under McClellan, the same being especially prominent in the battle of Rich Mountain. Mustered out at the end of the three months service, he once more took up the routine of business. In 1862, upon the call for "three hundred thousand more," he laid down his pen, applied to his uncle the Governor, for a commission, and was appointed major of the 105th. He served as such until the advance from Murfreesborough in June 1863, when the command of the regiment fell upon him by reason of Colonel Tolles' absence. He held it from that time until the regiment was mustered out. He was promoted to lieutenant-colonel to date from the death of Colonel Hall, July 10, 1863, to colonel February 18 1864, but not mustered because the regiment was below the minimum required for a full set of field officers. He was made brevet lieutenant-colonel March 13, 1865 and was mustered out in command. He participated in nearly all its operations, was severely wounded at Chickamauga and had three horses killed under him, one at Perryville, one at Chickamauga, and one on the New Hope Church line, near Big Shanty, Ga.

As an officer he was quiet, unostentatious and especially noted for his unremitting care for the health and comfort of those under his command. He married soon after the close of the war and settled in business in Akron where he has remained ever since. He has been so successful a manufacturer and banker that he is now about to retire from business. He has one daughter and two grandchildren, without which he declares, "No home is well furnished." Colonel Perkins is regarded with peculiar fondness by the survivors of his regiment, whose re-unions he always attends but such is his modesty that few would imagine that he was its commanding officer for two years of active service. He has always been active in educational and municipal affairs. He is a member of the Ohio Commandery of the Loyal Legion.

of the white laborer only those who looked for special pecuniary advantage from speculation skilled employment or mechanical superintendence, went from the North to the South In but three of the states of the North, was one-tenth of the population of southern birth in 1860, in not one of the Southern States was one-fiftieth of the population of northern birth The two tides of life had flowed on from east to west, side by side, having one language, one religion, one name, but only mingling a little at the edges So dissimilar were they, that one said, from his place in the Senate that year "There are two hostile bodies on this floor which are but types of the feeling that exists between the two sections We are enemies as much as if we were hostile states I believe the northern people hate the South worse than the English ever hated the French and there is no love lost on the part of the South "

The cleavage, which first showed in the establishment of the Confederacy, had long existed in the characters of the two peoples and the divergent institutions of the two sections The laws, customs and institutions of the North were shaped by freemen in the furnace-heat of free-thought and free-speech. The public-school was everywhere, opportunity was untrammeled. The institutions, laws and policy of the South were shaped by slave-owners to promote the interests of the slave-holders, the free-laborer was despised. Every official belonged to the slave-owning class, free-schools were unknown, free-speech was repressed by the law and the mob To proclaim liberty was a crime in half the states of the republic, to teach a slave to read or write, a felony The North had come to hate slavery as a sin against God and a crime against man, the South counted the right to enslave inherent in the white race, by Divine ordainment, and resented the feeling against it at the North as the result of envy and malice They regarded the constitution as a compact between the States, specially intended for the preservation of this institution The people of the North generally regarded it as an agreement between the people of the several States for the benefit of all the people

There were, also two conflicting views of government which became potent factors in this miracle of seemingly peaceful dismemberment One insisted that the Government of the United States was a nation established by the people, and having all the powers of self-preservation, control of its citizens and defense of its territory which are incident to sovereignty. The other insisted that the United States were only a federation, a pact between the several states, each one of which remained sovereign and might at will withdraw from the Union ; and that allegiance to the state was paramount The southern man regarded every effort to re-establish the power of the general government as not only a blow at the rights of his State, but an invasion of her soil, as well as her sovereignty The border Southern States still hesitated more from fear of the consequences to themselves than from any lack of sympathy with the principle or purpose of secession The State-Sovereignty sentiment of the North and the dread that a people especially devoted to the arts of peace had of intestine war, kept the North silent and the government passive

Neither section appreciated the qualities of the people of the other. The North thought the people of the South were mere braggarts , the South thought those of the North were mercenary cowards The one regarded the new government as a piece of bravado, a mere bubble intended to extort concessions The other looked upon the apathy of the North as conclusive evidence that it would make no resistance to dismemberment Thus the two sections, long before estranged and separated by tendencies which raised a more insuperable barrier between them than sea or mountain could offer, taunted and jeered each other both unconscious of the bloody destiny that lay before them One counted it an immutable truth that all men had a right to be free, and regarded the other as an aggressor against this universal liberty, the other believed the white man's right to enslave to be indisputable and counted any imputation of this theory an invasion of individual privilege and collective prerogative. So, two peoples, acknowledging two governments, regarded each other askance over an intervening belt known as the "border states," whose people were divided in sentiment, some clinging to the old and others welcoming the new

Thus the country stood vaguely expectant, when on the twelfth day of April, 1861, the guns of the new Government opened on the flag of the old which waved over Fort Sumter Instantly, the shadows which had blinded the people of both sections were lifted All saw the gulf which separated them The North sprang to arms, the South exulted in the opportunity that lay before it to teach its ancient enemy the lesson of its superiority. The border states hastened to declare their preference Virginia, North Carolina and Tennessee went with the new Confederacy, making eleven states which acknowledged its supremacy Kentucky and Missouri remained with the old Union, formally, at least, but it was with a divided sentiment, which extended a hand to each of the opposing civilizations

So the battle was joined between slavery and "state-sovereignty" on one side, and liberty and nationality on the other The conflict was between two peoples, one regarding the other as rebels, and esteemed, in turn, by them as invaders Each, from its own point of view, was right, each, from the other's point of view, was wrong Precisely what "the fathers" meant by the words of the constitution will never be definitely known What an overruling providence intended, the outcome of strangely-ordered events leave us not in doubt Which of these two contrasted impulses was technically right in its construction of the instrument which both cited in support of their action will ever be a mooted problem, which stood for justice, the rights of man and the better civilization, the future will not question.

III.

RECRUITING.

SOME idea of the times and the character of the people of that day, especially in the region from which the Thousand was drawn, can be given by a brief outline of the method by which enlistments were secured. Recruiting, up to that time, in the State of Ohio was under the charge of a committee appointed by the Governor, in each Congressional District, one man in each county.* These men not only served without pay but often, perhaps always, at great personal sacrifice. They were usually men of mature years and decided character, but without political or selfish ambition. These men, each acting in his own county, with such as he might associate with him, adopted a policy of procedure for the district, assigned the quotas to the different towns, recommended officers, and, in short, formed a volunteer council, which was one of the many instances of voluntary organization to assist the government and supply the defects of

*—A full account of the Military Committee of the 19th District of Ohio will be found in the Appendix.

statutory provisions, which that period so rich in examples of the strength and efficacy of the self-governing idea, can afford.

Recruiting was effected by the officers thus appointed, through personal solicitation and the holding of what were

MAJ. CHAS. G. EDWARDS.

CHARLES G. EDWARDS was born at Sodus Point, N. Y., May 11, 1836. Received a good common school education; was employed as clerk in an importing house in New York City, in 1853; came to Youngstown, Ohio, in 1859, where he engaged in the drug business until the firing on Fort Sumter in 1861. In April of that year he enlisted in Company B, 19th Ohio Infantry in the three months' service. In June, 1862, was commissioned Captain of Company A 105th Ohio Volunteer Infantry; was wounded three times at Perryville, Ky. In May, 1863; was relieved of command of Company A and detailed as acting field officer; was commissioned major July 16, 1863, and lieutenant-colonel February 18, 1864, but not mustered because the regiment was below the limit entitling to a full set of officers. Was also brevetted

termed war-meetings, in connection with the county committee and with the aid of prominent citizens in the various towns. No pecuniary inducements were then offered to secure enlistments save the government bounty of one hundred dollars for three years' service, and the regular pay of thirteen dollars a month. To have appealed to the sense of personal advantage would have provoked only laughter. The farm-laborer was getting twice as much with board and all home comforts, as the soldier was offered to face the perils of war. Such a thing as treating or other convivial influence was almost wholly unknown as an element of the recruiting service. Very few of the young men who recruited the Thousand had any inclination if they had opportunity to employ such influences. As a matter of fact, to have done so would have destroyed all hope of success, for no Western Reserve mother and very few Western Reserve fathers would have permitted or encouraged their sons to entrust their lives to the control of an officer known to be an habitual drinker. The writer recruited the larger part of Company G, traveling from town to town, holding personal interviews by day and public meetings usually at night. In the month he was engaged in this service he held more than forty public meetings. Not once was the question of personal gain alluded to save in objection by some man who said he could not deprive his family of the earnings needful for their support. Well may they have demurred. Nearly a year afterwards one of these men gave the writer thirty-six dollars three months pay—lacking three dollars which he reserved for emergencies—and

lieutenant-colonel U. S. V. for "gallantry in the Atlanta campaign." He commanded the regiment after Colonel Perkins was wounded at Chickamauga September 21, 1863 until the return of Colonel Tolles on November 20, 1863. He was also in command of the regiment during the pursuit of Hood October and part of November, 1864. He was continuously with the regiment except when absent from wounds, and was mustered out with it as major on June 3, 1865, at Washington, D. C. He is an active and honored member of the Loyal Legion, Minnesota Commandery. In 1870 he moved to Minnesota, has served four terms in the legislature as state senator, was a delegate at large to the National Republican Convention held at Chicago, 1888. In 1889 he was appointed Collector of Customs for the District of Minnesota.

asked to have it expended for the benefit of his family The three months pay with the addition of one dollar and fifty cents, bought one calico dress for the wife and one for each of two little girls one barrel of flour, fifty pounds of sugar one ham three pounds of tea, a pair of shoes for each, and two cords of wood

This is a fair sample of the relation between the cost of living at that time and the soldier's wages. Few if any of the soldiers' families, in this region at least, suffered during the war Men and women voluntarily taxed their own little surplus to provide for others who had less Those who could give nothing else gave their time and labor. Wives, mothers and sweethearts who had little to spare looked out for other wives and mothers who had not enough. In all the land there was a feeling of neighborship which has never been equalled—a neighborship which showed how the strain of common peril draws a free people together If the soldiers' families had been dependent on the soldiers earnings, thousands would have starved Yet our enemies termed us "Lincoln's hirelings," and today the children and grandchildren of those whom we endowed with the rich inheritance of a restored nationality and an undivided national domain, find pleasure and ofttimes profit in denominating the Federal soldier of a third of a century ago, a "mercenary

As illustrating the character and incentives of the men who enlisted in the 105th Ohio, the following account of one of those "war-meetings furnished by a correspondent may be taken as a sample of many The northern volunteers were mainly men who left their responsibilities, prospects and homes with extreme reluctance and only when they felt that duty and honor imperatively demanded the sacrifice

On the night of August 13, 1862, a war-meeting was held in the little country village of Orwell, Ashtabula county, to endeavor to fill the quota of a dozen men or so apportioned to the township The town had been fully represented from the start in actively engaged regiments and had come to realize something what war was, so that men who desired a closer acquaintance with it had become very scarce. The bounty stage had not yet been reached, and if a few dollars was offered it was done with apologies to the recipient as "a little provision for unexpected expenses." A little later the public became more familiar with the idea in the light of an equalization of burdens, which divested the transaction of some of the repugnance with which it was at this time regarded.

The men who cared for military glory or adventure had had ample opportunity to gratify their longing. The excitable or impressible had all been gathered into the ranks and it was realized that every recruit would be secured with increasing difficulty. Extraordinary efforts were made to effect the object of the meeting. Eloquent speakers from a distance joined forces with officers resplendent in new uniforms who had been sent home to urge enlistment. The line of argument or persuasion took the form of assurance that with the great accessions to the Northern armies now being made, the insurgent states would be quickly overwhelmed, "the shell of the Confederacy crushed" and after a few months at most, of a sort of picnic excursion, the "brave boys" would return covered with glory to their happy homes. The eloquence was all wasted. The meeting was a failure and about to adjourn with but a single recruit of doubtful availability when Horatio M. Smith, a clerk in the village store, who had been a silent listener, arose in his place and in a few brief sentences deprecated the mistaken policy of underrating the resources of the enemy and the perils of war, and thus unintentionally, no doubt, misleading men and especially boys who might rely more on what was told them than on what they knew as to the necessity for more troops. He said in effect, that he believed the war was only fairly begun, that if the colonies numbering but three millions of inhabitants could maintain for seven years a war against the mighty power of England in the height of her glory, the seceding states, numbering some ten millions of as bold and warlike a people as the earth produced, with four millions of slaves to work for them and keep their armies supplied, could not be overcome in a few months, if ever that their people were under the domination of leaders who claimed and exercised the right to rob their neighbors, black, brown, yellow or white, of the fruits of their labor, of their wives, children, and even of their lives in the name of Christianity and civilization, that the war meant not only restoration of the Union, but the extinction of that crowning infamy of the Republic, American slavery, that the time had not yet come to abolish this relic of barbarism, but if the North was true to itself it soon would come, that the armies of the South were being augmented by conscription as fast or faster than ours by volunteering that at any time they were likely to hurl an army across the borders of our own State and compel us to decide on our own soil the issues of the war, if we did not meet them and compel the question of armed secession to be decided on slave territory, that the men were certainly coming with guns in their hands and we must meet them on our feet or on our knees, must fight them and whip them or run away from them or submit to them, and must choose very quick which alternative we would take that war was not recreation, but the most serious affair a man could engage in, that it meant trial and privation cold, hunger sickness, wounds, and often death, that anyone who thought this too high a price to pay for the security of mothers, wives, children, and home, should not enlist as a soldier, that he himself was ready to meet the issue at once in the only way brave men could meet it, and he hoped ten other men would go with him from Orwell that night to join the 105th Ohio in which they had so many friends and relatives.

In as many minutes, ten white-faced men had walked up to the table and signed the paper which gave their services for three years or during the war to the defense of their country

Loving hands were busy in hurriedly packing into carpet-bags a change of underclothing a pair or two of stockings, a bottle of "Pain Killer," a little "housewife" with needles and thread, a roll of bandage and some lint and in every bag wrapped in a shirt or handkerchief, a Testament or Bible In an hour they were in wagons on the road to the camp at Cleveland, fifty miles distant, which was reached in the morning, just in time to permit them to join the regiment of their choice In a week they were on the way to the front, in little more than a month, they were veterans who had seen more war than many soldiers did in years and few of them saw the homes they left so unexpectedly that night until after three years of fighting and thousands of miles of marching, they returned when the flag they loved floated in undisputed sovereignty over the whole land. But at what tearful cost! Of those who made that journey from Orwell to Cleveland, how many were laid to rest in graves far from the mothers who kissed their boyish cheeks for the last time that night How many of those who returned missed the welcome of a voice that had been the dearest in the world!

This account has been condensed from a contemporaneous narrative How true a picture it was every one whose memory reaches back to that time can well avouch. The meeting in Orwell is but a type of thousands held at that time when pulses beat faster than ever before

IV.

THE RANK AND FILE.

THE men who took the oath of service on that August day of 1862, were fresh from their shops and harvest-fields. A few of them enjoyed the proud distinction of having seen service. The colonel had a scar upon his forehead, a reminiscence of the battle of Shiloh. The lieutenant-colonel had also won promotion fairly by a year's service as captain in another regiment. The major had been a lieutenant under the first call for troops, when it was hoped that ninety days would end the war, a hope he fervently shared; but, seeing it did not, he thought the time had come to go again. Four of the captains had records of previous service; three in the war then going on and one in the war with Mexico. Six of the lieutenants were also what were then esteemed veterans. They had seen service, and some of them had seen the hot glare of battle. A few of the enlisted men had also responded to the three months' call. On account of this, they were mostly made orderly sergeants. For the rest, field, staff, and line, the whole rank and file, were raw products of the life of the Western Reserve. Two-thirds of them were farmers' sons, who, up to that time had been at school, at work upon their fathers' farms, or employed by the month by some neighbor preparatory to setting up for themselves. There was one lawyer and five law-students among them; one minister, some dozens of clerks, two medical students, and a hundred or more teachers. Eighty-five per cent. of them were of native parentage. One-fifth of those of foreign birth who had missed the advantage of free-schools, signed the muster-roll with a cross. Only

CAPT. GEORGE L. RIKER.

GEORGE L. RIKER was born in Queens County, N. Y., October 11, 1830. He attended the schools of New York City until he was seventeen, when he removed with his parents to Livingston County, N. Y., and in 1850 came with them to Painesville, Ohio. He was commissioned captain Company D 105th O. V. I., with which he served until the fall of 1864. He was wounded at the battle of Perryville, Ky., and again during the siege of Atlanta. In February, 1864, he was commissioned major, but not mustered, the regiment being reduced below the minimum by casualties of service and not entitled to a

one who was native-born made his mark. There were no rich men in the regiment, probably but one worth more than ten thousand dollars, and, perhaps, not half a dozen who could claim more than half that valuation. At the same time there were no poor men among them. Every one was self-supporting, or belonged to a family of substantial means, or engaged in profitable industry. Of those who worked for wages, the average monthly stipend was at least double the pay the soldier received. Of farm-laborers, the lowest rate reported by nearly two hundred survivors, was fourteen dollars a month and board the recipient being a boy of seventeen. From that amount the wages of farm-laborers ranged up to twenty-five and thirty dollars a month. Clerks received from thirty to forty dollars and board, teachers from twenty-five to one hundred dollars a month. There were half a dozen college-students, and more than a hundred students of the various academies in the region from which the regiment was drawn, enrolled in the different companies.

This region comprised the five easterly counties of the Western Reserve, the northeasterly counties of Ohio—Ashtabula, Trumbull, Lake, Geauga, and Mahoning. In all of them there was not a town of more than one or two thousand inhabitants, and but one that laid claim to the title of city. It was almost wholly a farming region. What manufactures there were, were of a domestic sort, scattered here and there in the villages and at the cross-roads. Eight years before, a railroad had crept westward along the southern shore of Lake Erie. The Mahoning valley had but recently been tapped by a railroad from Cleveland, opening up its treasures of iron and coal. With these

---

full quota of officers. He resigned in September, 1864, having participated in every battle and skirmish in which the regiment was engaged up to that date. After his return he engaged in mercantile pursuits. In 1879 he was appointed light-keeper at Fairport, Ohio, which position he still holds. He has twice been elected mayor of the village and a member of the Board of Education for the same. He was engaged in a profitable manufacturing business when he entered the service.

exceptions, there was not a mile of railway in the whole five counties. Many of those who came to take the oath of service had never seen a locomotive until ordered to report at the rendezvous. The Lake Shore road cut the northern tier of townships in two of the counties—Ashtabula and Lake. The recruits from the southerly towns came in wagons along the level roads that stretched between fertile and prosperous farms to the railway stations in their various counties. One of these squads had a rather quaint experience with an incorrigible gate-keeper on a plank road, who refused to let them pass without payment of the customary toll. Being soldiers in the service of the State, they refused to accede to his demand.

There was a hot argument. The gatekeeper was obstinate; the embryo soldiers indignant. The incident was characteristic of the time and the spirit of the people. The gatekeeper was bound to do his duty; the young men cared nothing for the trivial sum demanded but thought it an insult to the service in which they were enlisted. There came near being a ruined tollhouse as the result, but someone broke the lock of the gate, and the wagons drove on with shouts of derision for the gatekeeper, who was what was then termed a "copperhead," and took this way to show his opposition to the war which was in progress.

It will help to realize the difference between the people of the two sections if we reflect that a Union man who had thus obstructed the march of Confederate soldiers to their rendezvous, would have been hanged as well as hooted. Even when exasperated, the northern man rarely lost his law-abiding character. Violence was almost unknown to the communities from which these young soldiers came.

During the months of July and August they had been recruited at their homes, in the fields, and at meetings held in the various villages, by officers who had received appointments which were to be exchanged for commissions when a sufficient number to constitute the regiment had been enlisted. Some, who had been loath to give their names during the harvest, now, that the crops were out of the way, felt free to enlist in what they termed the cause of "Liberty and Union," in the hope that by such sacrifice the period of strife might be reduced. It was strange how they always spoke of "Liberty *and* Union," invariably putting the most important word first, showing conclusively that union was regarded by them chiefly as a means of establishing and securing liberty.

There was, perhaps, less of a warlike spirit in the region whence they came, than in almost any other part of the country. Not a few of them were noncombatants in principle, men who would have endured a buffet without returning a blow, and who hated war as the worst evil that could afflict any age or nation. But love of liberty had become the very life-blood of this people. Throughout the whole country the Western Reserve of Ohio was a synonym for intelligence and freedom of thought. Whenever the foot of the slave, fleeing from bondage, struck the white roads that led northward through its green fields and sheltering woods, he was in no danger of losing his way until he stood upon the shore of the blue waters of Lake Erie and saw the signal flying that would bring into the offing some faithful captain, who would undertake to set him ashore somewhere in the Queen's dominions, where liberty was not a question of color. They had been reared to believe that "resistance to tyrants is duty to God," and counted any force that deprived a man of his natural rights as tyranny, not less, but rather more to be condemned, when done by many than when it was the act of one. One of the counties from which this Thousand came, was the home of Benjamin F. Wade and Joshua R. Giddings, pre-eminent among the champions of liberty and justice in that day—"Benighted Ashtabula," as it was termed in mockery and as it proclaimed itself in pride, having, as was claimed, the lowest rate of illiteracy of any county in the Union.

The counties composing the famous Nineteenth Ohio Congressional district were those from which the Thousand was recruited. The battle of liberty had already been fought out in its homes and schools. A few pro-slavery men still lived, and scowled and snarled among them, but "free-speech, free-soil, free-men," had been the watchword of the great mass of its people long before it became the slogan of a party.

The Whig stronghold became a "Free-Soil" outpost, without changing its party allegiance or its representative in Congress. When the House of Representatives expelled him for an affront to the slave-power, which then dominated the government, they returned him again with an increased majority, in token of their approval. So intense was the sympathy of its people with the cause of liberty that it sent its sons in great companies to keep the plains of Kansas against the aggressions of slavery, and "John Brown, of Ossawattamie," located somewhere in its umbrageousness, one of those hiding-places, in the solitude of which he evolved the plans, absurd and impotent as they were, of what he deemed a divine mission, as no doubt it was—a mission predestined to failure, and which could only have succeeded through failure. Some of the Thousand remembered having seen this man, like his Master great in his hate of wrong and in loving self-sacrifice for the right; and like Him, too, in failure of His earthly effort and the fate which befell, but unlike Him in the means He employed. Both were condemned by the law for proclaiming a truth greater than the law. The sunlight of the Master's stainless cross fell on the servant's blood-stained gallows. Both showed the way to liberty, and they who went forth to battle for the freedom of the slave, sang of the Master:

"As He died to make men holy,
Let us die to make men free,"

and of the Martyr, who deserved death by the law, and like Him, triumphed over the law:

"His soul goes marching on."

The words of a boy of nineteen, who was one of the Thousand, show the force of these influences with peculiar vividness He writes

> My first lively interest in the great question at issue between the North and the South was roused, I think, by a visit, to my father's house, of John Kagi, the right-hand man of old John Brown, of Kansas, who was killed, later, in the ill-advised Harper s Ferry undertaking I had known young Kagi well, as an intimate friend of my brother, Horatio and a frequent visitor at our house, when I was a lad of ten or twelve, and he a young man of twenty or twenty-one just before he went to Kansas from his home in Bristol, O He was then a remarkably handsome youth—tall; slight, amiable, refined and in every way most attractive He went to Kansas to teach school and seek his fortune Perhaps a year before the Harper's Ferry affair, he returned for a brief visit. A singular change had been wrought in his appearance and character His laughing eyes had become cold, stern and watchful , his mobile smiling woman's mouth was set and hard , his straight, black hair was streaked with gray and a white lock showed where a bullet had plowed his scalp He had no thought or word for aught but the outrages of the pro-slavery men upon the free-state settlers in Kansas He spent but a few days with his family, then hurried back to what he considered his post of duty. I heard little more of him until his tragic death at Harper s Ferry. I was, however, so impressed with his earnestness and the thrilling recital of events in Kansas that it has always been difficult for me to regard the firing on Sumter as more than an episode in a war which had begun years before on the western plains

So the lad who had listened to Kagi, with the brother, Horatio who was his friend, stood in the ranks of the Thousand, and became, finally, Captain Horatio M Smith, the distinguished quartermaster, honored with the special confidence of General Thomas, and Corporal William O

Smith, who was to his elder brother as was Benjamin of old to Joseph.

Another, a mere lad, was one day riding with his father along the road which skirts the southern shore of Lake Erie, when a steamer came close in-shore, loudly blew her whistle and lay tossing in the offing.

"See, my son," exclaimed the father, "that boat has come to take off a fugitive slave! That is the signal flying from the mast. I heard something about there being 'black birds' around, last Sunday, at church. If we hurry, we may see them go aboard."

CORP. WM. O. SMITH, CO. K.*

He brought the horses to a sharp trot around the point that lay beyond, and the wondering boy saw a colored man and a woman with a child in her arms, clamber on board the steamer, which hoisted its boat quickly up, and, with the echoing groans which marked the working of the old low-pressure engines, went on her way up the lake.

"Thank God!" said the father, standing up in the wagon, reverently taking off his hat and raising his right hand. "Thank God, another family is rescued from the hell of slavery!"

The son never knew whether it was by accident or design that he was brought to witness this scene. It was a dangerous thing at that time, even on the Reserve, to give aid or comfort to an escaping fugitive. Nothing more was said; but there is reason to believe that the stern-faced

*See Appendix.

father knew the peril of the fugitives, and if the boat had not arrived that day, he had arranged to take them at his own risk, in his wagon that night to a noted "station" on the "underground railway," just across the western line of Pennsylvania. The boy was one of the Thousand also with the lesson fresh in his memory.

V.

THE SWORD-BEARERS.

N all armies there are two classes—commissioned officers and enlisted men. The former carry swords and direct; the latter constitute the fighting strength. The regiment is the unit of force in an army; that is, it is the lowest organization which is complete within itself. The companies of a regiment have a certain organic relation to each other, and to the whole of which they are constituent parts. They may be separated and detached, but they are still part of the organization, are carried on its rolls, and return to it at the expiration of their "detached service;" with the regiment, it is not so. It may be taken from one brigade, attached to another or assigned to a distinct service, having no farther relation to the organization or its brigade companions.

The life of a regiment is that of a permanent community composed of ten families. Each family has its own place and its own specific quality and character. This special character of the company may, in some instances, depend not a little upon the men, but it is necessarily determined very much more by the quality and character of its officers. There is, perhaps, no relation in life in which the character of one man is reflected so clearly in the lives of other men as that of the commander of a company, in the soldierly quality of the enlisted men under his command. A colonel may impress his personality, to a certain extent, on all the companies of his regiment, but his influence

CAPT. ALFRED G. WILCOX.

ALFRED GOULD WILCOX was born March 31, 1841, in Madison, Lake Co., Ohio. He lived on a farm, attended the common schools and academy until fifteen years old, then entered Oberlin College, and was in the Junior year when the call for troops came, under which the 105th was organized. He was commissioned 1st lieutenant of Company F, which was raised jointly in Lake and Geauga Counties; participated in all the raids, battles and skirmishes in which the regiment was engaged; was promoted to captain and assigned to Company F, on the 13th of January, 1863, and was mustered out as such, having remained in command of same for nearly three years. Soon after the war, having chosen the profession of editor and publisher, he served an apprenticeship as city editor of the Cleveland *Leader*. He afterwards formed a partnership with Captain J. H. Greene, and bought the *Journal*, of Fremont, O. Later, he bought the *Telegram*, of Richmond, Ind. Here he built up a flour-

amounts to little in determining the moral tone of his men and holding them up to a high standard of efficiency, unless supported by the immediate commander of each company. It is only this man who can encourage and inspire the men under his immediate control to the best effort, the highest valor and the most unflinching endurance of privation and fatigue. Of this truth, the Thousand afforded a notable example in that veteran captain who had learned a soldier's duty on the plains of Mexico, who after the most arduous service the regiment ever saw and one of the most exhaustive marches ever performed by unseasoned troops, made report of his company: "Present or accounted for, *ninety-eight!*" Why was it, when the ranks of others were so depleted? Of course, the fact that they had done less marching than the others counted for much, but he had counseled his men to throw away everything they could spare, at the outset; when he saw a man exhausted, got another to help him; spared no opportunity to get a foot-sore one a place in a wagon, and by so favoring the weak and encouraging the strong to help them, he brought his company into camp without the loss of a man, captured or straggled on the march. It is a matter of sincere regret that the utmost exertion has failed to secure the portrait of an officer of such excellent promise as Captain Robert Wilson, of Company H, who fell, pierced by three bullets, on our first battlefield at Perryville.

---

ishing business, at one time owning and publishing also the *Courier* of New Castle, Ind. Not in the best of health, he sold his properties, and in the fall of 1872, removed to Minnesota. Locating in Minneapolis he became manager of the *Daily News* and afterwards of the *Daily Tribune*. Later he began publishing subscription books for *The Household*, of which, one, *The Buckeye Cook Book*, has had the enormous sale of nearly 1,000,000 copies. In connection with these publications he started *The Housekeeper*, which at the time of its sale by him in 1887, had reached a circulation of 120,000, a number unapproached by any similar publication. During the time he was carrying on these enterprises he became owner of a tract of fertile prairie lands of Minnesota, and became interested in farming and stock raising, and few men have done more for the agricultural interests of the State than he. Following these lines, with varying fortune he has led a life remarkable for energetic and persistent work and manly achievement. He lives in Minneapolis, and is an active member of the Minnesota Commandery of the Loyal Legion.

The character of an army depends upon the quality of these units of force, the regiments; and the regimental character must always be determined, in great measure, by the quality of its officers. They are the nerves by which the purpose of the commander is communicated to the mass; and if they are deficient in spirit, knowledge, or determination, when it stands in the forefront of battle, those who place dependence on it will be sure to suffer disappointment. The soldier looks to his officer, not merely for orders, but for example. Drill and discipline are only instrumentalities by which the efficiency of men and officers are alike enhanced. Drill merely familiarizes both with their respective functions; the use of discipline is only to establish confidence between the enlisted man and his officer. If that confidence already exists, it requires very little drill to make the recruit a soldier; if it has to be created, the habit of obedience must take the place of personal confidence.

CORP. LUMAN G. GRISTE.

Who were they to whom the destiny of the Thousand was committed? In every case they were the product of the same conditions as the enlisted men—field, staff, and line were the neighbors and kinsmen of the rank and file. The Colonel, born thirty-one years before in a little

---

LUMAN G. GRISTE was born at New Hampden, Geauga County, Ohio, June 18, 1841. Enlisted at eighteen in Company G, was appointed corporal; detailed as Judge Advocate's clerk during August 1863; wounded at Chickamauga, September 21, 1863; discharged February 24, 1864; graduated from Cleveland Homeopathic College, in 1874. Has practiced his profession at Twinsburg, O., since that time.

country village, had been educated in the public schools, had worked his way to some prominence at the bar, had been elected prosecuting attorney of his county, had gone west to Minnesota, half a score of years before its boom arrived, and had just returned to his old home when the first gun was fired on Fort Sumter. He raised a company for one of the earliest Ohio regiments, the Twenty-fourth, and had distinguished himself five months before in the bloody conflict at Shiloh. Short, compact, resolute, alert and self-reliant, he possessed in a remarkable degree the qualities which would have secured distinction as a military commander had fate not cut short his career. Within two months, he rose to the temporary command of a division, not by favor but by the hap of battle which, in a single hour, made him its senior officer. He never came to the command of the regiment again, but won deserved fame by his brilliant handling of the brigade of which it was a part. If he did not always win the love of those under his command there was none who could withhold admiration for his soldierly qualities or fail to feel a thrill of pride at the thought that he belonged, in a sense, to us.

The Lieutenant-colonel, five years older than his superior officer, tall, slender, courteous, with flowing black beard and keen, flashing eye, was an ideal soldier of another type. The counting-room and the village store had been his college. He had left a desolate hearthstone a year before to give what he deemed a shattered life to the service of his country. Never had soldier a nobler ideal. A constant victim of pain, he never shirked a duty or spared himself exposure. Sometimes irascible in camp he was a model of cheerfulness upon the march, nothing daunted him and no hardship was too great for him to endure. In battle his calmness approached the sublime. If the Colonel dreamed of stars as he had good right to do, the Lieutenant-colonel's aspiration never went beyond the eagle, which he, no doubt, hoped to wear, the joy of battle, the fame of brilliant achievement and a soldier's death — which he neglected no opportunity to win.

The Major was twenty-six, of auburn hair, pleasant face, calm, earnest eyes, and quiet, retiring manner. He seemed, at first glance, hardly fitted for command. For a time, the Thousand thought him almost a supernumerary; but there was a firmness about the smiling mouth under the tawny mustache and a flash that came sometimes into the great brown eyes that served well enough to check familiarity, and there was never any need to enforce obedience. It was thought that the Colonel was sometimes inclined to be imperious with his second in command, but he was complacency itself to the sunny-faced Major. Was it because that officer was close akin to the governor of the state, whose favor was not a thing to be despised by one ambitious of promotion? Let us not inquire too closely.

PRIVATE C. K. RADCLIFFE, Co. F.

The Thousand was composed of men not overburdened with regard for rank. The life from which they came was that stronger phase of New England life found at the West, which retains, perhaps in an aggravated form, the peculiar New England quality of a jealous self-esteem. They obeyed with readiness, because that was a soldier's

CHARLES K. RADCLIFFE was born in Mentor, O., a stone's throw from the little Disciple Church which President Garfield used to attend. He was seventeen years old when he enlisted as a private, and at that time was a shoemaker's apprentice. He served continuously until the army crossed the Chattahoochie River. Here, utterly worn out with the hardships of service he was sent to the rear, none of his companions expecting ever to see

duty, and treated their officers with respect, because they respected themselves. The quiet Major grew in their regard upon a basis of mutual esteem, which was not at all abated when he had held the command longer than both of his superiors. He had no special liking for military life, no desire for promotion, no thirst for glory, no hope for ulterior advantage. Without political aspiration, endowed with sufficient earthly possessions, he simply did his duty because it was his duty, and regarded the Thousand the less honored by his leadership than he by the confidence they bestowed. He had no lack of self-respect, but his orders took as often the tone of request as of command.

Three better types of the citizen soldier it would be hard to find in any army.

The subalterns were simply fair samples of the life from which the regiment was drawn. Of the ten captains, one was a professor in an academy, one a minister, two were students, one was a mining superintendent, three or four had been engaged in mercantile pursuits. They were mostly men approaching middle life, their average age being thirty-three years. Of these only one remained with the regiment until the close of the war—Captain Charles D. Edwards, of Company A, afterwards major, lieutenant-colonel, and brevet-colonel when mustered out. Two were killed, one died, four resigned, and two were dismissed.

The twenty lieutenants were of the average age of twenty-five years. They were nearly all students or clerks

---

him again. He was captured with the forage train near Murfreesboro, Tenn., June 21, 1863, and released on parole a few days afterwards.

The close of the war found him little more alive than dead. He went to Missouri to engage in farming, made no money but recovered his health, took a course in a business college, ran a paper at Baldwin, Michigan, was city editor of *The Commercial*, Toledo, O., and in 1889 was appointed mail agent. He has held many places of honor and trust in the towns where he has resided, his party, the church and the Grand Army. He now lives in Detroit, Michigan. It is to Comrade Radcliffe that the 105th owes the first attempt to write its history. He kept a daily journal and the newspaper account he gave of the service of the regiment is full of life and incident, and surprisingly correct when we consider the circumstances under which it was written.

Six of them were college graduates, or college students. Seven were mustered out as captains, four died during the service, eight resigned, one was dismissed.

The men these officers commanded had been their neighbors, schoolmates, friends. No wall of exclusion separated them; rank made little difference in their relations. They found it not difficult to command, for the only deference they exacted was the formal one their position required. Save in a few instances, they directed rather than ordered. The enlisted man sought his officer's tent for counsel as freely almost as his comrade's. On the march, they chatted familiarly as they had done at home. The friendships that had existed remained unbroken. The man in the ranks had almost as much pride in his friend who carried a sword as if the emblem of rank had been his own. Perhaps he was his brother or his cousin. Not unfrequently the orderly sergeant messed with the commissioned officers. Why should he not? In education, wealth, and all that society counts essential to gentility, save the accident of temporary rank, he was often their equal, sometimes their superior. Even in rank, he was likely at any time to rise to their level. Of the line and staff officers mustered out with the regiment at the close of the war, all but eight had been mustered in as enlisted men.

Few of the officers found it necessary to resort to exclusiveness or punishment to secure the respect of those under their command, and in those cases respect did not always accompany obedience. Obedience, indeed, became habitual, but it was the willing obedience of the intelligent man, not the slavish submission of an inferior based on fear of punishment. Because of this, the Thousand became noted for the parental character of its discipline. It had an enviable reputation for good order and prompt obedience, but was especially distinguished for the mildness and infrequency of its punishments.

From the point of view of the regular army officer, all this was horribly bad form, but the theory of discipline which prevails in our regular army is purely monarchical and aristocratic. Despite the many gallant and noble officers it contains it is in theory and in practice a disgrace to the republic. When the ranks shall be made the only door to West Point, and every soldier shall have an open field for preferment, it will become the most efficient army in the world; then desertions will cease and the expense of recruiting be avoided, since the best young men of the nation will seek the army as a desirable career. It is a change that is sure to come, since it is dictated by every patriotic consideration. The country cannot afford either to rear aristocrats or to deprive the men in the ranks of the soldier's just reward—the right to wear a sword when he has fitted himself for the duties of command.

Neither the officers nor men of the Thousand were saints, but they were fellow-soldiers as they had been fellow-citizens, and in the main, self-respecting soldiers, as they had been self-respecting citizens.

VI.

THE THEATER OF WAR.

HE theater of war was of almost unprecedented extent, and altogether unique in character. Roughly designated, it may be said to have been bounded by the Potomac, Ohio, and Missouri rivers on the north, and by the Atlantic and Gulf coast upon the east and south. It was divided by the Mississippi. That portion lying east of the great river was marked by certain peculiar combinations of natural conformation and artificial roadway, which were at every stage of the conflict of prime importance, and, in the main, determinative of the strategy of both armies.

Its most important physical feature was a rugged mountain region roughly triangular in form, its base extending from Harper's Ferry, on the Potomac, westward to the neighborhood of Portsmouth, on the Ohio river, and its apex resting at Stevenson, in Alabama. The northern and western sides of this triangle are each about three hundred miles in length, and its southeastern side more than five hundred miles. This region embraces nearly all of West Virginia, the western portions of Virginia, North and South Carolina, the northwestern part of Georgia, and Eastern Tennessee and Kentucky. It is composed of a great number of elongated peaks or overlapping ranges, having a general trend from northeast towards the southwest. These are divided into two general groups, separated from each other by a depression, which extends longitudinally from Lynchburg, Virginia, to Stevenson, Alabama.

The northern part of this depression constitutes the bed into which are gathered the tributaries of the James river, flowing eastward through the passes of the Blue

MARSHALL W. WRIGHT, R. Q. M.

MARSHALL W. WRIGHT was born August 27, 1818, in Conneaut, O. His father was a native of Massachusetts, his mother of Connecticut. He was the oldest son, and very early in life had to help support the family. School advantages were almost unknown. He pursued his father's occupation, that of tanner, and was married March 26, 1844. In 1847, he moved to Dorset, O., and followed farming for six years. He was elected Sheriff of the County of Ashtabula, in 1853, and served two terms. In 1857 he removed to Kingsville, Ohio, and has since resided there.

He has five children and eighteen grandchildren, and in April, 1894, celebrated his golden wedding. He was appointed lieutenant and quarter-master

Ridge Almost interlacing with these are the headwaters of the Clinch and Holston rivers, these, uniting, form the Tennessee, which, flowing to the southwestward, bursts through the mountain barrier in the northeastern part of Alabama, where it whimsically abandons its southwestern course, which, continued would lead to the Gulf of Mexico, three hundred miles away, and lazily and uncertainly pursuing the arc of a great circle, falls into the Ohio at Paducah, almost as far to the northward

---

of the 105th at its organization, and served as such until April 13 1864 when he resigned on account of ill health

Quartermaster Wright furnished a very necessary ingredient of the morale of the field and staff of the regiment He was a man of mature age, who had occupied positions of honor and trust, was of influence in his county, well-known and highly esteemed throughout the district from which the regiment came, of incorruptible integrity, unimpeachable good will for all, without a suspicion of self-seeking, easily approachable, of invincible good nature and having that most delightful of all faculties, the power of making everyone feel that he was his friend without being the enemy of anyone else He was a man of easy temper, not remarkable, either for executive ability or irrepressible energy, but altogether remarkable for readiness to encounter any difficulty, and for unfailing good nature under the most disheartening and depressing conditions He was every man's friend, as ready to cheer and condole with a teamster, or a footsore soldier, as with any officer of the regiment His wide acquaintance throughout Ashtabula County enabled him to do many acts of kindness for the friends and families of the soldiers which he was never too busy or weary to undertake To the sick of the regiment he was a benison, to everyone a friend

That he was able to spare time for these unnumbered errands of mercy and cheer, without the duties of his position suffering from neglect, is due to the rare qualities of the men who were his assistants and immediate subordinates Probably no regimental quartermaster ever before had two as efficient quartermaster sergeants as Horatio M Smith and George W Cheney or a commissary sergeant of such unpretending faithfulness or scrupulous exactness as William J Gibson a commissary who when the ration for each man during the siege of Chattanooga fell to less than five hard tack each for eight days had the self control and rigid sense of justice to give himself only the four and a half he dealt out to the others It seems a small matter to a man who has enough to eat but that half-cracker which Sergeant Gibson broke off from his own ration and cast back into the aggregate at a time when men knelt about the place where rations were issued and picked up the crumbs which fell upon the ground, represented more self-denial than can well be understood by those who have not been in like conditions

With such assistants and his own inexhaustible amiability, Lieutenant Wright was no doubt the best-liked quartermaster in the army, as he was easily the best-known and best-loved man in the regiment—not only by the men in the field but by their wives and children at home—as he continues to be until this day

This great longitudinal depression divides, not very unequally, this vast mountain region into two parts, each with an eastern and western declivity, both laterally pierced by innumerable narrow and tortuous valleys lying between irregular and precipitous mountain walls. The eastern portion is termed, indifferently, the Blue Ridge or Alleghany mountains. The western range is called collectively the Cumberland mountains, and, in its lower part, the Cumberland plateau. The eastern range was at that time practically impassable for an armed force throughout its whole extent, from the passes where the James river breaks forth in the rear of Lynchburg to the tortuous defiles through which the railroad steals from Chattanooga to Atlanta. The western side of this double-ended trough is pierced with some half dozen intricate and difficult passes, only one of which, known as Cumberland Gap, lying a hundred and eighty miles almost due south from Cincinnati, was supposed at the outbreak of the war to afford a really feasible route to the valley of the Holston, or East Tennessee. The struggle developed the fact that at least three others were actually available, while the elevated plateau into which the lower part of the Cumberland range expands, was cut by numerous difficult but practicable defiles between the head of the Sequatchie valley and the debouchment of the Tennessee river. The whole region is sometimes denominated the Appalachian mountains.

Along this median depression which separates the Blue Ridge from the Cumberland range, ran a railroad linking Richmond, the seat of Confederate power, with the southwestern states of Tennessee, Alabama, Mississippi, Louisiana, Texas, and Arkansas. Along the eastern slope of the Alleghanies ran also, other lines of railroad, connecting Richmond with Atlanta and the southeastern states of the Confederacy. The strategic effect of this conformation in conjunction with these railway lines was, first, to make the three northeastern states of the Confederacy unassailable from the northwest except through the northern outlet of the valley of East Tennessee, in the rear of Lynchburg, or around the southern end of this impervious rocky chain, along the railroad leading from Chattanooga to Atlanta. Because of this the Confederate forces in Virginia, North and South Carolina had no need to guard against attack from the rear, but could concentrate their whole strength against the enemy in front.

In the second place, this depression with the railroad running through it, served as a covered way by which the forces of the Confederacy might be quickly and safely concentrated on any part of their line which chanced to be threatened and returned before the enemy could take advantage of their absence. It was on these lines, running through Vicksburg, Corinth, Murfreesboro, Chattanooga, Atlanta, and Knoxville and uniting in the field of operations of the army of Northern Virginia, that nearly all the great battles of the war were fought.

This double-walled, impregnable rampart, extending three hundred miles southward from the Ohio, and five hundred miles southwestward from the Potomac, of necessity greatly enhanced the defensive capacity of the Confederacy. One has only to imagine the Appalachian mountains removed so as to permit access at almost any point on this long line, to realize how easily an army moving through West Virginia or Kentucky might, in connection with an attack in front have compelled the evacuation of Richmond.

As things were, however, an army operating from the Ohio river as a base, had open to it only three lines of approach to the Confederate territory: (1) through the gaps of the Cumberland range into East Tennessee; (2) along the line of the Louisville and Nashville railway to Stevenson or Chattanooga, thereby turning the southern end of the Appalachian mountains, or, (3) along the course of the Tennessee and Cumberland rivers to the same strategic line.

At the outbreak of the struggle, the Confederates

seized and held the southern portion of Kentucky, the center of the army of occupation being at Munfordville and Bowling Green, its right at Cumberland Ford and Barboursville, under General Zollicoffer, covering the road to Cumberland Gap, and its left at Fort Donelson on the Cumberland river, which with Fort Henry, twelve miles away on the Tennessee, was heavily garrisoned and relied upon to hold those rivers against both the Union land and naval forces These positions were admirable for defence, and equally admirable for an attack by the Confederate center It was natural, therefore, that the Federal commander in Kentucky, General Robert Anderson, and his successor, General W T. Sherman, should be apprehensive of such an attack, and desirous of strengthening his own center at Louisville This policy was continued by General Buell who was assigned to the command of the army of the Ohio, embracing the forces in Kentucky and Tennessee east of the mouth of the Cumberland, in November, 1861

In the meantime General George H Thomas, in command of the Federal left at Somerset and Camp Dick Robinson, was urging an advance by Cumberland Gap into East Tennessee, to seize the railroad running from the Confederate capital along the valley of the Tennessee, so as to both interrupt communication with the southwest and turn the right of the Confederate army in Kentucky by demonstrating against Chattanooga General Ormsby M Mitchell, who commanded at Cincinnati at that time, was enthusiastically in favor of this movement, declaring that to hold East Tennessee, with its intense Union sentiment, was "equivalent to placing an army of fifty thousand men at the back door of the Confederacy" President Lincoln, with that unerring insight which was the distinguishing quality of his genius, also approved this movement, and recommended to Congress an appropriation to build a military railroad from Lexington to Knoxville via Cumberland Gap for the transportation of men and supplies in order that this all but inaccessible cleft in the mountain wall might be made · an impregnable citadel of liberty We know now how true were the President's intuitions, and how just were the views of the commanders who urged this course. But the country had not yet learned the wonderful sagacity of Lincoln, and the modest Thomas and impetuous Mitchell were both distrusted for the very qualities which would have made them of inestimable value to the national cause had they been given the scope and recognition they deserved The one was doomed to perish in practical exile in a useless command on the South Carolina coast, the other to wait until the very last hour of the great conflict for the recognition of his merit

The influences which were to shape the action of the army under General Buell were destined to come from other sources than its commander It may be doubted if he was intellectually capable of a successful initiative Overestimating always his opponent's power and dwelling persistently on the strategic advantages the enemy possessed, he forgot everything that made in his own favor, and really allowed the movements of his army to be dependent on those of his opponent, to a degree, perhaps, unprecedented in military history Such a line of action can never succeed except in a purely defensive warfare—and even a Fabius needs to be able to strike at the proper moment and to strike with all his force

By some curious misapprehension of the character of General Thomas, who commanded the forces opposed to his right wing, General Albert Sidney Johnston was induced to sanction an advance under Zollicoffer, an advance justified, perhaps, by political hopes, but wholly indefensible from a military point of view. The result was the battle of Mill Springs, fought on the nineteenth of January, 1862, resulting in the first Federal victory of the war at the West Zollicoffer's force was not only defeated, but also driven across the Cumberland, exposing Johnston's flanks in a manner which, if followed up, must have compelled him to fall back to the line of the Cumberland river Instead of pursuing this advantage, Buell ordered his victorious subordinate to retreat

Little more than a month later, February 2, 1862, however, events occurred which were fortunately beyond the control of the trio of scientific soldiers—McClellan, Halleck and Buell—who then commanded the three great armies of the Union The department under the control of the latter, though not strictly bounded in his assignment to command, extended westward only to the mouth of the Cumberland River Beyond that was the Department of Missouri, with General H. W Halleck in command General George B McClellan as commander-in-chief of all the armies of the United States, exercised a general supervision and control These three men were pre-eminent among the officers of the Federal Army as theoretical soldiers As military critics, they were, perhaps, unexcelled in their day Their very excellence as theorists, however, not being coupled with that resolution and audacity which are essential to enable a commander to win battles or overcome an enemy, became a source of weakness rather than of strength The trained imagination, which is the peculiar quality of the strategist had in them been developed without the modifying influence of actual warfare or a corresponding development of that pugnacious spirit which inclines a commander to make up in celerity of movement, vigor of attack or stubbornness of resistance, any fortuitous advantage he sees that his opponent might have, but of which it is not certain that he will be able to avail himself Probably three men were never before associated in the chief control of a nation s armies who so closely resembled each other in capacity to overrate their opponents, minify their own advantages, and out of imaginary molehills create insuperable obstacles

It was an instance, on an almost unprecedented scale, of an army of lions led by a trio of hinds—not that either of these men lacked personal courage any more than they lacked military skill, but the fear of failure was with each so great as to overwhelm that dogged determination to win, on which success in war must always finally depend A mere scientific soldier may organize an army, may decide what strategic movements are preferable upon a definite theater of war, or may plan a successful campaign , but the man who commands an army and controls its movements should be, first of all things, a resolute and determined fighter

Despite the paucity of troops in the vast department under his control, the Confederate commander in Kentucky, General Albert Sidney Johnston, had posted at Forts Donelson and Henry an army of more than 20,000 men which should have been sufficient to hold them against three times their number This was a matter of supreme importance to General Johnston, for on the maintenance of this position depended his own ability to hold Southern Kentucky and Middle Tennessee These works were on the extreme eastern verge of General Halleck's Department of the Missouri, and, as such, were a part of the District of Cairo, then, fortunately, under the command of a soldier who had no paper reputation to paralyze his impulse, but who had every incentive, as well as the native resolution, to undertake great things, even when apparently impossible of achievement. This man, then quite unknown to fame, had gotten the idea that, by an unexpected attack, the weaker of these strongholds, Fort Henry, might be taken, and that the other might either be carried by immediate assault, or, being fully invested, might be compelled to capitulate before it could be relieved For a month he had importuned his superior, General Halleck, to allow him to pursue this course

On the first day of February he received permission to make the attempt , on the second, he started with fifteen thousand men to attack the two strongest military positions west of the Alleghanies, garrisoned by nearly twice as many men as he commanded , on the sixth, Fort Henry surrendered , on the twelfth, Fort Donelson was invested , on the sixteenth, it surrendered. Fifteen thousand prisoners and more guns than the besiegers had were captured. This achievement marked an epoch in the war. Not only had a new man appeared, but Ulysses S. Grant was a new type of soldier in our army—the type which used the forces he had, instead of waiting for what he might desire. It was the first great victory of a great war, and the army which capitulated at Donelson was the largest armed force ever captured, up to that time, on the continent. Because of these things and the brief time it occupied, it will ever be regarded as one of the most brilliant campaigns in military history. On the nineteenth, three days after the surrender of Donelson, Halleck, jealous of Grant's unexpected success, recommended the promotion of one of his subordinates, General C. F. Smith, over him. On that same day the President, wiser than his scientific advisers, recommended, and the Senate confirmed, the man, who first "organized victory" for our arms, to the rank of Major-General of Volunteers. The junta of military critics had failed; the fighting soldier had achieved the impossible. From that hour his course was upward, every step a victory, until victory culminated in conquest.

The inevitable result of the fall of Donelson was that the forces in front of Buell melted away in a night. Bowling Green was evacuated the day Donelson was invested. On the twenty-fourth of February, Buell's forces entered Nashville unopposed. He at once began to caution his subordinates not to move too rapidly. Early in March he was ordered to Savannah, on the Tennessee river, to join General Grant in his intended advance on Corinth, Mississippi. So deliberate was his march, however, that only a small portion of his army arrived in time to take part in the first day's battle of Shiloh.

From that date until early in June, preceding the time our story opens, the army of the Ohio, except one division under Mitchell, a brigade under Negley, and a few scattered outposts in Kentucky, was part and parcel of the roving farce which Halleck was conducting under the loud-sounding title of the "the Siege of Corinth," not that Corinth was besieged or even half-invested, but in six weeks the great strategist moved his army fifteen miles, almost without opposition, captured a deserted city, allowed his enemy to escape unhurt, and then—marched back again!

In the meantime, General Ormsby M. Mitchell, a soldier of the Grant type, who believed in doing something besides getting ready, being left at Murfreesborough, with only three brigades, had overrun Middle Tennessee, captured Decatur Huntsville and Stevenson, in Alabama, and held the line of the Tennessee River to Bridgeport, only twenty-two miles from Chattanooga. This "Gibraltar of the Confederacy" was at that time practically undefended. The highest estimate of the Confederate forces there was "about ten thousand men." As a fact, its garrison was less than half that number. East Tennessee was bare of Confederate soldiers and the people were clamorous as they had been from the first for Federal forces to come and occupy this all-important position, whereby the rear of the Confederate army in Virginia might be threatened and their most important line of communication between their eastern and western armies wholly destroyed. Negley, with one brigade, was actually in front of Chattanooga, only the Tennessee River lay between his lines and the most important position the Confederates held west of Richmond. General George W. Morgan, with twelve thousand men, was on his way to East Tennessee via the Cumberland Gap. Mitchell was begging for reinforcements in order that he might invest Chattanooga before it could be relieved. If the "Siege of Corinth" had continued a little longer or Mitchell had been reinforced by even a single brigade, he would, in all probability have captured Chattanooga. General Morgan asked that Negley might continue to demonstrate in its front, to prevent the enemy from throwing a force into East Tennessee. But General Buell's orders on leaving Corinth on the sixth of June, were to march via Decatur and Huntsville to take Chattanooga and occupy East Tennessee. Unfortunately, he was also ordered to repair the railroads leading thither. To this last work he addressed himself with ardor; the more important task he seems almost to have forgotten. Negley was at once ordered back to McMinnville, Mitchell was directed to repair the Chattanooga and Nashville Railroad and the whole army was scattered in small detachments along the lines of railway converging on Nashville. For two months Buell crept on toward his objective, building railroads, distributing bridge-guards, erecting stockades, returning fugitive slaves, and giving daily advice upon the conduct of the war. He was an officer of inconceivable industry in a literary way, and most unfortunately for his fame, his dispatches have been preserved with unusual completeness.

On the first day of August, General McCook was only six miles nearer Chattanooga than Mitchell had been in June. Both were cautiously feeling their way toward that city. General G. W. Morgan was entrenched at Cumberland Gap. Bragg had collected an army of fifty thousand men at Chattanooga. Kirby Smith held East Tennessee with thirty thousand. Buell had an invincible belief that Bragg's purpose was to advance upon Nashville, and first made his arrangements to meet and engage him at Altamont, on the summit of the Cumberland plateau, where there was neither forage nor water, and which was all but inaccessible to an army, even with no enemy to overcome. Then he decided to retire his army on Nashville, still confident that his opponent could have no other objective. On the day after the Thousand was mustered in, August twenty-second, Kirby Smith, having turned the Federal position at Cumberland Gap, arrived, with fifteen thousand men, at Barboursville, Kentucky. Buell thought it a feint to divert attention from Bragg's advance upon Nashville, and hastened his preparations for retreat. Five days later, Bragg began his march, unopposed, from the head of Sequatchie valley by Sparta to Carthage and Gainsborough, on the Cumberland River, which he crossed, unopposed on his way to Kentucky.

Two days after Bragg had started on his march Buell telegraphed to the commanding officer at Murfreesborough: "Could a good battlefield be chosen about Murfreesborough, affording position for the flanks and rear of a large army? Report in as much detail as possible in cipher."

Having thus advertised for a battlefield he gave the order to concentrate on Nashville, leaving Bragg to pass undisturbed through a difficult region scarce a score of miles from the left of his army and cross the Cumberland at his leisure. In this retreat, General Buell displayed his best qualities as a commander. His arrangements were, perhaps, the most perfect ever made for such a movement. As if on review, his army moved in the exact order prescribed for the various divisions and detachments. From Huntsville, Decatur, Bridgeport, Stevenson, Battle Creek, McMinnville, Decherd, and all the scattered intervening posts, the retreat began on schedule time and was conducted with admirable precision. It was one of the most masterly retreats ever planned, as why should it not be, since there was none to oppose or obstruct, to hasten or hinder? In order to secure its complete success, General Buell asked, with urgent importunity, that Grant would send, with all possible haste, two divisions to swell his army, already greater than that of the enemy from whom he fled, while that enemy romped leisurely down the western slope of the Cumberland mountains into the fertile plains of Kentucky. This was done, and the movement was completed without the least variation from schedule time. Not a man or a wagon was lost, as, indeed, none could well be, unless they strayed from the line of march, since there was no enemy in front or rear for half a hundred miles, save one who was marching away from Nashville as eagerly as Buell was pressing toward it.

When his army was finally encamped upon the banks of the Cumberland, Bragg had already crossed that river, and was preparing to fall upon Munfordville. Whether the commander of the Army of the Ohio stopped in his march to the rear to inspect the battlefield for which he had advertised near Murfreesborough or not, is not now ascertainable; but that he still believed that Bragg was merely maturing some fell plan to compass his destruction, there is abundant evidence, as also that it required the whole force of the national administration to start him from Nashville on that leisurely march he finally made so close upon the rear of Bragg's army that the dust of their passage was hardly settled when his advance guard arrived. Only the most consummate skill could have avoided a collision with the army in his front, and inferior to him in numbers, or delayed his march long enough to permit the junction of the Confederate commander and his lieutenant in the heart of Kentucky.

It was at this juncture of national affairs that the Thousand, the day after they were mustered in, reported to Major-General Horatio G. Wright, commanding the Department of Ohio, at Cincinnati, and were ordered to cross the river at Covington and wait for arms and equipments.

VII.

ON SOUTHERN SOIL.

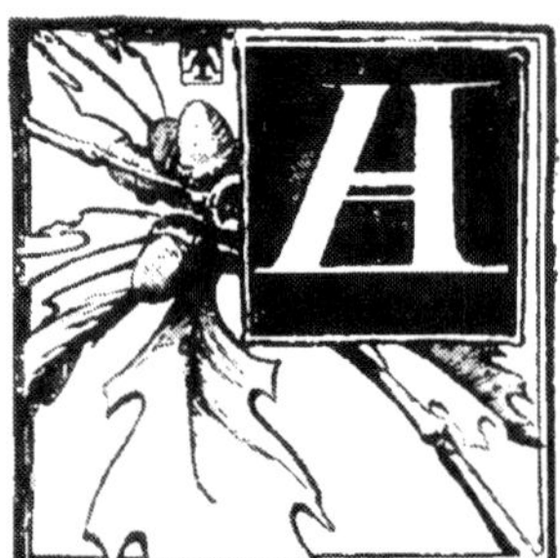

LIGHT, wavering mist hung over the Ohio river, shrunk almost to its lowest stage, when, in the early dawn of its second day of service, the Thousand crossed the Fifth-street ferry and clambered up the ungraded hills to the pleasant streets of Covington, Kentucky. It hardly needed the sight of blue uniforms, swords, and muskets, in the streets and at the ferries, to tell us that we had reached the theater of war. Two or three turtle-backed gunboats, lying at anchor in midstream, looned out of the fog, their ports open, the smoke lazily lifting from their funnels, an armed watch showing on their decks. They seemed like grim black dogs, ready to leap on their prey; and our hearts exulted at the thought that the skill and ingenuity which freedom fosters had provided the cause of liberty with such formidable weapons. Slavery furnished abundant supplies for the armies that fought for its perpetuity; but its existence had starved and crippled that mechanical skill and inventive genius, on the development of which depends the power to construct the delicate and ponderous instrumentalities of modern warfare. Had the Confederacy possessed the constructive capacity and mechanical skill of the North, with its advantages of position, the war for the restoration of the Union would, in all probability, have been a hopeless failure. But the hand which holds the lash is rarely skillful with the chisel or the lathe, and the wrong done to the slave brought its own fruitage of weakness to the master.

We landed on the Kentucky shore near where the water-works now are, and climbed the hillside without forming ranks. Company G was the first to set foot in Dixie, and as we passed one of the cottages, which clung to the sharp slope, an aged woman, standing in the door, saluted us with a wave of the hand, and said:

SERGT. JOSEPH R. WARNER, CO. G.

"God bless you, boys, and bring you all safe home again!"

Many uncovered at this first greeting on southern soil, and Sergeant Warner, whose heart was ever quick to acknowledge kindness, answered for all:

"Thank you, mother, and may you be here to see us when we come!"

The line was formed on Greenup street. While we rested on the curb, the red sunlight began to show through the silvery haze, telling of drought and heat. An elderly gentleman came along carrying a market-basket. He

---

JOSEPH RITNER WARNER was born in Erie County, Pa., in 1836; attended Kingsville, O Academy, and was studying law in Ashtabula, O., when he enlisted in Company G. He managed to stagger through the "Hell March," but was never well afterwards. He was urged to accept a discharge, but instead asked that he be reduced to the ranks and detailed as a clerk. He served in that capacity during the whole war to the surprise of every one who knew his physical condition. For many years he has been one of the most efficient clerks in the Pension Bureau, at Washington, D.C.

paused to inquire where we were from and to learn the names of our field officers. As he passed on some one told us that it was "Mr. Grant, the father of the fighting general." One of the "boys,"—a specimen of that sort of boys who never grow to be men, except upon the field of battle—made as if to filch an ear of corn from his store. Just then the fire-bells began to ring. "Wait awhile," said the old man, good-naturedly, "and you will get a much better breakfast. Covington gives her defenders one good meal as a send-off, and those bells are ringing to let her people know that another regiment has arrived."

The city made good its pledge of hospitality; the tables in the market-house may not have groaned with the viands spread out upon them, but some of the Thousand did before they were cleared off. It was a long time before they were to have such lavish hospitality forced upon them again.

During the day Mr. Grant came again. He chatted with the men as freely as with the officers. Why should he not? He was part and parcel of the life from which they came. He was very proud of his already famous son, but not offensively so. It was not long before he learned that the young Major's "Grandmother Tod," was the wife of Ohio's first chief justice, who was his own early benefactor, whose kindness his great son was unostentatiously to link with his own fame by frank acknowledgment in the book that resulted from that last heroic conflict with adverse fate, which was finished on Mount McGregor. But the father did not wait for the son's acknowledgment. He had the Colonel and the Major to dine with him, and the Thousand thought all the more of their major because his grandmother had befriended the father of General Grant, and had him 'apprenticed to the tanner's trade.' So far does reflected glory shine!

When we had finished our repast, we turned our attention to securing and distributing our arms and equipments. By some curious inconsistency, Commissary Sergeant Gibson had been left in Cincinnati, almost without assistance, to attend to the transportation of the arms, and camp and garrison equipage of the regiment. In nothing does the inexperience of the volunteer show itself so frequently as in inability to properly utilize the officers of a command. Here was a regiment having a full quota of officers, yet the important work of transferring these essential stores was left to a sergeant of the non-commissioned staff. A year later, so serious and arduous a duty would only have been entrusted to an officer of high rank, with an adequate force at his disposal. Almost any other man in Sergeant Gibson's place would have demurred at the magnitude of the task imposed; but his idea of a soldier's duty was "not to reason why;" and if he had been ordered to bail out the Ohio river with a pint cup, he would have gone at it with a quiet persistency, which, if it did not achieve success, would certainly have deserved it. Poor fellow, as he lugged and tugged at his Sisyphean task for the next three days, sleeping at night on the piles of stuff he moved by

WILLIAM J. GIBSON, COM. SERGT.

WILLIAM JAY GIBSON was born near New Castle, Pa., June 18, 1838, and spent his boyhood on a farm. His father being accidentally drowned and his mother dying soon afterwards, the lad was thrown upon his own resources at an early age. When scarcely fifteen, with most of his worldly effects on his back, and $10 in his pocket, he set out on foot for the academy at Kingsville, Ashtabula County, O., ninety miles distant, where he was first pupil and afterwards a teacher. He volunteered under the first call for 75,000 men, but the company with many others, was not accepted. He resigned his position of assistant principal of Kingsville Academy and enlisted as a private in

day for though he had some volunteer helpers no guard was provided. he little thought that the people of the city where he toiled an obscure private soldier would for many years welcome with delight his daily work in the editorial columns of one of her great journals

The enlisted man in our volunteer army may not have carried his commission in his knapsack he may have even failed of all recognition or been treated like a dog and a scullion by those who were his inferiors in all but rank but he carried under his hat, sometimes, the capacity to set things even afterwards Many a colonel has been outranked by scores of the privates of his regiment since their muster-out, and Gibson's pen has given the commissary sergeant of the Thousand a fame which no sword in the regiment won for its wearer

The equipment of the Thousand occupied three days Who that has ever witnessed the result does not recall it with a smile? If anything has been omitted from the soldier's outfit that could rattle, flop, pull, drag, torture, and distort the wearer it would be difficult to guess what it might be When he has donned his cartridge-box, heavy with forty rounds, adjusted as well as may be his waist and shoulder belts has hung his haversack protuberant with three days' rations on one side and his canteen upon the other, has slung his knapsack upon his shoulders the straps sawing away at his pectorals as if bound to amputate his arms or has rolled his blanket and

---

Company G August 7 1862 He was promoted to commissary sergeant at its organization and mustered out with the regiment June 3 1865. Contrary to the usual custom of regimental commissaries who tarried in the rear with the supply trains Sergeant Gibson usually marched and camped with the regiment and during the Atlanta campaign he took his chances with the rest in the trenches Though often under fire he was never wounded and had the rare good fortune never to be sick or off duty for a single day during the three years service

At the close of the war, he spent several months in one of [illegible] of Pennsylvania then removed to Ann Arbor where he graduated in the literary department of the University of Michigan in 1869 For several years thereafter he was a reporter and editorial writer on the Detroit *Post* and Detroit *Tribune* In January, 18[illegible] he became associate editor of the Cincinnati *Times-Star* a position he still (18[illegible]) holds

hung it across one shoulder, with, perhaps, his tent-cloth and poncho strung the other way, to maintain the harmony of the ensemble his picturesque hideousness is not entirely complete until he reaches out his hand, grasps his rifle, and, with that poised upon his shoulder, realizes, both in his own feeling and the eye of the beholder, the immense distance between the citizen and the soldier We very justly boast of the inventiveness of our people, but no appreciable amount of ingenuity has ever been wasted on the equipment of our soldiers The pack-horse has a saddle to keep his load in place, but the soldier has to carry his pack without any such muscle-saving and spirit-saving device Perhaps if wars do not cease too soon the government may some time grow paternal enough to consider the soldier's health and comfort, as well as the cheapness of his equipment

With military togs came military terms Titles took the place of names Shoulder-straps and chevrons began to assert themselves Men came to be known by companies rather than as individuals All the "Misters" disappeared with our first parade under arms Drilling was incessant, despite the bustle attendant upon arming and equipment, the making out of the duplicate and triplicate vouchers for everything required by army regulations

The streets were filled, early and late, with awkward squads, each one's awkwardness proving an encouragement to the other It may not be true that misery loves company but ignorance does and nothing encourages a raw recruit so much as the sight of a still rawer one There were not many drill-masters, for the best part of the officers were as untrained as the men, but each one taught his fellow what he knew When the squads were dismissed drill went on in the quarters What one failed to catch his comrade showed him how to do It is amazing how much was accomplished in this way, especially in the manual of arms, in the three days in which we lay at Covington

VIII.

THE "HELL-MARCH."

"On the March."

It was a time of intense excitement,—the conscious hush before a storm of threefold fury. The Federal army was in widely separated localities; with Pope in Virginia; where the disastrous campaign of the peninsula had just ended; with Grant in Mississippi, and with Buell in Middle Tennessee; while eight thousand men under General George W. Morgan occupied an impregnable position in Cumberland Gap. All at once, the country awoke to the fact that this force was in danger; the Confederate general, E. Kirby Smith, had collected an army in East Tennessee. What was he going to do with it? The military experts generally agreed that his purpose was to besiege General Morgan in the gap, try to cut off his supplies, and starve him into surrender. General Buell thought the movement against General Morgan was merely a feint, and that the force collected at Knoxville was intended to co-operate with Bragg on an advance into middle Tennessee. Both were half right. It was Bragg's first intention to drive back Buell's left, cut his line of communication, the Louisville and Nashville railroad, and compel him either to fight at a disadvantage or retreat across the Tennessee. In the meantime, Van Dorn was to attack Grant, Kirby Smith to invest Cumberland Gap, and, after its reduction, invade Kentucky in order to prevent troops being sent to the support of Buell

On the 9th of August, however, General Kirby Smith had suggested to Bragg a change of plan by which, instead of trying to reduce the work at Cumberland Gap he should only invest it on the south with a sufficient force to prevent the enemy's advance, while, with his main army, he should march through Big Creek and Roger's Gaps, concentrating at Barboursville Kentucky, and advance immediately on Lexington He also suggested that General Bragg, instead of operating directly against General Buell, should content himself with cutting that General's line of supply, and then turned northward, advancing by forced marches so as to unite their armies at some point in Kentucky, and move on Cincinnati or Louisville before any sufficient force could be provided for their defense

This magnificent plan of campaign excelled, both in boldness of design and evident and unquestionable feasibility, all other aggressive campaigns of the war It proposed to throw an invading army upon the wholly undefended center of a long line, both of the wings of which were fully engaged, and, at the same time demonstrate upon the flank of the enemy's chief armies in such a manner as either to compel a battle on the most disadvantageous terms, or, the abandonment of all the territory that lay between the Tennessee and Ohio rivers Whoever might have been at the head of the Army of the Ohio, the success of this plan if properly supported and vigorously carried out, would have been extremely probable with Buell in command, it was morally certain. Had it succeeded, the result would have been to transfer the line of active operations from the banks of the Tennessee to the Ohio, it would have added the State of Kentucky to the territory of the Confederacy and might, very reasonably, have turned the scale of final victory in its favor Had it been properly supported and conducted with the same boldness and enthusiasm with which it was conceived and initiated, its author would have become to the Confederate cause what Grant was to the war for the Union, the one great captain whose achievements dwarfed all others and bore down criticism with the unanswerable argument of results accomplished

The plan had two defects. (1) its author was inferior in rank to the general with whom he was to be associated, and to whom he was to be subordinate in its ultimate execution, (2) the force under the command of the officer having the initiative and most active, if not most important part to play, was entirely disproportionate to the magnitude of the work entrusted to him. Had Kirby Smith been given ten thousand more men, or even one more division and Morgan's cavalry, and had General Bragg moved a week earlier, as he promised General Smith he would, had he, even, starting when he did, contented himself with destroying Buell's communications masked Munfordville instead of waiting to reduce it, and pushed on to a rendezvous at Louisville, on a certain day, there is no reason to doubt that he would have found that city in the hands of his coadjutor on his arrival

The Federal military authorities were at first inclined to adopt the views of General Buell as to the strength and object of the army under Kirby Smith, concentrating at Knoxville, in East Tennessee After a time, the impression gained ground that it was intended to operate against General Morgan at Cumberland Gap, by cutting off his supplies Then the popular sentiment was aroused to apprehension of an actual invasion of Kentucky with a possible movement against Cincinnati and Louisville, both of which important points were almost wholly defenseless General Buell was ordered to take measures for the relief of the force at Cumberland Gap. He replied, as usual, with an argument against the step required Nevertheless, he sent General Nelson, with three brigadiers of his division, to do whatever might need to be done

With the knowledge that Smith had actually marched apprehension gave way to an excitement closely verging on panic. On the 16th of August, the Secretary of War telegraphed the governors of Ohio, Indiana, Illinois, and Michigan, begging them to send troops at once to Cincinnati and Louisville; on the next day, Governor Tod promised four regiments in five days. The Thousand was the first instalment on this pledge. On the nineteenth, the Department of Ohio was formed, and General Horatio G. Wright assigned to command, with orders, first, to relieve General Morgan, and then to see that General Buell's communications were made secure.

CORP. ROBT. A. ROWLEE, CO. C.

The discharge of this duty implied, first of all, the creation of an army of sufficient strength to resist whatever force Kirby Smith might have, and, secondly, its disposition in such manner as to baffle any movement he might make. Of such an army, the governors of the States named, furnished, with marvelous readiness, the raw materials.

But it is not an easy thing to create an army even with an abundance of the best material. It requires something more than men and arms; it needs a leader and an esprit

ROBERT ALLISON ROWLEE was born in Wethersfield, Trumbull County, Ohio, November 15, 1841. Enlisted as private in Company C; was promoted to corporal, December 18, 1862, and served as such to the close of the war. He was in every march, battle and skirmish in which the regiment was engaged but received no wound. Since the war, he has resided in Lorain, O., where he has been prominent in municipal politics, church work and charitable organizations, in many of which he has held high rank. He is of such youthful appearance that he has to carry his discharge in his pocket to make strangers believe that he really "fit through the war."

which shall pervade its every particle. There are two methods by which, given men and arms, an army may be created one is by the tedious process of daily drill, continued until the soldier becomes a machine and obedience a habit, the other is by the leadership of one in whom every soldier has an unfaltering confidence The one requires time—the other, a MAN Napoleon made his raw levies veterans in a day. One who has best described his method, represents an old soldier as saying to a newly-arrived conscript

"What is it to be a soldier? To march, to load, to aim, to fire! To die, if need be, without a word One learns it in a day The Petit Corporal does the rest!" This is the secret: courage, a little skill, a world of faith

The ability to transform a mob of brave men into an army which can win victories is the rarest of all qualities, and especially rare in professional soldiers The study of military science seems to blunt the power on which above all other qualities, success depends Grant had it, because he assumed that his men were as willing to do their duty as he was himself "Stonewall" Jackson had it, because his men saw in him an invincible determination and a confidence in himself, which no failure could daunt and no obstacle baffle He achieved apparent impossibilities because he lacked the power to doubt. Others developed it in greater or less degree as the war went on General Wright was not of this type As a cool, level-headed, faithful organizer,—a man who kept all the threads of a great work, suddenly thrust upon him, steadily in hand, never once losing sight of any part by absorption in any other part, his administration of the short-lived Department of the Ohio will always remain a testimony of the highest soldierly steadfastness and remarkable executive ability

Few men have ever done so much under such hopeless conditions as he accomplished in his first month in this command He had not, however, the power to inspire men to supreme exertion or, if he had, did not feel at liberty to take his hand off the throttle of the great engine under his control long enough to lead an army against the enemy which threatened the line committed to his care. To his credit be it said, however, he knew the man who could do this very thing, and begged again and again, that Sheridan might be sent to command the army opposite Cincinnati. "Sheridan," he wrote to Halleck, "would be worth his weight in gold." Given Sheridan to command the raw levies, General Wright promised that he would speedily drive Kirby Smith out of Kentucky. Had his prayer been granted how different would have been the history of the next two months!

Instead of Sheridan General Wright had as commander of his Army of Kentucky, Gen. William Nelson, a man, in spite of many excellencies, peculiarly unfitted for the task assigned him. Impetuous and daring to a fault, he lacked the power of conciliating and inspiring others. Long service in the navy had poorly prepared him for the command of volunteer troops, unless, by experience, they had come to appreciate his good qualities and overlook his harshness and severity. He lacked breadth and scope and was without that subtlety which previses an enemy's purpose or the self-control which foils an opponent by skilful disposition whenever doubt exists with regard to his strength or purpose. He treated his superiors with arrogance and his inferiors with brutality. If invective could have destroyed he would have annihilated both his enemies and his friends. Such a man, no matter what his military capacity, was certainly not likely to succeed in the command of raw troops, whose intelligence he insulted with profane diatribes, whose ardor he cooled by harsh rebuke, and whose effectiveness he well-nigh destroyed by lack of confidence.

Besides this, he was an especial favorite with and admirer of, General Buell, by whom he had been relieved from the command of his division, then lying at McMinnville, Tennessee, early in August, when the rumor of an invasion of Kentucky first arose, and with three of his brigade commanders, Generals Manson, Cruft, and James S

Jackson, assigned to command the forces in this State. Before he arrived, however, the Department of the Ohio had been created and General Wright assigned to it. This department embraced Kentucky, Ohio, Indiana, Illinois, and Michigan, and put General Nelson and his forces under General Wright's command. Whether Nelson regarded this as an affront to himself or to General Buell, it is certain that he did not act in harmony with his new superior, his conduct and language sometimes verging upon insubordination. Thoroughly imbued with the views and policy of his old commander, he seemed unable to rid himself of the idea that General Buell was still in control of his movements. It was no doubt largely due to this unfortunate bias in favor of his commander, that General Nelson's disposition of the forces in his new command was, apparently, in direct violation of the orders of his department commander, and resulted in useless and inexcusable disaster.

SERGT. JOHN F. HUMISTON, CO. E.

Hardly was the last belt-plate issued and the voucher for it signed, when the Thousand were ordered to the front.

It was a hot, dusty ride to Lexington, eighty miles to the southward; but they were eager eyes which scanned

JOHN F. HUMISTON was born in Charleston, Portage County, Ohio, in 1839. His parents moved to Chester, Geauga County, where he lived until the breaking out of the war. He enlisted in the 7th Ohio regimental band in July, 1861, and was discharged in June, 1862. Re-enlisting in the 105th he became a sergeant of Company E, and was mustered out with the regiment. He went to Minnesota in 1872, and is now engaged in the hardware trade at Huron Lake, Jackson County, of that State.

from the roofs and doors of crowded freight-cars the unaccustomed scene. What was the ineradicable stamp which slavery left upon the land and people which it touched? Hardly a score of the Thousand had ever been on slave territory before, and each felt at once its strange unaccustomedness. The houses, the fields, the people gathered at the stations, all bore the impress of another life. It was a surprise almost, to hear the same language spoken, and one noted, instinctively, that the master had bound the slave's limbs, the slave had put his seal upon the master's tongue. It was "Dixie land," we felt its charm though we did not define the cause. The grass was parched and sere upon the softly rounded hills, the pools were dry, the low branching oaks showed brown and dusty under the summer sunshine, the wild wormwood grew rank and green above the stubble, the shorthorns roamed restlessly about, vexed with thirst and stung with flies. It was rich and beautiful, the famous Blue Grass region that unfolded itself before our appreciative gaze — but the Blue Grass region lying parched and glistening in the heat and dust of an almost unprecedented drouth.

Yet even then, when at night we made our first bivouac on a sloping hillside, with a fringe of noble trees upon the crest, a tiny stream trickling from a placid pool that lay below a great spring-house, through the mossy stones of which its waters fell, a spacious mansion in a stately grove upon the opposite hill, with its white "slave quarters" glistening in the moonlight, there was not one among them who did not feel, not only that he was in a foreign land, but that he had never looked upon a fairer scene.

From the mansion there was no greeting. An overseer, with a chronic snarl upon his face, came to inquire and object to our intrusion. A colored woman sold milk and butter at the spring-house until there was no more to sell. After the guards were set, black figures stole softly down from the "quarters," crept up to the sentinels, who, scrupulous in the discharge of their duties, kept the sergeant of the guard busy bringing them to the officer on duty They came into his presence with soft, apologetic steps, making excuse as the instinctive knowledge of character which slavery gave, taught them to do, asked a few questions, answered cautiously such questions as were asked, showing clearly that prescience of a result, which the wisest and most hopeful dared hardly anticipate, which marked the slave's view of the situation everywhere After a little, they slipped away, one by one, the officer making no attempt to detain them

The harvest-moon shone brightly on the rows of sleeping men, each one of whom had his new rifle close beside him Were they not on the very theater of action?

This was the military situation when, on the 25th of August, Adjutant Robbins reported the Thousand to General Nelson, in command of the District of Kentucky, at his headquarters in Lexington, eighty miles due south of Cincinnati, on the road to Cumberland Gap Fifteen miles beyond runs the Kentucky river, ten miles farther on is the town of Richmond, just beyond which were camped two brigades under General Manson, numbering about seven thousand men There were troops at Lancaster, a brigade at Nicholasville; some regiments at Versailles, a camp at Frankfort, and two brigades at Lexington These, with Dumont's division at Lebanon and other points on the Louisville and Nashville railroad, constituted the Army of Kentucky under General Nelson's command General Boyle, at Louisville, and the garrisons of Bowling Green and Munfordville received orders directly from General Wright, the department commander The troops in and about Lexington, General Nelson estimated a few days later, at sixteen thousand men Seventy miles beyond Richmond, at Barboursville, lay the Confederate general Kirby Smith, with the force he brought through Rogers and Big Creek Gaps. He was twenty-five miles to the rear of Cumberland Gap, where the Federal general, George W. Morgan, was shut up with seven thousand men

There were two unknown quantities in this situation first how many troops had the Confederate general? second what did he intend to do with them? As to the first, General Smith's force had been reported all the way from fifteen hundred to thirty thousand men. They were veterans; the Federal forces about Lexington were all raw levies. General Wright seems to have thought Cincinnati was the Confederate objective. General Buell thought Smith intended to march westward, cut the railroad, and join Bragg in his expected movement on Nashville. General Nelson agreed as usual, with General Buell. Indeed, his despatches read like an echo of his old commander's thought.

The day before August 24th General Wright gave General Nelson this order.

If the enemy is in force, get your troops together and do not risk a general battle at Richmond, unless you are sure of success. Better fall back to a more defensible position, say the Kentucky river, than risk much.

To this General Nelson had replied from Lexington, on the same day.

The enemy variously estimated from fifteen hundred to eight thousand at or near Richmond. I fear it is Kirby Smith that has come up. I will go to Richmond myself tonight.

Clinging fast to the hypothesis that General Smith's objective was the Louisville and Nashville railroad, which he wished to cut, en route to join Bragg in his expected move upon Nashville, General Nelson seems to have concluded that he would march west from Rogersville and London, rather than advance on Lexington, through Richmond. To meet this purely hypothetical and wholly absurd movement, instead of obeying the explicit order of his department commander, he directed Dumont to march to Danville, and sent Jackson with his brigade to Nicholasville, intending to concentrate at Lancaster to intercept the enemy. Had his views of the Confederate general's strength and purpose been correct, the combination he planned might have been well enough, as against a superior force of veteran troops, under an enterprising leader, it was a movement which should never have been attempted

The simple fact is that General Nelson believed General Smith's strength did not exceed eight thousand men, that being the number of the two divisions which had made the wonderful march through Roger's Gap under his immediate command, entirely omitting from his estimate Heth's division of seven thousand, who came through Big Creek Gap, the brigade of cavalry which preceded them, and the five thousand from Stevenson's command, with which General Smith had been reinforced Because he chose not to believe these reports, he felt at liberty to disobey the command of his superior

While the Thousand slept in their first bivouac, General Bragg's order for his army to move out of the Sequatchie valley by way of Sparta, en route to Glasgow, Kentucky, was being carried to his corps commanders On that night, Buell's adjutant-general, Colonel Fry, telegraphed from the headquarters of his chief, who was waiting to be attacked at Decherd, Tennessee, to General Rousseau, at Huntsville, Alabama: "No fight, Bragg is very slow, if he wants one, he can have it We are all ready

Bragg was indeed "slow,"—a whole week behind the date he had fixed to begin his march to meet Smith in Central Kentucky; but it would be still another week, when he had crossed the Cumberland river without opposition, before the credulous and self-conscious Buell would believe that he was going to Kentucky instead of coming to fight him upon a battlefield near Murfreesborough, for which he made special inquiry four days later, as we have seen

There were four days of quiet camp-life—the very poetry of war The tents were pitched in a magnificent grove a hundred acres of brown pasture, baked with drouth until it echoed like a tiled floor beneath the tread, served as our drill-ground We mocked at rumors of impending peril, because we heard that our commander did so and read the veracious reports which appeared in the journals of the North. War news was manufactured far more readily then and in more slipshod fashion than would be tolerated now. Anything to fill a column, the more startling and improbable it was the better, seemed to be the rule. In that way, the men who fought the battles became terribly tangled in regard to what really happened and what was reported to have happened. Not seldom the latter has gone upon the record as veritable history and the former been forgotten or regarded as merely fanciful.

The days were full of duty, study and drill for officers and men alike. Squad and company movements, the manual of arms and the simplest of battalion maneuvers were practised with the utmost assiduity. No such luxury as target-shooting was indulged, nor was volley-firing permitted, except to the guard, who were allowed to fire their guns when relieved from duty. Because of this privilege, detail for guard duty was then as eagerly sought for as it came afterwards to be avoided. Fortunately, most of the regiment had been used to firearms from boyhood. The routine of loading was somewhat different but the general handling of the piece was the same. Our arms were the Springfield muzzle-loaders, an excellent weapon of its kind. But one cannot help wondering now, why was it not until June, 1863, that the magazine rifle was first used in action by our soldiers? It was not because they were not procurable, for a half-dozen firms were pressing their adoption on the government. There were two reasons given: one that there was a job behind the delay on which the fortunes of some of our statesmen depended; another, that the officers of the regular army thought it an unjustifiable extravagance to put rapid-firing guns into the hands of volunteers. They insisted that only long training could prepare the soldier to use the muzzle-loader effectually, and, of course, a much longer period would be necessary to teach them to load and fire a breech-loader. The reasoning was not entirely without fault, but it is characteristic of the class to which it was attributed, that one is inclined to believe both stories, and conclude that our army was deprived of more efficient weapons for two years, by the combined forces of prejudice and profit Possibly, neither is the true reason; perhaps it was genuine fear that the more intricate mechanism of the magazine breech-loader unfitted it for army use At any rate, the fact remains, and the Thousand learned its manual with the cheerful ring of the iron ramrods in the empty barrels, to aid the officer in timing his commands in firing-drill

On the 30th of August, the ninth day after muster-in, the regiment was engaged, between drills, in drawing the last of our equipments, blankets, overcoats and shoes Hitherto, we had had only a half a blanket apiece, and even this supply was somewhat short, but in the dog-days a little cover suffices Most of the men had supplied themselves with rubber ponchos The heavy double blankets which the placid quartermaster and his hustling sergeant deposited in every company street looked terribly burdensome to the perspiring soldiers, whose knapsacks were already full to bursting with the clothing which a generous government had heaped upon them with a too lavish hand They had no more need of overcoats and double blankets in August, in the very stress of a Kentucky drouth, than they had for foot-stoves or warming-pans, but they had not yet learned to limit their demands to their necessities, and having a chance to draw supplies, supposed the correct thing was to take all that was going Whoever ordered requisitions for winter clothing at that time, earned some deserved curses during the six eventful days that followed, and many more, afterwards, when the men came to realize how this extra clothing had eaten into their pay accounts

The issue was but half-completed when the long-roll sounded for the first time in earnest. How the palpitating drums throbbed and echoed! How the quickening pulses answered! In all the world there is nothing like this instant, imperative call to arms In a moment all else is forgotten

"Fall in!" echoes from end to end of the camp The men lounging in their shirt-sleeves run for their clothes and equipments. Officers rush to their quarters and don their side-arms All over the camp is the buzz of wondering inquiry, the snapping of belt-plates, and the hum of hurried preparation Orderlies align their companies and begin their roll-calls The adjutant passes down the line giving a hurried verbal order to each company commander

"The regiment will move in an hour in light marching order, with two days' rations and forty rounds of ammunition!"

The rations were unobtainable, but the ammunition was distributed, and the quartermaster ordered to follow with the rations There were rumors of a fight in progress The rumble of artillery had come to us on the sultry air just as the afternoon drill began, some said it was artillery while others thought it thunder There had been four heavy detonations in rapid succession, and then silence

Just as the sun went down the Thousand marched out of its first camp on its way towards a field of battle where the fight had already been lost. It was our first march. The road was the rough stone pike so common in Kentucky and Tennessee It was past midnight when we halted, a dozen miles from Lexington, and throwing out pickets in front and on the flanks, lay down in a cornfield in line of battle and slept until dawn Then we moved forward nearly to the Kentucky line where we halted to allow the shattered fragments of a defeated army to pass us to the rear

This time it was not the unexpected that happened what had been clearly and unmistakably indicated, had occurred Kirby Smith had marched from Barboursville on the morning of the twenty-seventh. On the twenty-ninth his cavalry had driven in General Manson's pickets That officer had formed his brigade and marched forward two or three miles, driving back the Confederate advance-guard in a sharp skirmish He did not send any order to

General Cruft, commanding the other brigade, two miles in his rear. It is evident that he shared the general belief, that instead of an invading force, the troops in front were a mere raiding party, which he coveted the glory of dispersing without assistance. So, instead of retreating as the department commander had ordered, behind the Kentucky river, he advanced with only half his force and gave battle. Elated by apparent success, he fancied that he had driven back the whole force of the enemy, and sent a message to the commander of his other brigade, that he could maintain his position and needed no assistance. So, a little army of less than eight thousand raw levies lay all night in front of double their number of veterans, gathering through the night to overwhelm them. As if this were not odds enough, the Union general had divided his little force into two parts, with an interval of five miles between them. Before the fight began he had reported to General Nelson, at Lexington, that the enemy had appeared in his front and he "anticipated an engagement." Nelson immediately sent orders to him not to fight, but to retreat on the Lancaster road. With his usual impetuosity, which counted an order made as already executed, Nelson, racked with gout, procured a buggy and started for Lancaster, lavishing curses upon all whom he conceived in any way responsible for the discomfort he suffered.

He expected, very unreasonably, to find Manson at Lancaster, where he arrived at half-past nine on the morning of the thirtieth. Instead, he heard the booming of cannon in the direction of Richmond. Procuring fresh horses, he set out in the direction of the firing, and stealing along unfrequented byways, at half-past two in the afternoon he came upon the field already lost beyond the hope of recovery. He rode among the fleeing fugitives frenzied with rage, raining curses and blows upon them, commanding them to stand and fight. A few obeyed, a wavering line was formed. The enemy advanced with their accustomed yell, there were a few hasty volleys, then the line gave way and the tide of fugitives surged to the rear, only to be hemmed in by the enemy's cavalry, which swarmed ahead of the wings and enveloped the doomed multitude as in a net. Wounded in the foot, raging with pain and chagrin, Nelson somehow escaped and reached Lexington during the night of the thirtieth. Cruft's brigade had been brought forward before Nelson's arrival on the field, and was involved in the general rout. The loss was 210 killed, 844 wounded, and 4800 captured. One-third of the Army of Kentucky had been practically annihilated. The blame, as usual, was laid upon the troops, who were said to have been "struck with a panic," and "being raw troops, broke and ran after a few volleys," instead of upon the rash and incapable general to whose blindness and flagrant disobedience of orders this great disaster was clearly due.

With this tide of defeat, the Thousand returned to Lexington, where they arrived at nine o'clock at night in the midst of a drenching shower, only to meet an order to go on picket. They had marched with hardly half a day's rations instead of the amount ordered, that being all the quartermaster could supply, and few had eaten since morning. These facts being reported, the order to go on picket was revoked, and they were directed to bivouac in the market-house, where coffee and an abundant supply of bread and meat were served to them. It was midnight when we sank to rest after our first march—a march of twenty-eight miles in less than thirty hours—on the rough pavement of the market-place, a foot-sore and weary multitude.

On the morrow, the evacuation of Lexington began. At eight o'clock we were ordered out on the Nicholasville pike. All day long the work of destroying government stores which had accumulated at this point went on. The smoke of their burning hung over the city, while clouds of dust rose from the roads to the westward leading to Versailles and Frankfort, on which our wagon-trains were already in motion. To the south and southeastward were other dust-clouds, showing the course of the main body of the enemy, who, having crossed the Kentucky river, were advancing on Lexington, and of Heth's division, which reached Winchester that afternoon The day was setting when the Thousand marched through the streets of Lexington—the last regiment of the Army of Kentucky on its retreat to Louisville, ninety-five miles away, as the crow flies, a hundred and more by the roads we were to take A small battalion of cavalry waited at the outskirts of the town for us to pass. They were to constitute the mounted rear-guard Some time in the night they missed the way and followed the first division of the wagon-train, which had taken another road, leaving us on the eleventh day of our service in the most trying of all military positions, that of rear-guard of an army fleeing from a victorious foe So far as the enemy's infantry were concerned, we had one full day's start of them. Their cavalry might, indeed, overtake us, but if we succeeded in crossing the Kentucky river before they did so, we would be secure from attack thereafter. This river flows through a deep and precipitous gorge, making it practically impassable, save by bridge or ferry, below a point nearly due south from Lexington If the enemy had crossed his main force to the right bank of the river, as seemed probable, we had only to cross to the left bank, at Clifton and Frankfort and destroy three or four bridges to be safe from his pursuit for several days If he divided his forces and left part upon the left bank, he would have this impassable barrier between them This it was not at all likely he would do When, therefore, we passed through Lexington and took the road to Versailles, we supposed the plan of retreat was to cross that river, destroy the bridges and ferries, and make it, at least, a temporary line of defense. The knowledge that before another nightfall we might be safe beyond this great defensive barrier buoyed us up with that strange confidence a soldier feels when he believes that his commander has outwitted his antagonist.

The day before, General Nelson, suffering from the pain of his wound and the chagrin of his defeat at Richmond, had relinquished the command of the Army of Kentucky. This devolved the command of the forces about Lexington either upon General James S Jackson, commanding the cavalry brigade, or General Charles Cruft, the junior brigadier in the disastrous fight at Richmond Neither of these officers being professional soldiers, desired to assume a merely temporary command at so critical a juncture General Horatio G Wright, commanding the department, therefore assumed the responsibility of usurping the constitutional powers of the President, and appointed Capt C C Gilbert, of the First regular infantry, a major-general, and assigned him to the command of the Army of Kentucky during General Nelson's disability At the same time, and in the same curious manner, Capt. William R Terrill, of the Fifth regular artillery, was made a brigadier-general.

It was under the command of General Gilbert, with Generals Jackson, Cruft, and Terrill as subordinates, that the retreat to Louisville was made No report of this movement is to be found in the Official Record of the War of Rebellion, either by the officer in command or any of his subordinates This is especially singular when we reflect that General Gilbert was a great stickler for regularity, and his command must have consisted of at least eight thousand infantry, with two regiments of cavalry and three batteries of artillery What accessions it received at Versailles and Frankfort is unknown Surely, so important a movement of so considerable an army at so critical a time, was not of so little importance as to be unworthy of a report The artillery was under the command of General Terrill The cavalry rear-guard was commanded by Captain Gay, who was soon after made chief of cavalry of the Army of Kentucky, and then assigned to the same position in the Army of Ohio He was another instance of a regular army captain assigned to high command without regard to the rank of his volunteer subordinates

It had not rained for many weeks save the shower of the night before, which had hardly reached a mile west of Lexington The dust lay ankle deep upon the hard, hot, limestone pike The forces that preceded us with their numerous wagons, had raised a cloud which hung over the road, shutting out even the walls and fences on either side The setting sun shone red and dim through the yellow mass. Each man was weighed down with knapsack and accoutrements We knew nothing of our destination, or the length of the march before us. Had the knapsacks been burned at the outset, many more would have reached the goal Men were invisible a few steps away, near at hand, they could only be distinguished by their voices There were frequent halts, but no rest. When the column ahead got jammed up on itself, we waited until it straightened out Sometimes it was a minute, sometimes ten or twenty minutes The yellow, acrid dust settled on beard and hair, got into the eyes and mouth, and burned the parched throat, while the perspiration made muddy channels down every face

The night fell hot and murky The dust-cloud shut out the stars. By and by the moon rose, the night grew chill, but still the dust rose in choking clouds The orders forbade details to leave the road in search of water Men were sent on in advance, in hope that they might fill the canteens before the wells were drained Long before midnight not a drop remained In spite of orders a few men were sent out to search for water It was a strange country The pools and streams were dry The wells had been exhausted by those in front Many of the people were compelled to haul water from a distance for domestic use These details returned empty-handed as the others had done About this time colored men came, one by one, and offered to bring water, to carry guns or knapsacks, — anything, if they could only follow us They were loaded down with canteens and accompanied by a few men started for water. An hour after they returned, staggering under their loads of dripping canteens Was ever water half so sweet! Yet we had scarcely begun to know what thirst is

The march would have been a severe one to seasoned unencumbered veterans, to these men yet foot-sore galled and weary from their first long march, and weighted down with knapsacks, overcoats, and blankets, in addition to ammunition and accoutrements, it was terrible. After a time, the men ceased to scatter to the roadside when there came a halt. They had no strength to spare, and the roadside was almost as dusty as the pike So they merely knelt down in their places, bowed themselves forward to relieve the strain on the straps that galled and cut into the shoulder, and slept In the moonlight they looked like heaps of dust, or pilgrims fallen asleep at prayer At the word they stumbled to their feet sometimes awake, sometimes asleep and staggered on The ambulances were soon full It was said, there were wagons somewhere in front in which those who were unable to go farther might be transported But when a man can go no farther such provision is of little good We were the rear of the column, back of us was only our own rear-guard and the enemy

There were several alarms during the night, firing off at the left, then at the right, then in our rear It was probably marauding bands of guerrillas, who set upon our men in search of water Once we were stampeded There had been a longer halt than usual The dusty fugitives knelt in the road or were stretched out beside it There was an uproar at the rear, the sound of galloping hoofs upon the pike There was a cry of "Rebs!" "Cavalry!" Every sleeping figure sprang suddenly to life Men ran over each other, stumbled, sprawled headlong, then rose and fled over the wall into an adjoining field; across that to a bit of wood When the pike was clear, a big gray mule came charging down it, frisking his tail, and making night hideous with his discordant bray. One lieutenant, who found himself, on waking, pinioned between two rocks had no sooner extricated himself than, impressed with the ludicrousness of the situation, he posted himself in the middle of the pike, and between roars of laughter began to shout. "Fall in, One Hundred and Fifth Ohio!" He was cursed with a gift of mimicry, and it may be that half-unconsciously he imitated the tones of his superiors, but he had no purpose to give offense, nor any idea that his levity would disturb any one's self-complacency, until a man who was tugging at a bridle-rein remarked that he did not "see anything to make such a damned clamor over," adding, "You seem to think it funny, but we shall never hear the last of that darned mule!"

Sure enough, we never have. At each reunion that beast is trotted out, and now everybody laughs at our "mule stampede." The lieutenant had to pay a sore price for his untimely jest, but in that case, as in many another, "he laughs best who laughs last."

The morning was already hot and lurid as the dusty column crept through Versailles, and after an hour's halt for breakfast, pressed on toward Frankfort. The enemy had followed the cavalry by way of Big Spring, so that our rear was undisturbed until we were in sight of Frankfort. The sun was going down when we reached the capital of Kentucky. It is but twenty-nine miles from Lexington by the most direct route. The one by which we had come was half a dozen more. It could hardly be termed a march; it was a flight.

For the first time the Thousand saw at Frankfort, the semblance of an army. The streets were full of trains. Lines of blue-coated, dusty men found their way between them or lay stretched upon the sidewalks. The cavalry came scurrying in upon their jaded horses, reporting the enemy in force only a little way out. Columns were marching heavily this way and that, taking positions covering the roads from the eastward. Guns were posted on commanding eminences. Despite the seeming confusion, there were not lacking evidences of order. For a half-hour we lay upon a gentle slope which overlooked the valley, and watched the dispositions made for defense. We could see the long line of wagons moving toward the bridge, and stretching from the bridge away westward. It was evident that there was to be no long delay at this point, and equally evident that it was to be held until the trains had crossed the river.

Thus far, we had known almost nothing of our commanding officers. We understood that we were in Colonel Anderson's brigade, and Gen. James S. Jackson's division; but as to what composed either the brigade or the division, we were without knowledge. Even now it is almost impossible to ascertain the facts. We knew that General Jackson was a Kentuckian, who had been in command of the cavalry of the Army of Kentucky before the fight at Richmond. Strangely enough, these two facts did much to inspire confidence in him. The raw recruit has always a most exaggerated idea of the efficiency of cavalry, and the Confederate general, John H. Morgan, had already made famous the Kentucky cavalry. Then, too, there was a bewildering intricacy in southern roads to those accustomed

CORP. BLISS MORSE, CO. D.

BLISS MORSE was born November 11, 1837, in Le Roy, Lake County, Ohio; lived on his father's farm until he enlisted in Company D, of which he was made corporal, and mustered out with the regiment in that capacity. He was in nearly all the operations of the regiment; was among those captured with the forage train on January 21, 1863, in front of Murfreesborough. The writer is indebted to him for the account given of the treatment accorded the enlisted men on that occasion. His home is now at Breckinridge, Mo.

only to the parallel roads and cross-roads of the sections and townships of the northwest. Going over the hills or around them, with no apparent regard to direction; crossed here and there by more or less used country roads, intersected everywhere with bridle-paths and private ways, the northern soldier, until he became accustomed to it, was sure to get lost whenever he tried to find his way anywhere except upon the main roads that led from one important point to another. We assumed that, being a Kentuckian General Jackson was able to meet the Confederate cavalry on even terms. We were to make his acquaintance that night, not altogether pleasantly.

As we entered the city, we found a company of fifty or more special constables ranged on each side the street and having in custody a number of colored men who had been taken, not without remonstrance, from among the ranks of the regiments which preceded us. These men were slaves who had taken this method to escape from bondage. They represented to their masters, and to every inhabitant of a slaveholding community, simply so much money. The taking them from their masters, or aiding them to escape was, in the estimation of people accustomed to the legal estate of slavery, the most infamous of crimes—a crime so despicable, indeed, as to debase the white man who was guilty of it, to the lowest possible level of popular contempt. Of this fact, the men who composed the Thousand were only dimly conscious. They knew, of course, that it was a technical violation of law to aid a slave's escape, but so absolutely antipodal was the state of society from which they came, that it was there looked upon as one of the least blameworthy of crimes, while to willingly aid in returning a fugitive to slavery would have exposed one to almost universal contumely.

The policy of the government in the early days of the war had been to return all fugitives who came into our lines; afterwards, the return of fugitives to disloyal owners in states in rebellion was prohibited, while in other states the army was forbidden to interfere with the operation of the state laws, that is, the Federal troops were to stand neutral, neither taking the slave from his master nor compelling him to return This policy developed a curious conflict of authority Of course, a commanding officer could not be required to admit every one within his lines who claimed to be in search of a fugitive, nor was he required to presume that every colored man was a slave Some officers naturally construed the general orders upon the subject freely in favor of the master, and allowed any one who claimed to be in search of a runaway free access to their camps Others construed them strictly in favor of the slave, and demanded not only the identification and location of the slave within their lines, but also proof of ownership, before they would allow the master to take him, except with his own consent In like manner, orders intended to prevent fugitives from seeking shelter in the camps, were construed to prevent the master from entering

In every Southern State the apprehension and return of runaway slaves to their masters was a profitable business Any one was authorized to arrest a colored man traveling without a written pass or duly authorized free papers and lodge him in jail A description of him was then published and the owner had to pay a certain sum for his apprehension, the sheriff's fee for advertising, board, and other legal charges Knowing that many slaves would seek to escape with the retreating army, a large force of deputies was set to watch the columns as the army passed through Frankfort, and arrest every colored man on the chance of his being a runaway Not only was this proceeding abhorrent to the sentiment of the northern soldiers, but they felt especially grateful toward those who had brought water and borne their burden during the terrible march of the preceding night No doubt the colonel shared this feeling At any rate, the command was halted, bayonets fixed, and with closed ranks and shouldered arms we entered the city A few colored men, still loaded with burdens, walked between the files The constables made a rush here and there The lowered guns obstructed them There were threats and blows, several of the men were struck, there was a rumor that one or two of the constables were hurt We marched on some of the constables following, and were halted on the pavement in front of the state-house. It was growing dark. Fires were lighted in the streets and water heated to make coffee when the rations should be procured A guard was set outside the line of gun-stacks. One or two frightened negroes were hidden under heaps of knapsacks and blankets, next the wall The constables watched across the way There was a clatter of hoofs, and General Jackson with some of his staff and a few of his body-guard, halted opposite the center

"Who commands this regiment?

In the temporary absence of his superiors, the major stepped forward and saluted

What regiment is it?"

"The One Hundred and Fifth Ohio

"I am told your men resisted the officers, who sought to arrest a lot of runaway niggers"

'A lot of men with clubs and pistols caused considerable confusion by trying to break through our ranks," said the major

'They were officers, sir," answered the General "Several of them were injured' His tones were loud and angry The men crowded up to the guard-line to hear The firelight shone on the guns and the bright trappings of the general's suite

"I understand some of the men were hurt, also,' responded the major

Served them right, they should not have resisted the officers of the law'

"The officers ought not to have obstructed our march," was the quiet reply

'Did they have any warrants?" piped a voice from the sidewalk A law student in the ranks was airing his acquirements

"It is not necessary—any man has a right to arrest a runaway negro in Kentucky," replied one of the staff

"You will put the men who assaulted the officers under arrest," the general commanded

The major bowed

One of the constables stepped forward and spoke to the general

"Could you identify him?" he asked "A slight man with a mustache, you say? Really, there seem to be several such here—looks as if they were mostly all boys," he added, with a smile, as he glanced up and down the firelit lines of dusty faces This remark was greeted by a laugh

"What has become of the niggers—the runaways?" inquired the general

The major shook his head

"How do you tell a runaway nigger from any other?" asked one in the crowd

"There is one of them now," interrupted one of the general's attendants, pointing to the right of the regiment, where Captain Edwards' servant, Ned, was preparing supper for the officers of Company A The general spurred his horse toward the man A dozen voices shouted to Ned, who turned to run

"Stop, you black rascal!" shouted the general "Who do you belong to?" he continued, as he reined up beside the trembling man, who stood, coffee-pot in hand, looking up at his questioner

"He is my servant, sir," said Captain Edwards, rising from the curbstone and saluting Edwards was the nattiest officer in the regiment, and despite the hard march we had been through, was as trim a soldier as one need ever hope to see

"Your servant? Where did you get him? I know the nigger—have seen him in Lexington Who do you belong to?" he repeated, addressing Ned.

The captain answered for him "I brought him from home, he is on the rolls as my servant"

"Be jabers," said one of Company A, coolly, "thin he belongs to Uncle Sam, the same as the rist av us!"

"Major," said the general to that officer, who had followed him down the line, "do you know that nigger?"

"I have understood that he is Captain Edwards' servant."

"Did he bring him from Ohio?"

"I don't know."

"Is he a free man?"

"I know nothing about it."

"You are all Abolition nigger-stealers," said the general, hotly. "I know the man; you can take him."

The constable advanced toward Ned.

"I don't see," said one of the onlookers, "that it is very much worse to steal a slave than to steal a free man, and not half as likely to be profitable."

"I wonder what old Abe would say to that sort of 'contraband' business," said another; in the darkness it was impossible to designate individuals.

These suggestions seemed to be not without weight to the general, whose new honors could only ripen into veritable rank by presidential approval.

"Never mind," he said to the constable, "I may be mistaken. Major, you will see that the man is forthcoming when he is wanted. We can't stop to hunt up everybody's runaway niggers, now."

He turned and galloped down the street, while Ned proceeded with his duties. There was no braver or more loyal soldier than Gen. James S. Jackson. He had served his country in the war with Mexico, was a member of the Thirty-first Congress, and was one of the first of the Union men of the South to spring to arms. This incident serves, feebly enough, to show the strength of sentiment which such men had to combat in the performance of duty. The country for which they gave so much, has been strangely unappreciative of a class who sacrificed more than any other for their devotion to it.

The incident shows how far apart in moral sentiment were the gallant general and the troops he led — the one fighting for the Union to save slavery, the other inspired by hope for its destruction It was a strange fate which decreed that the last sight that met his eyes should be the very "nigger-stealers" whom he contemned, rushing forward into the jaws of death to execute the last order that fell from his lips

It was ten o clock when the weary detail brought with dragging feet the rations they had been hours in seeking Coffee was quickly made, a half-cooked meal was eaten, and we sank again to slumber At two o'clock we were roused by whispered orders. The city was quiet save for the careful tread of moving columns and the steady rumble of wagons crossing the bridge on the pike beyond Our destination was now clear Frankfort, lying on both sides of the Kentucky river, offered a fairly good defensive position against the progress of an enemy upon the right bank of the river, to which the Confederates had evidently crossed. A very small force by destroying the bridges, could here delay a pursuing army for several days If the retreat was necessary, as it no doubt was, to leave the bridges standing after we crossed, would be the gravest of military crimes But the authorities of Kentucky protested against the bridges being burned So they were left standing until the enemy, in turn, found it necessary to retreat Then they were burned

The foot-sore and exhausted soldiers were with difficulty roused from sleep. It is little wonder Within four days they had marched seventy miles, laid in line of battle one night and marched all of another Every foot was blistered, every muscle was sore Heavy with sleep they staggered to their places in the line, the stronger aiding the weaker ones There were moans and curses Some of the stoutest of yesterday were now the faintest Slowly we dragged our way to our position in the retreating column and stumbled painfully along in the darkness. With the dawn came the sound of firing in our rear. The enemy's cavalry had crossed the bridge we kindly left standing for their accommodation A line of battle was formed upon a range of hills that lay across the pike The men cheered as they filed out of the cloud of dust, at the prospect of being allowed to fight As we flung ourselves upon the ground in the line of battle, it was with the feeling that we would rather die than retreat farther But the enemy did not attack As a matter of fact, his force was insignificant, but having once underestimated his strength, our officers had now gone to the other extreme and greatly overrated it

Several times during the day, this maneuver was repeated The march grew more and more difficult with each hot and dusty mile. Men dropped unconscious from heat and thirst Water was still scarce Every well and spring was drained Men crowded about them, pushing, scrambling, often fighting for a few muddy drops. Tormented by heat and thirst, and almost smothered by dust, we dragged through the long hours of that day, bivouacking at night by the roadside, with no water save what was found after a long search in some stagnant pools two miles away

At one o'clock came the order to move, and we again plodded on, halting every few minutes, the men dropping on their faces in the dust, would be asleep almost before the command was given When the word came to march, many of them would rise and stagger on, still asleep That day we marched until eight o'clock at night, and then bivouacked, for the first time since leaving Lexington in a green field with plenty of good water The next day, September 5th, a little after noon, we reached the suburbs of Louisville, where we were to remain in camp for a month

The Thousand had been under arms continuously, on the march, on picket or in line of battle, ever since the sunset of August 30th, six days, less three hours. In that time, they had marched about one hundred and forty miles, an average of twenty-three miles for each twenty-four hours During this time, they had slept in line of battle on the night of the thirtieth, three hours, five hours in Lexington, the night of the thirty-first, marched all the night of September first, halted six hours in Frankfort the night of the second, halted five hours the night of the third, slept eight hours the night of the fourth, making in the whole six days only twenty-seven hours of sleep The heat was overwhelming, the dust suffocating, the hot lime-stone pikes scorched the blistered feet Water was very scarce and of the poorest quality Such a march would have been a trying and terrible ordeal for the toughest veterans

After three years of service, more than two hundred of the survivors have testified that it was the severest work required of them At its close, hardly one-third of the regiment was fit for duty. Scores were permanently disabled The ultimate loss was greater than that sustained in any action in which the regiment afterwards participated It is fitly designated the "Hell-March" It was a terrible experience for men who had hardly marched a mile before, and whose service only numbered fifteen days when it was ended

General Nelson in the meantime, had arrived at Louisville and soon after resumed command With his customary impatience, he made a great clamor over the fact that a considerable number of men had straggled from the column on this march, and been captured and paroled by the enemy These he denounced as cowards and malingerers, as if their fault had been wilful, and not the natural result of exhausted nature That a column of eight thousand infantry, all of them troops of less than a month's service, should make such a march with a loss of less than five hundred men, is to the credit, rather than the discredit of the regiments of which it was composed The irate general, however, demanded that the severest punishments be imposed upon all such. Moved by this action of his superior, no doubt, Colonel Hall, forgetful of the strain his men had been called upon to bear, ordered that the entry, "straggled on the retreat from Lexington," should be placed on the muster-rolls against the names of all who fell out, and that they also be deprived of six months pay The order itself was a military offense hardly less grave than that charged against its victims Leaving out of consideration the fact that the colonel had no power to make an order depriving an enlisted man of pay at his own discretion, it should be remembered that these men were condemned, without trial, for an offense of which most of them were not guilty By far the greater number were undoubtedly permitted to leave the ranks to go in search of water, by the officers in command of the companies. Wandering about in a strange region, faint with prolonged exertion and loss of sleep, they sat down to rest, expecting soon to proceed upon their quest or renew the task of overtaking the regiment Exhausted nature would have its way, and they did not waken until summoned to surrender by our pursuers. In a case which came under the writer's own notice, a man from whose shoes blood had oozed at every step for miles, was told by his captain that if he left his place he would lose his position as a sergeant When he could endure no longer, he fell out, exclaiming "I cannot take another step!" The rear-guard missed him in the darkness, and he was captured Probably only a small proportion of those who fell under this sweeping and unlawful condemnation, were physically able to complete this terribly exhausting march The order was afterward revoked through the intervention of Governor Tod, who saw both its injustice and illegality Military law is of necessity, arbitrary in character, but only the rankest despotism punishes without a hearing

IX.

THE SCHOOL OF "DOUBLE DUTY."

A MONTH had elapsed since the long-roll first sounded in the camp of the Thousand—twenty-six days after the "hell-march" ended, and forty-one days after they were mustered into service—when the order came for them to march again, this time in the golden October weather, on that campaign which resulted in the wasted bloodshed of the short, sharp, and shameful battle of Perryville.

The interval had been one of absorbing interest, especially to the little army of untrained citizen-soldiers which constituted the garrison of Louisville. The retreat from Lexington had been contemporaneous with the defeat of Pope in Virginia, followed swiftly by the first invasion of Maryland, culminating in the battle of Antietam and the surrender of Harper's Ferry. At the time, Van Dorn moved on the rear of Grant's position in Mississippi, united his army with that of Price, and the battles of Iuka and Corinth quickly followed. These movements made it impossible to withdraw any considerable force from the Federal armies, either in the east or the west, to strengthen the center, with its two imperiled bases, Cincinnati and Louisville.

Had Kirby Smith advanced at once on Covington, there was nothing to prevent his making a lodgment on the south bank of the Ohio, opposite Cincinnati, by the time the

Thousand reached Louisville. The distance was about the same as Gilbert's column marched, and there was no force which need have delayed him an hour, but he waited to decide what he would do, to hear from Bragg, and to gather recruits for his army in Kentucky. So the golden moment passed. What might have been accomplished almost without the loss of a man, a week later became impossible.

On the day the Thousand reached Louisville, Bragg was crossing the Cumberland river with an army of forty-five thousand men at Gainesborough, Tennessee, Buell, with fifty-five thousand, was at Murfreesborough, Tennessee, Nelson, at Louisville, had seventeen thousand men of all arms, Smith, at Lexington, had about twenty-five thousand, with forty pieces of artillery. In front of Covington there were hardly five thousand men, and these seem to have been under no responsible head, merely separate commands reporting to department headquarters. But weeks were cycles then. The next day, one whose literary fame has almost overshadowed his military renown, Gen. Lew Wallace, was assigned to the command of the forces opposite Cincinnati; and on the next, General Simpson, with an army of laborers, was ordered to complete the system of fortifications on the neck of ground south of Covington, devised and begun by Gen Ormsby M. Mitchel, nearly a year before. Within a week the spades and rifles of the tens of thousands of "Minute Men," who poured in from Ohio and Indiana, had made Covington impregnable to any force the Confederates could send against it.

Louisville was still in peril. Had Bragg advanced by forced marches, ordering Smith, with whom he was in easy communication, to concentrate before this city leaving Heth to demonstrate toward Cincinnati, instead of delaying his advance six or seven days in order to capture Munfordsville, he might have been in front of Louisville on the eighteenth, at least six days ahead of Buell. The Federal forces in that city, less than thirty thousand raw troops, could not have held it against the assault of nearly twice their number of veterans for an hour.

This is what might have been; what the country saw was possible, and what we, who were camped about the city, expected would occur. What really happened was that this host of men—who hardly knew "Right-face" from "Shoulder arms," whose feet were blistered, bodies worn, and spirits shattered by a retreat of incredible celerity and hardship—were hustled into brigades and divisions, and made veterans in the harsh but effective school of double-duty Into the trenches at three o'clock, standing to our arms until day was well advanced, at work on fortifications one day; on outpost duty the next, worried by incessant alarms; drilling every moment, when not otherwise employed, practically besieged, though only confronted by a few bodies of cavalry and a light battery or two of the enemy! Here we learned not only the duties of the soldier, but also the equally important economics of army life—how to cook, how to tent, how to sleep in the midst of alarms, how to stand guard, how to serve on picket, how to live, in short, for to-day's duties, indifferent to what the morrow might bring. We had already formed the acquaintance of the ubiquitous and indestructible "hard-tack," our first issue of which, made on the day after our arrival at Lexington, was declared by one of the Thousand to be "the very last of a lot left over from the war of 1812" The fact that one of them, mailed to his friends at home by a member of the Thousand on that day is still in a good state of preservation, and is the recipient of three hearty groans when exhibited at each reunion of the survivors, would seem, at least, to give color to his conclusion.

It is hoped that before another great war shall come, there will be instituted a system of scientific inspection of food supplies for the army as rigid, at least, as that applied to the steel-plates of our navy, since the knowledge of fraud in their preparation has become public The purchase of food after a mere cursory inspection by an unskilled officer, who judges only by appearance, is one of the evils of which the American soldier may justly complain A qualitative analysis of one issue of hard-tack, made by one of the largest firms with which our government dealt at that time, showed such quantities of pipe-clay or ground white soapstone, as to lead a physician, who saw the results, to declare that thirty days of such food was enough to endanger the life of the strongest man This adulteration was unquestionably one of the causes of disease of the alimentary system in the Northern army, and it is quite possible that this diet of alum and pipe-clay is, to a large degree, responsible for the strong showing of intestinal disease among the survivors There is a poetic justice in the idea of a nation being taxed for pensions to soldiers whom it allowed to be poisoned while fighting in its defense.

However good the soldiers' rations may be, the change from home-cooking to army-cooking, done by an open fire, with only sheet-iron kettles and frying-pans for kitchen outfit—with hard bread and salt pork as the chief staples—is a serious one, involving almost as great a risk as battle itself Take, for instance, our commissary, who was not only a scholar, but also a vegetarian, who had not tasted animal food since his boyhood, and never thought he would again Necessity has small regard for theory, however, and a raging appetite compelled him to eat the rations he served to others One day a friend found him busily engaged in stowing away two pieces of hard bread with a savory bit of pork between

"Hello, sergeant," he exclaimed, "I thought you were a vegetarian?"

"So I am," was the reply between bites 'Are we not assured on the best authority that 'All flesh is grass'?"

It was the good fortune of the Thousand to learn adaptedness to the new conditions during that month of pleasant weather—the lull between the first great march and the beginning of its first campaign

Some events occurred during this interval of peculiar interest to the Thousand. It became part of a brigade which was assigned to the command of Captain William R Terrill, of the Fifth regular artillery, then recently appointed a brigadier-general of volunteers He was a Virginian by birth, and had at least one brother in the Confederate service He had been a classmate of Sheridan's at West Point, and is said to have been one with whom that pugnacious cadet had a personal difficulty for which he was soundly disciplined Everybody seemed to wonder at Terrill's being in the Federal army A story in explanation was afloat at that time His father was said to have been a zealous divine of the Old Dominion, who when his son left home for West Point, presented him with a Bible and made him promise to read it every day and never fail in his duty to the Stars and Stripes When Virginia seceded the good parson would have had his son consecrate his sword to the cause of disunion; but the young officer answered him that he could not break the oath he had sworn at his father's request on the Bible he had given him

It is a pretty story, and might well be true There must have been something very attractive about him to account for the warm friendship between him and Lieutenant C C Parsons, for whom he secured an assignment to command the magnificent battery of seven twelve-pound brass Napoleons, which he organized for service with his brigade, the men and officers being volunteers from the various regiments of the brigade, a large number including Lieutenants Cumings and Osborne from the Thousand Parsons was a *chevalier sans peur et sans reproche* His quickness of perception and fertility of resource were destined to play a rare part at the critical moment in two great battles, but promotion did not, in his case, keep step with merit After the war closed, covered with honors and brevets, he was for some years adjutant of West Point. After that he became a minister of the Protestant Episcopal Church, and as rector of the church of Memphis Tennessee, fell a victim to the yellow fever when that dread scourge smote the city. Between him and Terrill there was a most tender friendship, and he, as well as all others who were familiar with him had the highest anticipations of the military career that awaited the loyal young Virginian. It may be doubted if their hopes would have been fulfilled even had he not met his untimely fate. He did not understand how to endear himself to the volunteer—especially, perhaps one might say, the Northern volunteer. His idea of command was somewhat too highly colored with compulsion to at once call forth the best efforts of an undisciplined soldiery, and he had little of that dash which made Sheridan instantly and always a leader of men. He commanded respect by scrupulous attention to duty, but awakened no enthusiasm in those under his command.

Our *compagnons en brigade* were the One Hundred and Twenty-third and Eightieth Illinois and the One Hundred and First Indiana, two of which regiments were to remain with us to the end, while the other, the Eightieth Illinois, was detached after six months and was afterward widely separated from us. With these was temporarily placed a detachment from various Kentucky regiments under Colonel Garrard, known as "Garrard's Detachment."

Hardly was the brigade formed and assigned to the division of Brigadier-General James S. Jackson than a grand review was ordered. Why anyone should wish to review troops who had never had a dozen days of drill, passes reasonable comprehension especially in heavy marching order. This review was a peculiarly unfortunate one, being anticipated with execrations and remembered with anathemas. The day was the hottest 16th of September ever known even in the sultry humidity of the Ohio valley. The thermometer was said to have reached 100° in the shade, but the Thousand had no thermometer and saw no shade that day. The line of march was long, the paved streets were glistering hot beneath the feet yet unhealed after the "hell-march", the unpaved ones ankle-deep with dust. As usual there were numerous delays, and then a killing pace to make up for them Everybody was ill-tempered, the officers because it is impossible that men should march well and wheel with precision without training, the men because the officers were nervous and irritable, all because the weather was hot, the service onerous, and the reviewing officer—exacting, to say the least The net result in the division was a dozen or two of sunstrokes and a score or two of breakdowns The ambulances were full before the reviewing-stand was reached and the march back to camp one of the sorriest sights an unsympathetic populace ever beheld

Some curious incidents occurred in spite of these conditions The colonel of the Thousand got a wigging from the reviewing officer because the colors of his regiment were not displayed, and when he replied that we had never received anything of that sort, was reprimanded for not having secured so essential an implement of war—a failure for which he was just about as responsible as the shortest private in the rear rank The admonition led however, to a queer consequence On the march back to camp the bearer of the State flag of one of the regiments in advance of us was found upon the roadside overcome with heat, the banner trailed in the dust yet tightly held in his unconscious grasp The impetuous young Brigadier leaped from his horse, seized the flag and when the head of our column arrived handed it to the colonel, with the remark

"Here is a stand of colors for you, see if your regiment can keep them off the ground!"

The colonel called up a sergeant and gave him the flag, as he did so, his eye fell upon the coat of arms on the reverse

"But this is a State flag, general," he said hesitatingly. "We are Ohio troops, not Indianians"

"No matter, keep the flag until I order it returned"

The order never came Some months after the colonel returned it to those to whom it belonged It was rarely if ever unrolled while in the possession of the Thousand. A few weeks afterward we carried it into battle, furled upon its staff and covered with a black case, only its gay tassels showing the colors inside. When we sent it back, it had some honorable scars, received in a conflict where the regiment to which it belonged was not engaged. It is perhaps the only instance that occurred during the war, of a regiment being in active service for six months, losing meanwhile one-third its numbers, before it was given a stand of colors, or of a regiment from one state being required to fight under the flag of another state.

Our quartermaster, a grave man of middle age, splendid presence, and imperturbable gravity, was ordered out of the line to report to the reviewing officer, who asked, with a profusion of ornamental emphasis, why his mules had not been "roached." Now, the quartermaster was a man of consequence at home, had been sheriff of his county, and was not yet accustomed to being hauled up quite so smartly. He knew a good deal about many things, but little enough about mules. If he had been sworn, he could not have told what "roaching" meant. It was evidently something that needed to be done to the mule, whether cutting off his ears or trimming his tail, he did not know.

THE QUARTERMASTER.

So he answered, suavely and at a venture, that there had been a good many things to look after, and he thought he would leave that "until the boys had got through swapping." As there had been a good deal of "swapping," and the teamsters of the Thousand had evidently not come off second best in their honest exchanges with the keepers of Uncle Sam's corrals, this naive confession proved the soft answer which not only turned away wrath but brought a hearty burst of laughter. The quartermaster was courteously dismissed and rode away with a light heart, the only thing that troubled him being that he did not yet know the meaning of the verb "roach." This he determined to find out. Calling his wagonmaster to his side, he asked, in his own inimitably mild way:

"Why didn't you have the mules roached before we came out?"

"I did my best, captain," was the apologetic answer of the chagrined mule-whacker, "but there is only one pair of sheepshears in the division, and I couldn't get hold of that."

"Just so," said the quartermaster, with a chuckle. He had learned that roaching is done with sheep-shears and not given himself away.

During this time one of the most deplorable tragedies of the war was enacted in the city. Brigadier-General Jefferson C. Davis shot and killed his superior, the commanding officer of the Army of Kentucky, Major-General William Nelson. Nothing perhaps shows the law-abiding character of the people from whom these great armies were drawn so well as the fact that during a war of such length so few personal altercations occurred between their officers. In this case, the insult was, no doubt, a grievous one. Just what it was it seems difficult to ascertain. Though the matter was the subject of investigation by both civil and military authority, no reliable account of what happened between Gen. Nelson and his assistant is at this time available. Knowing the vehemence of Nelson's character, it is easy to believe that his language was not measured by the strict rules of courtesy, and he is said to have accompanied his words with a blow. At any rate, the homicide which followed did not interfere with the subsequent career of his slayer.

How did this tragedy affect the Thousand? The death of their late commander was announced in general orders. They had already read it in the newspapers. They stood decorously at parade-rest while the adjutant read the words

recital of the dead man's honors and achievements. Then the parade was dismissed. The officers sauntered to their quarters. They were talking of the dead commander as they laid aside their arms. Presently the sound of shouting was heard. The officers looked out of their tents. The men were cheering and tossing up their caps in the company streets. On the right and left, in the camps of other regiments, the same thing was being done.

"Orderly!" cried the colonel, "What is all this noise about?"

"The men are cheering General Jeff C. Davis, sir," replied the soldier, with a salute.

"Cheering Jeff C. Davis! Call the Officer of the Day!"

There was no need. Long before that functionary appeared to receive instructions the clamor was over and the men were quiet in their tents. The men of the Army of Kentucky had expressed their opinion of its late commander. It did not accord with that given in general orders, yet, perhaps, both were true, in part. The one was a judgment on his patriotism, which none could doubt, the other on his conduct to those subject to his power, which may have been too severe. It should not be forgotten, however, that those who had been longer under his command loved the stern old fighter despite his harshness. At that very moment, one of his old regiments was under close guard across the river lest they should break out and kill the man who slew him. They remembered the tender words he had spoken as they filed past him to engage in their first battle on the bloody field of Shiloh. These others remembered only the story of his wild, unreasoning rage as he rode among the shattered remnants of the force overwhelmed at Richmond through his own stubborn disobedience, and the terrors of the "hell-march," for which he was but half responsible. It was a brutal thing, this exultation in the death of a brave man, besides being a glaring military offense. There was talk of punishing the regiments which took part in it But it is difficult to punish an army especially one that is doing double duty in presence of the enemy.

The Negro question came up again, also In a few days it was to be put at rest forever by that proclamation of President Lincoln, which was the beginning of the end, a proclamation so far-reaching and tremendous in its import that it stilled almost wholly, for a time at least, the bickering which had filled every Federal camp on Southern soil The colonel was a soldier full of soldierly ambitions but he was to the core in favor of liberty He would not disobey orders or transgress the law, neither would he take a step beyond them to promote the master's interest One claimed a colored man who had taken refuge in the camp of the Thousand as his slave, the colonel demanded proof of title, proof in writing, since as a slave could only be sold by deed, title could only be shown by deed The claimant, instead of complying, brought an order from the commanding general that the Negro should be delivered up The colonel had, in the meantime, learned that the colored man was really free, but, having lost his free-papers, or had them taken from him, had been seized and sold for being at large without them or a pass from some white man, and declined to obey the order. The general threatened arrest for disobedience, the colonel threatened to report the general to the President for conspiring to kidnap a free man It was a bad dilemma in which to place one whose promotion yet lacked that most essential ingredient—the President's nomination So the order of arrest never came

There was another case

"Your old master has not long to live, and it seems as if he could not be satisfied unless he has you with him," said a gentleman to a young colored man he had traced to our camp "I think you will be free when the war is over, if not before, but if you will come back now and take care of him, I promise you your freedom at the end of a year, anyhow."

There was a strong resemblance between the two which suggested a nearer relation than master and slave The gentleman was evidently sincere, however, but as a contract with a slave would not be binding, he offered to give his written pledge to the officer, whose servant the other claimed to be, that he would do as he promised. The officer advised the colored man to accept; the two left the camp together, and both did as they agreed A similar case occurred afterward in which the quartermaster, who was one, in those days, whom all men trusted at sight and were never deceived, conducted the negotiations between a loyal master and a slave who had sworn that he would never return to bondage alive There were queer experiences in an "abolition regiment" in a loyal slave state. No doubt, in some cases, the letter of the law was violated in aiding slaves to escape even from loyal owners; but in no case, within the writer's knowledge, was any colored man incited to attempt escape by any member of the Thousand.

X.

THE BAPTISM OF FIRE.

HAD Bragg arranged for the greater part of Smith's army to be in position before Louisville on his arrival, that city might even yet have been carried by assault before Buell's army could intervene for its relief. In this way, and in this way only, could the loss of six days at Munfordville have been atoned. But Bragg, having reached Bardstown, forty miles from Louisville, on the 22d of September, four days before the arrival of Buell's advance-guard, was attacked with the same atrophy of purpose which had paralyzed the energy of Smith on his arrival at Lexington. Both were frightened at the success of their own brilliant strategy, and both were deceived with the hope of mustering thousands of recruits from the people of Kentucky, to whom they addressed at once appeals, which, read in the light of the present, seem ludicrous enough. They assumed that the people of Kentucky were ground to earth beneath the heel of a cruel and barbarous invader, and only waited an opportunity to rise *en masse* and fall upon their oppressors. As a matter of fact, while divided in sentiment, the people of Kentucky, instead of suffering hardship, had been enjoying a period of unprecedented prosperity. Never had horses, cattle, mules, wheat, and corn brought such good prices or found so quick and sure a market as during the year and a half of Federal occupancy of the State

Even the Confederate sympathizers did not appreciate the strategy of Smith and Bragg at its full value, and the recent Confederate victories in the east had not had time to have their full effect on the general sentiment in Kentucky They needed assurance that the armies which had appeared so suddenly at their doors would not presently melt away as quickly as they had come Victory alone could have brought any considerable number of recruits to the Confederate arms General Bragg halted to reconnoiter, to determine what the army in his rear would do, to verify Kirby Smith's report of the state of affairs in Kentucky; to note the effect of the proclamation he scattered, even to the intrenchments about the city Two days later, the head of Buell's army was at the mouth of Salt river, two days more and his dusty veterans were marching through the streets of Louisville. The old Army of the Ohio was united with the new Army of Kentucky with triumphant shouts which told to the thin line of Confederate cavalry on their front that all reasonable hope of conquering the city was at an end From that time the question was not what the Confederates might achieve in Kentucky, but with how little loss they might get out of it. No doubt. if a general like Grant or Sheridan had been in control of the Federal forces, Bragg would have at once realized this fact and begun his retreat along the line he afterwards pursued. But he knew the mental infirmity of his opponent, and counted on it to afford him abundant time to retrace his steps or, perhaps, opportunity to win a decisive battle

With this view, he began leisurely arrangements to compel his opponent to meet him on a field of his own selection With his right resting at Salvisa, his left at Danville, and his center at Harrodsburg, he occupied a position hardly twenty miles in length, one flank resting on an impassable river and the other reaching to the rough country known as Muldraugh's hill, a region utterly unfitted for military operations on a large scale, covering thereby all the roads leading into Middle and Eastern Kentucky, along which his retreat, in case of discomfiture, must lie To attack this position, General Buell would have to advance his left and fight at or near Salvisa, or divide his army and expose his own communications by advancing his right through the rough country on the Confederate left Knowing the peculiar caution of General Buell, Bragg confidently expected that he would advance his left toward Frankfort and swing his right round toward Harrodsburg He did not anticipate, however, that this movement would begin before the 10th of October He, therefore, ordered Smith to join him about that time at Lawrenceburg or Salvisa with all his force, except Heth's division, which was to be left to unite with Humphrey Marshall and continue the demonstration against Cincinnati This, with Stevenson s division, which was coming from Cumberland Gap, via Danville, would give him an army of about fifty thousand men, all veterans, to oppose Buell's somewhat larger army, one-third of which were new troops. Under these circumstances, he felt so confident of at least holding his position and, perhaps, crippling his adversary, that he did not hesitate to predict that "the great battle of the west" would be fought at or near Salvisa

General Bragg's forecast of his opponent's moves was curiously at fault. Instead of hesitancy and delay, General Buell manifested an almost unexampled vigor, and, instead of caution, his plan of campaign was characterized by the utmost boldness It was based, however, on an utter misconception of his adversary's purpose Arriving in Louisville, General Buell had found the whole country aflame with anger at his failure to meet and drive back the army of General Bragg With a larger force under his command, moving on interior lines, it was the universal belief that he ought not to have permitted Bragg to cross the Cumberland river into Kentucky; that he ought to have succored Munfordville, and that he ought to have engaged the army of Bragg before he had opportunity to unite with Kirby Smith. In all this the public censure was entirely just

An intelligent people are good strategists, and maps are terrible enemies of military fame General Buell found in Louisville not only an enraged people, but also a government finally worn out with his excuses, evasions, and lethargy. The order for his removal only waited the arrival of General Thomas to be delivered. The prospect of being superseded by his own subordinate seems to have inspired him to an activity altogether unprecedented in his military career. In four days he had reorganized his army, or rather combined it with the Army of Kentucky, and planned a campaign, which he avowed himself ready to embark upon without delay; so that when General Thomas arrived, that supersensitive soldier was able to allege this fact as a reason for declining the proffered command.

The plan of organization was defective in that it practically removed Thomas from responsible command, making him a mere figurehead, having the title of "second in command," but without authority or discretion In Thomas' place and in command of the strongest and most important corps of his army, he put C C Gilbert, whose rank was a matter at least of doubt. Under him were the most distinguished and experienced division commanders of that army, Sheridan, Schoepf and R B Mitchell—men who would naturally resent being placed under a man whose title to such rank was at best questionable and who had done nothing whatever to entitle him to such preferment The army was composed of three corps the First, or left, under Maj.-Gen. A. McD McCook ; the Second, or right, under Maj -Gen. Thomas L Crittenden, and the Third or center, under Gen C. C. Gilbert. Each corps was composed of three divisions and most of the divisions of three brigades Three divisions were unattached to any corps. There were three brigades of cavalry, while the artillery comprised about two hundred guns. The whole composed an army of fifty-eight thousand men

Buell's purpose seems to have been to drive Bragg out of Kentucky along the route by which he had entered, rather than to force him to give battle or attempt his annihilation. To effect this, he sent Dumont with fifteen thousand men and Sill's division of McCook's corps, numbering eleven thousand men, by the Shelbyville pike to demonstrate against Frankfort. The Second corps under Crittenden, with whom went Thomas, "the second in command," as a sort of supernumerary adviser, marched straight on Bardstown, which was supposed to be the center of the enemy's position. McCook with the other two divisions of the First corps, marched as if in support of Sill and Dumont, to Fisherville, turned there southeastward and advanced to Taylorsville, Bloomfield and Mackville. Masked by these two columns, Buell, with the Third corps under Gilbert, marched to Shepherdsville, thence diverging to the eastward, joined Crittenden at Bardstown. The apparent purpose of this was to compel Bragg to withdraw by Lebanon or Hodgensville. In the latter event, Gilbert would march directly to Elizabethtown instead of diverging toward Bardstown.

Bragg, possessed by his own pre-notions, and attributing to his opponent as full knowledge of his own position as he himself had, was entirely misled by these dispositions. Fully informed as to the movements of the First and Second corps, and the advance of Sill and Dumont toward Frankfort, he concluded that the movement of Crittenden and a part of McCook's corps on Bardstown was a feint intended to occupy his attention while Buell, with the Third corps, in connection with Sill and Dumont, advanced upon his right. This being in accord with what he deemed the best strategy, he determined to circumvent it by overwhelming Thomas before he could be reinforced, and then, by a quick march to his right, to form a junction at Salvisa with three divisions of Kirby Smith and give battle to Buell. Had he known of the march of the Third corps via Shepherdsville, refused his left and fallen with his right on the flank of Sill and Dumont, bringing the two divisions of Smith which were at Frankfort across the Kentucky river to engage them in front, he would have effectually foiled Buell's design and compelled him to retreat to Louisville or fight under great disadvantages. If, then, Buell had marched north by Harrodsburg, Bragg would still have had a secure line of retreat open to him north of the Kentucky river This misconception of Buell's movement led Bragg to mass his left wing and one division of his right at Perryville under General Polk, with orders to attack at daylight on the 8th of October

General Polk, better informed as to the enemy's movements, urged the concentration of the whole army at Harrodsburg before making an attack, or at least that the whole Army of Mississippi should be united for that purpose Bragg decided, however, to retain Wither's division to act in connection with Kirby Smith's army under his own command, against Buell's right, which he still conceived the more important line of the Federal advance The result was the bloody but useless and indecisive battle of Perryville.

The advance began at daylight on Wednesday, the first day of October Everything was propitious, save a scarcity of water in a part of the region through which the march was made. The roads were dry and hard, the weather was delightful, the men in the best of spirits The gums and maples were aflame upon the hillsides The brown oak-groves were gashed here and there with golden hickories The dogwoods showed like gleams of yellow fire under the darker leafage The corn was shocked or stood ripe in the fields. Stacks of hay and oats dotted the landscape Herds of cattle browsed upon the stubble-lands, on which the rag-weed grew rank and brown, protecting the herbage underneath The oaks that lined the pikes had dropped their polished acorns in shining circles on the hard macadam while the walnuts along the country roadways had covered the little-used tracks with yellowish-green globes, which, crushed beneath the feet of thousands, gave forth a pungent odor. The woodbine and the sumac flaunted gaudy banners in the hedgerows. Here and there, tobacco was ripening on the hills or hung in barns from which the winds brought the spicy fragrance of the aromatic leaf. The hemp lay in long rows about the shallow ponds where it had been spread to dry. Fairer skies or more delightful surroundings army never had upon a march.

In such a region an army of sixty thousand men shows like an innumerable multitude. On every road, winding through the brown fields and among the rounded hills, were long lines of blue. The flash of polished steel caught the eye in every direction. Long trains of white-topped wagons shone through clouds of dust upon the pikes. The troops marched, sometimes in column along the roads, sometimes in line through the fields. Flags waved in the mellow sunlight. Generals with their body-guards, richly dight, rode here and there. Horsemen abounded, aides and orderlies, and messengers; cavalry in squads and squadrons going everywhere without apparent purpose. What life their presence gave to the scene! That they were the eyes and ears of the army none could doubt, though they are sometimes myopic eyes and queerly placed ears. The infantry, with that spirit of banter that always prevails between the different arms, insisted that the restless riders were quick to hear what happened at the front and anxious to see what was going on in the rear. The artillery trundled steadily along the roads. The sound of drum, and fife, and bugle mingled with the rumble of wheels and the braying of mules. Now and then, the roar of a cannon or a ripple of musketry served to remind us that the light troops of the enemy were keeping touch of our front and watching carefully our advance.

The Thousand was part of the Tenth division of the First corps, consisting of two small brigades, the Thirty-third and the Thirty-fourth, the former commanded by Brig.-Gen. William R. Terrill, the latter by Col. George Webster. With the former was Parsons' battery; with the latter the

Nineteenth Indiana Battery. We marched east to Fisherville, and thence to Taylorsville, which we reached upon the afternoon of the fourth. On the fifth, which was Sunday, we lay in camp, and on Monday marched to Bloomfield, going on to Mackville on Tuesday through a very rough country. Our five days' rations were exhausted on Sunday. On Monday and Tuesday we subsisted on parched corn, with a small supply of bacon seized by the quartermaster at a plantation which we passed. Water was very scarce and very bad. There was some heavy firing to our right toward evening, and we were ordered to prepare for battle on the morrow. Only a few of the canteens were filled that night.

General Buell failing to encounter the enemy at Bardstown, as he had expected, had abandoned his previous hypothesis of Bragg's movements, and concluded that he would offer battle at Danville. He accordingly pushed Thomas, with Crittenden, toward Lebanon and advanced Gilbert to Springfield and McCook to Mackville. On the seventh he advanced Gilbert on the Springfield pike to within three miles of Perryville, meeting sharp resistance which led him to believe the enemy would offer battle at that place. Ordering the right and left to close on the center, he prepared to attack the next morning.

This order was received by General McDowell at half past two on the morning of October 8th. It directed him to march at three o'clock. This was manifestly impossible, but his *corps* was under arms at daylight, and about six o'clock the Tenth division moved along the old Mackville pike toward Perryville, nine miles distant, marching slowly and with frequent halts, over a difficult road. The day was very warm. About eleven o'clock we halted in column by division on the right of the pike, a half mile in the rear of the Russell House, on the battle-field of Perryville. Two brigades of Rousseau's division of the First *corps* were in the lead that day, the Tenth division having cut off the other —Starkweather's—it was in the rear. Our battery came up and halted near us on the left of the pike. Rousseau's advance brigades were posted in line of battle to the left of the Mackville pike, where it crossed Doctor's Fork, a tributary of Chaplin river. This point is a mile and a half west of Perryville, and the line of battle extended due north along a wooded slope which fell away to the eastward. To the left of this line, some four hundred yards, McCook ordered a battery to be placed on a knoll in an open field, fronting northward. This was the position our battery was destined to occupy. Before it was ordered forward there was some firing on our right front.

At length the order came for the battery to go to the front. How we envied the eager comrades as they swung themselves into their saddles and dashed forward at a sharp trot! The sun was hot and the horses' flanks were covered with sweat from the day's march, but they were in fine fettle, and one did not wonder at the flush of pride on the gallant Parsons' face as the guns filed past him and took their way along a narrow country road toward the left front. The fire of battle was in his eye and one guessed that the trot the bugle sounded was less because of any emergency in the order he had received than of his own impatience for the fray. It was then about one o'clock and there was in the air that curious feeling which assures even the dullest mind that a conflict is surely impending. Probably there were but two men in the whole army who doubted that an engagement would occur within the hour. General Buell, who irritated by the fact that the first corps had not arrived at the time he had named, had declared it to be too late to fight a battle that day, and retired to his quarters two miles in the rear, and the commander of the Third corps, who was already striving to prevent his division commanders from engaging the enemy. Upon the extreme right, Crittenden was ordered to advance very cautiously and put himself in touch with Gilbert's right, ready to attack the next day.

It takes two to arrange a battle, as well as to make a bargain, however, and Bragg, who had arrived upon the field about the same time with McCook, had given his voice for a fight that day The enemy's dispositions had already been made for an attack upon Gilbert's left flank, about where the Mackville pike crosses Doctor's Fork The posting of Rousseau's two brigades to the north of the point selected for the main attack, created an impression that McCook was endeavoring to turn their flank, and Maney was hurried to the extreme right. Donelson was ordered to move in that direction as he advanced, unmasking Stewart, while Wharton's cavalry was pushed across Chaplin river to demonstrate on the rear of the Federal army It was the appearance of this cavalry which induced McCook to refuse his left, and order Parsons to a position commanding their movements He anticipated an attack upon his train, which was yet strung out on the Mackville pike at the mercy of any force which should pass our left

These counter movements had been going on ever since the head of McCook's column arrived upon the field. Almost at the same moment when Parsons' battery reached its position and opened on the Confederate cavalry on the north, Maney's brigade, one of the most noted in the Confederate service, having surmounted the almost percipitous banks of Doctor s fork, appeared in line of battle on the crest of a wooded ridge, hardly two hundred yards from the left of the battery Advancing to the edge of the wood, they opened a deadly fire. Previous to this, the One Hundred and Twenty-third and Eightieth Illinois, with Garrard's detachment, had been ordered forward and came into position on the left of Rousseau's line, angling back in rear of the battery The guns were quickly shifted to bear upon the enemy thus unexpectedly appearing within easy rifle range , the One Hundred and Twenty-third Illinois was ordered to charge, and the fight was on, hot and furious

The other regiments of the brigade had already disappeared from view when the order came for the Thousand to move forward About the same time, the other brigade of our division, with Harris' battery, the Nineteenth Indiana were ordered to the right front of the corps So the line of battle of the First corps consisted of one brigade of the Tenth division on the right, then two brigades of the Third division, then, the other brigade of the Tenth division, except the Thousand not yet in line, refused so as to front northeast, and then, with a wide interval, the other brigade of the Third division, in our left rear, on eminences on either side of Wilson's Creek, the bed of which was then only a mass of dusty shale. The formation has been praised as a wise one, especially that of Starkweather's brigade This was selected by Starkweather himself without knowledge of the country in his front. Had he posted his men along the country road which ran nearly east and west a quarter of a mile in his front, his left resting on the Perryville road its thick stone walls would have constituted an impregnable rampart from which he could not have been dislodged This road ran hardly two hundred yards west of Parsons' position and was the natural cover for the battery's support How it managed to escape McCook's and Jackson's notice it is impossible to conceive, except upon the hypothesis that they were expecting an attack from the north and not from the east.

We followed along the same country road by which the right of our brigade had advanced, marching with a quick step Thirst and fatigue were forgotten The Thousand had on its report that morning six hundred and forty-five names The detachment of one hundred skirmishers and three men from each company sent out in search of water, together with the ordinary details, left its actual number scarcely five hundred

On we went, down a slight declivity, up over a crest into the woods beyond The firing grew heavier, the rattle of musketry mingling with the roar of cannon. We stood at rest a few moments, listening to the unaccustomed din The woods hid everything except the puffs of smoke on a crest away to our left where a battery of the enemy was posted. Occasionally we saw a shell burst in the air.

We crossed a field, following the ruts the battery had left, entered a lane, went up a slope on the other side of which was a scattering wood. An aide met us, shouting a frenzied demand for haste.

"Double-quick!"

We dashed along the crest, down the other side, past a corn-field on our left, along a narrow lane and through a gate into an open-wooded glade. We had come near half a mile on the double-quick. The men were panting.

"Halt!"

On a little knoll to our right front, the battery was firing with frenzied rapidity. The shells from the enemy's battery flew over our heads and cut the limbs of the trees by which we stood, sending down a shower of acorns. Bullets pattered about us. We could see the artillerymen dashing back and forth as the smoke lifted from the guns. Men were coming back from the hell which the crest hid from our view, some wounded, some stragglers. Somebody suggested that the guns were empty, and the order to load was given in some of the companies. Our division and brigade generals were standing, unmounted, just in the rear of the battery. Both had accompanied it to the position assigned and remained to watch its action, General Terrill leaving the duty of posting his brigade to his staff officers. He was by training, almost by instinct, an artilleryman, and his battery's action eclipsed in interest the maneuvering of his brigade. When Maney's brigade appeared in line of battle in the woods upon its right, as it stood facing northward, advancing with a steady fire until they reached the fence a hundred yards away, its peril absorbed his whole attention. Ordering Colonel Monroe of the One Hundred and Twenty-third Illinois, to charge the enemy's line, he remained beside the battery, directing and encouraging the men in its operation.

When the Thousand came up, the right of the brigade had fallen back, and the enemy, checked by the hot fire which greeted them, had halted in the edge of the wood along the fence below. The battery stood alone upon the crest of the hill, half its guns silenced, its men and horses being cut down by the fire of the enemy. It was said the order to withdraw the battery had been given. Even then it was too late. A mounted aide pointed out our position and rode beside our adjutant at the head of the column as we advanced. A caisson, the horses of which had become unmanageable, dashed through our line to the rear.

"Forward!" The colonel's voice rang like a clarion above the din of conflict. He sat upon his horse as we filed past and uttered a word of cheer to each company. His hat was pushed back from his forehead and showed the scar received at Shiloh glowing red upon his smooth, white forehead. Few who saw him then will ever forget his calm and masterful presence.

The head of the column passed through a gap in the fence that ran along the edge of the wood, filed to the left, and passing twenty yards in rear of the battery, marched on until the right companies were beyond the shelter of the little knoll on which it stood. Our path was strewn with dead and dying men and horses.

"Front!"

The command brought us facing to the rear while the bullets were whistling by us like hail, and men were falling in the ranks of the three right companies. The others were a little sheltered by the crest of the hill on which the battery stood.

"About face—forward—guide center!"

In the center were the colors of the One Hundred and First Indiana, close-wrapped in their black case, but as stoutly advanced as if they had been our own. The regiment to which they belonged was not in the fight, having been sent as guard with the division train to obtain supplies.

We faced by the rear rank; advanced in line to the crest of the hill in the teeth of the leaden storm that swept it. There we first saw the enemy, two lines of gray in the edge of the brown woods scarce ninety yards away. Puffs of smoke and jets of flame shot out from the undergrowth and along the fence.

"Halt! Commence firing!"

Our left companies, the right of our line as we stood faced to the rear, overlapped the battery. General Jackson fell just as we advanced. Some of our men fell to the rear to pass the group that knelt about him. The left was refused, because of the overlapping of the enemy's line and the conformation of the ground. Those whose guns were loaded fired; the others made haste to load. Men fell, sometimes with a groan, sometimes without a sound. It was slow work loading and firing with the old muzzle-loaders. The air seemed full of flashing ramrods. One and another staggered wounded to the rear. The line-officers went back and forth encouraging, directing. We stood alone, a thin line of blue, in the open field. The enemy were mostly under cover. On our right the nearest force was along the wooded ridge to which the rest of our brigade had retired. To the rear, near half a mile, was Starkweather with his veterans. Then we first heard the rebel yell we were to hear so often afterwards. The gray line burst from the wood and rushed up the slope.

LIEUT. H. H. CUMINGS, (1863.)

"Forward!" cried Terrill. "Do not let them get the guns!"

His face was flushed with agony at the thought of losing the battery of which he was so proud.

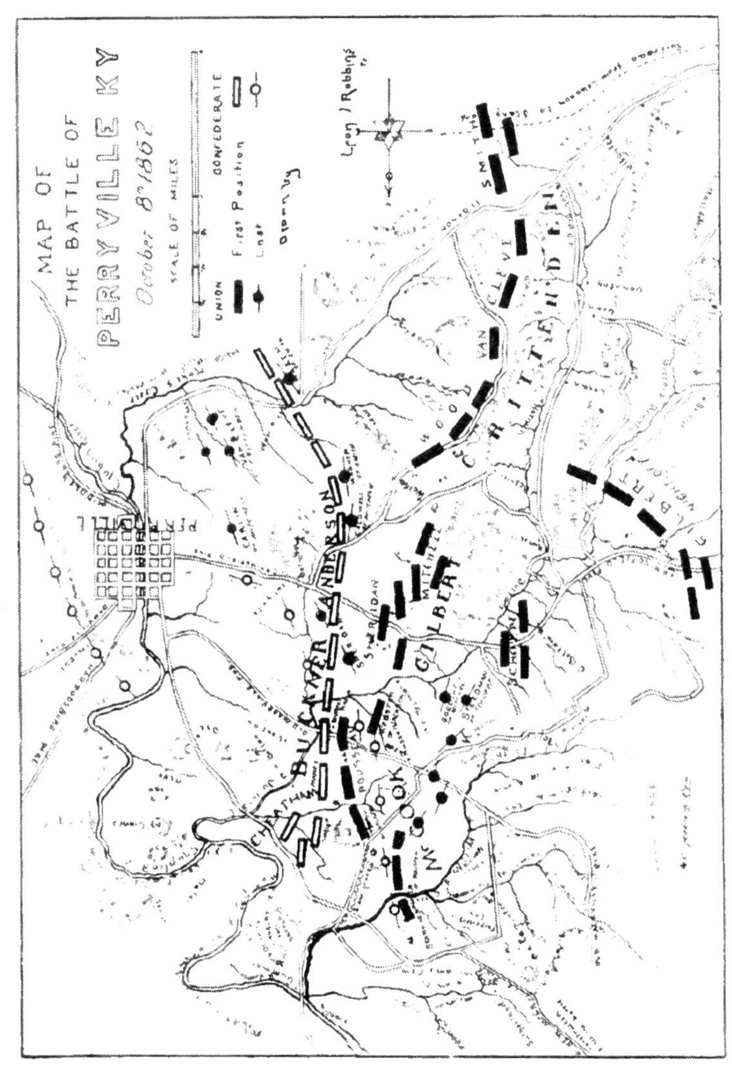
MAP OF
THE BATTLE OF
PERRYVILLE KY
October 8th 1862
SCALE OF MILES
UNION
CONFEDERATE
First Position
Last
Drawn by
Leon J Robbins
PERRYVILLE
BUCKNER
ANDERSON
CHEATHAM
GILBERT
CRITTENDEN
SMITH
VAN CLEVE
WOOD
SHERIDAN
MITCHELL
SCHOEPF
McCOOK

"Charge!" commanded the major, whose horse having been shot, was on foot with the left companies There was a clang of bayonets. The left companies surged forward to the front of the battery Cummings, of ours fired the two right guns, double-shotted with canister, full in the faces of the enemy, then almost at the muzzles of the pieces, and with his few remaining men dashed through our ranks to the rear under cover of the smoke. We would have cheered them but were too busy with our own work to give more than a flash of the eye to their gallantry When it lifted, the enemy had faltered half-way down the slope Our fire was too hot for them to stand. They fell slowly back and began firing again

Seeing the uselessness of the unequal conflict Terrill gave the order to retire to a fence which ran along the edge of a wood in our rear. It was done with reasonable steadiness, considering the fact that we left one-fourth of our number dead to mark the line we had held We rallied at the fence, and when the enemy showed above the crest of the hill, renewed the fight. Just here our adjutant who rode a chunky, serviceable but not showy stallion, having turned to see that all the men got the order to retire, found himself face to face with the Confederate line Turning, he charged down the little slope to the fence, not stopping to hunt any of the numerous gaps. Indeed his head was down and the bullets buzzing like bees about his ears, so that he had eyes or ears for nothing else The stallion charged manfully to the fence, but had been too well taught to break bounds The adjutant himself, was no fence-jumping cavalier, but one glance behind showed him that something must be done With a lift on the reins he plunged the spurs into the sides of the old bay, who rose to the occasion and would have bolted to the rear, if one of the men had not hooked on to his rein Thereupon, the adjutant dismounted, being then the only mounted officer left with us the brigadier being on foot and his staff either dismounted or on duty elsewhere Putting up a wounded man in his place, with another clinging to the stirrup, the adjutant sent his fiery steed to the rear and took orders indifferently thereafter, from Gen Terrill and Col Hall, both likewise dismounted.

The three right companies, not hearing the order to retire, were cut off, but under command of the gallant Edwards, the senior captain, now thrice wounded, fell back farther to the left, and rallied behind the stone fence that marked the roadway The left and center, now mere shattered fragments, retired under the command of General Terrill, by whose side marched our colonel. After the belt of woods was passed, we entered a corn-field, the enemy followed sharply and their bullets cut stalk and leaf and rattled the kernels from the drooping ears beside us, every now and then claiming a victim Here Terrill ordered a march by the flank to unmask Starkweather's regiments which lay upon the crest of the hill above us Some did not hear the order and were still facing the enemy when a magnificent volley-fire by companies, rang out in our rear, while Stone s and Bush's batteries opened on the pursuing enemy. As we flung ourselves upon our faces and crept around the flank out of this maelstrom of fire we could but exult in the skill of our comrades whose level volleys cut the serried stalks in their front like a sickle of flame.

Two hundred yards back of Starkweather's right, we formed a new line under the personal direction of General Terrill. Here we began to compare notes and try to determine the fate of our comrades. The three right companies were almost wholly missing Where were they? After a time they found their way to us, having been cut off in falling back. Where was the rest of the brigade? General Terrill thought it had been wholly dissipated His attention had been so taken up by the battery, that he had quite lost track of the regiments which had swung back before the Thousand came upon the field and he had been so absorbed in the working of the guns that he had little idea of the severity of the attack He did not realize we had held our position until every third man had been killed or wounded. He was very much depressed, thinking not of what his men had done, but

ADJT. A. M. ROBBINS.

AMBROSE MASON ROBBINS was born in Niles, Ohio, June 27, 1837, graduated at Allegany College, Meadville, Pa., June 28, 1858; enlisted as private in Company B 19th Ohio Volunteers, April, 1861. After the expiration of the three months' service was admitted to the bar of Ohio, at Warren, Trumbull County, in July, 1861; appointed 1st lieutenant and adjutant 105th O. V. I., August 1, 1862; served, with regiment until March 28, 1863, when he resigned on account of disability; was appointed Chief Clerk and Deputy Marshal 19th Congressional District of Ohio, on the adoption of the Conscription Act, in the fall of 1863, and served as such until November, 1865. He was in the dry goods business from 1866 until 1873, and since that time has been in the iron business. Since 1885, he has resided in Cleveland, Ohio. He is a member of the Loyal Legion, Ohio Commandery.

of what he had failed to accomplish and of the stain he feared would fall upon his honor as a soldier

At our right, the magnificent diapason of battle rose and fell The bullets flew over us, and now and then a shell went shrieking by. In our front the enemy was repulsed again and again Many of our men crept forward and taking their places in the line on the crest above, joined in the fire upon the enemy Some of the line-officers borrowing the rifles and cartridges of their dead comrades, did likewise. Our number grew constantly as those who had been scattered found their way to our new position As the day drew to its close, the young brigadier began to hope that his command had not been so completely shattered as he had feared One and another reported having seen large numbers of the other regiments fighting with Rousseau in the woods at our right. Then we heard that our lieutenant colonel, Tolles, had come up with his skirmishers and joined the Eightieth Illinois, in position somewhere toward the right With reviving spirits Gen. Terrill's interest in the conflict which raged about him again awoke Drawn as it seemed by an irresistible magnetism he walked toward the battery now hotly engaged upon the opposite hill three hundred yards away. As he climbed the slope toward it he was struck by a shell, and died almost before a friend could reach his side

The battle was over for the Thousand Its division and brigade commanders had been stricken almost in its ranks Its colonel now commanded the brigade, to-morrow he would command the division, being the senior officer left alive in it. Yet it was but forty-eight days since he was mustered as colonel As the sun went down we watched the flashes in the wood where Sheridan was driving back the victorious enemy, and witnessed the last terrible onset when the enemy's line, pushing Rousseau's exhausted regiments back fell on the fresh line of Gooding again and again, but failed to drive him from the position he held When Starkweather retired we formed with his troops on the new line It was a mile back of the line we held when the battle began. The whole left wing had been driven in, so that our front was now near the point where we had halted in column on our arrival on the field. More than eight thousand men, friends and foes, lay dead and wounded on the ground which had been so stubbornly contested. The Thousand little knew how hot a conflict they had shared, or how honorable a part they had borne in it. General Bragg, with the echoes of Shiloh fresh in his memory, said: "For the time engaged, it was the severest and most desperately contested engagement within my knowledge." And General McCook declared it to be "the bloodiest battle of modern times for the numbers engaged on our side." Of less than 13,000 troops of the First corps engaged, 3,299—more than one-fourth—were killed, wounded, or missing. Of the whole army less than half had been engaged. The moon rose and lighted up a veil of silvery mist that hung over the field of strife. Out of it came the moans of the wounded. Campfires shone through it here and there and watchful pickets sent a challenging shot into it now and then. Through it came the steady rumble of wheels and hoarse tones of command. We thought the enemy were preparing to renew the attack instead of fleeing to avoid ours. All night anxious groups went up and down our lines seeking their own commands or inquiring for friends who would never again report for duty. Long past midnight the detail sent out for water returned with full canteens. It was the first water we had tasted since the fight began.

Would we fight upon the morrow or not? We waited anxiously for the day to break, for the sun to rise. The enemy did not attack. We received no orders. Then by twos and threes our men began to sally forth in search of lost comrades. The enemy had departed. On the stony pikes three miles away could be heard the steady roar of their swiftly-driven trains. Three days afterwards, we started in slow and cautious pursuit. In three days more, we had found their rear guard. They were safe across Dick river, whose precipitous banks forbade pursuit. Such was General Buell's view. Bragg and Smith retreated unhindered through Cumberland Gap; their army was shipped by rail to Murfreesborough, and before Buell had recalled his scattered forces Bragg was threatening Nashville. He had driven the Federals out of Middle Tennessee, captured 25,000 prisoners, 81 cannon, 27,000 small arms, 1,200 wagons; killed and wounded 7,000 Federals, and gotten off scot-free with a larger army, better provisioned and equipped than when he marched out of Sequatchie valley on the 29th of August. He had done this in the face of a superior force of the enemy and with every advantage of position in their favor. To compensate for its lost opportunities, the Army of Ohio had a new name and a new commander.

CAPT. L. DWIGHT KEE.

The battle is one thing; its history another. History says truly that the battle of Perryville was a Confederate victory. An army of twenty-five thousand fell upon one of

L. DWIGHT KEE was a teacher of wide repute in the southern part of Ashtabula County where the 105th Ohio was mustered into service, and he was commissioned captain of Company I. He was a man of distinguished presence, high character and quickly mastered his duties. He was shot through the head at the battle of Perryville, Ky., forty-eight days after the regiment enlisted. He was greatly beloved by his men and universally respected by the officers of the regiment. It is a matter of regret that no fuller details of his life have been furnished for these pages.

fifty thousand, drove in every part of the line it attacked, killed and wounded more than four thousand men; captured eleven guns and five hundred prisoners, and so paralyzed its enemy that when it fell back he dare not pursue until three days had intervened and there was no longer any danger of renewal of the conflict. To the Federals it was not a very important engagement: they merely lost four thousand men and gained nothing. To the Confederates it was one of the most brilliant victories their arms achieved; the men they lost were simply the price paid to dislodge the enemy from the line of the Tennessee. It was not only a decisive victory but an exceeding small price to pay for the advantage gained. How did it happen to be so cheaply won?

There are two answers: the one that which history gives, the other that of common sense. History says it was a Confederate victory because "the raw troops upon the left broke and fled in confusion at the first fire." More than a score of reputable historians who have treated this campaign make substantially this statement. In this case history is not only false but most absurdly and ridiculously false. There were only two brigades of raw troops in the left wing of the army at Perryville. These composed the Tenth division. Their whole number was 5,557. The one was on the extreme right of McCook's line, the other on its extreme left.

It is simply impossible that the failure on the part of two small isolated brigades to hold their respective positions should have enabled twenty-five thousand Confederates to overpower fifty thousand Federals, or have prevented thirty thousand fresh troops from pursuing and destroying an army which twenty thousand had repulsed with great loss, after a fight of unusual severity.

How did such a mistake occur? General Buell's report* of the battle declared that "the suddenness and strength of the attack and the loss of two of their gallant leaders, Jackson and Terrill, caused some of the new troops of the Tenth division to fall into disorder, and threw the weight of the battle on the Third division."

It is probable that this statement was largely based on the language of the young staff officer who reported the part taken by the Thirty-third brigade in that day's fight. Of course, General Buell did not speak of his own knowledge, for he knew nothing of the fight until it was nearly over, and then did not deem it necessary to come upon the field. Speaking of the Thousand in its first position this staff officer says * "In spite of the efforts of the officers most of the men broke and fell back in great confusion." Speaking of the same regiment and some of the One Hundred and Twenty-third Illinois, in our second position, he says "Here the conduct of some of the officers was disgraceful." Lest there should be any mistake in regard to what regiments he includes in his condemnation, he adds immediately "The Eightieth Illinois and Garrard's detachment behaved well." These serious imputations which have thus crystallized into history, compel a plain statement of the conditions affecting the conduct of these brigades, and especially of the two regiments thus officially denounced.

These brigades—the Thirty-third and Thirty-fourth—were posted on the extreme left and right of the First corps, about a mile apart. Gen. James S. Jackson, the division commander, remained with the Thirty-third brigade. They were all new troops, but that does not excuse them from any obligation to be good troops and brave men. If they were not such they deserve condemnation; if they were, those who set this ball of obloquy in motion deserve to bear the shame of traducing brave men under cover of fortuitous rank.

The fact that one of these brigades lost nineteen per cent and the other twenty-two per cent of their entire strength that day establishes, at least, a strong presumption that General Buell was in error in ascribing to them the misfortunes of his army, more than half of which was not used at all. The fact that every brigade along the front of the First corps was forced from its position and driven back nearly a mile, makes the selection of these new brigades for invidious rebuke, at least ungenerous Of course, not as much is to be expected of troops that have been in service less than three months as of veterans, and if they did anything like as good service in so hot a fight they were entitled to praise rather than censure Now, the plain truth is that these two brigades lost more men than the whole Third corps, and each of them more than the entire divisions of Sheridan and Mitchel respectively, which have always been deservedly applauded for their magnificent conduct on this field

Let us go a step farther In the nine brigades which were actively engaged that day there were forty-three regiments. Of these, at least thirty were veteran organizations All alike were driven from their positions, except those of the Third corps who came in after the First corps had been repulsed Of these forty-three regiments, there were five which lost more than two hundred men each, the Tenth Ohio, 229, the Ninety-eighth Ohio, 229, the Seventy-fifth Illinois, 225, the Seventy-ninth Pennsylvania, 216, the First Wisconsin, 204, the One Hundred and Fifth Ohio, 203. The four regiments whose losses were next highest were the Twenty-first Wisconsin, 197, the Fifteenth Kentucky, 196, the Third Ohio, 190, the One Hundred and Twenty-third Illinois, 189 Three of these regiments—the Ninety-eighth Ohio, the One Hundred and Fifth Ohio, and the One Hundred and Twenty-third Illinois—belonged to the contemned "new troops of the Tenth division" It is not possible that troops who had been in service less than sixty days deserved to be singled out for opprobrium after such losses

The staff officer referred to above, the acting adjutant general of the Thirty-third brigade, especially stigmatizes the One Hundred and Twenty-third Illinois and the One Hundred and Fifth Ohio, and particularly commends the two other organizations in the Twenty-third brigade The simple truth is that these two regiments, constituting but sixty per cent of the strength of the brigade sustained seventy-eight per cent of its entire loss in killed and eighty per cent of its loss in wounded The One Hundred and Twenty-third Illinois lost almost twenty-six per cent of its reported strength, and the One Hundred and Fifth Ohio thirty-two per cent. of its reported strength, or thirty-eight per cent. of the number actually engaged The Eightieth Illinois lost only eleven per cent of its strength Garrard's detachment lost none killed, and but six wounded This is not said to contravene the statement that these latter organizations behaved well, but only to show that the stress of battle fell less heavily upon them, making good behavior a much easier matter

The brigade has been blamed for permitting its battery to be captured It is said, that the men of the battery deserted Lieutenant Parsons while he was trying to bring one of the guns to bear on the enemy It may be true: but it must be remembered that those men had only had their horses two weeks and their guns only ten days They had never fired a shotted gun, and hardly a hundred blank cartridges until that day So fierce was the attack that there was only time to change direction of part of the guns the others remaining as at first posted, trained to the northward. Yet they stood by their guns until they lost almost forty per cent of the whole number engaged It will not do to asperse the manhood of such men The simple truth is that the loss of the battery and whatever confusion occurred in the regiments blamed for such loss, were the plain and evident results of unaccountable negligence in assigning it an untenable position and of grave mismanagement of the infantry which this initial error occasioned

The battery was posted on the extreme left of a line facing eastward, with its guns pointing to the north. The enemy had already attacked the front of the line near where the right of our corps rested on Doctor's Fork This fact should have put Generals Jackson and Terrill on the alert in expectation of an attack from that direction Ninety yards east of the battery's position began a heavy wooded slope. No skirmishers were thrown forward, nor was any examination made of this wood. Just beyond the crest, at that very moment, lay one of the most noted brigades of the Confederate army. They had only to climb the slope on the other side, deploy into line under cover of the wood and advance to the edge of the wood, along which ran a high rail-fence, to make the battery's position wholly untenable. No sooner did they open fire and the peril of the battery become apparent to General Terrill, than he ordered the One Hundred and Twenty-third Illinois, which had just been rushed into position at the double, rear rank in front, to charge the enemy's line. Such an order was justifiable only to gain time to withdraw the battery or for the arrival of expected succor. As an attempt to carry the enemy's position, or repel their attack, it was simple madness. The front already developed by their fire was more than double that of the assailing force. They were under cover in a thick wood with a high rail-fence along its edge. The perfectness of their cover may be judged from the fact that one of the Thousand said to the writer: "I can see nothing to shoot at but the smoke of their guns. Shall I aim at that?" Against such a position, held by more than double their number, the One Hundred and Twenty-third was thrown across an open field. That they should be repulsed was inevitable, that there should be confusion was natural. No troops ever fell back after such repulse, under a withering fire, leaving one-fourth their number behind, without confusion. Instead of sneers and blame they had bravely earned encomium.

On the repulse of the One Hundred and Twenty-third Illinois, the One Hundred and Fifth Ohio was rushed in like manner, rear rank in front, to the extreme left of the new line, advanced into the open field, and assigned the hopeless task of repelling a greatly superior force posted under cover. It is more than probable, considering what was actually accomplished by the Thirty-third brigade that day, that, if they had been posted under cover along the fence at the edge of the wood thirty or forty yards in the rear of the battery and there allowed to await the enemy's attack, instead of being pushed into the open in detail, rear rank in front, the enemy would have been unable to dislodge them As new troops, unaccustomed to tactical maneuvers, common sense demanded that they should be so handled as to avoid confusion therefrom as much as possible

The fear of losing his battery evidently blinded General Terrill to all other considerations Instead of posting the infantry of his brigade in such position as to prevent the enemy from securing the fruits of their surprise, he thought only of regaining the guns already lost by neglect of ordinary care in posting them Skilled soldier as he was, he did not show on the one field of battle where he held high command that power of instant adaptation which is essential to success

This is not said in blame Truer or braver men than General Jackson and General Terrill never lived, and they had no more sincere mourners than the officers and men of the Thousand They were the victims of a strange oversight, whether their own or another's cannot now be determined General Jackson fell before there was time to do anything towards remedying this mistake The peril was instant and overwhelming He met it like a man and gave his life to redeem the error The same is true of General Terrill No man in his command could have any desire to cast blame upon him, all most willingly shared his misfortunes All that is desired is to call attention to the fact that "the new troops of the Tenth division" should not be blamed for the mishaps made inevitable by the failure to reconnoiter the position of the guns

But there is another witness who ought in justice to be called to testify of the conduct of the Thirty-third brigade that day—the enemy

Maney's brigade, of Cheatham's division of the Confederate army of Mississippi,† which was in our front was composed of the Forty-first Georgia, the First, Sixth, Ninth, and Twenty-seventh Tennessee It had no need for a scapegoat, and no prejudice against new troops It was already famous as a fighting brigade and maintained that reputation to the end of the war Its loss that day was one-third greater than any other brigade on the Confederate side Until they passed the strip of woods in rear of the knoll on which Parsons battery stood, not a single shot was fired at them except from the guns of that battery and the rifles of the Thirty-third brigade The commander of every regiment in that brigade made a full report of its part in the fight What is their testimony? Major John D Knight, of the Forty-first Georgia, speaks of our fire as "most terrific and deadly Just at this place,' he says speaking of their position in our front, "our regiment sustained half, if not two-thirds, their entire loss during the battle' That loss was one hundred and fifty-one, including *six color-bearers* The first Tennessee was "in the rear of the left of the brigade," and so lost "only three or four at this point.' Colonel Porter, commanding the Sixth Tennessee, reports "It was here, at the fence and between it and the point where the battery was in position that this regiment sustained its greatest loss *Here was the hottest part of the engagement*" This regiment's loss was one hundred and seventy-nine, including *two captains and three color-bearers*, killed before they reached the crest of the knoll Major George W Kelsoe, of the Ninth Tennessee, speaks of our fire as "a most galling' one and mentions that the commander of his regiment, Lieutenant-Colonel Buford, was wounded and *two company commanders and the color-bearer killed* in their final charge upon the battery The loss of this regiment was one hundred and fifty-four Lieutenant-Colonel W Frierson, of the Twenty-ninth Tennessee, speaks of our fire as "such a storm of shell, grape and Minié balls as no troops scarcely ever before encountered,' which, if hardly correct, is certainly emphatic This regiment had *two color-bearers killed and a third mortally wounded* Their loss was one hundred and eight out of two hundred and ten engaged

Thus the dead and the living of our victorious enemy testify that if the men of the thirty-third brigade were new soldiers they were stout fighters As for them we can truly say that it was an honor which even the memory of defeat cannot dull, to have been christened veterans by the onset of such valorous foes as Maney's Confederate brigade

---

* THE REPORT of General Buell upon the battle of Perryville, dated a month after his removal from command is found in Part I, volume XVI, Series I of the Official Records' of the Union and Confederate Armies" pages 1023-1036

The report of General A McD McCook who commanded the 1st Army Corps dated October 18th, is to be found on pages 1038 1044 of the same volume

The report of Brigadier General Rousseau, commanding the Third Division, is found on page 1044, and the part especially stigmatizing the troops of the Tenth Division on page 1046

The report of Captain Percival P Oldershaw General Tenth Division is to be found in the same volume pages 1059-1062

The report of Captain William P Anderson, A A G 23d Brigade is to be found on page 1062 of the same volume

The report of Colonel Albert S Hall, commanding 105th O V I, is to be found on page 1064, and also again in the appendix of this volume

The reports of the officers commanding the regiment constituting Maney's Brigade, Cheatham's Division of the Confederate Army of the Mississippi, may be found in the same volume, beginning on page 1113 continuing to page 1119 General Braxton Bragg's report of this battle may be found on page 1088 volume XVI Part I, Series I of the 'Official Records

---

† IT MAY BE interesting to know that General Hardee, commanding the left wing of the Confederate Army, claims the capture of this battery The repulse of the Tenth Division for the right Brigade of his command in his report on page 1121 of volume 16 part I of the official records will be found this statement 'This combined attack was irresistible and drove the enemy in wild disorder from the position nearly a mile in the rear Cheatham and Wood captured the enemy's battery in front of Wood, and among the pieces, and amid the dead and dying was found the body of General James S Jackson, who commanded a division of the enemy at that point " Evidently General Hardee was determined to claim all that was in sight Cheatham's division were the only troops engaged in the attack upon the troops of the Tenth Division, in this part of the field though it is possible that in the advance afterwards made by Wood upon the left of Cheatham he may have passed over the same ground

XI.

BETWEEN THE ACTS.

THE loss of Parsons' Battery was a serious blow, not merely to the self-esteem of the brigade, but especially to the regiments, whose officers and men had volunteered to form this organization. The following account of Captain Cummings, now Commander-in-chief of the Grand Army of the Republic, Department of Pennsylvania, of the organization of the battery, its service and the life and death of its accomplished Commander will be of interest to the reader:

PARSONS' BATTERY.

Parsons' Battery was organized from details of men and officers taken from the 105th O. V. I., 80th Ills., 123d Ills. and 101st Ind. while in camp in Louisville, Ky., early in Sept. 1862. Col. A. S. Hall asked for volunteers from our regiment to join the battery. Among the officers who volunteered were 2nd Lieut. W. H. Osborn of Co. I and myself. The battery was commanded by Lieut. Charles C. Parsons of the 4th U. S. Regular Artillery. It had five Napoleons or light 12 pounder brass guns, one three inch rifled Parrott and two 12 pounder howitzers. The organization of this battery was the idea of Brig. Gen. W. R. Terrill who commanded our brigade. He had recently been promoted from captain of battery M 5th U. S. Artillery and was an enthusiastic artillerist. He had achieved much distinction with his battery at Shiloh and won his promotion thereby. Lieut. Parsons was a man of singular purity and

CAPTAIN H. H. CUMINGS.

HENRY HARRISON CUMINGS was born in Monmouth, Ill., December 1, 1840; was son of Charles and Emily (Amsden) Cumings; was great grandson of Benjamin Cumings, who was private in the Hollis, N. H. Company of Colonel Prescott's regiment, at the battle of Bunker Hill, and afterwards lieutenant in a New Hampshire regiment, with Washington at Brooklyn and about New York, and at Princeton. He is also, on the maternal side a great grandson of Lieutenant Abram Amsden, of the Vermont troops in the Revolutionary war. He removed with his father to Madison, Ohio, in 1852; worked on his father's farm summers and attended school winters, first at the district school, then at Madison, Ohio, Seminary, then at the Grand River Institute at Austinburgh, Ohio. He entered Oberlin College in the freshman

sincerity, an able and accomplished officer, a graduate of West Point Military Academy and in every respect a man of most admirable qualities and character Gen. Terrill spent much time with the battery and paid great attention to its equipment and the drill of its officers and men, and we were rapidly getting into shape to do effective service At Perryville the battery in going into action immediately preceded our regiment and unlimbered on the ridge where our regiment fought

We were overwhelmed by the enemy in a very short time, before it was possible to get all the guns into position I commanded one section composed of two 12 pounders and that day my section had the right of the battery and went into position on the right of the line just at the right of the position that the 105th Ohio soon took Being on the right we were able to stay by our guns longer than the other detachments of the battery The last gun fired from the battery was my right gun, which I fired with my own hands Gen Terrill was with us, directing the working of the guns during most of the short engagement Gen. Jackson passed me and spoke to me but a moment before he fell. The enemy took all our guns except one howitzer, which being in the rear did not have time to get into action

---

class in 1859, taught school winters and studied the rest of the time at Oberlin until the last of June, 1862 when he left college to enter the 105th but was graduated with his class (that of 1862)

After the war he came to the oil country of Pennsylvania and in June, 1866, settled at Tidioute, Pa, where he has since resided He has been engaged in refining oil in pipe line transportation and in various operations, chiefly western land speculations, banking, and in recent years lumbering in southeast Missouri, in connection with the Missouri Lumber and Mining Company, of which he is president, at Grandin, Mo He has never held office except the non salaried local offices of his town, many of which he has filled among which he has served as president of the Tidioute School Board for some ten years a position which he still holds (1895) and is proud of As a citizen he has always felt much interest in the success of the Republican party, and has served as a member of the State Central Committee and as delegate to many political conventions among them the Republican National Convention at Chicago, in 1888 He is a member of Colonel George A Cobham Post G A R, and of the Loyal Legion Commandery of Pennsylvania At the encampment of the Grand Army Department of Pennsylvania for 1895 he was unanimously chosen Department Commander which position he now holds

In trying to limber up one of our guns, when the infantry fell back, the driver and every horse attached to the limber were shot dead and fell into a heap I saw them the next day, lying on the field as they fell The enemy pulled our guns off the field but were unable to take them away and they were the next day recovered by our troops

After the battle the battery was disbanded, the officers and men returned to their regiments. Lieut Parsons served with distinction in command of batteries H and M 4th U S Artillery at the battle of Stone River and on detached service elsewheres, was on duty at U S Military Academy, West Point, for some years after the war, resigned and entered the Episcopal ministry and died of yellow fever at Memphis, Tenn, in 1878 His death fittingly closed his worthy life and illustrated the noble character of the man I add the tribute paid to his memory at the time of his death by the *Memphis Avalanche*

(*From the Memphis Avalanche, Sept 1878*)

A MARTYR OF '78

Death aimed high when his fateful dart struck down Charles C Parsons, late colonel of the United States army and rector of Grace Episcopal church Yet the mark was fair and near and bared for the blow

Into the room of disease the Christian soldier marched The hand which had applied the match to cannon on the battlefield lifted the dying head, cheered with prayer the departing soul day and night. To his own fated exposure, this man invaded the strongholds of the plague, carrying help to the body and the soul of many stricken men Death struck hard and true The chivalrous soldier, the honored shepherd of a flock, the courteous, polished West Pointer, the favorite friend particularly of the young of Memphis, was borne to his last resting place Over his grave, in marble let this be cut

"A MARTYR OF '78

He died for the people against whom he had fought."

Capt Cumings is probably mistaken in regard to the recovery of the guns Lieutenant Wm B Turner that day in command of Smith's Mississippi Confederate Battery which operated upon our extreme left, says in his report of this battle, "I immediately opened an enfilading fire on them, at the distance of 250 or 300 yards, with canister, and continued it with shell and spherical case as the enemy retired This continued until our forces had so far advanced as to be between our battery and the enemy's infantry when we commenced replying to a battery of the enemy, which had annoyed us considerably, opening upon us with guns of heavier caliber than ours as soon as we commenced our firing. I continued this until I received orders from General Cheatham to cease firing, and our infantry advanced and took the battery opposing us (This no doubt refers to one of the batteries on Starkweather's line, though he is in error in regard to the capture —T) I then advanced the battery to a position farther to the front to open on a battery which was firing on Captain Carnes' battery, when I received orders from General Cheatham to withdraw my battery to the rear

"After night I received orders from Capt M Smith to send my horses and limbers to the front, and withdraw some of the enemy's guns which had been captured the enemy having taken off most of their limbers with their horses I brought off all I could find (excepting two caissons which were disabled) amounting to five 12-pounder Napoleon guns (brass), one 12-pounder howitzer gun (brass), and one 6-pounder Parrott gun (steel) with two limbers and two caissons without limbers, filled with ammunition for the Napoleon guns During the night, I exchanged my two 6-pounder guns for two of the Napoleon guns together with the ammunition, and the next morning, on our leaving for Harrodsburg, my men, by order of Capt. M Smith dismantled the guns which we were unable to take with us "

These were, evidently, the guns of our battery The entire number of guns captured that day according to Gen

Bragg's report, was twelve There is an error of one in this as ours was counted as an eight-gun battery though but seven were captured Of these two of the Napoleons were taken by the battery serving with Maney's Brigade

In part 2, volume XVI, Series I of the official records, will be found the following, showing the farther disposition made by the confederates of the two guns captured from our battery and given to Maney's battery

Headquarters Army of Tennessee
TULLAHOMA, APRIL 8, 1863

BRIG GEN GEO MANEY, *Shelbyville Tenn*

General I am instructed by the commanding general to advise you he wishes your battery composed of guns taken from the enemy You will, therefore, turn over one of your guns turned over to you from Captain Semple's battery to the reserve He also directs that the names of four of the bravest Tennessee men who were killed on the field be inscribed upon guns The man to engrave them will be in a few days at your camp, to whom you will give the names of men to be engraved and report the same to the general commanding

Very respectfully, your obedient servant
H OLADOWSKI
Lieutenant-Colonel, Ordnance Duty

Headquarters Maney's Brig Cheatham's Div , Polk's Corps
CAMP NEAR SHELBYVILLE, APRIL 10 1863.

LIEUTENANT COL H OLADOWSKI,
Chief of Ordnance, Army of Tennessee

Colonel Your note conveying directions of the commanding general in reference to my battery, was received this morning The gun from Captain Semple's battery will be turned over to the reserve whenever commanded

The instructions of the commanding general as to the inscription of names on the pieces is highly gratifying to me, and will be appreciated by my entire command Your note expresses that

The names of the four bravest Tennessee men who were killed be inscribed upon guns

I feel it proper to mention in this connection that while my command at Perryville contained four Tennessee regiments, each one of which can afford many names eminently deserving the appropriate honor designated the Forty-first Georgia was also part of my brigade at the time, and participated with the Tennessee regiments, and with like valor and devotion, in the severe conflict, resulting in the capture of a quantity of the enemy's artillery, further, it may be noted, this was the only regiment, not of Tennessee in the entire division engaged on our extreme right and I must add as my conviction, the Southern Army lost neither a truer soldier or more amiable and admirable gentleman on that field than Col Charles A McDaniel, the commander of that regiment

If it be the desire of the commanding general to bestow a compliment encouraging and appropriate to the Tennessee troops through my brigade as a medium, the inscription should properly be limited to the names of Tennesseeans, but if the purpose be to honor the fallen braves of this particular brigade, then justice, far more than any generosity, will strongly direct attention to the name of Col McDaniel for an inscription

I respectfully and earnestly suggest, that, as the battery complete will contain just one gun for a suitable name from each of my four Tennessee regiments it would be a profound gratification to me to be allowed the privilege of inscribing the name of Col McDaniel on one of the guns captured by my brigade at the battle of Murfreesborough, the gun to be presented to some Georgia battery, as a token of respectful memory on the part of my command for a gallant soldier of a different State from themselves, who gave up his life fighting side by side with them, for the results, whatever they be, of usefulness to the country or honor to themselves, achieved on the field of Perryville

Very respectfully, etc ,

GEO MANEY Brig -Gen l Commanding

The author has made some effort to trace these guns farther but has been unable to do so.

Some of the experiences of members of the Thousand connected with this battle are worthy of record.

Corporal Norris L. Gage of Company G., a handsome young fellow, slow of speech but of a specially courteous manner, being twice wounded in the heat of the fight, turned to the lieutenant in rear of his position, using his rifle as a staff, and asked with the habitual salute: "Lieutenant, can you tell me where I can find a hospital?" The officer could only point to the rear and ask "Are you badly hurt?" "Twice" was the reply, and he added, regretfully, "I'm afraid my fighting days are over." So they were; disabled by his wound, the Thousand saw him no more.

CORP. N. L. GAGE.

Captain Byron W. Canfield of Company E., was one of the brightest and pleasantest officers of the regiment, fond of a jest and always making light when others were inclined to murmur. While we were at the lane in rear of our first position a bullet struck him just at the angle of the forehead, plowing a furrow along the parting of his

---

NORRIS L. GAGE was born in Sheffield, Ohio. At the time of his enlistment he was attending Kingsville Academy, preparing for college. He was twice wounded, almost at the same instant, at Perryville, October 8, 1862. After his recovery, he was engaged in various clerical pursuits for some years. He afterwards entered the service of the Santa Fe Railway; then engaged in mining in California, and for several years past, has been interested in various railway enterprises.

hair Picking up his hat which the bullet had knocked off he turned to his first sergeant who stood beside him and pointing to the wound, asked with a grin, —

"Moffatt, do you see any brains?" "Lord, no,' replied Moffatt, who was as much of a wag as his captain. "Did you think I'd got a microscope?'

Comrade Charles Radcliffe relates that while the fire was hottest the men in the front rank of Company F, to shield themselves a little behind the crest of the knoll, knelt down or rather crouched down to load While in this position the man upon his left was struck and sank down in a heap Leaning over him to inquire how badly he was hurt, a bullet cut his right sleeve and made a flesh wound in his arm If he had not leaned over to aid his friend it would have struck him full in the breast

---

The Major s horse was wounded and became unmanageable Though he had two other horses shot under him during his service, he always refers to this one, with special regret because of "a bottle of excellent whiskey which was in one of the holsters " Telling his loss to Hartzell, the wag of the line, that worthy screwed up his face in the peculiar way that always preceded a jeu d esprit, and replied

' You see Major, the disadvantage of being too temperate I might have lost the bottle, but the whiskey—never!"

"Sachie," a young soldier of Company G whose name as enrolled on the roster, was Eaton, though no one ever gave him that appellation, was the life of his company and, indeed, of the whole left wing, through his irresistible tendency for "turning to mirth all things of earth " Just before we came into action that day, while the Thousand was halted under the oaks through the branches of which the enemy's shells were flying now and then, Sachie turned to the officer near him with a countenance of ludicrous concern and said, in a hesitating manner and with his inimitable lisp

"Lieutenant, if you think it would be all the same to Uncle Sam, I d like to knock off about half a day!"

A lieutenant who got separated from his command just as it entered the corn-field after passing the woods in rear of the battery, having been stunned by the explosion of a shell which buried itself in the ground near him, found the enemy in uncomfortable proximity when he became conscious again and made a dash into the corn-field The fire was very hot and he was in instant expectation of being struck as he pushed on, dodging from row to row with the idea of confusing the aim of those who were firing at him, for of course, he thought the whole Confederate army had their eyes on him Presently a sharp stinging sensation on his right side told him that he had been hit He wondered that he did not faint or feel any serious inconvenience As he neared the crest of the hill, however, he felt the warm blood trickling down his side and concluded that he had been seriously hurt In a little while he passed round the left of Starkweather's right regiment then hotly engaged with the enemy who were in his rear, and found the fragments of the brigade, in their new position General Terrill sitting upon a log the picture of utter woefulness

Some of his comrades sprung forward at his approach and one of them who had been a medical student hearing of his hurt proceeded in the masterful way which superior knowledge inspires, to examine the same The hole in the blouse was found, the blouse and vest and shirt removed, there was a twinge of pain and then a grunt of satisfaction from the operator. Fortunately for the lieutenant he wore a silk undershirt The ball was evidently somewhat spent and though it penetrated the outer clothing, had merely imbedded itself with a fold of the silk, a little way into the muscle and came out with the cloth with a sudden jerk The medical student was delighted and those who had gathered round congratulated the new comer upon his rare good luck

"But how came there to be so much blood?" asked the bewildered fellow

"Blood," said his friend "You haven't lost a spoonful"

"Haven't? Why it ran all down my side" was the reply.

The friend clapped his hand upon the other's clothing. Sure enough, it was drenched. He drew his hand away; looked at it, smelled of it; then sat down bursting with laughter.

"Coffee!" was all he could say.

Sure enough the thrifty lieutenant had filled his canteen with coffee that morning and had treasured it with exceeding care. The bullet had passed through the canteen about the middle before reaching him and the jar of his motion had slowly spilled the coffee through the holes it made which, as it trickled down, he had mistaken for blood.

H. E. PAINE, Musician.

Comrade H. E. Paine tells how he and another drummer boy being on duty with the stretchers for the first time in action that day, were half-compelled and half-persuaded, by an officer of another regiment not even belonging to our division, to go into the fire-swept space between the contending lines, to bring off his wounded brother. He went with them to point out the way, but when he came near took shelter behind a tree and left the drummer boys,

---

HENDRICKS E. PAINE was born in Le Roy, Ohio, in 1845. He came of good fighting stock, having no less than three near relatives of the same name who rose to the rank of brigadier-general in the war of Rebellion. Because of his youth and delicacy of frame, he was unable to enlist until he joined the

to rescue his brother, which they did. They are not sorry now that they did it, but only the new recruit could be induced to undertake such a foolhardy thing.

The disappearance of Sergeant Joseph George, is one of the mysteries of that battlefield which will never be unravelled. He was, with the exception of Jerry Whetstone the tallest man in the regiment. He had been in the three-months service and was in all respects a model soldier. During the fight in our advanced position, he loaded and fired with the utmost coolness. When we fell back into the wood he took his stand behind a tree and continued to fire upon the advancing enemy. When, convinced that it was useless to attempt any further resistance to the strong line advancing upon us General Terrill gave the order to fall back the writer went and gave the order to George and some others near the lane fence who had not heard it. George's answer was "Just as soon as I have one more shot."

None of the regiment ever saw him again. He was not among the dead on this part of the field and whether he was killed or wounded and captured, no one knew, until his name was found among those interred in a national cemetery. There was rumor of a very tall man found among the dead of the Seventy-ninth Pennsylvania, which came to the knowledge of the writer afterwards when on duty with one of its officers, but he was unable to verify it. As that regiment was in our rear, it is more than probable that Sergeant George fell back through the corn-field and took his place in their line and was the tall stranger who attracted attention and fell while fighting with them.

105th as a drummer. He was a universal favorite because of his fine appearance obliging character and close attention to duty. He was a special favorite with Colonel Tolles, who was never tired of doing favors for the bright lad, who had found a way to overcome his gruffness. He was transferred by special order of the War Department to the headquarters of his uncle, General E. A. Paine, in February, 1863.

After the close of the war, he became interested in oil and finally settled at Scranton. He is engaged in various business enterprises, he is a member of the Board of Trade—a bank director and one of the foremost citizens of that prosperous city.

No man of the regiment will ever forget the agony which settled afterwards into deep dejection, of Lieutenant, afterwards Captain Spaulding, whose brother, Asa, was killed in this engagement. As we faced to the rear and advanced in line, the lieutenant left his post long enough to rush to the other flank of the company and grasp his brother's hand

"Be a man, Asa!" were his only words, to which his brother responded "I will"

We found him lying beside the oak where he had fired his last shot with a bullet through his head A year afterward, as we bore the brother from the field of Chickamauga, he said as he listened to the roar of guns in our rear "I am glad I am not leaving Asa there!" Little did the gallant soldier realize how near was his meeting with the young brother whose death had hung so heavily upon his heart — all the more heavily because the lad had enlisted against the protest of his sister whose only hope these two heroic brothers were

---

Captain Edward V Bowers of Company K was one of the oldest men in the Regiment He was a minister of the Gospel, a Methodist perhaps, of gentle, courteous nature, a little stooping in the shoulders, with a hint of grey in his beard His habit of life had fitted him better for remonstrance than command It was nothing less than a misfortune that he was not made our chaplain instead of the man who drew pay as such In that position he would have been a blessing and an honor to the regiment As captain of Company K he was careful and anxious for the health, comfort and welfare of his men, but not being smart in appearance, or an adept in mastering his tactics, he was the object of some cheap wit among certain of the line officers who were greatly his inferiors in fact, and by no means a favorite with the Colonel. He was scrupulous in the performance of duty, but did not always realize the necessity of form and discipline. He used to invite those of his men who desired to do so, to unite with him in his evening devotions, until informed that it was "prejudicial to good order and military discipline" to pray with his men though quite permissible to swear at them

It was on the field of Perryville that the sterling qualities of this curiously misplaced man appeared The writer will never forget the calmness with which he stood in his place uttering words of encouragement to his men quite unmoved by the leaden hail that hurtled past Turning to the officer nearest him, he said with characteristic self-depreciation

"If any orders should come please let me know I think I do not hear as well as some"

After the battle was over that night, Captain Bowers gathered a few of the more religiously inclined of the regiment about him and in a little depression of the hill on which we lay, held a service of prayer It was very quietly done, but when the notes of a hymn reached the ears of the Colonel, now commanding the brigade, he sent at once to "stop the racket that old fool Bowers was making to draw the enemy's fire on us!"

Aside from the fact that not a gun had been fired for hours and that the roar of a shattered army moving toward its new lines was all about us, it is altogether probable that the Colonel's angry command could have been heard farther than the words of the softly-chanted hymn

---

Elbridge T Early of Company K was shot in the hip and also in the head at Perryville His wounds called forth a letter of commendation from Col Hall, which was well-merited, as some extracts will show Early was taken sick and sent to the hospital in Lexington, where he was with several others when the enemy took the city and the retreat to Louisville began Col Hall writing after Perryville, said "A week passed by and no tidings came from them; almost another, and still no tidings when one morning young Early reported for duty, no parole disgracing his pockets When he learned the city (Lexington) was being abandoned, though reduced by fever, he crawled from his cot and made his escape from the hospital and the city; and evading the enemy at Paris and Cynthina, avoiding the roads, and traveling by night through the woods and fields, he at length made his way to Covington over one hundred miles From thence he came to Louisville and rejoined his regiment

"He was much worn down, and greatly enfeebled, but the fire of patriotism was yet beaming in his eye, and the unconquerable spirit of a true soldier, could be seen in every motion

"On the first day of October, the bugle sounded the advance, and all were directed to remain who did not feel able to participate It was the long-roll for battle, and Early, though still feeble, would not remain behind He was with us—shared our fatigue, our hunger and our thirst He knows what it is to march, after being two days without bread, subsisting upon corn and bacon eight miles without water, and then without resting, to participate in the bloodiest and most desperate battle of the rebellion He fought in the front line, and though wounded in the hip, kept fighting still, until stricken down by a ball, piercing his temple No man could conduct himself more gallantly He is entitled to a proud place in the affection of all patriots "

Six months afterwards comrade Early was discharged and is yet living, treasuring the letter of his old commander as a priceless heritage By accident the name is given both in the Roster and the tables as Elbridge F Early This was not discovered until the plates had been cast

---

Ira Nye, of Company F, was one of those strange instances of presentiment fulfilled that are to be found so often in the soldier's experience as almost to cease to be regarded as notable From the very date of his enlistment, he insisted that he would be killed in the first engagement. This impression he repeated about the time the regiment left Louisville, and when nearing the field of action bade his friends in Co E farewell, saying to one of them that his hour had come He did not let this feeling influence his conduct, but went bravely on and was shot through the heart in our most advanced position Writing home some time before, he said he wished to be remembered as a good soldier" The man who faces the enemy with the certainty of death in his mind, certainly deserves to have this modest ambition realized

---

In preparing the foregoing account of the part of the 105th Ohio in the battle of Perryville the author has been greatly assisted by the recollections of more than fifty of the survivors who kindly responded to his request for the same. While, in the main, agreeing with each other there were some glaring and irreconcilable differences In such cases there was nothing to do but accept the weight of evidence In one case, the most positive averment of one man was expressly contravened by more than twenty others in an equally positive manner

The charge made upon Terrill's and Starkweather's brigades by the three brigades of Cheatham's division and Liddell of Buckner's, was regarded as of such unusual and desperate character as to deserve extraordinary honor as the following order will show:

GENERAL ORDERS, Headquarters Army of Tennessee,
No 1 TULLAHOMA, TENN Nov 23 1862

1 —The several regiments battalions, and independent companies engaged in the ever-memorable battle at Perryville Kentucky on October 8, in which they achieved a signal victory over the enemy numbering three to their one, and drove him from the field with terrible slaughter and the loss of his artillery will inscribe the name of that field on their colors The corps of Cheatham's division which made the gallant and desperate charge resulting in the capture of

the enemy's batteries, will in addition to the name, place the cross cannon inverted

By command of General Bragg

GEORGE WM BRENT,

Assistant Adjutant General

XII.

A STIRRING WINTER.

"A VETERAN."

THE glare of battle in one hour transforms the recruit into a veteran. It does not teach him tactics. The wheelings and facings of the drill-ground, the combinations of battalion and brigade evolutions may still be mysteries to him, but the inexpressible something which distinguishes between the recruit and the veteran has transformed him into a soldier. He has not learned how to maneuver but he has learned how to fight. When once he has stood up to be shot at, all the rest of his education is mere form; he is already a veteran, knowing that which lies beyond drill and discipline and is the real marrow of a soldier's life.

Perryville was the last of the autumn battles. The Thousand buried its dead and marched, three days afterward to Danville, twelve miles away, where it lay eight days, when the brigade was ordered in hot haste to Lebanon, Kentucky, to repel an anticipated attack by the rebel general, John H. Morgan, who having slipped to the rear of the Federal columns which were cautiously escorting Bragg out of the State, was at his favorite occupation—cutting lines of supply, capturing trains and detached posts General Buell focussed his attention on this pestiferous antagonist with a celerity and energy in curious contrast with his demeanor toward Morgan's superior. He did not seem to realize that the way to dispose of Morgan was to destroy Bragg

This was the beginning of months of weary chasing after the bold cavalier, whose excellent mounts and thorough knowledge of the country enabled him easily to elude the 'dough-boys,' who, though many times his number, tramped up and down, and back and forth along strange roads, in rain and snow, by night and day, seeking and finding him not, save when, now and then, he pounced down on some undefended train or unsuspecting post Then there was a sudden flurry, a sharp skirmish, a quick surrender, and the restless partisan was far beyond pursuit before the lagging infantry could be started after him

There is something ludicrous in the method that was adopted to protect the long line of supplies and the exposed flank of an army operating nearly two hundred miles from its base, against the incursions of mounted rangers, issuing from the defiles of the Cumberland mountains, and retiring thither when pursued Indeed, the aversion which our government showed to the enlistment and proper employment of cavalry in the early days of the war is wholly unaccountable, unless one keeps in mind the fact that there was a general belief among army men of the old school, that rifles and sharp shooters had destroyed the efficiency of cavalry as a fighting arm Instead of cavalry we had, therefore, a multitude of little infantry posts, interspersed, now and then, with one of greater strength composed of infantry and artillery, while regiments, and sometimes whole brigades, were detailed as guards for the immense trains made necessary by the transportation of supplies over great distances Every bridge on every line of railway had its little stockade and guard of five, ten, fifty, or a hundred men, whose duty it was to prevent its being burned, or the track torn up by "bushwhackers" or "guerrillas," as the bands of disaffected partisans were termed. Against raiding parties of one or two thousand, with a few pieces of artillery, they were no protection whatever Middle Kentucky and Tennessee were one vast network of such little posts

All the Union armies of the first year were put into the field with hardly enough cavalry to serve as couriers and orderlies On the other hand, the Confederates, from the beginning, gave great prominence to this arm It is true they did not learn how to use massed bodies of cavalry much sooner than we did; but their partisan horse, from the outset played an important part in all their movements They not only covered the front of every advance and the rear of every retreat but were our teachers in that species of warfare which was denominated "raiding

Gen John H Morgan, in boldness and fertility of resource, was easily the first of the Confederate raiders Much of his success was, no doubt, due to his second in command Basil Duke, whose subtlety so admirably supplemented his leader's dash and enterprise Gen Duke was termed, sometimes, "the brains of Morgan," and there were times when that leader seemed in need of more than he carried under his own hat, but it cannot be denied that he was bold, adventurous, full of resource and of amazing fortitude He had too, in a superlative degree the quality of attaching men to him These qualities fitted him for the role of a partisan leader—a role in which he was rivaled only by Forrest Dividing his forces, Morgan swept almost at will, along the hard stone pikes or obscure country roads, gobbling up the guards, burning stockades and bridges tearing up the railroads, and every now and then surprising some of the stronger isolated posts Truth to tell he had not much stomach for a fight, and little enough skill in ordering one But if he had been a better fighter, he would, in all probability, have been a less valuable raider His function was not to fight but to confuse, circumvent and annoy And this he did with admirable efficiency

Today he would drive in our pickets, tomorrow capture an outpost fifty miles away, and the next day, perhaps, burn a transport on the river as much farther in another direction. With the march to Lebanon, the Thousand became a part of this exacting, unsatisfactory warfare.

"Move with the regiment to Lebanon! Start immediately, make forced march! Reach Lebanon to-morrow, and defend the place against Morgan's cavalry," was the first of many orders of like character.

We reached Lebanon in time, so did plenty of other troops. In three days there were enough there to have eaten Morgan's men, horses, saddles, and all, but Morgan was somewhere else. Then we were ordered in like haste to Munfordville, the scene of Wilder's surrender three months before. Almost before we arrived, the pioneers were rebuilding the railway bridge he had destroyed. It was terribly cold, we crowded into a few of the buildings which had escaped the general destruction, and shivered about the fires we built of what we could pick up. In a day or two we were provided with tents and remained here a month, engaged in constant drill, with occasional expeditions to obtain forage for the animals. During this time the Tenth division of the Army of the Ohio was reorganized by assigning to its command Gen. Charles C. Gilbert, who, having figured for two months as a major-general, and as such been in command of the most important corps of the Army of the Ohio, had laid aside one star, and was now only a brigadier. Garrard's Kentuckians were detached and the Nineteenth Indiana battery transferred to the Thirty-third brigade. This organization lasted a few days only. On the 1st of November, 1862, the Army of the Ohio became the Fourteenth corps, its field of operations the Department of the Cumberland, and its commander, Maj.-Gen. William S. Rosecrans. Maj.-Gen. Joseph J. Reynolds was assigned to the command of the line of supply along the Louisville and Nashville railroad.

Munfordville may well be regarded as the high-school

in which the training of the regiment and brigade was completed. Next to a fight or a forced march, the colonel of the Thousand loved a brigade-drill, and well he might, for in that he showed at his best. His voice was of such remarkable carrying power that he handled a brigade with little assistance in the transmission of orders, while his eye was so accurate in judging distances that few of those confusing halts occurred which are apt to mar the course of such maneuvers.

The Thousand was fortunate in having a lieutenant-colonel who was, in some sense, a martinet. Little given to severity, he had a passion for orderly details. Every visible phase of camp-life received his constant attention, and any irregularity in the laying out of streets, the pitching of tents, the fixing of a guard-line, or the policing of a camp was sure to meet his eye and call forth a reprimand. As a tactician he was almost perfect, and his pride in the appearance of the regiment made him indefatigable in drilling them. From frosty morn till purple eve, through all the autumn days the echo of serried footsteps filled the camp. Company drill and guard mounting he scrutinized with care, and woe to the careless or uninstructed officer who made an error or permitted a straggling movement. In maneuvering a battalion, he was an ideal commander. Mounted on his black horse, his slender, soldierly figure, dark, pointed beard, keen, black eyes, and sharp, regular features, gave him a most distinguished appearance. His shrill, almost piping voice, at first provoked mirth from its grotesque inconsistency with his martial countenance and figure. When one became accustomed to it, the very shrillness of his tones constituted one of his distinctive excellences. No matter what the clamor his commands came distinct and clear, cutting rather than overwhelming other sounds. Whatever the Thousand owed to others its excellence in drill, its habit of instant obedience, and the thorough discipline for which it came to be well reputed, were due in the main to the indefatigable efforts of Lieut.-Col. William R. Tolles.

We graduated from this school in haste after thirty days. Morgan was again in the saddle along the old route from the head of Sequatchie Valley to Middle Kentucky, so it was said. We were sent to Glasgow, Kentucky, to receive him. Three days we waited and he came not. Then a trooper arrived in hot haste to tell us that the ubiquitous raider had entered an appearance at Hartsville, Tennessee, fifty miles away, whither we were ordered to proceed without delay. We pushed ahead, laughing all the time at the absurd figure we cut in this ridiculous chase of cavalry by infantry. Sure enough, when we reached Hartsville, we learned that Morgan had captured the garrison and departed before the order came for us to pursue. We remained in this region a few days hunting for him, where we knew he was not, or at least thought he was not.

CAPT. RIKER.
1863.

THAT was our first Christmas in the service which we celebrated here. Who that shared that jolly rout will ever forget it? Perhaps the war furnished no more characteristic revel. It was a warm, sunny day like the early spring of the North. There were many rabbits in the old fields where the brown sedge-grass made excellent cover. Lieutenant-Colonel Doan of the One Hundred and First Indiana, the biggest and warmest-hearted old boy in the brigade, preferred a request to the colonel-commanding that his regiment might be allowed a Christmas rabbit hunt. Straightway the matter was taken under advisement; the commanders of the other regiments were consulted, and it was finally determined to organize a big hunt for the brigade. The regiments were accordingly mustered under arms, each man equipped also with a stout stick, and having been marched to a favorable location, pickets were thrown out to prevent surprise; then each regiment stacked arms, formed a hollow square, faced inward, took distance at ten steps apart, and began to march toward the center, beating the cover as they went. It was a jolly hunt, abounding in shouts and ludicrous contretemps. Many rabbits were killed, many more escaped; there were broken heads and bruised shins, for one cannot be sure who is behind the rabbit at which he strikes; but nobody minded such things, and few who engaged in it will recall a scene of more hilarious merriment. Each regiment got enough of the soft-eyed victims to flavor the Christmas stew with which we were regaled that night. The One Hundred and First Indiana was reported to have made the highest score on account of the colonel's being the best judge of a rabbit-cover; though an officer of the Thousand who stole out of the line and took post on the side of a ditch which led up to a big swamp was said to have made the largest individual bag.

Imagine his surprise when, months afterward, one of Morgan's captains clapped him on the back, he being then a prisoner, and reminded him of the place where he had hidden to intercept the cunning cotton-tails, who, escaping the round up, were seeking shelter in the swamp. A scouting party whom Morgan had sent to spy out the land and let him know what chance there was of surprising our brigade, was, it seems, at that very moment hidden in the swamp; they even considered the question of making a raid on the lone rabbit-hunter. The gray-coated captain remarked that he reported to "the Old Man," which was the pet name Morgan's men gave him, that it was "no use trying to surprise a command which, even when they went hunting at high noon, never took off their equipments nor got a hundred steps from their gun-stacks." It was a compliment of which our colonel had every reason to be proud.

Perhaps as a result of this report in regard to the alertness of our brigade, a day or two after, we were notified that Morgan had concluded to go to Glasgow after all, and that a determined and elaborate effort was to be made to set a trap into which he would be sure to fall. So many bodies of infantry were to close in on him at Glasgow that he would have to run over some of them in trying to get away. We, therefore, hustled back, via Scottsville, but the much-sought-for raider was not at Glasgow when we arrived. We were then rushed over to Cave City, where he had just been doing some mischief; sauntered down to Bowling Green, and from there to Nashville, and on to Murfreesborough, Tennessee, where we came just too late for the great battle of Stone's River.

GEN. JOSEPH J. REYNOLDS.

Here the Thousand became part of the Second brigade, Fifth division, Fourteenth army corps. The grave and earnest Thomas, best-loved by his soldiers of all the generals of the great war, commanded the corps whose acorn-badge came afterward to typify his character. We called him "Pap Thomas" sometimes, but not so often nor so flippantly as many have supposed. By his staff he was known as "Slow-trot," because he was not given to galloping save

JOSEPH JONES REYNOLDS was born in Indiana in 1822; graduated at West Point, class of 1844; was assistant professor in the Military Academy from 1845 to 1855; and Professor of Mechanics in Washington University, St. Louis, until about the outbreak of the war. He was appointed a Major-General of volunteers and assigned to the Fifth Division of the Army of the Cumberland, on its organization, under General Rosecrans, in the fall of 1862, which command he held until after the battle of Chickamauga. When General Thomas succeeded to the chief command, General Reynolds was

when there was need of haste Some of our generals did a deal of galloping, not only on the march and in battle, but also in their reports. Thomas never galloped on paper and not often on the road

General Reynolds, who commanded the division, was of the same unassuming type Quiet, slender, scholarly, he was a model of soldierly courtesy, which embraced the enlisted man as well as the wearer of shoulder-straps He never returned a salute carelessly, or as if it were a mere matter of routine but always as if he felt it a personal greeting, which it gave him pleasure to acknowledge Though a strict disciplinarian he was easily approachable, and no commander ever had a more thoughtful care for the welfare of his men

---

appointed Chief of Staff In the re-organization of the army by General Grant he was thrown out by questions of rank, and was assigned to command in the department of the Gulf In 1864 66 he commanded the Department of Arkansas He was greatly beloved by the men of his command His memory is held in special reverence by the survivors of the Thousand of whom he spoke in terms of especial praise in his report of the battle of Chickamauga In some manner, due probably to his promotion to Chief of Staff about this time, the regimental reports of the Second Brigade in that battle were lost after reaching his hands It is quite possible that they may yet be found among the records of the Department of the Cumberland

XIII.

A MIDWINTER CAMPAIGN.

WINTER campaign, even in the latitude of Tennessee is sure to be attended with many difficulties and uncertainties. Just sixty days after its organization, the army of the Cumberland fought its first battle, on the last day of 1862 and the first day of 1863, by the banks of Stone's river, thirty miles southeast of Nashville, Tennessee, on the railroad running to Bridgeport. It was without any strategic preliminaries. The Federal army simply marched out of Nashville to assail the enemy in position at Murfreesborough. Each general planned to attack by the left flank. The Confederate commander got his blow in first. Both probably acted under a mistake. The Union leader thought the Confederate forces very much demoralized by the failure of the invasion of Kentucky. The Federal view of that movement was that Bragg had been driven out of Kentucky, his army beaten, dissipated, and utterly worn out with a long and profitless march.

This impression was no doubt confirmed by the stories which spies who came into our lines as deserters were instructed to circulate. The bait was swallowed by the commander of the Army of the Cumberland with eagerness. Perhaps one reason it was so fully credited was that General Rosecrans' chief of scouts seems to have been under a curious hallucination in regard to the spirit and discipline of the Confederate forces

The Confederate commander likewise misconceived the temper of the Federal army It is a curious fact, that the spirit of the soldiers of the Army of the Cumberland rose higher with each strategic check or seeming disaster in battle The Confederates believed it greatly demoralized by its retreat of two hundred miles its bloody check at Perryville the recapture of Cumberland Gap, and the constant cutting of its line of supply by Confederate raiders On the contrary, the spirit of the army was never better than when it set out on the Murfreesborough mid-winter campaign The retreat had irritated every man from the division commanders down to the dullest private, Perryville, instead of being a victory, as the Confederates called it, was merely an accident General Bragg did not realize that it was the commander of the army, and not its soldiers, who was demoralized by his onset, and so naturally concluded that what fifteen thousand did at Perryville, fifty thousand could do with equal ease at Stone's river He knew his own army regarded the march into Kentucky as a brilliant strategic success rather than a failure, and all envied the divisions which albeit with enormous loss, had driven back and held in permanent check three times their number on the Kentucky battle-field.

Impelled by these mutual misapprehensions, the two armies joined battle, the long, thin line formation of the Federals inviting a repetition of the tactic so successful at Perryville The attempt to apply it developed the man of the Army of the Cumberland The right wing, now under McCook, as was the left at Perryville, was rolled back upon the center, just as in that battle, but in the center was Thomas Neither dismayed by disaster nor confused by unexpected conditions, he bent his energies to hold what was threatened and regain what was lost In the face of an enemy already flushed with anticipated triumph, he formed a new line, at a right angle with the original one, and thus, doubled back on the center, presented a wall of fire and steel, against which the enemy's forces vainly dashed in recurrent waves until darkness came to end the bloody strife.

Late that night the commander of the army summoned his generals to consider the question of retreat. Thomas, worn with the fatigue of the day, but confident of the morrow, gave his voice against retreat, and, during the discussion that followed, fell asleep leaning against the wall in the corner of the log-house in which the council was held. Near midnight, he was awakened by his chief and asked if his corps could protect the army in its withdrawal to a new position. "The army cannot retreat," was his reply, and leaning back he resumed his slumber. He did not argue, he did not question; he merely *announced* his conclusion. The commander sallied forth with McCook to hunt for a position in the rear. Whether convinced by what he saw, or yielding to the conviction of his great lieutenant, he abandoned the idea of retreat, and the battle which seemed lost at sunset was won before the coming noontide.

LIEUT. HENRY ADAMS.

HENRY ADAMS, the youngest son of Asael Adams, late of Warren, Ohio, was born April 29, 1835; educated in the public school of that city, he devoted himself to a business career, and for some years had been teller of the old Western Reserve Bank, when in November, 1862, he was appointed a second lieutenant of the 105th, and assigned to Company G. He joined the regiment near Bear Wallow, Ky., and was immediately appointed Brigade Commissary of Subsistence on the staff of Colonel Hall. He was prostrated by sickness, brought on by exposure and fatigue, and died on February 20, 1863, in hospital

Despite his many brilliant qualities, General Rosecrans was not well-fitted for important, independent command. He did not fear danger, he only feared defeat. Over-confident before the battle was joined, the roar of conflict seemed to confuse his energies and paralyze his judgment. His only thought was to seek a means to extricate his command from impending destruction. His fear of disaster was so great that he would have abandoned the field of Stone's river to avoid it, as he did Chickamauga in order to provide a way of escape for the fragments of the army he thought was overwhelmed. In both cases, Thomas supplied the nerve which his chief so woefully lacked.

The battle of Stone's river, having thus been won by the hardest, the Army of the Cumberland lay confronting the Confederate forces for nearly six months. Except frequent reconnoitering of its flanks, this army of a hundred thousand did nothing from midwinter until midsummer.

We held the left center of the Army of the Cumberland. It was a favorite theory with General Reynolds that a volunteer command should be given variety of service. The monotony of camp life, he thought, brought home-sickness, which is the worst enemy of a soldier's efficiency. During the five months we lay at Murfreesborough, he provided for his men such a variety of duty as made the campaign that followed an enjoyable holiday. Nine times in those months, one or both, of the brigades of Reynolds raided the right of the enemy's position. Lebanon, Smithville, Carthage, Readyville, Auburn, Liberty, Statesville,

at Murfreesborough, Tenn. He was the only civilian given a commission in the regiment. Of him Colonel Hall wrote after his death to his brother, Whittlesey Adams, Esq.:

"The whole Brigade was astounded at his death. No man ever in so short a time more tenderly endeared himself to soldiers than did Lieutenant Adams, to my entire command. Affable, prompt, cheerful, always ready and supplied with all commissary stores that the department could furnish, to his business education and habits the duties of his position came naturally and he enjoyed the exercise of them with a high satisfaction. He mastered the rules and regulations governing his duties at once, and entered upon duty with the exactness of a long experience. His efficiency as an officer, and the upright and spotless character which he ever bore, won for him a name which will be sacred to us all."

McMinnville, the whole region that lay between our left flank and the Cumberland river, was scouted and raided so thoroughly by our infantry, that Stanley and Minty had some opportunity to mass the small force of cavalry and hold it ready to act as occasion might require. A brigade of mounted infantry was organized also,—ludicrous and resonant, but easily subsisted, of unequaled endurance, and having hardly more need for a roadway than a goat. Poor, despised mule! How little credit your virtues receive! The horse is a creature of song and story, but who has sung the praise of the mounted infantry mule? Wilder's "Mule brigade" was part of our division. No military experiment ever paid better than the "Jackass brigade," which, though it made a deal of noise in those days, has blown its own horn but little since.

From January until June, 1863, the Thousand was a part of the Army that lay encamped about Murfreesborough, Tenn. Aside from the incidents that have been related there were others that greatly affected the regiment. The duty was steady and considering the season of the year might be termed onerous. In addition to daily drill, picket and camp guard, there was work on fortifications, loading and unloading supplies, and two tours as train-guard to Nashville. The water was bad and somewhat too abundant in our first camp; in one to which we removed it was excellent.

There were great changes in the personnel of the Regiment during this time. Before the first day of June, 1863, nine months after muster-in, eleven officers had resigned, one had been dismissed, two had been killed. Of the rank and file, fifty-six had been killed, seventy-eight had died, and 197 enlisted men had been discharged for disability.

Those in hospital who never rejoined increased this number so that more than one third of the regiment had either been killed, died, or been discharged since its muster. The number detached with the sick, who afterwards recovered, had reduced the number present for duty to about one half the original complement.

Among the deaths, the most notable was that of Capt. Ephraim Kee, of Co. B, on the 16th of January, 1863. He was a young man of great promise; just ready to enter college at the time of his enlistment. He had been a fellow-student with the writer and many others of the regiment at Kingsville Academy. While there his attainments as a scholar were very marked, as was his poetical talent. Big, tawny giant as he was, there was an undertone of melancholy in his disposition that always surprised his intimates by its apparent lack of cause. On this account most of his poetical effusions were of a serious character. Two poems of his, in the possession of the writer, are entitled "A Vision" and "The Dying Student." Both dwell upon a life cut short before the attainment of its dominant ambition, its controlling idea. This thought he was to exemplify in his own death.

CAPT. EPHRAIM KEE.

On the 15th, of January 1863, he was the ranking officer in the picket detail of the regiment for that day. The writer was the second in command. Who the other commissioned officer was is not known. Capt. Kee and the writer were not only old friends, but their companies were next to each other on the left. The day was bright and pleasant and the night which followed clear and cool. Each officer had four hours' duty and four off at the reserve. The two officers joined their blankets and made one bed at t e foot of a great oak. He came off duty about ten o'clock and lay down. When the lieutenant went on duty at two o'clock, he complained of thirst. The other handed him a canteen, which had been lying on the ground and showed the rime upon its woolen casing He drank freely When the writer came off duty, he had been removed to camp, hardly conscious Before night he was dead A congestive chill had removed a gallant officer who would gladly have died in battle but chafed at the very thought of perishing by disease

The following extract from the poem entitled "The Dying Student" above referred to, will give some idea of his poetic quality as well as of his impetuous and ambitious character Had he lived, he would no doubt, have made a name in literature

Oh, sooner far that Death might call
When rising tempests spread a pall
    Of darkness o'er my head
When vivid lightnings flashed on high
And rolling thunder shook the sky
    And all was wild and dread

Oh, I would die midst fire and smoke
"And shout and groan and saber stroke"
    Upon the crimson plain
When armies proud with maddened strife
In wild disport with human life
    Heap up the piles of slain

But ah, 'tis vain It may not be
Yes I must die, and soon with thee
    Fair world for aye must part!
The cold sweat stands upon my brow
My feeble pulse beats slowly now
    And lead-like sinks my heart

His was the most promising intellectual life of the regiment and the feeling of every one who knew him, was that the possibilities of a great career had been cut short He was succeeded in command of Company B, by his first Lieutenant and bosom friend, A D Braden, who having been in the three months' service, was of right, entitled to be Captain at the outset, but gave way to Kee because of his great friendship for him Indeed, it is said that both expected to be lieutenants under Captain John Reeves*, through whose instrumentality this company was raised. For some reason, he was not mustered and the two young men, to whom he was greatly attached, became captain and first lieutenant respectively.

Our first Chaplain, Rev. Aaron Van Nostrand, joined us here, held two or three religious services, was taken sick and died soon afterward, Feb. 27, 1863.

Another death was that of Lieut. Henry Adams. During his brief service with the regiment, he was on duty at Brigade headquarters as Commissary of Subsistence, but became known to the regiment as a genial and courteous gentleman and faithful soldier.

At this camp, after six months of service, when it had lost one-third of its members, the regiment finally received a stand of colors. Why this essential feature of regimental organization was so long in reaching us it is hard now to discover. There is a rumor that Gen. Kirby Smith or Gen. John Morgan, or some other meddlesome confederate confiscated the first one sent us, but the truth seems to be that the regiment got so far ahead of its own requisitions or was pushed forward so fast that its equipment had no time to catch up with it. At least the first time it paraded under its own colors, was well past the midwinter solstice, and was made the occasion of one of the most ludicrous things which happened during the war.

The fact has already been noted that our colonel was inclined to find his way into print whenever occasion offered, sometimes making occasion where one did not happen to exist. He was by nature and inclination a politician

---

JOHN REEVES, JR. was born in Washington County, Pa., in 1815, and was, therefore, forty-six years old when he was appointed Captain in the 105th Ohio. He resided in Howland, Trumbull County, Ohio, and was a man of great influence and pronounced character. It is said that the necessary number of men to form the company were enlisted in ten days. He spared neither time nor money in the work. Just why he was not mustered with the regiment is not known. He was one of the men who went to California in '49, and was for thirty years consecutively chosen a Justice of the Peace in his town. He was also Treasurer of his county, dying in 1894, at the age of seventy-nine.

Entertaining no hope of a permanent military career, his eyes were always to the advantages to be derived from military service, in a political way. The winter of 1862—63 was a time of very serious political disturbance in some por-

LIEUT. ALBERT DICKERMAN.

ALBERT DICKERMAN was born March 26, 1840, at Masonville, Delaware County, N. Y., and is a descendant of Thomas Dickerman, who came to this country from England, in 1635, and settled at Dorchester, Mass. His grandfather, John Dickerman, was a soldier in the Revolutionary War, under Captain James Blakeley and Samuel Fletcher. The subject of this sketch attended district school until he was sixteen years old; after eight years, only in the winter, working on the farm summers. Attended Norwich Academy, at Norwich, N. Y., two terms. At the age of seventeen he moved with his parents to the vicinity of Cleveland, Ohio, and worked one season as a market gardener. From the autumn of 1857 to July 1862, he was studying and teaching, a part of the time at Chester, Ohio, and about six months at Oberlin O.

tions of the North. The Knights of the Golden Circle were making strenuous efforts to rouse disaffection the draft which had become necessary in some states was unpopular the financial outlook was unfavorable in the extreme and all the forces opposed to the prosecution of the war were crystallizing for a final effort to embarrass the government compel the disbandment of the armies and the recognition of the Slave-Confederacy The presentation of the new colors afforded an opportunity, in the opinion of the colonel for expressing the views of the soldiers on these subjects At the dress parade of the regiment, on the 16th of February, therefore, resolutions were read by the adjutant and adopted unanimously, after a speech from the commander of the brigade, by the officers and men of the regiment The resolutions though pitched in a most exalted key undoubtedly expressed the exact sentiments of the whole command The really ludicrous thing about it is the idea of a military organization mustered under arms in the most formal way, listening to a set of resolutions propounded in effect by the commanding officer and read and certified by the adjutant and then being called upon to vote on the same Probably no one desired to vote against the resolutions but if he had he would hardly have dared to do so Had the regiment resolved itself into a mass-meeting electing its own officers it would have been some-

---

and about a year and a half in Missouri In July 1862 he enlisted in Company E 105th O V I was mustered with the regiment at Camp Cleveland was appointed sergeant major and served in that capacity until March 29, 1863 when he was appointed adjutant and served in that capacity until the close of the war

After muster out he studied law at the Union Law College in Cleveland, Ohio and was admitted to the bar in June 1866 In August of that year he located at Hillsdale Mich, where he lived until the spring of 1883 While there he served for three years as director of the public schools for four years as Circuit Court Commissioner, for four years as Judge of Probate, and represented the county in the State Senate during the General Session of the Legislature in 1881 and the Special Session in 1882 practicing his profession in the meantime In the spring of 1883, he moved to Muskegon Mich and in 1887 was elected Circuit Judge of the Fourteenth Judicial District and took his seat in 1888 At the expiration of his term in 1894, he declined a re election and moved to Watsonville Cal where he now (1895) resides

what different, though political resolutions hardly accord with good order and military discipline. Only a few days afterwards the major part of the officers of the regiment were threatened with arrest for signing a respectful protest against an act of injustice to one of their number. These resolutions, given in a note below,* were carried home by the worthy gentlemen who brought the colors and no doubt brought consolation to many a loyal heart which never stopped to consider the circumstances attending their adoption. Late as it was in our service when we received our colors, they are now among the most tattered and war-worn of the hundred odd battle flags which the Buckeye State treasures with deserved honor.

The promulgation of these resolutions was among the last acts of Adjutant Robbins who was compelled by a painful injury received in the performance of a duty accidentally imposed upon him during a leave of absence, to tender his resignation. He was succeeded by Lieut. Albert Dickerman, promoted from private of Company E, to be sergeant-major some months before, and now March 29, 1863 promoted to a lieutenancy and appointed adjutant, in which capacity he served till the close of the war. He was a man of strong character and brilliant qualities, systematic, prompt, cool and courageous, one of those men who never lose their heads nor forget nor omit any routine duty. His career since the close of the war has fully justified the promise of his military service.

*The following are the resolutions adopted at this characteristic military mass-meeting at which all the participants were in uniform and under arms.

WHEREAS, Rebel sympathisers in some portions of the loyal States have represented that the Army of the West was in favor of a compromise with the rebels in arms, and was opposed to the policy of the administration in the conduct and management of the war. Now, therefore be it solemnly resolved by the officers and men of the 105th Ohio Volunteers:

1st. That the war was begun by a slaveholding aristocracy who planted upon the negro, deemed themselves too good for democratic institutions, and is waged by that aristocracy for the purpose of dismembering the Republic, and erecting out of its territory a separate and independent nation.

2d. That to the army has been confided the duty of conserving and preserving the United States one and undivided and that trust shall be executed at whatever cost.

3d That the Fathers who made the Constitution, intended to give the Government power sufficient to protect itself from a foreign and domestic foe and that the Army will construe that Constitution to possess power ample for that purpose and execute it, in that construction, against all its foes

4th That we regard as public enemies those persons in the loyal States who are seeking to create dissensions and interpose constitutional quibbles against the prosecution and management of the war, and that they are only professing respect for that Constitution to enable them to prostitute its forms for the aid of the rebellion, and for the final humiliation and destruction of the nation

5th That the preservation of the integrity of the nation, and the honor of its arms, is paramount to all other considerations and that we will never leave this soil until the last rebel is dead or bows in honest submission to the authority of the United States, and the foundations of the Temple of Liberty are laid anew upon the basis of Democratic equality, that beneath its shadows generations of a better race may celebrate the achievements of the armies of the Republic

6th That the policy of the administration in the conduct and management of the war, is most heartily approved, and that we welcome to our assistance armed bodies of men of whatever color, who will aid us more speedily to rid the country of that aristocracy, who ungrateful for its blessings, are waging a causeless war for the destruction of the nation

7th That we are proud of the noble patriot who as Governor of our beloved State, sustains the Government with a heart—divided only by his watchful care for the wants of the Ohio volunteer

8th That with the most exalted confidence in the President, in the Secretary of War, and the generals over us we resolve, lastly That every achievement of the army shall be laid upon the altar of an undivided country, and redound to the glory and lasting permanency of free institutions and that inspired by this, we will endure without a murmur, whatever of hardship or exposure may await us until the nation's last foe shall breathe no more, and final victory bring enduring peace

HEADQUARTERS 105TH OHIO,
MURFREESBOROUGH, TENN, 17

I hereby certify that the above is a true copy of the series of resolutions unanimously adopted by the officers and men of the 105th Ohio Regiment, on dress parade, February 16, 1863

Lieutenant A M ROBBINS,
Adjutant 105th Ohio

XIV.

GOBBLED.

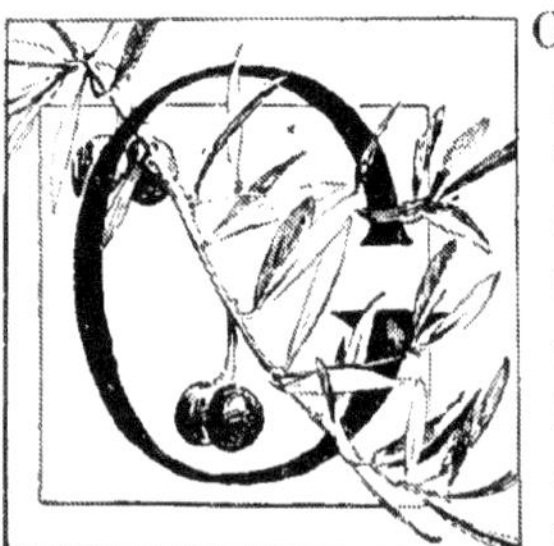

OBBLED! That was the term applied to those detachments on which the enemy's raiders swept down in overwhelming force and through surprise or overwhelming numbers made resistance vain or impossible. The Thousand was one of the many regiments to have this opprobrious term applied to it because of the surprise of a detachment belonging to it. It is a curious thing that this surprise resulted from obedience to the explicit commands of its colonel who though the most alert and careful of commanders, was possessed with a very strong desire to outdo others. This desire, accompanied with a belief induced by the representations of a trusted follower, that there was no enemy in our immediate front, led to the unfortunate mishap it is now our duty to record. If Morgan had little opportunity to make long raids after the advance of our army to Murfreesborough, and the winter rise of the Cumberland river, he made abundance of short and audacious ones. Along our whole left, from the Manchester pike to the Cumberland river, his restless partisans were ever ready to take advantage of any leas opportunity. Fully informed of every movement as they were by sympathizers within our lines, they pounced now upon a picket, now upon a train, and again on an unwary post. After chasing him for months, the Thousand found him one day when they least expected that pleasure. In the gray dawn of a January morning, a forage party left its camp It represented the brigade though the detail was from the Thousand except the wagons and drivers It numbered one hundred and twenty men, under the command of a captain with two lieutenants

At that time, foraging meant only the procurement of corn and fodder for the animals no supplies for the army itself were obtained in this manner Until within a very brief period each brigade commander had sent out his trains for this purpose with such guards as he deemed necessary In many cases in order to secure a quick advance it had been customary to mount the guards in the wagons drive out at a rapid trot hastily gather and load the forage, and return before the enemy had time to collect a force to send against them Accidents had sometimes resulted from carrying guns loaded and capped in wagons in this manner, and orders had been issued that each forage detail must be composed of a sufficient guard and also a " loading party of four to each wagon " and that this party should remain with the wagons but never be allowed to ride in them " outside the lines of the army "

The question was what constituted " the lines?" Was it the infantry pickets or the cavalry videttes regularly maintained on all the roads at a distance of a mile or two beyond? The detail from the Thousand was what was termed the "loading party,"—one hundred and twenty-eight men for thirty-four wagons It was intended to constitute part of a larger train which was going out on the Liberty pike under a heavy guard from Wood's division The detail from the Thousand should have been ordered to report to the officer commanding this train, since it was only as a part of it that the brigade commander had leave to send his wagons outside the lines at all But no such orders were given the captain in charge On the contrary, when the detail reported at brigade headquarters in the early dawn of the mid-winter morning, that officer was informed that the brigade wagon-master had located a particularly nice bit of forage out on the Liberty pike, which could only be secured by "getting ahead" of a big train which was going in that direction that morning The captain in command was, therefore, charged to leave the train to the wagon-master's guidance, who had an order directing the pickets to pass him with train and guard

This wagon-master occupied an anomalous position at brigade headquarters. While really a private soldier, he apparently enjoyed the confidence of the colonel to quite as great a degree as his commissioned staff He was a man of infinite resource and impregnable assertiveness His life had been so full of adventures that a very willing tongue hardly found time to recount them He was a survivor of the Mexican war, in the course of which he had achieved many marvels Since the Thousand had been in service hardly a day had passed in which he had not been the hero of some romantic incident His acquaintance with the general officers on both sides was remarkable for its extent and familiarity As a scout and spy, he went within the Confederate lines at will, talked with the utmost freedom with officers of the highest rank had hair-breadth escapes going and coming, and had killed nearly as many "rebs" as Samson boasted of having slain Philistines, some were unkind enough to say with the same weapon. How he gained such ascendancy over the Colonel, no one has ever been able to explain It is scarcely possible that he believed in the wildly-incredible tale that the wagon-master told about three female correspondents who served as troopers in Morgan's command for the mere pleasure of informing him of the movements of that bold raider, or the other wondrous narratives with which he was so well supplied Unfortunately, the wagon-master's most remarkable feats were always performed when no one else was nigh, and though a redoubtable scout, he took good care not to reveal any movements of the enemy which were not already clearly developed Altogether, he was a fairly good wagon-master, a really good forager, and kept the colonel's table abundantly supplied with whatever the country afforded. In short, he was a handy man to have about headquarters—never handier than on that 21st day of January, 1863.

That this man should be put in virtual command of the train excited no surprise; and when, after reaching the

Capt. Byron W. Canfield.

Byron W. Canfield was born in Chardon, Ohio, where he was engaged in business at the outbreak of the war. He enlisted in the 105th Ohio, as captain of Company E. Was wounded at Perryville, and was in command of the forage detail captured on the 21st of January, 1863. He was dismissed from the service without a hearing but afterwards restored by order of the War Department, it being conclusively shown that instead of violating orders, he obeyed them literally. He was very popular, and many of the officers signed a protest against his summary dismissal, though they incurred the serious displeasure of the brigade commander by so doing. He is now a resident of Indianapolis, Indiana.

picket-line on the pike, where the train had already arrived, he renewed the Colonel's urgency for haste, and insisted that the men should be mounted in the wagons, so as to proceed at a trot to the cavalry outpost, in order to "get ahead of Wood's train" and gather in the forage he had marked down, there would not have been a moment's hesitation, but for the fact that one of the lieutenants accompanying the detail was a captious fellow, who insisted that the Colonel had no right to send a train beyond the pickets without a guard as well as a "loading detail." Some of the men grumbled also, for it was no pleasant thing to ride in an empty army-wagon with a canvas cover drawn over the hoops, along a hard-frozen road, at a sharp trot, on a cold morning But the Captain obeyed the orders he had received, and the men were told off as far as they would go, four to a wagon the captious lieutenant being put in the rear wagon with three men

The train bounded resonantly over the hard pike at a brisk rate, the wagon-master riding ahead with three or four cronies and a lieutenant, Stambaugh, from our battery. None of the guns were capped and but few of them were loaded Some two miles out we climbed a wooded hill on which the wagon-master had asserted we were to find the cavalry vidette Just as the head of the train reached the top of the hill, a few shots were fired—two or three, perhaps half a dozen in all Then all was quiet. The drivers stopped because the wagons in front were halted There was no outcry, no confusion, no orders Supposing the train had halted for the purpose of forming the detail as a guard, the lieutenant in the rear wagon scrambled out and ordered his men to form in line and load their guns It is a matter of some seconds to charge a muzzle-loader with cold, numbed fingers. Before it was accomplished, men in blue overcoats came riding along the train The wagons started on The officer supposed these were some of the mounted men who rode in advance with the wagon-master.

"What are the orders?" he asked.

"Surrender!" was the reply and he found himself looking into the muzzles of three or four cocked revolvers The lieutenant glanced around at his men Their guns were not yet loaded, their bayonets were in their scabbards It was useless to resist—there were no means of resistance His sword, which he had drawn when ordering his men into line, lay across his arm The demand for his surrender was repeated, a shot whizzed past his ear. The enemy outnumbered his little squad four to one. He gave his sword a toss into the thicket, turned and clambered into the rear wagon, now again in motion The whole affair had not occupied two minutes, perhaps not one

Colonel Hutcheson, of Morgan's command, with a hundred and sixty men, wearing the blue overcoats of Federal soldiers, had surprised and captured the vidette, and prepared an ambuscade on the wooded hillside for the train they evidently expected. The mounted party in advance had ridden confidingly up to a group of blue-clad soldiers on the pike whom they took to be the Federal vidette, only to find themselves confronted by Confederate revolvers The shots fired were a signal for the troopers, hidden in the woods on either side, to close in on the train They quickly covered the drivers with their pistols, and ordered them to drive on. There was no opportunity to learn the number of our captors, and no chance to resist them if we had known We were practically as helpless as if bound hand and foot A few of the men crawled out of the wagons and escaped—perhaps half a dozen in all. The Colonel had yielded to the wagon-master's importunity, the Captain had obeyed the Colonel's orders, and the Lieutenant had obeyed the Captain's We had got "ahead of Wood's train," and Morgan had "got ahead" of us So we dashed on at a sharp trot toward the enemy's lines and the prisons of the Confederacy

The men were paroled and released at McMinnville The officers were kept a day or two in the house of a scholarly Unionist who had been compelled to seek safety within our lines The Confederates had scattered his fine library, each one taking whatever he chose, and throwing the others on the floor Out of the debris the Lieutenant rescued three volumes smeared with red clay from the boots of careless troopers. These he was permitted to carry with him into the prison to which the officers were sent, probably because they were written in Spanish, and so of little interest to those having us in charge They served to lighten many a weary hour in Confederate prisons

The wagon-master escaped during the night, before reaching McMinnville, found his way back to camp, and made a formal report, the glittering inaccuracies of which showed how well fitted he was for a much higher position It gave a thrilling account of his own achievements, told how he "emptied three saddles" with his revolver, and finally engaged Colonel Hutcheson in a hand-to-hand contest with his saber, actually "disarming him." What more he might have done, there is no telling had not that officer, in rapt admiration of his desperate valor, exclaimed "For God s sake, sir, do not throw away your life!" Yielding to this pathetic appeal, the wagon-master surrendered, and so lived to make the report which is the only bit of official history that has been preserved in regard to the matter. Curiously enough, its says nothing about the Colonel's orders to "get ahead" of the other train On the contrary, it declares that the Captain ordered his men into the wagons during the wagon-master's absence, quite ignoring the fact that neither officers nor men desired to ride in the cramped, lumbering army-wagons in such weather, and that the only reason for mounting them was the need of haste to enable us to reach the cavalry outposts in advance of the larger train in order that the forage the wagon-master had spied out might be secured

Acting upon this report, while Captain Canfield was still a prisoner-of-war, without any hearing or opportunity for defense whatever, he was dishonorably dismissed the service, the department commander expressing regret at his inability to "inflict the extreme penalty of the law upon one so deserving an ignominious death." At the same time, the commanding general took occasion to exonerate Colonel Hall from "all blame or censure" in connection with the affair.

Things turn out queerly in war, sometimes. The Captain was a brave officer, who had never shown any inclination to skirk a duty or disobey an order. A bullet had plowed along the parting of his hair at Perryville without in any wise disturbing his composure. What interest had he in headlong speed, and why should he order his grumbling men into wagons that freezing morning? Yet the subaltern was guilty of a crime worthy of death, and the superior officer exonerated even from censure! Why not? The superior prepared the evidence on which the finding was based. There was no court of inquiry, and the subordinate was not permitted to be heard. In fact, he was then an inmate of the famous Libby Prison, and the news went near to ending his life. When the matter came to be reviewed by the War Department, the

LIEUT. ALONZO CHUBB.

ALONZO CHUBB was born in Pittsford, Monroe County, N. Y., October 25, 1823; moved with his parents to Michigan in 1838; learned the printer's trade and afterwards engaged in carriage making in Detroit. Moved to Painesville, Ohio, in 1852, and was engaged in manufacturing wagons when the war began. He recruited by far the greater number of Company D, of which he was made 2d lieutenant. He was captured with the train near Murfreesborough, Tenn., January 21, 1863, and was for several months confined in rebel prisons at Atlanta and at Libby Prison at Richmond, Va. He was wounded at the battle of Perryville and again at Chickamauga, and

dismissal was annulled, the department holding that the captain obeyed orders, and ought not to be held responsible for the consequences

From one point of view, this mishap of the Thousand was a great blessing to the army of which it was a part Six days afterward, the general commanding issued a general order regulating foraging and forbidding the very things which were before permitted An attempt was made to compel the men who had been captured to return to duty in violation of their paroles, which it was contended, were in some manner irregular. The men protested that they ought not to be compelled to violate their oaths, but this manly protest was unheeded It was an unpleasant episode—just as needless and inexcusable as the great slaughter for which the general himself was responsible eight months after that very day But there is a vast difference between the punishment which is fit and proper for a captain of the line and a major-general—an act which makes him who wears two bars upon his shoulders "richly deserving an ignominious death," is at best, only an error of judgment, which it is almost an offense to impute to the wearer of two stars.

The following account of this unfortunate event by Corporal Bliss Morse, of company D, is given especially because

---

resigned in November, 1863 He moved to Ionia County, Mich, in 1864, to Manistee County in 1867, where he has since resided He has been supervisor of his town, Probate Judge of the county, and is now Justice of the Peace and Sunday-school Superintendent and hopes to celebrate his golden wedding in 1896 His portrait taken at seventy-one seems hardly older than when he was in service

In his army life, Lieutenant Chubb did not always decline to partake of intoxicating beverages He had lost the two middle fingers of one hand and his favorite jest when asked to imbibe was to put this hand, with only the first and little finger on it, beside the glass and say, "Only two fingers, if you please!" The joke was always new and usually convulsing On the way from Atlanta to Richmond as a prisoner of war, the officer in whose charge we were, a genial Confederate captain, was so enamored of its fun, that he must needs have Lieutenant Chubb out at every station where he stopped long enough to visit a saloon, to show the Yankee method of measuring a drink The persimmon whisky," which abounded in the Confederacy made this a trying ordeal to the lieutenant, but the efforts he made to entertain his host were at least commendable It must be admitted that the favor showed to him greatly excited the envy of his *compagnons de voyage*

the enlisted men among the survivors desire to express their appreciation of the course of General John H Morgan in ordering their release on parole and, in particular, the kindness of Captain John H Green, under whose charge they were in the march to Carthage, on the Cumberland river

"On the morning of January 21 1863, when the detail was made, as we stood in line before his quarters, Colonel Hall said

'Boys, you ought to be good for five hundred of them—infantry against cavalry—every time!'"

So we might have been, had we been on foot His remark shows that he was conscious of the danger of sending us out in advance of Wood's train

Into the wagons we got—some of our guns were loaded some not, I think, but we rode along pretty full of glee Just before we got to that cedar forest where we were surprised we passed on our left a few cavalry dressed in our uniform I believe they were Rebs They seemed to be estimating our number, looking at us closely, riding slowly. I think they returned to their command around that cluster of cedars These men had our overcoats on and that disarmed suspicion When the train stopped the cavalry rode down the line revolvers in hand shouting Surrender! surrender!' I think the transfer was made rapidly I rode in the same wagon with Captain Canfield, Lieutenant Chubb and I have always thought you were in the same wagon, too, but in that I must be mistaken, I suppose

We rode, I should think about twelve miles, to where a road went to Liberty, there Captain Canfield, Lieutenant Chubb and yourself were separated from us, our arms were also turned over The iron around the hoofs of those mules went clickety-clack over that twelve miles of pike as fast as I ever rode The coming night was my first experience in mule-riding At Smithfield, we got some bread and meat to eat about midnight We then resumed our ride, continuously all night and until next day noon when we reached McMinnville We were quartered in the Court House As we rode in, an old gray-bearded man said

"Uncle Sam is a good Quartermaster for we uns!"

The mules and wagons were corralled (One of those very wagons we got back at Jonesboro, near Atlanta)

We stayed Thursday night Friday night we were paroled and in the afternoon were on our way with escort to our lines near Carthage on the Cumberland River. That Friday evening at midnight, we camped among the hills, some fat bacon and flour was issued to us for supper We made a dough of the flour wet with bacon fat, then we wound it on sticks, some on staves or boards, and baked it by the fire. Saturday afternoon we had dinner of corn bread and meat, just the same fare as the officers in command When we came to streams too deep to wade, we mounted on the horses behind our 'brothers in gray ' Saturday night we stayed at a church-house near Alexandria, Tenn The captain in command sat up all night and wrote each of us a separate parole As we were travelling along Sunday morning, a little ahead of our escort,—(for we were under very good officers) Jackson, Sill and myself, stopped at a little log house for something to eat A man and his wife lived there, they had eaten their breakfast, some bread, turnips, potatoes and the shank of a ham was what was left We were welcomed kindly As we ate, the wife stood by her husband s side—looking up to him she said

"John, doesn't it give you great satisfaction to feed these men?" In that log house, with that affectionate look and tone, I have often thought marriage was not a failure. Passing along toward the river, we met an old woman who said.

"God bless, you, boys! I have a boy in your army "

We were ferried over the Cumberland River at Carthage. The officer commanding the escort made us a little speech, saying he had tried to treat us just as he would like to be treated were he a prisoner, but if he met us on the field of battle, would fight us as hard as ever We gave him three cheers and thanked him We then made our way to Louisville, a few to Camp Chase; some were returned to their regiments from Louisville Rosecrans did not regard their paroles "*

*The following is a copy of the parole given to one of our enlisted men and the order of General Rosecrans in regard thereto

HEADQUARTERS MORGAN'S DIVISION
McMINNVILLE Tenn

I the undersigned, belonging to the United States Army, having been taken prisoner by the Confederate States Cavalry under General John Morgan, in consideration of my being released on parole (whereof this is my witness), do solemnly swear not to bear arms against the Confederate States during the present war until regularly exchanged, under penalty of death, nor will I disclose anything that I have seen or heard in the Confederate Army to its prejudice

Sworn to before me this 23d day of January 1863 By order of General John H Morgan

(Signed) ALBERT A CHAMPLIN
Private Company E ' 105th Ohio Vols

Teste JNO H GREEN, Captain and A A A G

HEADQUARTERS DEPARTMENT OF THE CUMBERLAND
MURFREESBORO April 16, 1863

Special Field Order No 103

EXTRACT

Albert A Champlin, Company E 105th Regiment of Ohio Vols, having been captured by the enemy, paroled and set at liberty without the *delivery* required by the Cartel agreed upon by the Government of the United States and the Confederate authorities for the exchange of prisoners during the existing war, cannot be claimed by the Confederates as a prisoner of war and is, by their failure so to deliver, released from parole and will report for duty with his command

By command of Major-General Rosecrans

H THRALL,
Capt and Asst Adj t-Gen l

XV.

MILTON.

SERGT. L. N. PARKER, 1863.

THE time came when Colonel Hall had an opportunity to pay the Confederate raider for the chagrin and disappointments that he had suffered at his hands. Just two months after the capture of the forage train, the Second brigade was ordered to reconnoiter our left front. The brigade, still composed of our old companions in arms, and a company of the First Middle Tennessee cavalry, marched north to Cainesville, and the next morning turned sharply eastward and advanced by a rough country road to Statesville, from which the enemy was dislodged, but fell back only a short distance when he took a favorable position and offered battle.

Satisfied that he was confronted by an overwhelming force, Colonel Hall withdrew his little army, not on the direct road to Milton, but to Auburn, thinking to induce the enemy to believe that he intended to retire by way of Readyville. Morgan, who had a theory that the safest road to take is that along which an enemy has just marched, set out the next morning by the direct road to Milton to make a raid across the Lebanon pike. So he reported, at least, but some doubt is thrown upon his purpose by the demonstration he made in our rear and his oft-repeated anxiety to "get a whack," as he phrased it, "at Hall's brigade," whose commander had irritated him by some slighting allusions, in published communications.

It must be confessed that the Confederate raider had received scant courtesy at the hands of our colonel who

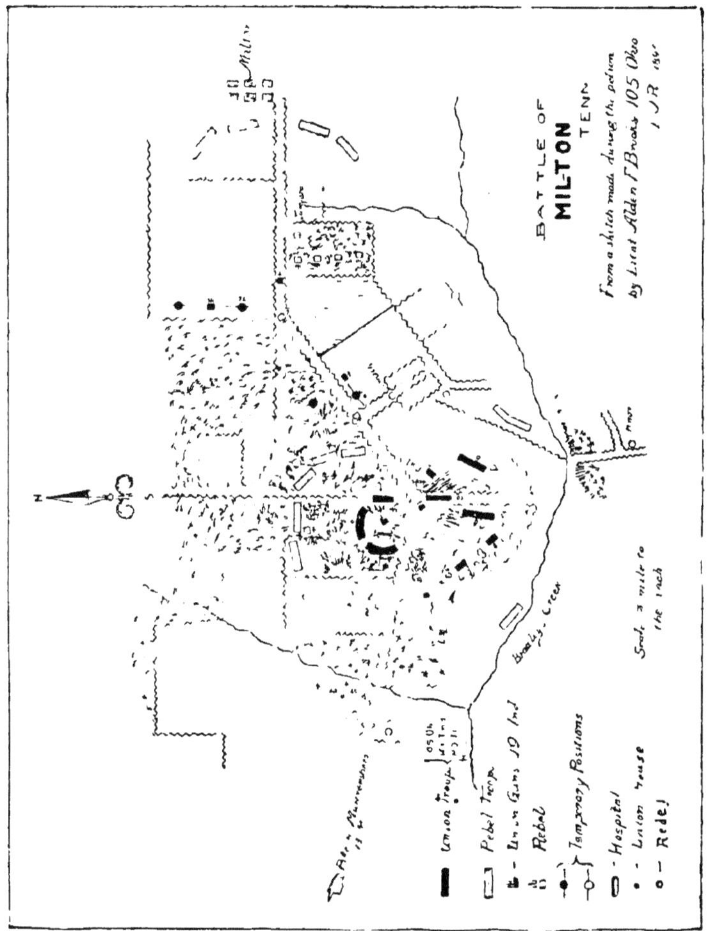

was not a little inclined to find his way into print, reporting his movements to the public as well as to his superiors often with somewhat uncomplimentary allusions to his opponent Some of these had stung the dashing Confederate leader, and both he and his officers were anxious to give battle to the Second brigade It is not strange that such taunts on the part of one who had thus far enjoyed small opportunity to prove his military skill or the prowess of his command, should annoy the great raider, who could justly boast that, month by month, for more than a year, his command had cost the Federal government a hundred times as much to replace the stores he destroyed as its support had cost the Confederacy So he repaid the colonel's jeers in kind, but waited impatiently for the time to come when he should have a chance to take a sweeter revenge

They were not the only men who seemed to think vituperation an important element of warfare. One of the most interesting features of that wonderful collection known as the "Official Records of the Union and Confederate" armies is the hearty good will with which even officers high in rank belabored their opponents with the pettiest diatribe and the most absurd recrimination. One finds it in the most unexpected places—in orders and reports, as well as in letters and despatches published for popular effect Some Federal generals spoke only of "rebs," while some Confederates refer to their opponents only as "Yanks" or "Yankees" There were a few who seem to have been too much absorbed in fighting their enemies to have had time for berating them, but some of the best soldiers were also the sturdiest detractors Both Morgan and the colonel of the Thousand might have found good examples among their respective superiors However, "he laughs best who laughs last," and the time had come when our colonel would get the better of the bluegrass raider in deeds as well as in words The pleasure of beating John Morgan in a fight of his own seeking, and with an inferior force, was to be his

The colonel was informed of his opponent's movement almost as soon as it began, whether through one of the wagon-master's female correspondents, who, as he solemnly avouched, not only wore trousers and rode with Morgan, but left letters for him in hollow stumps and knot-holes where, only an eye of preternatural keenness would find them; whether these fair, false ones, whom some were so incredulous as to deem purely mythical, gave the information which started us on that early morning march to Milton or not, it would be hard to determine; but the wagon-master has not refused to admit that he was inside the Confederate lines that night, while others thought him asleep, and that he learned thereby all the plans and purposes of the Confederate leader.

COMRADE L. NEWTON PARKER.

Personally, the writer believes the information came from a detachment of Morgan's command whom he sent out to engage our rear, while he pushed forward with his main body on the Milton road to intercept us. This force ran into a vidette of Captain Blackburn's company of Tennessee cavalry, which had been posted just a little out of Statesville to give information of the enemy's movements. The colonel was, perhaps, occasionally inclined to lay undue stress on the hypothetical, but he was always vigilance itself. Sometimes, we thought the bullet that grazed his

---

L. NEWTON PARKER was born January 27, 1842, in Wayne, Ashtabula County, Ohio. He was educated at district schools with the exception of two terms at Oberlin, and one term at Kingsville Academy; taught district schools and worked on farm, until enlisted in 105th O. V. I., August 8, 1862; was twice wounded at Perryville; stunned (entirely senseless for a time) by exploding shell at Milton, March 20, 1863; was mustered out with regiment as first sergeant of Company I; has been twice elected township clerk, twice Justice of the Peace, three times assessor, once county surveyor. He was never absent from his command except while in hospital

cranium at Shiloh interfered with his dreams, and called his sleeping men to arms, when there was little need; but it is certain that no enemy could ever come near a camp of his without being discovered, unless they came with wings So by daylight we were on the move. Then appeared the good results of our long marches and fruitless chasing after Morgan. We were matched that morning against his Kentucky thoroughbreds, and beat them into Milton, eight miles away It is true the head of his column reached the junction of the two roads just outside the town a little before we did, but our advance regiment was on the heels of our cavalry, and Harris' guns well up to the front. It looked for a time as if the enemy might attack us then and there, but we pushed on through the town in the early morning and took position at Vaught's Hill, a wooded eminence, three-quarters of a mile beyond.

The enemy advanced to the attack before the regiments were all in position, but the battery held them in check until our formation was complete The Eightieth Illinois had the right, the One Hundred and Fifth Ohio supported the battery upon the pike, the One Hundred and Twenty-third Illinois was on the left-center, and the One Hundred and First Indiana on the extreme left

The military instinct of the colonel commanding the brigade was shown in the instant selection of this splendid position, and a life full of soldierly promise reached its climacteric on that bright spring morning, when, sitting on his horse on the wooded slope of Vaught's Hill, he posted his brigade, almost without the aid of the staff officers, his magnificent voice echoing above the din of the opening

---

from wounds, after Perryville He kept a diary during the whole term of service, wrote it out more fully soon after the close of the war and was careful to note each day's movements and position To this journal and also to Comrade Parker for assistance no other man could have rendered, the author is under great obligations and the reader in debt for the character of this work

We are fortunate in being able to present two views of this esteemed comrade—one while he yet wore the chevrons and one as he appears today—the Mentor of the Survivor's Association

battle. His whole force numbered only fourteen hundred men, while the enemy had at least twenty-five hundred He was fourteen miles from Murfreesborough Seeing himself thus outnumbered, he dispatched a courier for reinforcements, with the assurance that he could hold the position as long as his ammunition lasted Lest this supply should fail, the men were instructed to hold their fire until the enemy were within close range. This comparative silence of the infantry, no doubt, led the enemy to over-rate his advantage He dismounted his cavalry, threw forward a strong line of skirmishers, and forming in their rear, charged again and again the left of our line Once it wavered, but the arrival of three companies of the Eightieth Illinois held it firm

For more than three hours the firing was very sharp, the enemy being repulsed in several assaults, then seeing the futility of attempting to carry the position before the arrival of reinforcements, his loss being very heavy, including General Morgan one of his colonels, and two lieutenant-colonels among the wounded, he withdrew, leaving four captains, two lieutenants, and sixty-three men dead or mortally wounded upon the field His loss was estimated at about three hundred in all He himself reported it "very severe especially in officers" Our loss was six killed, forty-three wounded, and seven missing Captain Buskirk, a very popular officer of the One Hundred and Twenty-third Illinois, was the only officer lost on our side One of the missing, a member of the Thousand, was captured, and after several months in Confederate prisons, was finally exchanged, and drowned, by the explosion of a boiler on a Mississippi steamer on his way home

Soon after the fighting had ceased, General Minty with two brigades of cavalry came up They made a reconnaissance beyond the town of Milton without finding the enemy On our return, we were greeted with much enthusiasm as the "fellows who had beaten Morgan"

This battle was of no great consequence either in numbers or results, but it was a very gratifying incident to the brigade and especially to the Thousand and their colonel It was not only a defeat of an old elusive enemy, and a victory against overwhelming numbers, but it was one secured by the skill of the commander and the quiet confidence of his men In all its elements, this little affair was peculiarly picturesque and romantic It wiped away the stain incurred by the surprise of his forage train and placed the colonel's feet securely on the ladder of deserved promotion Had not death intervened, there is little doubt that he would soon have received the star he coveted as well as the brevet which came just in time to give eclat to his obsequies

Of this engagement Colonel Hall made the full and characteristic report to General Reynolds commanding the Fifth Division Center, Army of the Cumberland, which is given below

SIR—Having completed the reconnaissance begun on the 18th instant I hereby report the operations of my command

I left camp with two days rations in the haversack and two on pack-mules with the following force One hundred and twenty-third Illinois Infantry Colonel James Monroe, commanding, 18 officers and 313 enlisted men, Eighteenth Illinois Infantry, Colonel Thomas G Allen, commanding, 18 officers and 365 enlisted men, One hundred and first Indiana Infantry Lieut - Col Thomas Doan, commanding, 19 officers and 353 enlisted men, One hundred and fifth Ohio, Lieut Col William R Tolles, commanding 18 officers and 245 enlisted men one section of the Nineteenth Indiana Battery, Captain S J Harris commanding and Company A of Stokes' cavalry, Captain (Joseph H) Blackburn commanding giving me a total strength of infantry of a little over 1 300 My orders were to ' reconnoiter the enemy and strike him, if the opportunity offers "

On the night of the 18th I occupied Cainsville, taking two prisoners, making that night an unsuccessful effort to surprise a small rebel camp and failing by the mistake of a guide

Early next morning I took the Statesville road, finding the enemy s pickets captured two of them At Statesville my advance was met by a force of 150 or 200 rebel cavalry a slight skirmish took place here, in which a sharpshooter from the One hundred and fifth Ohio mortally wounded one of (J M) Phillips' rebel cavalry The enemy retired slowly down Smith's Fork toward Prosperity Church on the pike I followed very cautiously, skirmishing the ravines, and upon reaching the pike wounded two of Smith's (Eighth) Tennessee cavalry and captured one Half a mile from this spot, down the valley toward Liberty, a regiment of rebel cavalry re-enforced by those whom I had driven from Statesville was in line of battle across the valley A small cavalry picket was also on the pike toward Auburn I rested my command at Prosperity Church about two hours

Becoming entirely satisfied that a large rebel force, under Morgan's command, was massed in the vicinity, and that I should be attacked by them the next day at the farthest. I determined to choose my own ground for the engagement, and accordingly at dusk I moved my command to the high ground to the rear of Auburn, bringing me three miles nearer Murfreesborough, leaving the rebel regiment wholly unmolested, by skirmishing my way to Auburn with forty or fifty rebels, whom I found had occupied the place during the afternoon. Of this force I wounded one or two, and they retired on the Woodbury road. That night the enemy's pickets confronted mine on every road leading from my position, and a large force advanced in the night from toward Liberty and encamped in the vicinity of Prosperity Church. Knowing that the enemy largely outnumbered me, I determined to draw him as near Murfreesborough as possible, and to reach a fine position near Milton, seven miles from my Auburn camp.

I moved at light, and upon reaching the high ridge, three miles from Auburn, halted twenty minutes to fill canteens and view the enemy's advance. He was two miles behind me, but showed himself in no great force. Making on this ridge some demonstrations which would indicate a purpose to stay there, I dropped suddenly down the slope toward Milton, and passed three and a half miles of open, level country, at a quick but steady step, occupying one hour, bringing me through Milton with the head of my column within 500 yards of the spot I desired to reach. Throwing two companies of the One hundred and twenty-third Illinois and half of Blackburn's company of cavalry into the edge of the town as skirmishers, and posting lookouts on my flanks and rear, I put a Napoleon into position, stacked arms, and awaited the enemy's pleasure. In twenty minutes his advance was visible in the angle of the pike, beyond Milton, about 1,500 yards away, and was promptly scattered by a shell from Harris. A few minutes later the enemy advanced, dismounted, and attacked my skirmishers in the village. By this time a large force was visible, and two heavy columns began passing, one to my right and one to my left, on the gallop. At this moment I started three messengers to the general to apprise him of my whereabouts, and to ask him for a re-enforcement of cavalry. Placing the Eightieth Illinois into position to take care of my right, and the One hundred and first Indiana my left, I drew my skirmishers gently back, re-enforcing them with three more companies of the One hundred and twenty-third Illinois, so as to cover the center, and set Harris to shelling each column as it passed, supporting his guns by the One hundred and fifth Ohio. As the heavy flank movements of the enemy made it necessary, I drew the whole command slowly back, converging my flank regiments to a line with my center along the top of the hillock, where I had determined to make a stand. The heavy column passing to my left was two or three times cut in two by Harris, but from the nature of the ground was enabled to pass out of range. The column on my right was forced to come nearer and run the terrible gauntlet of Harris' fire, which killed and wounded them at every shot, and finally ran against a volley from the Eightieth Illinois, which killed and wounded some thirty men and eight horses, and but for an unwarrantable delay on the part of the officer commanding the Eightieth Illinois, in giving his men orders to fire, would have been substantially destroyed. As it was, the terrible raking given it by the artillery, and the volley from the Eightieth Illinois, which it finally received, quite effectually extinguished its valor and boldness, so that a thin line of skirmishers and part of Blackburn's little company was all that was necessary to control them thereafter.

Each of my regiments came into position on the crest, just as I directed, without confusion or delay; but there was no time to spare on my left. Here the enemy dismounted, and advanced with all the precision, boldness, and rapidity of infantry drill. The blow struck the One hundred and twenty-third Illinois. The first attack was at once repelled, but the enemy, quickly re-enforcing his line of skirmishers renewed it with double force and determination, rapidly advancing his main line At this moment some confusion was manifest in the One hundred and first Indiana, but the gallant example set the men by their field line, and staff officers, by the unflinching One hundred and twenty-third Illinois and the opportune arrival from the right of five companies of the Eightieth Illinois and one of Harris' guns, enabled me to check the disorder Every man returned to his post and fought to the last The enemy gained no advantage, the advance he made by it cost him dearly

The enemy now opened on my center with four pieces of artillery and vigorously attacked my rear but was repulsed at the rear by Captain (W S) Crowell, with one company of the One hundred and fifth Ohio, and Captain Blackburn's company dismounted The enemy's artillery assisted in driving the enemy from my rear The engagement was now general My line encircling the hillock, inclosing us within five acres of space, was entirely surrounded by the enemy, and every reachable spot was showered with shot, shell, grape, and canister Meantime Harris was not idle, with one gun on the crest, he swung it as on a pivot, and swept them in every direction, and Lieutenant (W P) Stackhouse with the other gun on the pike, swept everything within his range Artillery was never better worked Again and again the enemy tried to break our devoted circle, and continued the unequal contest upon me steadily from 11 30 a m till 2 15 p m, when, seeing it was of no avail, he drew off his cavalry to my front leaving but a small force on my flanks, and, desisting from the attack with small-arms, continued to play his artillery till 4 30 p m, when he finally withdrew it also He however, continued to so occupy the ground outside of my line as to prevent me from taking his slightly wounded or the arms left by him He collected the most of them and took away all the men, except those in rifle range of my lines that were not dead or mortally wounded The enemy left upon the field of men and officers, sixty three, including four captains and two lieutenants, dead or mortally wounded, and from an interview with four surgeons, left by the enemy, I learned that the wounded carried away cannot be less than 300, among whom were many officers, including General Morgan, slightly wounded in the arm, Colonel (J W) Grigsby, arm broken; Lieutenant-Colonel (Thomas W) Napier, thigh broken. Lieutenant-Colonel (R M) Martin flesh wound in the back and many officers of lower rank I am myself satisfied, from a personal examination of the ground, that the enemy's loss is not less than 400 To this could easily have been added a large number of prisoners if my cavalry re-enforcements had reached me in due time

Colonel Minty, of the Fourth Michigan, commanding cavalry re-enforcements, reached me about 7 p m, at dark and after the enemy had wholly left I am most credibly informed that Colonel Minty received his order to re-enforce me at about 1 p m, and I submit to the inquiry of my superior officers why it should take Colonel Minty six hours to make the distance of thirteen miles over one of the best roads of Tennessee The gallant Colonel Hambright, with his brigade of infantry reached me within thirty minutes after the cavalry had reported

I have brought into camp fifty-three stand of arms, taken from the enemy, ten prisoners and eight horses The wounded and prisoners who fell into our hands represent nine regiments including three of mounted infantry, and there were at least three regiments of the enemy held in reserve during the entire engagement, one mile in front The total force of the enemy could not have been less than 3 500 The surgeons declined to disclose the force and one wounded officer placed it at 4 000 Among the enemy's dead was a mulatto killed on the advance line fully uniformed and equipped My loss is as follows Killed one captain and five enlisted men wounded one lieutenant and forty-one enlisted men prisoner one enlisted man missing, seven enlisted men

Of the number wounded but few are serious, and many will not need hospital treatment The missing were all inside the lines when the engagement began They undoubtedly ran away to the rear, and are either captured or are in the woods on the way to this camp

The detailed reports of regimental commanders are forwarded herewith, together with a plan of the route passed over and of the field of battle

I directed the citizens to bury the rebel dead and brought my own into camp

The hard fighting of the day was done by the One hundred and first Indiana and the One hundred and twenty-third Illinois but I feel profoundly thankful for the prompt and gallant co operation which every officer of the command gave me, and too much praise cannot be given to the men of the entire command for their soldierly conduct Captain W R Tuttle of the One hundred and fifth Ohio, my acting assistant adjutant-general, and Lieutenant Sandford Fortner, of the One hundred and first Indiana my aide-de-camp, rendered me the most valuable assistance on every part of the field Captain Blackburn, of the First Middle Tennessee Cavalry, deserves special praise for his daring and efficient conduct during the scout and engagement I desire also to make special mention of Private J H Blackburn, Company A, First Middle Tennessee Cavalry, for the prompt and intelligent execution of my orders in bearing my dispatch from the point of attack to division headquarters, at Murfreesborough, and also of Private Edward Potter, Company E, One hundred and fifth Ohio for the faithful and prompt management of my train of pack-mules, so placing them that not an animal was lost, and for his valuable assistance as an orderly on the field

I have the honor to be, very truly, your obedient servant

A S HALL
Colonel, Commanding Second Brigade

XVI.

A MIDSUMMER JAUNT.

T was the 24th of June when the campaign against the Confederate position at Tullahoma opened. Grant had Pemberton by the throat in Vicksburg, having intervened between him and Johnston with whom lay the only hope of relief of the beleaguered city. Lee had just entered Maryland for a second trial of his curious strategic hobby, an advance upon the rear of Washington, Baltimore, and Philadelphia, by the upper fords of the Potomac, with no other possible means of egress from the enemy's territory.

Two of the chief armies of the Confederacy were thus in mortal peril. It was essential that the third, which was under Bragg, at Tullahoma, should not be allowed to detach any considerable force to the assistance of either. Under these circumstances, General Rosecrans was peremptorily ordered to advance.

The enemy held what has been called "the line of Duck river." Properly, it was no line at all, merely a position with two exposed flanks and a range of hills with somewhat difficult passes in front. These passes were too far apart to admit of mutual support by the forces holding them, in case of attack on either, and did not converge upon a common center within supporting distance, so as to constitute an effective line of defense. The position was essentially weak, also, in the fact that the enemy might turn either flank without uncovering his own, while at the same time steadily approaching his objective. Indeed, this had already been done by General Reynolds, two months

SURGEON JOHN TURNBULL.

JOHN TURNBULL was born in Cedarville, Greene County, Ohio, March 10, 1840. His grandfather was an officer in the British Navy. He attended the public schools and Jefferson Medical College of Philadelphia, Pa., from which he graduated in the spring of 1861. He immediately enlisted as a private in Company A, 17th O. V. I., for three months; was promoted to hospital steward and mustered out after four month's service in West Virginia; served gratuitously for nearly a year as volunteer assistant surgeon with 65th O. V. I., and the "Minute Men" of 1862. He was appointed assistant surgeon of the 105th, and joined at Tullahoma, Tenn., July 4, 1863. He had charge of the health of the regiment from that time until the close of the war, the surgeon, Dr. Charles N. Fowler, being constantly on detached service as medical director. At the battle of Chickamauga, Surgeon Turnbull was on duty with the regiment during its furious charge. Two men were

before, when he seized McMinnville and should have been supported by the whole army in holding possession of it

When, on the 23d of June, McCook advanced toward Shelbyville on the right, and Crittenden toward McMinnville on the left, both threatened the spinal cord of Bragg's position—the Memphis and Charleston railroad which ran in his rear It was then that the chain of hills behind which Bragg had sought refuge after the fight at Stone river, became a fatal hindrance to the operation of his army. If he threw his force on Crittenden, McCook would advance to Huntsville and Thomas would crush his center, if he attacked McCook, Crittenden would seize Decherd, destroy the bridges, and prevent the use of the Nashville and Chattanooga railroad in his retreat It is little wonder that Bragg hesitated. Liberty Gap, in front of McCook, and Hooker's Gap in front of Thomas, were the salient points in the ridge of hills in front of Tullahoma They were only six miles apart, but each was twenty miles from Tullahoma, the center of the Confederate line Both were strongly fortified, but either might be turned by infantry.

When McCook began his demonstration against the former, on the 23d of June, a great part of the force holding the latter was withdrawn so as to be within supporting distance of the threatened point Thomas, moving at daylight on the twenty-fourth, with Reynold's division in front, Wilder's mounted infantry brigade being in the lead, found Hoover's Gap practically undefended When Wilder's skirmishers drove in the pickets, there was a scattering fire, then a wild clangor of great guns, seemingly fired at

---

shot while he was dressing their wounds After the battle was over, he was left to look after the wounded, was captured and after two weeks released and sent through to our lines at Chattanooga While thus a prisoner, and serving friend and foe alike, a squad of Confederate cavalry robbed him of coat, hat, boots, money, case of instruments all he had, except shirt and trousers, giving him an old pair of shoes Because of the resulting exposure, he was for several weeks in hospital at Chattanooga in a very critical condition Since the close of the war, Dr Turnbull has pursued the practice of his profession at Bell Brook, Ohio He has been a member of the town council, president of the Board of Education, and has served the Democratic party as a legislative candidate

random, then a strange silence. What did it mean? Wilder did not hesitate. Pushing forward his line, he was soon in possession of the Gap. Rushing on to where a sharp crest gave a favorable position in rear of the enemy's works, he posted his brigade on each side of the road, his battery of

CAPT. ANDREW D. BRADEN.

ANDREW D. BRADEN, who succeeded Captain Ephraim Kee in command of Company B, was one of the most justly esteemed officers of the regiment. Of a rare modesty, he needed to be sought out to be known. He served in Company C, of the 9th O. V. I., in the three months' service in West Virginia, and was mustered as First lieutenant of Company B, 105th, with which he remained until the regiment was mustered out. From September, 1864 until February, 1865, he was Acting Judge Advocate of Baird's Division, 14th Army Corps, but remained in command of his company and marched with it. After the close of the war, he engaged in the practice of his profession, at Canton, Ohio, where he still resides. He was appointed postmaster by President Harrison and served one term.

howitzers upon it, and sent back for reinforcements, while Harris, with unerring instinct, threw his guns upon two commanding eminences a little in their rear. Hardly were these dispositions made when Hardee's columns were upon them.

The Second brigade was the next in rear of Wilder. We had been halted where the country road forks toward Liberty Gap, a mile or more in the rear. The sounds in our front seemed to have puzzled every one. Off at the right we heard the echo of McCook's guns. It had rained steadily for hours: everything was dripping wet; the men held their guns beneath their arms under their shining ponchos. The water ran off the muzzles. Hat brims were turned down; the cloaks of the horsemen dripped as they splashed back and forth in the muddy road which lay between two yellow torrents. General Reynolds threw his two remaining brigades into half-distance columns on the left of the road, evidently to make way for those

M. L. MAYNARD, MUS.

MILTON LEWIS MAYNARD was born in Hambden, Geauga County, Ohio, September 22, 1834. Previous to enlistment, he worked as carpenter, summers, and taught district schools winters. Having a fondness for mathematics he devoted much of his attention especially to its higher branches. He enlisted in Company E, 105th, August 11, 1862, with which he served as chief musician of the regiment until the close of the war.

There was a firmness and gravity about the man, which commanded the respect of all, and as his duties brought him into personal relation with

in the rear. A big oak-tree, low branching and dense, grew just at the fork. General Reynolds took position under it. Staff officers were dashing back and forth. General Thomas, with his staff and body-guard, came forward at a sharp trot and joined him. The two talked earnestly together for a while, then Thomas dismounted, sat down upon a stone at the foot of the oak, took out his knife, cut a shoot that grew near, and began to whittle it. Presently there came a roar of artillery from the front. Soon the distant rattle of musketry mingled with it. An aide dashed up, splashed with mud from head to foot. He reported eagerly to General Thomas. That officer heard him, still whittling. Then he rose, threw the stick away, put his knife in his pocket, and turned toward Reynolds. We were too far away to hear his words, but it needed not much acumen to guess them.

He swung himself into the saddle, the two officers saluted, then bugles sounded and orders echoed along the massed columns of Reynolds. In an instant we were on the march, with Reynolds and his staff splashing along the muddy road in our front. Back in the hospital the colonel of the Thousand, tossing on a bed of pain, was bewailing the fate which kept him from the field of conflict. He had gathered his last laurels. Colonel Robinson, of the Seventy-fifth Indiana, was in command of the Second brigade. There had been a change in the brigade too. The Seventy-fifth and Sixty-eighth Indiana had taken the places of our old brigade companions, the Eightieth and One Hundred and Twenty-third Illinois. We could hear the steady roar of the Spencer rifles that had been given to Wilder's

every man in the regiment, he was one of the best known and most highly esteemed men in the command. It was proper, therefore, that when the Survivors' Association came to be formed he should be chosen as its secretary, which place he has held ever since. Not only has he the confidence of his comrades, but his fellow citizens of Geauga County have also manifested their esteem for him in electing him County Surveyor for six consecutive years, and County Assessor for two consecutive terms. He resides at Chardon, O., blessed with an interesting family, one of whom is a veritable "Daughter of the Regiment," having been the honorary secretary of the Survivors' Association for many years.

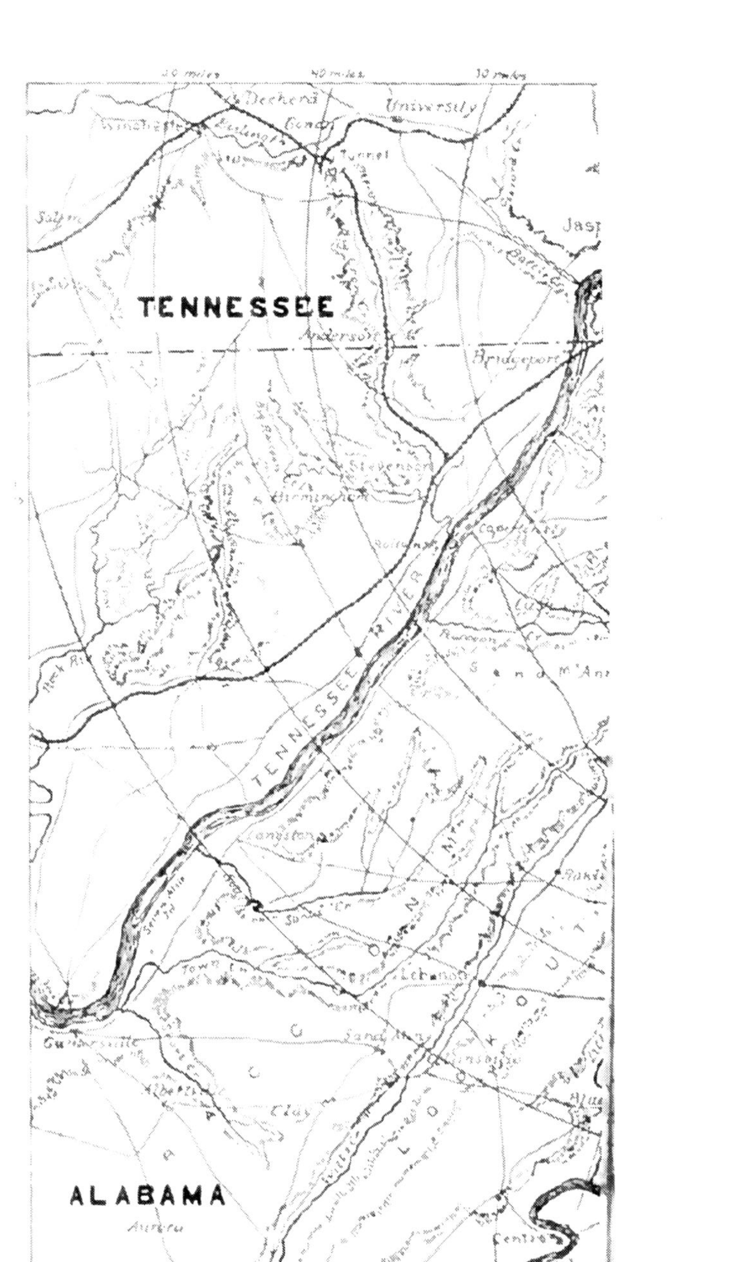

Drawn from the official map by Leon J. Robbins

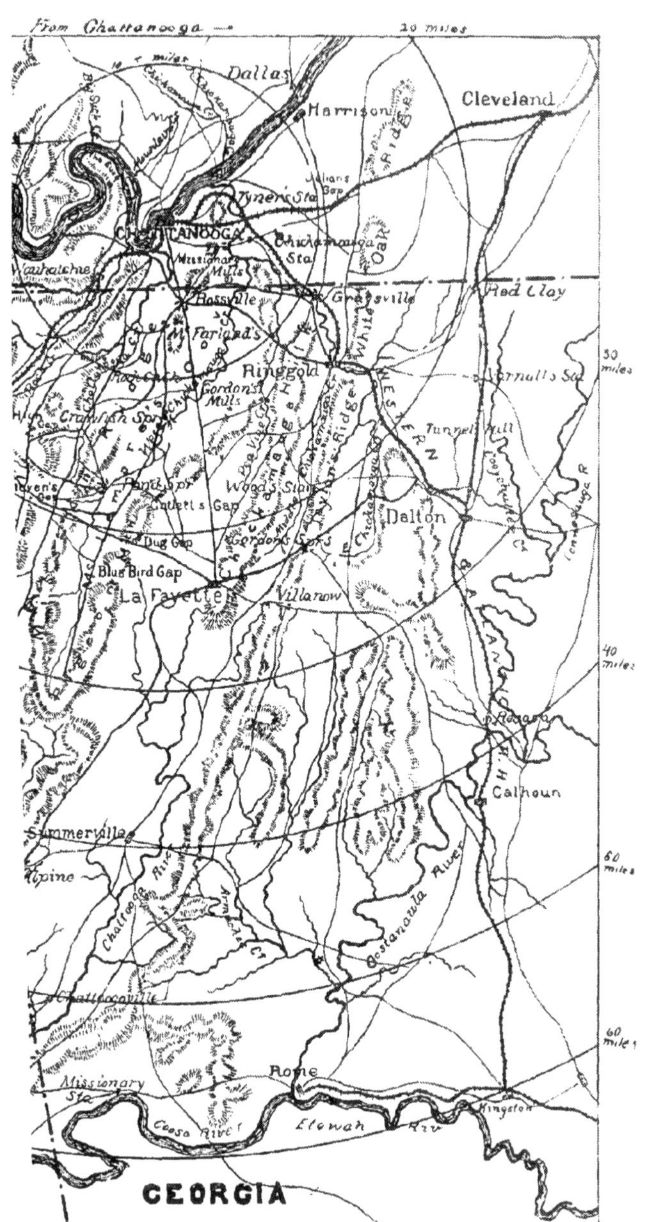

From Chattanooga
20 miles
Dallas
Harrison
Cleveland
Tyner's Sta
CHATTANOOGA
Chickamauga Sta
Missionary Mills
Rossville
Graysville
Red Clay
Ringgold
Gordon's Mills
Crawfish Sps
Tunnel Hill
Woods Sta
Dalton
Dug Gap
Blue Bird Gap
La Fayette
Villanow
30 miles
40 miles
50 miles
60 miles
Resaca
Calhoun
Summerville
Oostanaula River
Chattoogaville
Missionary Sta
Rome
Kingston
Coosa River
Etowah Riv
GEORGIA

men and were first used in action that day, as we double-quicked along the slippery road to their support. Soon, we deployed to the right, advancing up a sharp, green slope, while Lilly's battery, the Eighteenth Indiana, dashed by us to the front. Regiment after regiment followed on our left. We reached the top of the slope, reformed our lines, and moved forward. The lieutenant-colonel was on leave, and our major in command. We entered the wood and found ourselves in rear of one of Wilder's regiments, which had been sharply engaged with a force they had already driven back. We passed through their lines and took position in their front. They had lost heavily and had exhausted their ammunition. We opened fire on the enemy, who retired into a wood that lay beyond a ravine in our front.

There was a splendid battle scene a little to our left, where Hardee's columns charged again and again the line which Wilder's repeating rifles held, while battery after battery, and regiment after regiment, hurried up from the rear to their support. It was in vain; no force which could have been hurled against them was sufficient to regain the pass, which had been lost by the temporary withdrawal of Hardee to meet the attack upon their left. The darkness fell suddenly, and we lay upon our arms in the dripping wood, with the dead and wounded friends and foes about us. The adjutant had much trouble with his horse, which, in the darkness, he had unwittingly hitched to a tree against which a wounded enemy had leaned and died. All night the stout bay snorted his discomfiture.

In the morning we advanced our skirmishers; the enemy retired. We had taken a splendidly fortified position, with the loss of less than a hundred men, and the campaign against Tullahoma was virtually at an end. Thereafter, it was a mere foot-race. The elements favored the enemy. For nine days it rained continuously. Swollen streams and bottomless roads delayed our advance across "the Barrens" in our front, whose soil is a mixture of quicksand and glue when wet. With the aid of the railroad. Bragg managed to transfer his army safely across the Tennessee. It was a flight rather than a retreat; guns, tents, and supplies were abandoned or destroyed. We entered Tullahoma on the first day of July, without firing a shot.

We tramped on after the fleeing enemy, through the mud and rain, with the echo of glad tidings in the summer air, for Grant had taken Vicksburg with the army that held it, and Lee, shattered and broken at Gettysburg, had with difficulty won the prize for which he fought — the privilege of retreating with heaviness the way he had come hoping for triumph.

XVII.

A WASTED OPPORTUNITY.

HE campaign against Chattanooga began on the 16th of August. The army of Rosecrans was the same which a month before had driven Bragg out of Middle Tennessee. The army opposed to it was the one it had dislodged, plus such reinforcements as it had received or might receive from the Confederate armies of the east and the west. Lee could spare a corps or more. Johnstone, in Mississippi, had an army practically out of business, now that Grant had taken Vicksburg, and the Mississippi river was in the hands of the Federals from its source to its mouth. All he could do was to prevent mere aimless raids into the interior, or guard against an advance on Mobile, which Grant was eager to undertake, but was not permitted by the myopic Halleck, who was anxious now, as he had been ever since the fall of Donelson, to keep this young giant of the west from climbing over his shoulders into supreme command.

Chattanooga, as a defensive position against an enemy occupying the right bank of the Tennessee, is essentially weak. An enemy might cross above or below the city, and might mass his forces to cross at either point without discovery. Bragg naturally supposed that Burnside, who was coming through Cumberland Gap, would co-operate with Rosecrans, and that Gordon Granger, who was concentrating toward Liberty gap, intended to unite with him and Crittenden in forcing a passage of the river north of the city.

This theory was confirmed by the activity of Hazen who with Wagner's brigade and his own, Minty's cavalry and Wilder's mounted infantry kept such a scurrying to and fro along the west bank of the Tennessee, as might well induce the belief that half the Federal army was hid behind Walden's ridge. Wagner tossed shells into the city from Moccasin Point, Hazen's men built pontoons at the mouth of North Chattanooga creek, while the cavalry scouted up the river as far as *London*, hunting for Burnside's left. Bragg mistook this feint for the serious attack.

It was the 29th of August before everything was in readiness for the crossing. Crittenden, with his corps was in Bragg's old hiding-place, the Sequatchie valley. Thomas stretched from Battle creek to Bridgeport, and McCook lay about Stevenson. The crossing was ordered to be made at these places simultaneously: Reynolds at Shell Mound, Sheridan at Bridgeport, and McCook at Caperton's, Brennan and Crittenden at the ferries above Shell Mound. For a week our division, which had become the Fourth Division of the Army of the Cumberland, instead of the Fifth, through one of those changes which seemed intended to prevent all *esprit de corps* in our army, except Wilder's brigade, had been lying in the Shelter of Battle Creek valley, only a small force with Harris' battery showing on the bank of the river opposite Shell Mound. Several reconnoitering parties had crossed and the railroad bridge just above had been burned. We had captured and built eight flat-bottomed barges in which to make the crossing. It began on the twenty-ninth, Colonel King, with a part of his old regiment, the Sixty-eighth Indiana, in the lead, and continued at the rate of four hundred men an hour until our division and most of Crittenden's corps had been transferred to the left bank of the Tennessee. Crittenden started direct to Chattanooga by the railroad, taking post at Wauhatchie, and feeling the enemy around the nose of Lookout mountain. On the 2d of September Burnside's advance and Hazen's scouts formed a junction at Kingston and Thomas and McCook began the ascent of those mountain ranges lying to the south of Chattanooga These are the Raccoon, or Sand mountains, lying between the Tennessee and the valley of Wauhatchie This range is ten miles wide at Shell Mound, and twenty miles wide at Caperton's. To the east of this, lay the Lookout mountain range, hardly half as wide, but much more rugged and precipitous, separating the valley of Wauhatchie from that of Chattanooga creek Beyond this latter was Missionary Ridge, a range of sloping hills lying between Chattanooga creek and West Chickamauga creek

Between this and that valley of Pea Vine creek are the Pigeon mountains, at the southern extremity of which is the town of Lafayette, Georgia, east of these is Middle Chickamauga creek, beyond which is Taylor's ridge, whose eastern slope is washed by the main fork of Chickamauga creek.

The Lookout mountain range and Missionary ridge had fair roads leading along their sandy crests to Chattanooga The valleys of the Wauhatchie, Chattanooga creek, and West Chickamauga had good roads leading in the same direction Thomas' corps was in front of Dug Gap, twenty miles from Chattanooga McCook, at Valley Head, was forty, and at Alpine forty-three miles from the same point

On the 4th of September the Thousand began its march from Shell Mound over the Sand mountains The weather was delightful, the autumnal brown of the oaks being relieved by the gold of the hickories that grew upon the slopes and the softer tints of the chestnuts upon the level plateaus which constituted the summit. The roads leading eastward were little used—hardly more than cross-country trails. There were heavy details for pioneer work, but even the artillery and wagons had to be held by ropes to prevent them from falling off the steep roadways, while the teams were doubled at the worst points, making slow work The night fell long before we reached the summit, and all night long, with torches and ropes, and shouts and jests, we dragged the lumbering wagons up the sharp incline

Cooper's Gap, the former leading to Dug Gap and the latter to Catlett's Gap in the Pigeon mountains on the road to Lafayette.

In the meantime, McCook with the right, had moved by a longer route, but somewhat easier roads leading from Caperton's bridge by Coshtown toward Valley Head, Alpine and Summerville which latter is only twenty miles from Rome, Georgia which itself is but twenty miles from Kingston on the Chattanooga railroad, the artery on which Confederate occupancy of Chattanooga depended.

"As soon as we hold that ridge" said General Thomas, pointing to the rugged side of the Lookout, "Chattanooga is ours!"

"And then?"

"Then we will fall back to the river, fortify Chattanooga, Bridgeport, Stevenson, put a brigade on the nose of Lookout, fill these places with supplies and in the spring swing by the right from Guntersville and Caperton's into the valley of the Coosa a force big enough to handle Bragg, leaving Burnside and another corps to hold the line of the Tennessee."

"And then?"

"Then Bragg will fall back to Kingston or Atlanta, but it will be too late. We shall cut the Confederacy in two again, taking Montgomery and Mobile,—and end the war! It is folly to act on the offensive in Virginia with such an opportunity here to pierce the heart of the Confederacy."

He spoke to one of his division commanders. A lieutenant of the Thousand, who had a request to prefer which the latter was kind enough to approve, and had been invited to accompany him to headquarters, listened wonderingly. They found the corps commander ready to take horse for a personal inspection of his advance. The time was inopportune for the request, which was never preferred. It was of little consequence then, of none at all now.

Years afterward this chance conversation served as a key to unlock the lips of the great soldier who should have been at the President's right hand—the Von Moltke of the War of the Rebellion. But the Bayard of the Cumberland had few friends at court. He thought himself distrusted because of his southern birth and scorned to organize a movement on Washington in his own behalf.

His prediction had not long to wait for fulfillment. On the eighth, we took possession of Lookout mountain and the road which ran along its level summit until twelve miles away it overlooked the Confederate citadel. Before even a soldier had time to ride down this mountain highway and question what his purpose might be, Bragg, sensible of the folly of trying to hold Chattanooga longer abandoned the "Gibraltar of the Confederacy" without striking a blow in its defense, and marched his army toward Lafayette, twenty-four miles distant.

On the ninth, the news of the evacuation of the Confederate stronghold swept along the valley of Wauhatchie, crept up the sides of Lookout, greeted everywhere with the cheers of an exultant army. Before the sun went down, McCook's men at Valley Head had heard it, and joined their shouts with our exultation. How the bands played up and down the valley that night! Why should they not? We had won a great victory, and driven the enemy from one of the most important strategic positions he had held, without firing a gun. We had only to march into Chattanooga, take position along the Tennessee river, connecting with Burnside on the left, and retiring McCook either to Caperton's or by Lookout valley, to compel the enemy to abandon Tennessee or give battle upon some part of an easily defended line.

On the 9th of September, the Army of the Cumberland had accomplished all it had set out to do—all it was prepared to attempt. It had only to turn the heads of Thomas' columns toward Chattanooga and withdraw McCook the way he had come, to complete one of the most remarkable campaigns ever planned. By the fifteenth, all the trains of the army might have been safely parked in the valley between Chattanooga and Missionary ridge. Instead of this, the order was given to push on and "attack the enemy in flank."

Thomas hurried to protest. He pointed out what had been won, showed what might be risked, what might be lost. Here were five fair roads leading to Chattanooga, less than twenty miles away. In forty-eight hours the objective of the campaign could be made secure beyond a peradventure. The army was not prepared for a farther advance. It was needful to secure its base, its material, its communications. He pointed out the unfitness of the terraine for an offensive movement toward Lafayette or Rome, the whole country being rough and broken, cut by transverse mountain ranges with few gaps, and those easily defensible, the whole region covered with dense forest or blinding chaparral, without available roads except the few that lead north and south in the valleys and on the crests, that mutual support of the flanks of the army would be almost impossible, that the army could only be supplied through Chattanooga and must at all events fall back there within a short time for mere want of subsistence, and especially that the enemy had the advantage of a railroad in his rear and could concentrate on either flank in half the time that would be required to collect a force to meet him.

It was in vain: the triumphant general was drunk with over-confidence. A good fortune so great as to be almost incomprehensible made him believe his luck invincible. His fancy pictured his enemy fleeing in confusion and disorder along the roads that crossed his front, the remnant rushing pell-mell to seek safety in Rome. This straggling crowd of fugitives he fancied he could annihilate by striking them in the flank with Thomas' and McCook's corps, while Crittenden fell upon their rear. Such fatuity was unaccountable until months afterward, the Confederate commander

"flanked him out of Tullahoma and Chattanooga" as easily as the hunter flushes a covey he has marked down.

The Confederate deserter was an institution which has received too little consideration. Taken altogether he was of far greater service to the southern cause than the best corps in the Confederate army. He was ubiquitous, willing and altogether inscrutable. Whether he told the truth or a lie, he was almost equally sure to deceive. He was sometimes a real deserter and sometimes a mock deserter. In either case he was sure to be loaded.

The northern officer was wholly unacquainted with the character of the southern "poor-white." With the usual arrogance of the well-informed, he looked with contempt on the man who could not read and write, who made small pretense of tidiness, who spoke the vernacular of the South with a drawl, and seemed more concerned about his supply of "terbacker" than the outcome of the war. These men, simple-minded, but true as steel and cunning as foxes, needed no padding of pretense to make themselves believed. They were not thought capable of deception. They came into our lines, told the stories they were instructed to tell, hung about for a while, were sent to the rear or slipped away, stayed at home a month or two, and then found their way back to their regiments.

Bragg's deserters did their work well. On the eleventh of September the Army of the Cumberland was hopelessly scattered. Crittenden was at and near Ringgold, twenty miles from Pond Spring, in front of which lay two divisions of Thomas' corps. McCook was twenty-five miles to the south of Thomas. Only the merest accident saved the army of Rosecrans from being destroyed in detail that day and the next. Negley and Baird were pushed across MacLemore's cove on the road to Lafayette. Bragg had laid a pretty trap for them, but Cleburne was sick, Hindman was slow, so the attack was not made in time. When it was made Negley, who did not believe in the demoralized condition of Bragg's army, seeing himself outnumbered, withdrew from

lap. The next day, September 12th, Cri
side of West Chickamauga creek and he
distance from Thomas, was only saved
by the fact that Polk did not believe any

man would so scatter an army in the presence of an enemy He feared a trap and refused to attack, though expressly ordered to do so and heavily supported

---

Morgan commanded the regiment, and General Franklin Pierce the brigade to which he belonged After the treaty of peace with Mexico Colonel King returned to Ohio and in the spring of 1849 crossed the plains to California Returning again, he was appointed postmaster at Dayton by President Pierce and after the election of President Buchanan the position was again conferred upon him. So general was the satisfaction given in the discharge of his official duties there was no competing applicant for the place

For many years, both before and after the Mexican war, Colonel King took an active part in all important matters connected with the militia of Ohio, and at the outbreak of the War of Rebellion, was colonel of the 1st Regiment Ohio Volunteer Militia, at Dayton, which city sent several organized and equipped companies into the field. On the 17th April, 1861, the day of the proclamation of the governor of Ohio calling loyal men to the defence of their country, Colonel King reported to Governor Dennison, and was immediately placed in command of Camp Jackson (near Columbus) then in a chaotic state, but which he soon reduced to form and discipline He was subsequently transferred to Camp Chase, where he remained in command until, without solicitation on his part, he was appointed by President Lincoln lieutenant colonel of the 19th regiment United States Infantry, with headquarters established at Indianapolis In the summer of 1862, when Kirby Smith invaded Kentucky, he took at the request of Governor Morton the temporary command of the 68th Regiment Indiana Volunteers and was sent to the assistance of Colonel Wilder, at Munfordville, Kentucky and participated in that engagement He was surrendered with his regiment and other bodies of Federal troops, to an overwhelming force It fell to his lot to deliver the post to the enemy, and the rebel general Bucker, who while a prisoner of war had been in his charge at Indianapolis, treated him with marked consideration

A beautiful incident connected with this capitulation was afterward disclosed The ladies of Greenburg, Indiana, presented the 68th regiment with a silken flag It was highly prized, and the regiment was loath to part with it When it was determined to surrender, Colonel King wrapped the colors around his body, under his clothing He wore them thus for thirteen days, saved them and the regiment bore them into the bloody fight at Chickamauga

After the 68th Indiana regiment was exchanged, the command was again pressed on Colonel King who (obtaining leave from the War Department for that purpose), accepted it In the summer of 1863 his health, which had been seriously impaired becoming somewhat re-established he again took the field, and was placed in command of the 1st brigade, General Reynolds Division, 14th Army Corps, commanded by General Thomas, at the head of which he distinguished himself during the advance from Tullahoma to northwestern Georgia, and in the effective crossing of the Tennessee River, his brigade being the first troops to cross, and capture Shell Mound, in the face of the enemy Just before his death he had been promoted colonel of the 6th Infantry United States Army He fell during the second day's fight

Few men more thoroughly commanded the confidence and respect of all who knew him than Colonel King He was a gallant soldier, a ripe scholar a good citizen a man of noble character and high sense of honor, and whose love of country was so true that he laid down his life at her call

The retreat of Negley with two divisions, served to half awaken Rosecrans from his delusive dream. McCook was called up; but instead of being sent straight through to Chattanooga by the Lookout valley road he was ordered to climb that range and join Thomas in MacLemore's cove. He arrived on the seventeenth. On the eighteenth the blow fell. On that day, the Confederate army having concentrated on its right, crossed West Chickamauga creek below the left wing of the Federal army and took position facing westward east of the road leading from Chattanooga to Lafayette. Crittenden was posted on this road at its crossing of West Chickamauga creek. Thomas and McCook were in the upper part of MacLemore's cove. Granger was at Rossville. The Confederate general's plan of attack was to wheel his right so as to intervene between Granger and Crittenden, overwhelm Crittenden and advance on Thomas and McCook shut up in the narrow confines of MacLemore's cove and either compel them to surrender or drive them back the way they had come. It was a splendid scheme, but miscarried, as Bragg's plans were apt to do, from too great minuteness of direction. At four o'clock of the eighteenth there did not seem to be a possibility that the Federal army could escape from the coil the enemy had cast about it.

Rosecrans' infatuation had well-nigh proved fatal to his army. Even then, had he known the true condition of affairs, he would probably have fixed his line of battle at Rossville where Thomas should have been four days before. The movement he decided upon in response to his opponent's initiative was simply to pass the center corps of his army in rear of his left by a night march, the right closing sharply upon it to be used as a reserve. Crittenden lay along the Lafayette road from its crossing of West Chickamauga creek, toward Chattanooga something like two miles including the front of Wilder's brigade on his left. Thomas was ordered two miles to the left of this, to form a line connecting with it east of this road. When in position, this made a line of battle four miles long and necessarily weak in many places Rosecrans still despised his enemy or he would not have risked the single-line formation which had cost him so dear at Stone's river The tales of the deserters were still echoing in his ears, and he thought Bragg's advance simply the desperate device of a defeated foe to slip in his rear and cut his communications

At four o'clock on the afternoon of the eighteenth, the Thousand lying at Pond Spring, eighteen miles from Chattanooga, received orders to be ready to march with three days' rations Already the movement had begun Baird's and Brannan's divisions were marching northward Just at sundown, two brigades of Reynolds' fell in behind them. Palmer followed us, in the rear of whom was Negley, while McCook closed up on the rear of Thomas It was a weird march over rough woods roads A cold wind blew from the north Where there were fields along the roadside the fences were fired and the column marched between lines of flame There were frequent halts The firelight shone on the rubber ponchos the men wore to shield them from the chill night wind Aides and couriers dashed back and forth A regiment somewhere in front struck up a song, and for hours the wooded cove echoed with the battle hymns of thousands who would never sing again At daylight we were at Crawfish Springs An hour after we halted for rest and breakfast at Osburn's Cross-roads Baird and Brannan were four miles ahead While we rested, Palmer filed past us Resuming our march, we halted about nine o'clock near a tan-yard The distance we had come was not more than ten or eleven miles, but a night march is always fatiguing The men stretched themselves by the roadside, for the morning sun was hot, and were soon asleep.

No one seemed to know where our position was All was doubt and uncertainty The ground was wooded, broken with low, transverse hills and irregular knolls The woods were open, but grown here and there with baffling stretches of dense underbrush. There were a very few small fields and indistinct roads. The ground in our rear was elevated, in our front slightly depressed. Palmer had taken position to the eastward of a road running north and south. He guessed it to be the Chattanooga road, but did not know. Suddenly firing began away to our left. The men awoke and listened, comparing views in regard to it. It grew louder and came nearer. Turchin was hurried to the left of Palmer. Presently our brigade commander, Colonel King, rode up and in slow, deliberate tones put the brigade in motion. We moved by the double-quick around a low wooded knoll, across an open field, faced to the right and advanced in line of battle. The One Hundred and First Indiana were on our right in the front line. The wave of battle rolled down the line toward us. There seemed to be an interval at our right; we were moved by the flank to fill it. It was the worst possible region in which to maneuver an army, being without landmarks or regular slopes, and so thickly wooded that it was impossible to preserve any alignment. Besides, there seemed to be, as we know now there was, an utter lack of fixed and definite plan, and a woeful ignorance of the field. Soldiers are quick to note such things, and one of the Thousand, seeing a group of officers in consultation, said he guessed they were "pitching pennies to decide which way the brigade should front."

There was a lull in the action. We lay in the edge of the wood. From a thicket a hundred yards away came a dropping but deadly fire. By and by, the turmoil deepened about us. There was no chance to use artillery save at close range. On our whole front there was hardly a place where a range of three hundred yards could be secured. Communication between the flanks was almost impossible. The winding roads were full of lost staff-officers. The commander of a regiment rarely saw both flanks of his command at once. Even companies became broken in the thickets, and taking different directions were lost to each other. Confusion reigned even before the battle began. It is folly to attempt to unravel the tangled web of that two days' fight. Even the part a single regiment took is almost untraceable. More than a hundred accounts of it have been prepared; hardly two of them are alike in essentials; very few of them reconcilable in details.

The enemy determined our movements for us. The line at the right of our brigade was either broken or there was an interval between us and the next division; it is impossible to determine which. There has been a thirty years' war of words upon the subject. Two generals have claimed credit for remedying the defect, and a third has written a volume to discredit both. The Thousand lay in position and saw the enemy's columns pass the right flank of our brigade. The One Hundred and First Indiana began to bend backward from the right like a willow wand; presently it broke. Then the line of the Thousand began to bend, in like manner refusing the right flank to the wedge-shaped tide whose fiery impulse was irresistible. The order to fall back was given by the brigade commander, who sat on his horse, immediately in our rear.

CAPT. E. ABBOTT SPAULDING.

E. ABBOTT SPAULDING was born in Monroe, Ashtabula County, Ohio, in 1837. He had just graduated at Western Reserve College, and begun the study of medicine when the war broke out. In 1862 he was commissioned a lieutenant of the 105th O. V. I., and assisted in raising Company G, of which he became second lieutenant. He was promoted to first lieutenant to date from the battle of Perryville and transferred to Company E, of which he became captain, on the resignation of Captain Canfield. He continued in command until wounded at the battle of Chickamauga, of which wound he died a few days afterwards. He is buried in the Federal Cemetery, at Chattanooga, Tenn. He was greatly loved and esteemed by the whole regiment.

"About face! Forward, guide center!" commanded the major. The center was at the apex formed by the doubled back right wing. The movement was sure to result in confusion. The enemy's fire was hot as the breath of a typhoon.

"Double quick!" shouted the brigade commander, and leaning his head upon the horse's neck, he spurred hardly faster than the blue-clad mass he led to the rear. Into an old field, across a road, through a thicket of pines, over a low ridge we ran and halted, whether by order or because every one was blown it matters little now. The ranks were quickly reformed. Some of the One Hundred and First Indiana were with us. Colonel King, with the light of battle on his face, looked younger than we had ever seen him before. The bullets still flew over us, and the clamor at our right front had grown fiercer. The roar of artillery mingled with the musketry. A staff-officer rode up and spoke to Colonel King. He pointed to the right and shouted: "The Sixty-eighth are over there!" It was his own regiment and he was deservedly proud of it. The roar of artillery deepened. We did not know where "over there" might be, neither did our commander, but as we changed direction and advanced to the right, we saw upon the side of a hill before us, in front of which stretched almost the only open space in that part of the field, a sight never to be forgotten. Two, three, four batteries (some say more, and some say less—probably twenty guns) were being fired with the utmost rapidity almost in the faces of the enemy, who charged, fell back, rallied and charged again in the teeth of the terrible storm. In a moment we were in line at the left, and just in the rear of the spouting guns. As the enemy retired we advanced. Until the sun went down we lay in line, firing now and then in answer to the scattering shots from the thick woods in our front. It seemed we were not far from our former position, but the dead and wounded that lay about us were not ours. From the former we took the canteens to assuage the thirst of the latter, and then cartridges to replenish our own boxes.

After dark there came from away upon the left the most terrible outburst of musketry, cut now and then with the roar of cannon, we had ever heard. We could only see the flashes as they lighted up the clouds above, but it seemed a thousand times worse than a fight by day as we sat in the murky darkness and wondered how it fared with friend and foe. It was Johnson's division repelling the night attack upon the refused angle of our left. This night battle raged for more than an hour, and then ceased as suddenly as it began. We put forward our pickets a little way to guard against surprise. We would have built breastworks if we had had axes and spades. A thousand axes that night would have made our line from end to end almost impregnable. But the few we had were five miles away on the Dry Valley road, on the way to Chattanooga. Soon after the fight upon the left was over, it being then past nine o'clock, we were marched, stumbling in the darkness, through the woods to a new position. Where it was we had no idea, save that it was on the slope of a hill, in the edge of a thicket, with a half-upgrown old field in our front. Some began at once to roll stones and logs into position to form a barricade, but most of the men sank down and were asleep as soon as the line was formed. Marching all night and fighting all day, left every muscle as sore as if it had felt the bastinado. There were rumbling sounds of artillery and ammunition wagons moving in our rear. From the front there was a frequent sound of chopping. How we envied the "Johnnies" their axes. Aside from these sounds, no one would have dreamed that a hundred thousand men were waiting to renew the slaughter when the sun should rise!

WITH the first ray of light, we b
gan work in earnest on our barr
cade. A heavy mist hung ov
the field. By eight o'clock w
had a respectable breastwork o
logs, and rails, and stones. The
we were ordered forward an
took position on lower ground
the east of a small field. Th
Thousand was on the right of th
second line; it's right in the wood
its left in the field. The righ
wing of the army had draw
back during the night and we we
at the angle it now made wit
the left. The battle had bee
raging on the left for half a
hour, when at ten o'clock, ad
vancing with a gradually increa
ing roar, it reached our fron

up the battle We could see it was a deadly fire The enemy halted, the men lay down in the shelter of the trees and for a time the fight went on, Indian fashion Gradually, the enemy's fire slackened and we saw that they had drawn back from our front

Soon there came a still fiercer uproar on our right Unknown to us almost the whole right wing had been suddenly ordered to the left The general who a week before had mocked at the need of securing Chattanooga, was now ready to imperil his whole army to hold the road which led to it The enemy's columns on their left where Longstreet commanded, were formed with care and moved to the assault like a tornado The mist had cleared away and through the sunlit intervals of the wood, we saw their flanks sweep by some two hundred yards away Rank after rank, with guns at the right shoulder, waving hats and with that rebel yell which served the Confederates in place of the English cheer, they poured on toward our right rear

Our division commander, Reynolds, rode hastily up and ordered Major Perkins of the Thousand to change front and charge this column in flank It was a desperate thing—three hundred against many thousands But the major did not hesitate or question The general rode forward with him, to the rear of our line, instinctively extending a hand in farewell as he commanded "Attention, battalion! Shoulder arms!"

Every man knew what was coming, but none hesitated Each man sprang to his feet

"Order arms! Fix bayonets! Right shoulder, shift arms!—Right wheel! March!"

The general said something as we marched away which was answered with a cheer. We went on through the dense chaparral until we were close upon the moving column Then came the order

"Charge bayonets! Double-quick!"

Almost with the word we burst on the charging host It must have been near the rear of the column

struck the end of a line which bent back and let us pass Two guns that were firing to the front were hastily turned on us the canister with which they were shotted scattering the leaves in our front like a covey of young partridges flushed by an intruder. We were upon them before they could reload The gunners and the infantry support fled to our left They evidently thought us the advance of a heavy column At length we ran upon a strong line lying in a dense thicket diagonal to our front, being nearest on the left and overlapping our flank

By this time we were much exhausted How far we had come we had no knowledge, certainly half a mile, the general opinion has always been that it was more Here we halted, reformed our line, dressing on the colors, and lying down, sheltered by trees and inequalities of the ground, opened fire on the line in our front When we started, the noonday sun was looking in our faces, when we halted, we still faced the south or nearly so Our loss had been nothing to what we had expected, yet quite a number had been killed, the Major, Captain Spaulding, and many others wounded The Major had returned along the way we had come That was now closed up The fire in our front grew hotter, the enemy seemed closing in on all sides of us except at the right. It was our turn to run, and we ran as fast as the nature of the ground permitted Almost every one has remarked that the distance we covered in returning was much greater than that made in our advance. It is no doubt true. The strange thing about it was that we came out into a part of the field entirely new to us We had crossed two or three roads in our advance The artillery fire which was on our right when we set out was raging still on our right when we returned, though we were facing the other way. Where had we been? Who can trace our path on that bloody field?

The question has never been answered The mere statement of its elements so stamps it with impossibility that the men engaged in it have been chary of alluding to

It was nearly night when a fragment of the Thousand stumbled across their division then marching toward Rossville, not long before that magnificent charge of Turchin's which cleared the enemy from our left rear. The delight of General Reynolds at seeing the men whom he thought he had sent to certain destruction was unbounded. When General Thomas rode along our lines the next day, he drew attention to the regiment and called up Captain Edwards to relate our strange adventure. When he had heard all the captain could tell, General Thomas turned to the regiment, then but a little company, and raising his hat said: "It was gallantly done!"

No wonder the men cheered, and have kept on cheering for thirty years in their hearts. To be praised by George H. Thomas, was reward enough for all they had suffered, both because he was not lavish of praise and this was openly given on the field, where he himself had displayed the highest quality of heroism. Reynolds mentions the the charge in his report, and is known to have been often puzzled over the seemingly unexplainable mystery.*

The writer suggests an hypothesis forced upon him by careful study of the situation. If the student of this most mysterious of modern battles, will place himself a little to the east of Poe's house, he will have our position when we wheeled to the right and started on our charge. The position assigned to King's brigade on the official maps is not the one occupied by it at eleven o'clock on the morning of the twentieth. We were then at the southeast corner of an open field, our right in the woods adjoining and our left in

---

*THE FOLLOWING is an extract from General Reynolds's report alluded to above:

"The 105th Ohio, Colonel Perkins commanding, and until this time lying in reserve, was ordered to face the enemy and go at them with the bayonet. The order was gallantly executed, the enemy was thrown back, and the receding regiments partly rallied; but the enemy returning with increased force and turning their right, these regiments were borne back, the 105th Ohio with them. The latter regiment carried off the wounded rebel General Adams, who had been previously captured by Captain Guthrie's company of the 19th Illinois."

Official Records, vol. XXX, page 441.

the open The front line of the brigade lay along the hedgerow on the east side of the field The right wheel brought us into the woods and we were in the woods continuously, except when crossing some open roadway, until our return Assuming that we started from the southeast corner of Poe's field, which was our probable position, that we advanced southwardly at least half a mile, that we withdrew by the right flank, that the distance we went in withdrawing was greater than that covered by our advance, that we were for some time undisturbed in the position we finally reached, and that Hood's column of attack struck our lines a little to the right of Poe's about the time we started, which attack was repelled by the accidental concentration about Snodgrass hill, resulting from the famous order to Wood, to "close up on Reynolds," it will be evident that we must have passed through some interval in Hood's column, or in its rear, struck some other force, probably Hindman, advancing diagonally across our track, and after engaging them for a time, escaping by the right flank, found our way into the rougher country west of Snodgrass hill, the enemy we had engaged following us until we passed beyond their left flank

It is admitted that this solution is apparently incredible, and would be impossible on any field not of such umbrageous character There seems to be no other hypothesis reconcilable with the known and incontrovertible facts, no other, indeed, that is not much more incredible In fact, we must have passed through and around the Confederate left, or pierced the line of fire with which Hood about that time encircled Snodgrass hill Such an achievement is unprecedented in modern warfare, and the fact that it was not attended with more serious loss does not detract from the merit of a charge which, for sheer desperation, has rarely been equaled, and for marvelousness of escape never exceeded

Reynolds' division was unfortunate in many respects in this battle One of its brigades, Wilder's, was not under his command at all; the other two, Turchin's and King's, were separated all the first day by Palmer's division, while on the second day, King's brigade was posted at the angle formed by the refusal of the right wing. Discussion has centered, especially at this point in both days' battles.

General Turchin, in his anxiety to strike Reynolds, has cast some slurs on King's brigade, apparently forgetful of the fact that this brigade lost more officers and men at Chickamauga than both the other brigades of the division,* and if it had done nothing more than check Hood's advance, as our charge did, until men and guns could be parked on Snodgrass Hill to beat him back, it would have performed a distinguished service. Among its losses were its gallant commander, Col. Edward A. King, who fell a victim to his eagerness to know the actual condition in his front. He sat just in rear of his line scrutinizing the enemy's position through a glass, when he was struck in the head by the bullet of a sharp-shooter.

That night our army was withdrawn to the Gap in Missionary ridge, where it should have been posted at the outset. Upon the second day it withdrew to Chattanooga.

Chickamauga was a battle almost unparalleled in modern times. Volumes have been written to prove how those who fought were marshaled. Such efforts are mostly vain. Those who commanded knew little more about it than those in the ranks. What happened under the shadow of the brown-leaved trees in that rugged amphitheater between Missionary ridge and West Chickamauga Creek, only the recording angel can truly declare. Confusion grows worse confounded with each attempt to reduce order out of im-

*The exact figures are especially pertinent in view of General Turchin's claim of the well-nigh unprecedented character of the services of the Third Brigade of the Fourth Division in this battle. They are:

First Brigade, Colonel Wilder, wounded, killed and missing	125
Third Brigade, General Turchin, killed, wounded and missing	43
Total First and Third Brigades	168

The Second Brigade, Colonel King, lost in killed, wounded and missing, 184. Official Records, vol. XXX, part I, page 173.

penetrable chaos. It was a soldier's fight, not a general's battle The woods in the rear of the line were full of stragglers, yet among them were few malingerers Broken into fragments, not only by the impact of the enemy's columns but by unavoidable loss of direction in advancing and retreating through woods and thickets, over irregular hills and along obscure and unmarked roads these men sought less frequently to avoid conflict than to engage in hopeful fight

On the first day, Reynolds and Hazen rallied in twenty minutes the flying regiments which Stewart's charge had driven back The men were not demoralized, they knew that when the enemy had broken through the line, it was useless to remain in the positions they held, but they rallied behind the guns without regard to whom the leader might be, and advanced to the attack without hesitation When the fire grew hot on the afternoon of the second day, on Snodgrass Hill, the stragglers in the woods beyond turned back and made their way with haste to the fire-wreathed crest. It was as if a magnet drew them to the focus of the fight. Every moment the line grew stronger, not only because troops were ordered to its support, but because men and officers wandering objectless in the woods rallied to the sound of stubborn fighting The woods in the rear of our line were full of moving columns, too, regiments and brigades going they knew not where, by roads it was almost impossible to follow Sheridan and Davis, Johnson and Van Cleve, Negley and Crittenden marched and countermarched through the baffling umbrage, following now a fancied path, now misled by the trend of a hill, going to the left with no knowledge where the left was; rushing to the right with only the roar of battle for a guide

At one time a division commander, Gen J C. Davis, and some of his staff, dashed into the Dry Valley road and endeavored to form the train-guards of other commands to go back into the swirl of battle with them Cumings, of the Thousand, writing in his journal that night, tells an

A brigadier-general, one of the best in our army, rode up to a group of soldiers in which were some members of the Thousand, on the afternoon of the second day, and asked if any one of them knew the location of his brigade, adding humorously, ' Somehow, the d——n thing has got lost!" It was literally true While he had ridden to one flank, a superior officer had moved the one he had left, and while he was seeking this, the other had fallen back Regiments, brigades, and, in one case a whole division, got lost and remained lost for hours

To the enemy, the difficulties resulting from the umbrageous character of the terraine were not so great, though still of serious character. They had some more or less capable guides, they were the attacking party, and all the roads from the fords and bridges of the Chickamauga led in the same direction Besides that, the area covered by their movements was much more restricted than that over which ours extended The distance between the Chattanooga and Lafayette road, along which our line extended, and West Chickamauga creek, was in very few places more than two miles, and was cut by numerous tributaries having a general easterly direction These things served to give some idea of direction, though even then it was almost impossible to preserve their alignment or maintain their relative positions

Chickamauga has been claimed as a Confederate victory because they held the field of battle, and as a Federal victory because the enemy did not recover Chattanooga Both claims are specious rather than veritable The purpose of the Confederate general was not to regain Chattanooga—that was only an incident His purpose was to cripple the Federal army, compel it to retreat the way it came, and incidentally regain Chattanooga In all these he failed He did, indeed, drive the Federal army from the position it hastily took to resist his advance but he did not care to attack it in the position to which it retired. He caused a very heavy loss to the Federals, but his own loss was even greater. In short, he neither destroyed the Federal army nor gained any material advantage over it. Indeed, the Federal army could afford to lose the seventeen thousand who fell at Chickamauga and hold Chattanooga where it was forced to go, rather than advance to Lafayette where its commander was eager to have it go.

On the other hand, those who claim Chickamauga as a Federal victory because Chattanooga was held ignore the fact that this city was no longer the Federal objective. It had been in our possession for ten days, during which time our army might have concentrated there without the loss of a man or the firing of a gun.

Now, that time has cooled the heat of partisanship, we see that the battle of Chickamauga was a useless slaughter, made possible only by Rosecrans' neglect of the urgent remonstrance of his great lieutenant on whom he cast the burthen of what he deemed a lost battle. History was not unkind, therefore, when it named the subordinate, "the rock of Chickamauga," but rather exceedingly charitable when it put its finger on its lips while the chief rode away from the field he thought was irretrievably lost.

PERHAPS nothing could show the character of this remarkable action more clearly than the following extract from the report of Colonel Wilder, commanding the First Brigade of our Division, made not to General Reynolds, who commanded the Division, but to General Rosecrans in command of the army, this Brigade having been detached from the Division since the middle of August preceding:

"I sent messengers," says Colonel Wilder, "to find General McCook. Lieut. Col. Thurston, chief of General McCook's staff, soon appeared and notified me that the line at my left was driven back, and dispersed, and advised that I had better fall back to Lookout Mountain. I determined, however, to cut my way to join General Thomas at Rossville, and was arranging my line for that purpose when General Dana (Charles A.), Assistant Secretary of War, came up and said that our troops had fled in utter panic; that it was a worse rout than Bull Run, that General Rosecrans was probably killed or captured. He strongly advised me to fall back and occupy the passes over Lookout Mountain to prevent the rebel occupancy of it. One of my staff officers came up and reported that he had found General Sheridan a mile and a half to the rear and left, who sent advice to me that he was trying to collect his men and join General Thomas at Rossville, and that I had better fall back to the Chattanooga Valley. I now at 4 p. m. [illegible]"

The significant facts appearing from this extract are that Colonel Wilder, a brigade commander of singular fertility and resource, who had been for a number of days moving back and forth over this ground, was utterly confused by the condition of affairs He was unable to find the corps commander, to whom he had been assigned, whose chief of staff was as much at sea with regard to the whereabouts of his chief as Colonel Wilder himself that an Assistant Secretary of War declared a battle to be ' a worse rout than the first Bull Run ' in which the percentage of loss on both sides was greater than at Waterloo, that everybody spoke of Thomas being at Rossville, while the fight at Snodgrass Hill was still raging at the hot est, and finally that Sheridan, the most impetuous and magnetic of leaders, ' a mile and a half in the rear, was *trying* to collect his troops " All this throws a powerful sidelight upon this phenomenal battle, and confirms the truth of the following extract from a private letter to the writer from General Richard W. Johnson, who commanded the Second Division of the Fourteenth Army Corps in that engagement, under date of April 17, 1895

' It appears to me that the battle was fought without a plan on either side, and whatever success we achieved was due to the persistent courage of our divisions, brigades and regiments, acting independently No man can write a correct *history* of that battle for it was fought in the woods and the heavy foliage and dense undergrowth prevented even colonels seeing the flanks of their regiments "

t on, which it had conquered
near losing through the inexe
ing general, who slipped away
battle, to look after his ponto
treat for the army he thought
ture. Here too, came the co
wings, McCook and Crittende
staffs, leaving only one of its
hearted Thomas who would no
to gather the shattered force
through the sun pierced chap
his calm presence and inflexible
army—an army without regim
—an army in which rank coun
grasped a gun—shoulder-strap
side in the long line—battle-fl
shadows almost touched—wh
gracious, with the stern light
upon his face, the master-spi
out appeals, without clamor, t
ence, turned doubt into determ

Again and again, the wave of Confederate assault swept against the unconquerable line on Snodgrass Hill The crowded second-growths that stood upon the slopes, were shot away as a reaper cuts the grain The dark, pine branches lay in windrows between the contending forces In the lull between recurrent shocks men gathered them, and heaping on them rocks and rails, even the bodies of the dead made low sheltering works behind which they waited renewed assault Along the line rode Thomas, showing no tremor, no fear, no doubt The men cheered, the clustered flags dipped in salutation, the officers gave over the work of direction, and each one picking up some dead man s musket buckled on his cartridge-box, and taking a place in the line, waited for the next pulsation of battle So, while Rosecrans and two of his corps commanders, waited through the sultry afternoon, a dozen miles away, for the shattered army to appear, the echoes of their guns, the dust that hung over the wilderness where they fought, and the few messengers that came and went, told that the fight was still on, and the "Rock of Chickamauga" was still unconquerable As the sun went down, McCook and Crittenden returned to the army which would not come to them The unorganized mass of individual valor which had repelled the enemy's last assault, had fallen back to the slopes about Rossville, and was slowly and sullenly sorting itself out into an army of regiments and brigades again It was one of the most marvelous things in the whole history of war—a scattered and disorganized army crystallized into a triumphant force by the magic of one man s will!

A considerable force had already reached Chattanooga; two brigades of the reserve, some regiments of cavalry, a number of batteries, which had made their way out of the confusing labyrinth of wooded hills, which composed the field of battle, into the Dry Valley Road, others that had crept along the country roads that crossed Missionary

When the night fell, the amphitheater which lies between Chattanooga and Missionary Ridge, along the Rossville Road and the Valley of Chattanooga Creek, was full of strange sights. Soldiers in squads, officers in groups, cavalry, infantry and artillery men, some going one way and some another, ambulance stretchers, wounded men walking with difficulty, men helping some comrade to escape peril of capture—a strange mass of fragments who pressed not hurriedly but steadily, some of them toward Chattanooga, and some of them back toward the army they had left hours before.

A lieutenant of The Thousand, who had been sent to the rear in charge of the wounded had picked up a wounded confederate, Brigadier-General Adams, and reporting him to the officer in command at Rossville, was ordered to continue with those in his charge to Chattanooga. Gen. Adams had been wounded several hours before and captured, it is said, by an Illinois regiment. For some reason or other, he had been abandoned. When the lieutenant and his men came near he cried out that two or three men who were standing by were robbing him. Their conduct and his condition seemed to justify this charge. Certainly some one had taken from him all the valuables

---

the place of their own lost commands. In the spring of 1864 he was detailed by special order of the Secretary of War to the duty of forwarding recruits from northern depots to the armies of the west, carrying back and forth large sums of money to be paid to the recruits on their arrival at destination ranging from $10,000 to $65,000 a trip.

He continued in this special service until the close of the war and justly boasts of having "handled" more bounty-jumpers and unwilling recruits who were induced to enter the service by high bounties in the later months of the war and to have lost fewer of those entrusted to his care than any man in the army. Among the curious incidents he mentions is the finding one of the Captains of the Thousand, Wm. G. Crowell, among a company of recruits, who having resigned because of ill-health had re-enlisted as a private soldier for a handsome bounty. Captain Hartzell travelled in the discharge of this duty over 40,000 miles and had all sorts of pleasant and unpleasant adventures. He was an inveterate wag who could always be counted on to find something funny in the most lugubrious circumstances. This quality has not forsaken him and at each re-union of the survivors of the Thousand he is expected to furnish them fresh food for their mirth and has never yet disappointed them.

he had. He was loading them with imprecations of unique and vigorous character. The men sullenly retired. The lieutenant who had been a prisoner of war himself, felt great compassion for his wounded enemy, but found that when he proposed to remove him, the vials of vituperation were turned on him as well. The general declared that it was simply murder to remove him from the field. Finding that his wound was well bandaged and mistrusting that his clamor was a ruse to prevent removal in the hope that his friends would prevail, the lieutenant persisted, and one of the men with him having secured a horse the prisoner was lifted into the saddle and with all care removed from the field. He got over his exasperation after a while, and when he bade the lieutenant good-bye, said he would like to give him a token of his good will, but the "damned rascals had not left him even a sleeve-button." So he asked his captor to cut off one of the buttons of his coat and if he was ever in the like plight within the confederate lines to send it to him and he would repay the courtesy he had received. The lieutenant did so and gave his prisoner the knife he used in order that he might not be without something to cut his tobacco, of which he made free use.

Two curious facts are connected with this incident. The Thousand has, in a way, always claimed the capture of Gen. Adams in its famous charge through the confederate left wing. Surgeon Turnbull who was then the slenderest of striplings, just out of his medical studies, quite unlike the portly practitioner he has since become, is still inclined to the opinion that he dressed Gen. Adams' wound in that charge. There is no doubt in the writer's mind that he is in error, and that the claim of original capture cannot be maintained. If any reliance at all is to be placed upon the maps and reports of that battle, Gen. Adams must have been wounded at least an hour before the charge was made and on a different part of the field. When the lieutenant found him he was at least a mile from the scene of the charge The officer whose wound Surgeon Turnbull dressed was probably a colonel of Stewart's Division who was carried off the field, but recaptured by a part of his own command Surgeon Turnbull was one of the bravest men the writer ever saw and his conduct in following the regiment in that charge and ministering to the wounded under the hottest fire just where they fell, was an act of heroic coolness which few even of his profession ever equalled He was ordered to remain and care for our wounded and in consequence was captured and held by the enemy for several days On being released, he was met just outside the confederate lines, by a squad of the enemy's cavalry, who robbed him and those with him, taking instruments, watch, money, coat, hat, boots, in short, as he quaintly reported, "about everything except his hope of salvation which was so small they did not find it"

The Thousand came into Chattanooga on the instalment plan So far as known, the Major, who had a close call for his life, being shot in the thigh by one of the men who threw themselves on the ground and were passed over in our charge, with those in attendance upon him was the first to arrive Fortunately for him, he was enabled to get back to Nashville before the way was barricaded and so escaped the crowded hospitals and the hardships of the siege which followed The lieutenant with the squad under his command, reached the city about ten o'clock at night and taking the wounded in his charge at the hospital, he reported to the provost-marshal and was assigned to duty with the men under his command on the road just at the left of the point where the building known as Fort Negley afterwards stood The duty consisted at first in halting those who came and forming them into ranks After a short time all those under his command, lay down and slept, the lieutenant with them No wonder, this was the third almost sleepless night with two days of constant and exhaustive conflict between The moonlit stillness was interrupted now and again by the roar of a gun on the yet troubled field of bat-

to his hands the day before, which shied, as well he might at the dilapidated squad which gathered round to shake hands with the rider, who thereupon remarked that the beast "hadn't got quite used to men in blue uniform yet" It was a better jest than it would now seem, for the blue showed by no means very clearly through the dust and grime of battle. Hartzell, the irrepressible wag, remarked that in his opinion "about the pleasantest way to fight a battle was as train-guard, a good way in the rear" He would have been the same jovial comrade under fire Cummings is now the Department Commander of the Grand Army in the State of Pennsylvania, and is just as modest and kindly as when with a single bar upon his shoulder, he pressed forward to shake hands with all, and ask after the dead and wounded of the two days' fight which he had heard but had not seen

On the morrow the army fell back to Chattanooga. How we watched its progress! One division after another was deployed into line on the plain between the city and Missionary Ridge, then wooded to its crest, save for a few clearings here and there Batteries were placed in position to resist an advance and a line of skirmishers thrown forward to the crest The members of the contingent already arrived had steadily increased They had been assigned a position and were on the outlook to greet their comrades It was well toward sundown when they came, at their head Edwards, the senior captain, on whom the command had fallen after the Major was struck Neatest of soldiers, as he was one of the bravest and most enduring, the struggle had told upon him. He was haggard and anxious. Yet he was the same courtly gentleman who has since adorned the senate chamber of Minnesota There were few jests then. Though resolute and determined, the soldiers of the Army of the Cumberland recognized that the peril was not over, and while they questioned of comrades they would never meet again, they nerved themselves for the struggle they knew must impend The next day the enemy appeared, our skirmishers retired, our lines were drawn back and the Siege of Chattanooga had begun.

XX.

THE SIEGE OF CHATTANOOGA

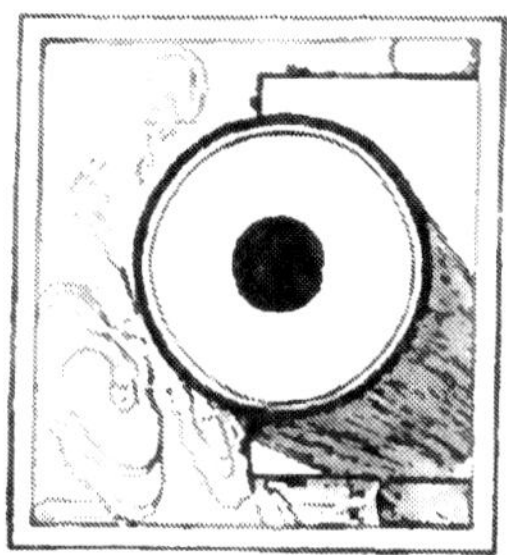

NE of the most deli
autumnal scenes was Ch
when the army of the C
fell back and began to
itself on the group of ca
hills, which the stragg
city occupied. The irr
of eastward fronting
which overlooked the
lay between the city and the half-encircling crest o
ary Ridge, together with the wide, swift river wh
its western side; Walden's Ridge rising behind i
point of Lookout Mountain just far enough away
yond the reach of effective bombardment by the a
that time, made a singularly difficult position t
assault, even before the erection of those works w
transformed it into a citadel.

If the place was held at all, it could only be
siege, or its evacuation compelled by cutting off it
It was beyond the range of effective bombard
Missionary Ridge or Lookout Mountain, while th
see river effectually protected it from assault on
half its circumference.

On the other hand, the supplies for the army
scant, and the line of supply was of the most exp
acter. The river and the railroad passing aroun
of Lookout Mountain constituted the chief mean

ing the railroad from Nashville to the Tennessee, by which all our material must come. It was then, and has ever since been a matter of surprise that Bragg having determined to invest Chattanooga, did not at once push forward

CAPTAIN HORATIO M. SMITH.

HORATIO M. SMITH was born at Worthington, Berkshire County, Mass., January 27th, 1835, and came with his parents in infancy to Ashtabula County, Ohio. He was reared on a farm in Orwell; attended district school and the Orwell Academy; taught two or three winters and at twenty-two entered a country store as clerk; was admitted to partnership a year or two later. After a few years he relinquished his interest in the store and engaged as traveling agent with a New York firm. He rapidly acquired a large country trade and was receiving a good salary when the war came on. He enlisted as a private in Company K, 105th O. V. I., August 13th, 1862; went into camp next day and on the organization of the regiment was made quartermaster-sergeant, which

a sufficient force to strike this line at its most salient point, the Valley of the Wauhatchie, so as effectually to intervene between the city and any relieving force. Events showed that if this had been done, the city would in all probability have been abandoned. There was nothing to prevent such a course. The enemy had only to cross from McLemore's Cove to the Valley of the Wauhatchie, by the roads we had traversed, and others open to them nearer to the city, to retake, and by aid of a little defensive work, easily to hold the eastern bank of the Tennessee.

There was no force between Chattanooga and Shell Mound sufficient to seriously contest such a movement and there was no reason why Bragg should hesitate to reduce his army before Chattanooga to that extent. A mere skeleton line was all that was required to hold the crest of Missionary Ridge, and as we have seen already, he had no use

---

post he filled until the regiment reached Murfreesborough where having been previously promoted to a lieutenancy, he was detailed early in 1863 as brigade quartermaster, in which capacity he served on the staff of Colonel Hall and his successors until after the battle of Chickamauga. In October, 1863 he was appointed by General Thomas, post quartermaster at Chattanooga and a few weeks later, depot quartermaster at the same place. About this time he was commissioned captain and A. Q. M. by President Lincoln and later by President Johnson, brevet major. He served on the staff of General Thomas at Chattanooga about eighteen months and at Nashville in charge of the cavalry depot about eight months. At this place he sold off at auction the horses and mules, many thousand in numbers in the department of the Cumberland after the dissolution of the army. At Chattanooga his duties were varied and onerous and involving not only the distribution of the vast quantities of supplies required by Thomas and Sherman, but also the direction of a small army of civilians employed in the construction and operation of numerous great repair shops, many saw mills, logging camps, wood yards and coal mines, the building of immense store houses, barracks, hospitals and other necessary structures. Steamboats and other river craft were reconstructed, the great permanent bridge across the river at Chattanooga built, the laying out and management of the National Cemetery attended to and its records kept. In short all quartermaster work not otherwise specially provided for was done by him. Many millions of dollars passed through his hands and the immense business under his control was conducted with such energy, economy and judicious adaptation of the means in reach to desired ends as to win for him the unstinted commendation of the sound and practical chiefs, General Thomas and Quartermaster Meigs.

After his return to civil life, Major Smith engaged extensively in the produce shipping trade with finally disastrous results which not only absorbed all his savings but involved him in an indebtedness which it was the hope and effort of his latter life to discharge.

for anything more His enemy was in no condition to leave the stronghold to which he had retired, and if he did, was too short of supplies to make any advance The only reason that can be given for this failure was a too confident belief on the part of the Confederate General, that all that was required, was to cut the line of supply at some point, so as temporarily to isolate the invested position. This he did by pushing forward a brigade to the point of Lookout Mountain, which cut off communication by rail and river, but did not suffice to prevent the landing of a relieving force below, which ultimately turned the left of the Confederate position and rendered its attenuated line wholly incapable of resisting the sortie of the beleaguered army

Two things in part excused, if they did not justify General Bragg's neglect to occupy with a heavy force the east bank of the Tennessee, from Chattanooga to Shell Mound, the one was a confirmed belief that the Army of

---

In 1876 the government having decided on the establishment of the great military post at San Antonio Texas ' Fort Sam Houston, ' Quartermaster General Meigs, himself one of the ablest engineers this country has produced, paid Major Smith the compliment of selecting him to superintend the entire construction of this most important work of the kind in America, and which consisted of a large area of parade and other grounds, barracks, quarters for officers, stables, shops, offices storehouses, water works and general provision for the accommodation of many thousand men and horses, who are permanently quartered or are occasionally mustered there This work which was accomplished to the fullest satisfaction of all concerned was completed only a few years before his death, which occurred in 1890, while on his way north in the hope of arresting a threatened relapse of the terrible "dengue" or "break-bone fever" from which he had been suffering

The army career of Major Smith was the most notable of any member of the regiment He not only rose from a private soldier to the rank of captain and A Q M in the United States army, without aid or influence from others, solely on his own merits and the recognition of his capacity, by those he served, but he so impressed General Thomas with his remarkable ability to organize, direct, control, overcome difficulties and to produce desired results, that he placed him in one of the most responsible positions in reference to the safety and efficiency of the Army of the Cumberland and the Army of the Mississippi, that of post and depot quartermaster at Chattanooga

That this country boy, with only the training of the country school and the country store, should have performed these duties, not only with efficiency, but with ease, shows what a genius he had for organization and detail In other respects he did not show remarkable powers He shone in fulfilling the orders of others rather than in achieving great enterprises of his own inception He was a genius of organization and detail Given a specific thing to do, there were few men who so easily and surely achieved the desired result

the Cumberland was so pressed for food that it would be obliged to evacuate Chattanooga as soon as the railroad was cut and the river obstructed so that boats could not ply between the city and Bridgeport. Another reason why he did not deem it necessary to intervene more strongly was the fact that he knew there was no Federal force of any importance which could be sent to the relief of Chattanooga nearer than Memphis or Washington, and from neither the Army of the Mississippi nor the Army of the Potomac was it supposed that assistance could be expected in time to afford effectual relief. The real danger to be apprehended, as Bragg thought, was from the junction of Burnside's army with that of Rosecrans, which he was careful to guard against by holding his own army well in hand between them.

That General Bragg's conclusions, while lacking the positiveness which characterizes the deductions of great military genius, were by no means unreasonable, will appear from the fact that almost the first act of the Federal commander was to assemble his corps and division commanders at his headquarters to consider the question of abandoning Chattanooga, crossing the river, and taking position on Walden's Ridge. There is no official record of this council, but one of the survivors asserts that the commanding general expressed no opinion, and no one among the subordinate commanders favored it. It is difficult to conceive what advantage was expected to be gained by such a movement, but the fact that it was mooted shows that Bragg was not unreasonably sanguine when he looked for the place to be evacuated before relief could come.

After this conference the work of defense began in earnest. The enemy had assumed position on Missionary Ridge, our forces falling back, burning the houses and felling the trees that intervened. A continuous picket-line was established along the whole front. The enemy's tents shone through the brown leafage on the slope and crest of Missionary Ridge. They brought some heavy guns into position and threw shells at our working parties. Lines of circumvallation were laid out and the army addressed itself to the work of preparing cover in case of an assault. The oaks that crowned the hills were cut down and used as supports in the bomb-proofs. Breast-works, ditches and covered ways were built. Forts and bastions rose at salient points along the line. The men worked eagerly but confidently. There was more or less of skirmishing every day, and frequent night alarms.

LIEUT. ALDEN F. BROOKS.
(From a pen-sketch by himself.)

On the third day General Rosecrans rode through the camp, making addresses to the soldiers at various points, where they trooped to hear him. It was not a formal military progress; just the general, a few of his corps and division commanders and members of his staff. His words

---

ALDEN F. BROOKS was born in Williamsfield, Ohio, April 3, 1840. At the age of fourteen he went with his people to Iowa, and soon after removed to Plattville, Wisconsin, where he attended school. At eighteen, being threatened with lung disease, his physician advised an overland trip to California, which he took in the spring of 1859. He spent a good deal of his time on this journey sketching and making topographical maps of the route. This experience afterwards was of great advantage to him in the service. He staid in California till after the war commenced, when he returned to Ohio and soon after enlisted in the 105th. He was with the regiment during the retreat from Richmond to

and demeanor were confident one may almost say boastful strangely at variance with actual conditions. His army was enthusiastically devoted to him. They had not yet had time to study the movements of the past month. The history of the Union Army since the 9th of September when the enemy surrendered Chattanooga had not then been written. We supposed the battle of Chickamauga to have been a necessity that it could only have been avoided by surrendering Chattanooga the objective of the campaign.

We did not know that Thomas had protested against the movement into McLemore's Cove and that we might have been in Chattanooga on the 15th without firing a gun, waiting to be attacked on the very ground we now occupied, after a loss of 17,000 men. Because of this we still believed in our commander, whose confidence, as usual, soon rose to the point of boastful exultation. He rode from camp to camp the shouts and cheers of his soldiers constituting a vote of confidence, which seems incredible when we reflect that he had left his army only a few days before in the midst of one of the most terrific battles, and come to

---

Louisville; was in the battle of Perryville, where he was wounded in the left hand. He was detailed Topographical Engineer of 4th Brigade, 4th Division, 14th A. C., on the staff of Colonel A. S. Hall. At the battle of Hoover's Gap he was the only Topographical Engineer who made a map of operations out of twenty or more engineers, and was recommended by Major General J. J. Reynolds for a commission and assigned to duty as Topographical Engineer on his staff. After the battle of Chickamauga he was detailed as draughtsman at Department Headquarters with Colonel Merrill; was mustered 1st lieutenant colonel at Ringgold, Georgia, in May, 1864; detailed Assistant Topographical Engineer on Major General Thomas' staff and joined the command at Marietta, Ga. Returned to Chattanooga after the capture of Atlanta and continued in charge of the engineer office at that point until detailed with T. B. Van Horn to survey and lay out the National Cemetery at Chattanooga. Was mustered out with the regiment. Went to New York in 1867 and studied in the Academy of Design; was also a pupil of Edwin White, the "American Titian"; removed to Chicago in 1870 and opened his first studio. In 1881 he went to Paris and was a year under Carolus Duran; exhibited in the Salon of 1882; since he has exhibited in New York, Boston and Philadelphia, also every year in Chicago. He has often received honorable mention and had the honor of being the only artist in Chicago who exhibited in both oil and water color at the World's Fair, 1893.

He was married in 1861 and has two daughters and one son. He resides in Chicago, Ill. He is the only member of the regiment who has achieved special distinction as an artist, and the portrait given above from a pen sketch of himself is his highest credential.

the city we were now exhorted to defend, in order to see that the means of escape across the river were prepared. This was not an escaping army. The roar of battle was in its ears but that general was right who declared in the council referred to, that though he had lost one-third of his division, those who remained were just as eager to fight as before. The army did not even know the story of those two sulphurous days under the trees of Chickamauga. They thought their leader had simply been forced to fight at a disadvantage and that the army had escaped destruction through his skill. It was a most fortunate belief. He made wonderfully inspiring speeches that day—considering the facts of the previous week. The work of entrenchment went on with increased earnestness. The Army of the Cumberland had done little fortifying heretofore, but now it wrought with the consciousness that safety lay at the spade's point. It is wonderful how soon the city became impregnable.

The enemy had taken possession of Lookout Mountain and established on the Point a battery which commanded the river and railroad below with a plunging fire, but did not reach the city. One morning we were waked by the explosion of a shell in the camp of our division. The enemy had put some heavier guns in position on Lookout Mountain, and by elevating them as high as possible, they were able to throw shot in a most uncertain manner, sometimes into our lines, sometimes just outside of them, and again clean over town and river among the teams parked on the other side. For a few days they fired pretty steadily. One could see the puff of white smoke, watch the shell with its little jet of white vapor and small black center, as it crept towards us seemingly very slowly. If it was likely to fall too near, all ran for the bomb-proof,—a useless precaution, since the height from which it fell, was such that the bomb-proofs would have been no protection. Indeed, those which fell among us buried themselves so deeply in the earth that no harm, to speak of, came from their explosions. There

The shell had knocked the prop from under the plank on which he had rested

The feeling of danger soon wore off, and every discharge was greeted with a derisive howl—each one merely glancing up to see if it was likely to fall in his vicinity It is amazing how easy it became to guess the point at which the shell would strike, and how little attention was paid to this bombardment There was a rumor that two men and eight mules were the net result of seventeen days firing, but that was probably an exaggerated diminution Still it is a fact, that though the Thousand lay in direct range between the battery and the bridge, which seemed to be the special mark for their shots, the writer never saw a man who was hurt by the bombardment and has no recollection of loss in the division through this useless cannonade

But if the bombardment was of little moment, an insidious foe which made much less noise, threatened us with something worse than mere defeat On its arrival at Chattanooga the Army of the Cumberland had hardly ten days' rations These, with very slight additions, were all that it had to subsist on for nearly forty days A long and devious road, over sixty miles of mud and hill, exposed to frequent attacks of the enemy s cavalry, lay between Chattanooga and the line of supply, the railway from Nashville to Bridgeport Over this only a meager and uncertain supply of food could be obtained From the first we were on what was termed "half-rations,' soon these grew less until one or two hard-tack a day were all that were obtainable and by and by, the time came, when the good-natured quartermaster could make no farther excuse and the conscientious commissary sergeant in making a last issue broke the fifth cracker in twain, as he issued his own ration—a little less than five for eight days! The whole five were hardly enough for a day—especially to men who for two weeks or more had not once had enough. Men picked up the kernels of corn scattered upon the ground where the few horses still left in the city were fed and ate them Officers who drew

ten, and by cooking it a long time made what is still declared by its partakers to have been a "savory mess." Duty and disease made heavy inroads upon men thus weakened. Starvation did not come, but his foot was at the opening of every tent. An officer of the Thousand was detailed with his company to go with the train that brought in the first loads of corn. As the lean mules dragged them up the slippery slope from the bridge, crowds of gaunt men eyed the yellow ears hungrily. At length there was a rush—the wagons were overturned and every man caught what he could carry of the precious stuff and ran. Several wagon-loads were thus "distributed" before one was allowed to pass. It was a terribly mutinous way of satisfying hunger, and the officer was put under arrest for not preventing it. There is no record of his punishment, and it is probable that his superiors regarded the offense, under the circumstances, as creditable rather than discreditable to him. The grim soldier, who was in command of the train, shouted for the men to fire upon their hungry comrades, but no one of his command heard the order.

By this time, the wooded knolls, which had made the city a thing of beauty, were bare. The oaks had been cut down for various uses, and the roots digged out for firewood. The enemy on Missionary Ridge, which had been

---

the Western Reserve. His father, Isaac, was a merchant. Young Mansfield attended the common schools and graduated from Poland College, afterwards learning the machine and moulder's trades. He enlisted as a private in Company H, 105th, in August, 1862. He was successively promoted to sergeant, second lieutenant and first lieutenant, breveted captain, and assigned to duty as A. Q. M. Fourteenth Army Corps at Chattanooga, Tenn. At the close of the war he became owner of the Darlington Cannel Coal Mines and operated them with other important plants. He was Justice of the Peace, Clerk and Treasurer of Darlington Township for eighteen years and has married 684 couples, represented his county three times in the State Legislature as a Republican, is Superintendent of Sunday School and elder of Presbyterian church, Vice-president of Beaver College and director in National Bank. His collection of orchids and wild flowers of Beaver county is very fine. He retains in maturer life the taste which made his journal of the war-time a collection of flowers of the region through which the army marched. In science, especially geology, he has made many new discoveries of plants and insects in coal formations, and he has a large collection of war relics.

wooded to the summit had made great clearings. The plain between had been almost entirely shred of cover and obstacles. Along the side of the ridge ran two and three irregularly parallel lines of dull red. They were the confederate works. From Bragg's headquarters flashed steadily back and forth to the signal station on Lookout Mountain orders and reports.

One day almost a month after the siege began they told the confederate commander that a new miracle had been performed which showed how foolish he had been in leaving the left bank of the Tennessee so weakly guarded. For the first time in the history of war the railway had been called upon to do its utmost. The most efficient railroad man of that time was Mr. Thomas A. Scott, who had won the highest renown as such, rising to the first vice-presidency of the Pennsylvania Railroad. He had been made Assistant Secretary of War in charge of transportation with almost autocratic power. When the Army of the Cumberland fell back to Chattanooga it was determined to transfer the 11th and 12th corps, under command of Gen. Hooker, from the Army of the Potomac, to Tennessee. Mr. Scott found here the opportunity of his life. In eight days he had collected the transportation and, over the worst of roads, in the face of incredible obstacles, had landed the two corps, in all 16,000 men with their artillery, transportation and equipments in Middle Tennessee. The blow at our own line of supply which Bragg had neglected to strike in sufficient force at the outset, was now impossible.

Still he did not strengthen his hold upon the left bank of the Tennessee, but contented himself with cavalry raids in our rear. Then Grant came and took command of the military division of the Mississippi. Thomas had already been raised to the command of the Army of the Cumberland.

Our division commander, J. J. Reynolds, had been made chief of staff and General Absalom Baird had been assigned to the command of our division. The Brown's Ferry attack

give us a lodgment on the left bank of the river and before Bragg could reinforce his left Hooker had crossed at Bridgeport and rations were again available for our hungry men

With the opening of the river came again our Lieutenant Colonel, but half-recovered from disease, yet eager to take part in the conflict which impended The army was reorganized, the spirits of the soldiers quickly rose from the depression incident to their condition, and all were eager for that wonderful fray which closed this most spectacular of warlike movements

Two of the Thousand were to leave their names connected in a singular way with the city in which we were thus closely pent-up Lieutenant Brooks, the artistic topographer of our division, was afterwards to lay out the beautiful cemetery, in which so many of his comrades lie one of the first interred therein being the gallant Spaulding, Captain of Company E, who, after being carried by the men who loved him devotedly, from the very front of the battle, was doomed to die in the hospital at Chattanooga

In all the transformations of this wonderful time, there is hardly a more romantic story than that of Horatio M Smith. A country boy, educated at a country school, he was a clerk in a dry-goods' store at the outbreak of the war The morning the Thousand was mustered into service he came into camp with a dozen recruits he had enlisted the night before, and driven forty miles that they might be on hand in time Because of the energy displayed, his business habits and attractive qualities he was made Quartermaster Sergeant Before we reached Chattanooga, he had been appointed Lieutenant and Brigade Quartermaster During the battle of Chickamauga, he especially attracted the attention of General Reynolds, on whose staff he served as a volunteer aide, instead of going with the trains Soon after reaching Chattanooga he was given charge of some buildings, in which stores were collected When the enemy began to shell us from the point of Lookout Mountain fearful that his stores might be ignited he gathered up a lot of empty barrels and placed them on the roof and along the sides, with a camp-kettle hung on each. It was a thorough job tidily done which very soon attracted the attention of General Thomas. Inquiring who had charge of the building the young lieutenant was ordered to report to his headquarters. In a few days he was mustered out of service with the Thousand having been appointed Captain and Assistant Quartermaster in the United States Army by special request of General Thomas and assigned to duty, first as Post-Quartermaster of Chattanooga and afterwards as Depot Quartermaster at that point. As such all the vast quantity of material required for the army of Sherman, during his advance on Atlanta passed through his hands. He built the permanent bridge across the river, ran the railroads centering there, the steamboats on the river, and at one time had an army of laborers and clerks under his control greater in numbers, than the division of which the Thousand was a part. The value of the stores that passed through his hands it would be hard to estimate and the ability and faithfulness with which he executed the trust imposed upon him were certified by every commander who had knowledge of them to be worthy of all praise. Thus while we waited for the great transformation scene which was to end this episode of the great war, fate was busy with the destinies of those who were her favorites or had the power to compel her favor by doing the right thing at just the right time.

There was no question of the army's ability to hold Chattanooga against the enemy and the scarcity of supplies came upon them so gradually that it was hardly realized until it was practically at an end. Instead of being demoralized, the army was in a peculiarly resolute and confident mood. This was strengthened by the character of the position, which, it was evident to the most inexperienced eye, could only be taken by regular approaches over a wide, open and peculiarly exposed plain. Only along the valley of

Chattanooga Creek upon the right, and from Orchard Knob on the left flank was such approach at all feasible. The former seemed the most probable line of approach, and if one had been there prosecuted with vigor in connection with the undisputed possession of the left bank of that stream and the wooded slope of Lookout Mountain beyond, it might possibly have compelled the abandonment of the city before the arrival of reinforcements and supplies.

It is evidence of lack of confidence on the part of the enemy that he lay for two months before the city, without either making an assault or opening any line of offensive works, occupying his men in fortifying the slopes and crest of Missionary Ridge and the slope of Lookout Mountain against assault. The reason which General Bragg gave for this course, that he was without siege artillery and that his transportation was taxed to the utmost to provide supplies in a region utterly exhausted, is no doubt sufficient in part at least, but much more importance should be attached to his stubborn belief that his enemy would be compelled to evacuate the city for lack of supplies. The result of this failure to attack, was that in the course of a few days every vestige of apprehension had disappeared among the soldiers of our army, who began to speculate not on how the enemy was to be resisted, but how he was to be overcome. None doubted that he would be attacked, but how the defensive works that stretched almost an unbroken line along the crest and side of Missionary Ridge were to be broken, it was not easy to determine. The peculiarity of the situation and one which should have negatived all idea of demoralization on the part of the Army of the Cumberland, was that the besieged were thinking all the time of attack, and the besiegers planning only for defence.

This is attested by the contents of half a dozen journals kept from day to day during the siege. Some passages from the diary of Captain A. G. Wilcox, of Company F, a graduate of Oberlin, and since the close of the war a successful publisher and business man of Minneapolis, very clearly exemplify what has been said besides giving an idea of the situation hardly attainable, except from contemporary narrative. It begins two days after the battle of Chickamauga.

Chattanooga, Tenn., Sept. 22, 1863.

Last night at midnight we fell back to this place. It is strong by nature, and a line of earthworks nearly completed extends around it. The Confederates threw them up to resist our expected attack, and left them for us to use in resisting them. It is being rapidly strengthened and completed. Captain Edwards, who has been in command of the regiment since Major Perkins was wounded (on the 19th), has shown himself a very capable officer. He has got the regiment into shape in a good position, and is, I think, anxious for another fight. I don't blame him. He took command at a hard time, and feels that he will not get full credit for what he did. He will probably get another chance soon. A demonstration is being made by the enemy on our left, but with a clear field for a thousand yards in front, a mountain on our right, and a formidable ridge on our left, we are ready for Bragg and his army. *Why could not Chickamauga have been fought here? If Bragg attacks he will not get away with enough men for another campaign.*

This modest and conscientious officer, with the roar of useless battle still in his ears and with pity for his dead comrades yet fresh in his heart, enters in his journal on the very first day after his arrival in the beleaguered city, the question which the future will always ask when it makes mention of that strange conflict in the woods of Chickamauga. The same night he adds:

9 p. m.—Skirmishing all along the line, but no serious fighting. At one time during the day, a rumor flew over the camp that the army would cross the river in retreat, and I never saw so gloomy a regiment. But now, with a good prospect for a fight tomorrow, the men are positively gay

To fight is not so bad, but to give up all that we have fought to win is terrible

Sept 23d, 1863

No fighting today, but large trains have been seen moving round our left. Rifle pits have been strengthened We worked Colonel Long s house into the pits and the fort on which our right rests Expect an attack tomorrow morning Ran up a flag over the fort today, and Harris battery fired a few shells at the rebel picket line, which was in plain sight One of the shells struck a chimney which remained standing after the house was burned to prevent its giving shelter to the enemy, behind which a rebel picket was located which was annoying our men The way they scattered when the chimney came tumbling down was funny enough to us and started a cheer along the whole line

Sept 24

At work on fort, slight skirmish this morning To-day, General Rosecrans rode along the line, and stopped here and there to talk with officers and men The way the men rushed out to greet him showed that he had lost none of his popularity among the rank and file on account of the disaster at Chickamauga The air was full of hats and cheers His personal magnetism might make him a successful leader in a charge, but he could never have checked a retreat and made the last stand at Chickamauga as Thomas did. The boys never throw up their hats for Thomas—I believe, in spite of his modest ways, he would rather like it if they did—but in a fight they are always glad to see "Old Pap' looking after things and will stay with him to the end Thomas is always cool and his men can't be stampeded To a casual observer, "Rosy" would seem to be the idol of the army, but if officers and men were to choose a commander by vote, I believe Thomas would be elected The only fear now is that Bragg may cross the river, threaten our rear, and compel us to follow him.

Sept 25

Rumors that Rosecrans came back to Chattanooga with the defeated wing of the army while Garfield joined Thomas where the unbroken portion of the line held the field until night Rosecrans of course, thought the battle was lost

Sept 26

On picket Rebels in sight and range but no shooting Heavy skirmishing to both right and left of us

Sept 27

Went across river to find company wagon and get mess chest Rebels have planted heavy guns and are preparing to starve us out Rumor says that Bragg demanded a surrender and threatened to shell the town The wounded are coming in under a flag of truce

Oct 2

Heavy rains It is reported that Lee is visiting Bragg, and that the advance of Grant's reinforcements have arrived (This probably refers to the arrival of Hooker's advance in Tennessee) Rebels have been moving all day from their right to left

Oct 3

Rumors of consolidation of 20 and 21 corps under Gordon Granger and military commission to investigate McCook and Crittenden for alleged misconduct at Chickamauga Rebels opened on us with 32 pounder from the slope of Lookout Three shots struck near our regimental line, but hurt nobody

Oct 6

Shelled us nearly all night Quiet on account of fog this morning No firing today Heavy cannonading in the distance That is accounted for by the absurd rumor that Longstreet's corps has refused to obey Bragg's orders and that Bragg had turned out the rest of the army to reduce him to obedience (This report was not only current, but very generally believed. It was said to have been brought by the ubiquitous "deserter —Ed)

Oct 7

Chilly rain. Rebel and Union papers predict that Bragg will make a desperate effort to regain this place Rations are scarce There is no corn within thirty miles and each train needs a division as guard Roads are almost impassable. Report that Hooker has won a small fight in Trenton Valley. Rebels in front are silent.

Oct 8

On picket Sentinels so near the enemy's picket that they can talk across the line No firing They pace their beats eyeing each other like deadly enemies as a part of the great machine of war, named the army, but personally disposed to be the best of friends For a time, papers and tobacco were freely exchanged, but that is now forbidden

Oct 9.

Orders came last night to be ready for a night assault. Rebel papers say Bragg's victory at Chickamauga is of no avail unless he routs us out of Chattanooga.

Oct. 13

Election today, 284 votes polled in regiment, all but one for Brough (Brough was the Union candidate for governor of Ohio.) The loyal majority in Ohio is expected to reach 75,000

Oct 14

Post at McMinnville captured with 585 men Rosecrans has ordered the officers tried, and says "No surrender must be the order for bridge guards and garrisons (This capture was one result of a Confederate cavalry raid on our communications Our cavalry under General Crook was so close upon them that they had time to do but little damage)

Oct 18

Official reports from elections give Brough 70,000 majority on home vote Curtin 30,000 in Pennsylvania and Iowa loyal by 15,000 Last night the rebels waked the echoes in the hills with their shouts over some news that suited them. Today we answer with cheers over the elections. With the backing of a loyal people the army will take care of the rebellion.

Oct. 21.

Today Rosecrans' farewell to his army was read at dress parade. Rumor that he goes to the Army of the Potomac, and another that he is removed for incompetency. The last is not credited and the former is not probable. Grand old General Thomas takes command of our Army of the Cumberland. General Grant becomes the head of the new Division of the Mississippi, embracing the army of the Cumberland, Burnside's Army of the Ohio, Sherman's Army of the Mississippi and Hooker's 11th and 12th corps. Rations short—less than one-third.

Oct. 22.

Picket today, our brigade covering the entire division line. Line runs along the bank of Chattanooga Creek. Could throw a stone to where the rebel outposts stand. Our general officers approach the line and rebel generals and staffs are frequently in sight. Killing men on picket is murder, not war. Our heavy guns have fired constantly today, and the shells bursting on the slopes of Lookout wake echoes which sound like musketry.

Oct. 23.

A wagon train of supplies came in today. Roads almost impassable. Mules are half starved and weak so wagons come light. Mules and horses are shot by hundreds to save from starvation. We must soon have Lookout, the valley and the river or starve.

Oct. 24.

Rumor says Grant is here and the cars are running to Falling Water, seventeen miles up the river. The change of commanders is an experiment. Twelve pounds of crackers, eight of meat and a little coffee for five of us for five days.

Oct 27

Brisk cannonading and musketry, this morning, at daybreak. General Turchin's brigade went down the river last night with some pontoon boats, surprised a brigade of the enemy, and drove them back after a sharp fight, clearing the river for our boats Men are starving here, saw a man today picking kernels of corn out of the dirt, and eating them He was the picture of misery. Men go to bed tonight without supper and get nothing more until day after tomorrow Mule-meat is considered a luxury

Oct 29.

Last night there was heavy musketry and artillery in the valley west of Lookout There were two distinct attacks and each lasted nearly two hours, with a lull between them. For a time the roar of musketry was appalling, as it came to us in the still night air Rumor has it that Hooker had gained an advanced position and entrenched, and that Longstreet tried in vain to dislodge him by his desperate attacks. Batteries on top of Lookout have been firing into that valley today There must have been an advance of our lines

Oct 31

Camp fires indicate an increased rebel force on the east side of Lookout. Boat up last night with 35,000 rations and will make a like trip every twenty-four hours Rebels sent a raft down and broke our pontoon bridge so that we get nothing today

Nov 4

The pickets still fraternize Yesterday the owner of one of a lot of horses which were pasturing between the lines went out to catch him, and he ran over to the rebel line The Yankee owner asked permission to go after him, and got the permission and the horse too, the rebel picket helping him to catch the horse and mount As he rode back to our lines, three rebel horses which had been feeding on the same ground ran into our lines and were caught and driven back to their owners. Such amenities would seem incredible to one not a soldier. Colonel George, commanding brigade, says Rosecrans *should never have fought Bragg at Chickamauga, but should have concentrated his forces at Chattanooga as soon as it was abandoned by Bragg and made a secure base of supplies.*

Nov. 12.

No rations accumulate at the landing. Wagon trains take supplies to the starving city, as fast as boats bring them. Refugees go north starved out, when they can. Deserters come in frequently, particularly into Hooker's lines, it is said. There is a good deal of sparring between our men and Hooker's, who are just from the Potomac. Our boys ask them if they are out of butter, and where their paper collars are, and call out All quiet on the Potomac. Hooker's boys think we have never had a battle in the west, only a few light skirmishes.

Nov. 18.

Cannonading and musketry in Lookout Valley yesterday. Rumor that an attempt was made to take Lookout but failed.

Nov. 22.

On night of the 20th we got orders to march at 4 a. m. with two days' rations and 100 rounds of ammunition. A few hours later, order was countermanded. Rumored that Burnside has been cleaned out, and another report that he is all right. Sherman's corps is here and has landed at foot of Mission Ridge next the river. Howard has joined him. Orders have come to move at four tomorrow morning. Rumor that Mission Ridge is to be taken. It looks like a Gibraltar, not to be taken by assault. The Colonel (Tolles) made a neat speech to the regiment on parade and intimated that we would meet the enemy again soon.

The Thousand slept peacefully that night in the camp which had been their home for two months. Every one knew that tomorrow would be the beginning of the end of a siege memorable in history for its bloodless character. That night about the camp-fires its incidents were rehearsed with the appreciative humor which comes only from high spirits. Aside from short rations there was even little of discomfort experienced by the besieged.

There were some quaint experiences, and more than one journal bears evidences of the scholarly leisure which the members of the Thousand enjoyed during those bright autumnal days. How did they get so many books to read? A school of some note had been located at this point, and a brother of Sergeant Warner had been a professor in it little more than a year before. It is possible that this may account for so many volumes of standard literature coming into the tents of the Thousand. They were men who could appreciate good literature, and there was little harm in borrowing what had otherwise surely been destroyed. Did they ever return them? There was none to claim them when we marched away.

SERGT. J. R. WARNER.
(1890)

One of the most curious incidents connected with the siege was the absolute disappearance of an immense stock of tobacco, which was stored in warehouses along the river. It is said that certain northern men who happened to be dwelling within the limits of the Confederacy, confident of its sudden downfall, had disposed of their possessions for Confederate money and investing the proceeds in "Lone Jack" and "Kinnikinnick," had shipped it to Chattanooga, as the point most liable to early capture by the Union forces, hoping thereby to make the exchange from Confederate currency into "greenbacks" not only expeditiously but profitably. There were said to be some hundreds of thousands of pounds of the fragrant weed, packed in little bales and snugly stowed in these warehouses. Immediately on the occupation of the town by our forces, the owners who had remained to be captured with their wares, made application for protection for their property, and an order was issued that a guard should be stationed in front of the premises. By some accident a line was drawn under the word "front," which the officer mistook for a mark of emphasis, and was so careful to obey that he quite forgot to station guards on the other sides of the buildings, which being thus exposed, were entered and the tobacco removed. So abundant was the supply that no smoker lacked a pipeful, even when it was impossible to get bread or meat for love or money; and many a survivor of that day believes that his ability to keep up the fatigue of picket every three days upon such meager fare was due to the soothing influences of this abundant supply of *Nicotiana*. Such theory would, of course, be scouted by those who seriously believe that tobacco is "is an Indian weed which from the devil doth proceed," but their objection will not change the veteran's belief.

Years afterwards the writer has been informed the owners sought to recover from the government pay for the tobacco thus converted into "Soldiers' Comfort" without the intervention of the sutler. Whether they succeeded in their suit is not known, but if the sum demanded was not too great, the government could well afford to pay for the same as a means of preserving contentment among the beleaguered soldiery.

The health of the army was remarkably good during the entire siege, and there was something in the situation the circling hills to the eastward, the great mountain hanging over us to the south, the swift, dark river which circled round the now barren promontory covered with red lines of earthwork, and formidable bastions dotted with white tents and populous with soldiery, that seemed to promote confidence and beget impatience. From the dark-visaged lieutenant-colonel, who returning from his sick leave, felt himself aggrieved that he had missed a fight, down to the youngest drummer boy, every one was full of anticipation of the victory we were to win when we should move against "the Johnnies."

The sentiment was greatly strengthened by the commingling of the men from the three great armies of the Union. Sherman's bronzed veterans fresh from victory on the Mississippi, with "Vicksburg" ever on their lips, and the natty soldiers of Hooker, with their handsome commander, and the long record of triumph and defeat of the Army of the Potomac, had come in hot haste to bring relief to the Army of the Cumberland. All of these, together with Burnside's Army in East Tennessee had been united under the command of the victor of Donelson, Shiloh, Vicksburg and a score of intermediate battlefields—these armies amounting to twelve corps, numbering, present and absent, over four hundred thousand men, and embracing four departments—constituted the largest military command ever held by an American up to that time—a command especially organized for the new military genius who was to pause for a brief moment at Chattanooga on his way eastward to supreme command on the Potomac to win new laurels.

Each army felt its honor peculiarly at stake in the conflict which impended. The Army of the Tennessee, held the left, strengthened by a part of Howard's corps. This was expected to be the critical point, and it was natural that Grant should assign the post of honor to his old soldiers, and his tried lieutenant, Sherman. Hooker was on the right charged either to make his way over the nose of Look out, or passing around it, to throw his force across the river and push forward against the enemy's right center at Rossville.

For a fortnight the bands of the opposing hosts had sounded defiance to each other from echoing crest to crest. The watchfires burned thickly along the now denuded sides of Missionary Ridge and on the eastern slope of Lookout. The battle of Wauhatchie gave the first decided advantage to the Army of the Potomac, but a brigade of our division (Turchin's) had won great glory in the Brown's Ferry affair, which though almost bloodless, was a matter of great daring, executed with coolness and skill; while the Army of the Tennessee had made one of the most remarkable marches in history, from the banks of the Mississippi to the crag-encircled arena on the Tennessee, fearful that the battle would be fought before they should arrive. Thus honors were easy with the soldiers of the three united armies, while the cavalry inspirited by their successful pursuit of the force sent to operate on our communications, was again massed and thrown to our left to divert the enemy from Burnside, whose exposed situation at Knoxville was a source of constant anxiety to the government and the general commanding. Everything was prepared, and the general on the success of whose arrangements all depended, walked quietly through the midst of his new soldiers and would have passed the camp of the Thousand unrecognized, had not Sergeant Parker, the most painstaking of diarists, who was to become the Nestor from whose decision in regard to the movements of the Thousand there is no appeal, happened to be on duty that day. A little while before, when Grant first came to Chattanooga, the Sergeant was a sitter in the tent of an army photographer when Grant came to be photographed to gratify the curiosity of an old friend who desired to see how he looked in the new command to which he had been active in urging his advancement. The photographer would have hustled the boyish sergeant out of the chair and his tent, too, for that matter, but the great General would not permit it So the blushing youngster was photographed while the commander of the Military Division of the Mississippi, the autocrat of half a dozen states, who held in his hand the destiny of the Union, waited his turn.

While the army waited confident and exulting, Grant wandered among the camps of his new army seeking to gather the spirit of the soldiers who were to act under his leadership on the morrow, to whom his features were yet only half known

XXI

BATTLE OF LOOKOUT MOUNTAIN

T. WALLACE
1863.

WHAT a glorious battle amphitheat
Never before were two armies muste
for conflict with such spectacular envi
ment! Never were the pride and p
of war displayed in such magnifi
setting! From the rebel signal sta
on the crest of Lookout Mountain, e
movement of our army, from the Va
of the Wauhatchie on the right to a p
opposite the mouth of Chickam
Creek on the left, was clearly visible,
cept where a spur of Walden's R
ome of Sherman's forces from view. It must b
a thrilling scene to the Confederate watcher, wh
moving flags told his commander, at his headquar
issionary Ridge, each significant feature of the mig
rama unfolding at his feet. In Wauhatchie Va
thing was astir. At the foot of Lookout men w
repairing the pontoon bridge, which had broken
before. The battery on Moccasin Point was thun
ngrily against the craggy face of Lookout. There
movement of troops in Lookout Valley, but wha
nded he could not discover. Beyond the river, to

redoubts, past the line of works, long since made impregnable to assault, and marched column after column, blue-clad and steel-crowned, into the bare, almost treeless plain

CAPT. WILLIAM WALLACE.
1894.

WILLIAM WALLACE was born near Belfast, Antrim Co., Ireland, January 13, 1841, and came to this country at an early age. From the age of 14 to enlistment, Aug. 21, 1862, was a clerk in a country store. Was enlisted as 4th sergeant of Co. I, and served as such until January 17, 1863, received commission as 2d lieutenant, and on May 2d, 1863, was promoted to captain of Company I, and remained with the regiment as such until the close of the war. Took part in all the marches and battles of the regiment; was never wounded or sick which enabled him to be present for duty at all times. On returning home, found that his old position as clerk, was open to him, which position he retained for 21 years; then engaged in mercantile business for himself for 16 years. Was auditor of Trumbull County from 1883 to 1890, when was elected to legislature to represent the Trumbull and Mahoning district; was on the State Board of Equalization for one year. At the organization of the Warren Savings Bank Company, was elected treasurer, which position he still holds.

that lay between our lines and the Confederate works at the foot of Missionary Ridge. Flags danced in the bright sunshine. Bands played. The air was full of shouts. The artillery along our whole line opened on the enemy. Thomas, with the Army of the Cumberland, was in the center between Chattanooga and the Ridge. Hooker with his troops from the Army of the Potomac, lay beyond Lookout Mountain on the right. Sherman with two corps of the Army of the Tennessee and Jeff. C. Davis' division of the Fourteenth Corps, lay on the west bank of the river opposite the north end of Missionary Ridge, ready to leap across and attack the most undefended point in the enemy's line. As they marched out upon the plain, the columns of the Army of the Cumberland deployed until an almost continuous line stretched from Chattanooga Creek to a point opposite the right of the enemy on Missionary Ridge. No wonder that the hearts of the Confederates throbbed with apprehension as they looked at this array. A soldier learns instinctively the science of war, and despite its apparent strength there was something in the position of the Confederate army which showed its soldiers that when its flank were turned as it was but too easy for an enterprising enemy to do, its center must inevitably break. The semi-lune stretching from the river above, along Missionary Ridge to Lookout Mountain, was strong in inaccessibility of its parts, but weak in power to protect its rear or strengthen quickly exposed flanks. The soldiers did not formulate these defects, but felt them.

Many changes had been made in the environment of the Thousand since we entered Chattanooga. General Thomas had been promoted from the command of the Fourteenth Corps to the Department of the Cumberland, which now embraced the Fourth, Fourteenth, Eleventh and Twelfth Corps. The two latter were nominally under General Hooker, who was thus really a second in command in the Army of the Cumberland. As it chanced, however, he vas at this time without the Eleventh Corps and had twc livisions of Sherman's and two brigades of the Fourteenth 'orps instead under his command.

General John M. Palmer was in command of the Fourteenth Corps. Our old division commander, J. J. Reynolds, iad been made Chief of Staff of the department, and in his

CAPT. D B. STAMBAUGH.

DANIEL B. STAMBAUGH was born at Brier Hill, Mahoning Co., O., April 6 38. Received a common school education. Working on farm when enlisted pril, 1861, in Co. B, 19th O. I. V., in three months' service. Enlisted as privat ith 105th, in July, 1862. Was mustered as 2d lieutenant, and promoted espectively to 1st lieutenant and captain. Remained with regiment until the lose of the war. Returned to Youngstown, O., and became identified with ie coal and iron interests of this valley, and is still engaged in it, also the ardware business and is president of the Stambaugh, Thompson Co.

place was General Absalom Baird, a younger man of fascinating personality and a splendid record. Our division was now the third of the Fourteenth Corps. To our brigade three regiments had been added, one of which furnished its commander, Colonel James George. So that when we marched out over the breastworks at the left of Fort Negley the second brigade of the Third Division consisted of the 75th, 87th and 101st Indiana, the 9th, 35th and 105th Ohio and the 2d Minnesota. On our left was Hazen's brigade of Wood's Division of the Fourth Corps. Before us, half-way to Missionary Ridge almost, was the chain of hills of which Orchard Knob is the most important. This was the enemy's advance position. Our guns fired over us at the enemy; the enemy's shot swept by us, doing little damage. Our old commander, Reynolds, rode past, while we lay in line, and singling out the regiment he rode along its front, reminding us of the charge we had made by his order at Chickamauga. We cheered him when he said we would soon have another chance at the enemy. It did not need a prophet or a Chief of Staff to tell us that. However, everybody was cheering at every opportunity all up and down the line. The enemy fired on us with some heavy guns on the Ridge, but their shots fell short. We saw them standing on their works and watching our maneuvers. It must have been an imposing sight to them. There were mustered on the plain that day, in full view of the enemy, nigh fifty thousand men, with more than one hundred guns, including the heavy guns in the forts along our line. The movements of these forces must have greatly magnified their apparent numbers.

We waited and speculated—Colonel Tolles standing beside his black horse, impatient for the fray to begin. Now and then a shot from the crest of Lookout was answered by our guns on Moccasin Point. Neither did any harm, but the echoes rolling back and forth added to the romantic character of the battle-scene. About noon the fire grew hotter on our left. Half an hour later Wood's Division moved to the assault of Orchard Knob We followed, supporting their right It was nigh half a mile away but when we reached the hills and looked back, the whole world seemed alive Waves of blue were swelling over hillock and plain, the great guns of the forts were belching harmless shots over our heads The enemy were fleeing to their next line of works a mile away, at the foot of the Ridge We had captured four hundred men, and had left one hundred dead and wounded on the way

From end to end of our line from those who remained in the works, from the Army of the Cumberland and the Army of the Potomac, from all who saw and all who heard, rose clamorous cheers over this first success in a movement which was to be so full of wonderful spectacles. The enemy looked down upon us from the crest of the Ridge and yelled back defiance We thought there was a note of doubt in the yell, as, no doubt, there was

The day closed bleak and dreary We could now clearly see the enemy's works Those at the foot of the Ridge did not seem very strong, but along its crest was a heavy line with batteries on projecting points which seemed to enfilade every foot of space between

---

It rained all night. In the morning the rebel pickets were in plain sight There was no advance but the cannonading from Fort Wood and all the forts along our line was terrific The batteries on our line of battle also opened fire upon the Confederate works at the foot of the Ridge The crest seemed alive with cannon whose shots plunged down upon us in the plain below, for the most part, harmlessly

Then came the echoes through the fog of shots up the river and we knew that Sherman had crossed and begun to hammer away at the end of the Ridge Troops were hurried along it to meet him, and Howard was pushed out to the left of Granger to make connection with him when he should drive the enemy back But the enemy did not drive

They held their position across the ridge and Sherman kept on hammering. Then behind us — over beyond the crest of Lookout — we heard the echo of musketry. What did it mean? The soldier soon becomes a strategist. As we lay and listened there was no lack of theorizing. It was the general belief that Bragg had concentrated on Hooker, who we knew had been weakened by taking away Howard's Corps, which was on the left of Granger. We did not know that Osterhaus' Division and two brigades of our own corps in part made up for their absence. Would the enemy succeed in driving Hooker out of the valley? After a little it became apparent that the fire was coming nearer. A white mist, the remnant of the night's storm, still hung about the nose of Lookout. Now and then the wind swept it aside, till we could see the crest, sometimes the palisades below. Anon the white veil would settle over it all and only the rattle of musketry would come out of the sunlit cloud. All at once it flashed upon us that this demonstration against the Ridge in our front was a feint and that Hooker was trying to take the Lookout — was taking it as we were soon assured. After a while faint cheers could be heard. How intently we listened! That's no corn-bread yell! went along the line, as every eye and every field-glass was turned toward the cloud-veiled Mountain. The artillery ceased firing, and the two vast armies of Grant and Bragg in breathless suspense awaited the outcome of the contest which both realized was no feint but a fight to the death. Again and again the "mudsill" cheer rang out, each time nearer the palisaded crest. Soon a faint grey line appeared on the open field on the slope of Lookout. Even with the naked eye, it was apparent that it was disorganized and falling back. Through the smoke and mist, the colors sometimes flashed. The gray masses fell slowly back, and a line of blue appeared. As the crimson of the old flag was recognized, Grant's army broke out into cheer after cheer, which must have been inspiring to Hooker's men and appalling to the enemy.

With scarcely a halt to reform, the line of blue moved forward General Hooker riding his white horse, following close upon the charging column The Confederates, fell slowly back, rallying and breaking again, until with a sudden rush they made for a line of works which seemed extended from the foot of the palisade down the slope between the timber and the open field Here they made a last stand, with a rush our brave fellows swept up to the works, but so stubborn was the resistance that for a moment it seemed to us that the lines and colors were intermingled and the assailants captured But the enemy's colors soon broke to the rear and disappeared in the woods The clouds settled down over the scene and only desultory firing was kept up Until night-fall and even after, a few scattering shots were heard on the slope Then all was still The audacity of the plan and the suddenness of its execution paralyzed the enemy, and amazed those who witnessed its execution.

But few soldiers ever see a battle We heard Chickamauga, but as for seeing it, it might as well have been fought in the dark Thousands of men, on both sides, saw Hooker s battle or all that the mist permitted to be seen. Those with field-glasses could see men drop out of the line, dead or wounded Without a glass one could only distinguish the lines and masses of troops by the gray or blue, and the crimson of the colors That night one of the Thousand wrote by the light of his camp-fire

"It is clear now that Bragg is outgeneraled and our communications cleared At this time 9 p m, the whole side of Lookout is ablaze with camp-fires, and the flashes of the rifles of the pickets show where the lines of the two armies rest

"When the Army recovered from its first feeling of amazement at the audacity of the plan which had been fought out with such dash and courage, enthusiasm was unbounded, and for hours the long lines rang with cheer after cheer which were echoed and re-echoed by Missionary

Ridge and by Lookout, until the whole valley seemed alive with shouting men. We expected to return to camp to-night, but have orders to sleep on our arms. This means a move to-morrow. Most of those who remained in camp have come out to rejoice with us over Hooker's victory above the clouds."

XXII.

MISSIONARY RIDGE.

On the Crest of Lookout.

From a War Time Photograph.

The morning showed the Stars and Stripes floating on the crest of Lookout. The army greeted them with cheers. Then the firing grew hot upon the left, rising and falling in refluent waves. By and by, we were moved past Fort Wood over to the left so as to join with Sherman. An hour after, we were in plain sight of the enemy's forces on Missionary Ridge, and there is no doubt that the moral effect of great bodies of men marching, counter-marching, and forming in line in their front, while a battle raged upon their right, and another impended on the left, had much to do with the victory that came afterwards. Apparently the Confederate position was impregnable to assault. Until Lookout Mountain was carried,

---

ON THE CREST OF LOOKOUT.

COLOR SERGEANT ANDREW GEDDES carried the colors of the 105th in every march and battle in which the regiment engaged, from the time they were

the Confederate soldiery had felt secure. With their dislodgment from that stronghold they lost confidence in the position they held, and our movements in the great amphitheater below magnified our numbers. A man rarely sees the whole of an army, and though the Army of the Cumberland had dwindled before the attack was made to hardly more than twenty thousand men, three times that number had first and last appeared in battle array upon the plain. The effect of fighting a battle on the right and another on the left, with seemingly undiminished numbers still remaining in the center, was to dishearten the Confederate soldiery to such an extent that when the assault came they broke and fled in a manner not less incomprehensible to their officers than to us. "You uns must have had mo'n a million men," said one of the prisoners to the writer. "I seed 'em a-marchin' an' counter-marchin' fer three days an' knowed ther warn't no use in fightin' that many!"

They had, too, the soldier's fear of being flanked. They expected the troops which scaled Lookout the day before would pass to the rear of Missionary Ridge and assail their left flank, and that Sherman would cross to the north side of South Chickamauga Creek and turn their right flank. General Jeff. C. Davis begged that he might be allowed to do this, and it is strange that his request was not granted by Gen. Sherman. Bragg's army would have been little trouble to any one after that day if it had.

Of the nine divisions belonging to the Army of the Cumberland on the field of battle, three were with Sherman and two with Hooker when the signal for the advance was given. Baird's, Wood's, Sheridan's and Johnson's divisions only remained, ranged from left to right in the

[illegible] ... Philadelphia, Pa. The p[illegible] ... from a photograph of him and the co[illegible] ... Lookout Mountain soon after its capture.

order named. There has been much controversy in regard to what the general commanding intended to accomplish when he ordered this assault. His own account of it is not entirely consistent with the impression one gathers from his

MAJOR-GEN. ABSALOM BAIRD.

previous orders. The probability is that it was a sudden inspiration,—a determination to make the move and abide the result—which so often decides not only the fortune of battle but all other human hazards. That he expected to divert so many of the enemy's forces from the right as to enable Sherman to reach his right rear and so end the contest is not unlikely. That he expected these four divisions to scale that shingly crest, four hundred feet high, sharp and steep, surmounted by a continuous line of works and enfiladed by sixty guns, is not within the range of probability. He knew with the unerring instinct of genius that the crisis of the fight had come and threw forward the only force at his hand to precipitate a conclusion.

It was three o'clock in the afternoon when the signal guns were fired on Orchard Knob. A lieutenant of the Thousand, half-disabled by a fall into one of the many ditches that lined our works, which had re-opened an old wound, was left in the camp which was kept by a small guard, and served as a base of supplies for our comrades in arms, to whom the cooks took every day, some part of the rations here prepared. Perhaps he was in command, but the duty was not onerous nor confining. He had never seen a battle before—only bits of battles which had come under his observation from his place in the line. Through the favor of an old commander he procured a horse and leave to serve as a volunteer aide-de-camp. This gave him the range of the field and in consideration of his disability, leave to do pretty much as he chose. During the two preceding days of battle he had been everywhere—watching, inquiring, delighting in the magnificent spectacle. He had been with Sherman on the left and made his way across the creek to meet Hooker's men as they swept down the north slope of Lookout. When the signal came he was on Orchard Knob. As the artillery broke forth in one long roar the whole line of the Army of the Cumberland from left to right sprang up and for a few moments seemed to advance in orderly array toward the works at the foot of the Ridge. When they came in close range they broke into a run. All the time, the enemy's artillery on the crest of the Ridge, was pouring into them a fire which it seemed must annihilate them all. Every one who saw it held his breath in wonder that they still kept on. As they neared the works, a line of smoke burst out on the gray hillside, another, and then we saw the Confederates scrambling up the steep incline towards the upper line of works. Every one drew a breath of relief. The upper works were still a line of flames and the cannon on the ridge still fired incessantly.

COL. WILLIAM R. TOLLES.
(From a Photograph.)

Would our men be able to hold what they had gained? That was the question in every mind. It did not seem possible. While we waited we saw here and there a stand of colors shoot upwards from the works; behind each a straggling wedge-shaped mass of blue! Another, another and another! The whole line was moving! Scrambling, falling, pushing on! First one flag would be in advance, and then another! How beautiful the white and crimson showed against the dull hillside! Now men grew pale as they looked on holding their breath! There seemed no sem-

semblance of order, only struggling crowds fired by a fierce rivalry to outdo each other! Here and there a mounted officer was seen! Up the sloping road which reached the summit just at the left of Bragg's headquarters, we could see through our glasses a man on a black horse riding as leisurely as if the air about him was not full of shells. On, on the wedged-shaped columns pressed while every heart stood still with terror! If they should be repulsed! If the enemy should hurl them back and follow them down the sharp slope! There was no reserve. Between Hooker, whose guns were just opening upon the enemy's left, to Sherman away across Citico on his right there was nothing to resist a counter charge should this be repulsed! Groans and hurried sighs burst forth from the pale, set lips of those who watched—veterans to whom what was being attempted before their eyes was a sheer, incredible, impossible thing!

The lieutenant shut his eyes in dread of what he might see. He beheld his comrades overthrown, hurled back, pursued! He heard a half-incredulous exclamation of surprise! A sigh of relief! He looked again! A flag had reached the crest! Another and another! Almost before they could be counted, in half a dozen places, the Stars and Stripes were planted on the line of red-clay rifle-pits that zig-zagged along the narrow crest! Then a shout went up from every spectator in the mighty amphitheater! Men clasped each other's hands! Clung to each other's necks! Shouted and wept and pointed to the Ridge where the enemy could be seen in hurried flight, while the victors, following hard upon them, sent back to us their cheers, feeble at first for want of breath, but continued and uproarious afterwards. As soon as he could spur across the plain the lieutenant was with his comrades. Knowing their position he had expected to find them decimated at the least. One killed and two wounded was the list of casualties! The God of battles had been kind, marvelously kind, not only to the Thousand, but to all those engaged in this wonderful assault.

How was it that this which seemed impossible was, after all, so easily achieved? Reference has been made to the demoralization among the Confederate soldiery caused by watching for two days an army greater than any of them had ever seen at one time before, maneuver on the plain, while they knew from the roar of battle that another great army was engaged on their flank.

Another thing which has been little considered no doubt contributed to the result. The steepness of the slope, rising out of a flat plain gave the fire of the Confederate artillery a plunging character which greatly diminished its effect, during the charge upon the lower works. When these were taken, both the artillery and rifle fire from the crest went very largely over the heads of our men. Every marksman knows the tendency to over-shoot under such circumstances. Every man that is engaged in the charge is positive that he never faced a hotter fire. No doubt it is true. Those who watched and those who climbed are alike able to testify to its intensity, and only the fact that the fire swept over them because the guns were not sufficiently depressed, can account not merely for the small comparative loss but for the achievement of so apparently impossible an undertaking.

But one who was in the charging line, and who wrote a day or two afterwards, his remembrance of what he saw and felt shall give the story of his experience.

"When the three guns were fired on Orchard Knob, we did not know what they meant and it was a moment before we started. I suppose there must have been some delay in passing the order. However, we got under way as soon as we saw the division on our right charging across the field towards the breastworks at the foot of the Ridge. The rebel skirmishers were soon scattered and fled at a round pace up the slope.

The fire of two batteries was concentrated on us and the shells burst thick and fast about us. Several had struck near but no one was harmed as yet. Across the wide field

enemy. Officers rode to and fro frantic almost seeking to restore order, fearful of the consequences The wave of men, drunk with the frenzy of battle, rolled and tumbled up the hill I glanced for a minute beyond our line, or our crowd rather, and saw *the old flag* on the crest of the next hill beyond As far as eye could reach the line of blue showed that while we had been watching the battle nearest us, the whole right moved by the same impulse, were sweeping up the slope Turning again I saw the men, who a moment before, were on the slope, now almost at the crest, and moving slowly and painfully, as if out of breath, but still going up The colors of different regiments, vied with each other for the advance. One brave color-bearer pushed on by painful steps, stopping now and then behind a tree for breath until he reached the rebel works The enemy's flag was waving there defiantly, but he planted ours beside it and the other flag went down Then other colors came up, and were planted on the works The enemy fled in wild confusion, and blue and gray covered the hill, pursuers and pursued The enemy were already leaving the point we hoped to gain Their artillery, four pieces, was taken, and a new section sent to reinforce it, was captured before it had unlimbered

Lieutenant Allen, who had been a sergeant in Parson's battery got some men together and turned these guns on the fleeing enemy

The first line was forming when we reached the top Colonel Gleason of the 87th waved his long arm and said, "Forward, my brave boys," but too slow for our Colonel Tolles, who, in his shrill voice, commanded, "'Tion, tallion! Der-hup! For'd, double quick—hup!" and the 105th became the first line of the brigade following the enemy Soon the gallant old 9th Ohio came up and halting we fired at the enemy who had been engaged with Sherman now turning on us, and in a few moments we had swept the Ridge

That day was the climax of the Colonel's life. Never before had his coolness and courage shone so clear. Unable because of weakness to breast the hillside with his men, he followed a road a little to our right, keeping even with our advance and cheering them by his words and his example. His horse seemed to know the importance of the occasion, too. Usually so full of fire, he was staid and quiet as if he knew the significance of the great conflict going on around him.

In our fight upon the crest, where we were saved from severe loss chiefly by a little depression over which we fired lying down, the Colonel stood by his horse, his hand upon the bridle, watching the fight. One of the line officers, too much excited to lie still, rose to his feet and waved his sword.

"Lie down!" commanded the Colonel.

"But, Colonel, you——" was the hesitating reply.

"It is my duty to stand," was the sharp reply, "and your duty to lie down!"

How it was I do not know. It seemed as if the fire, even at Perryville, where we lost one third of our number in thirty minutes, was hardly fiercer than we faced here; yet, when we came to sum up the casualties in the whole brigade, but four were killed and only a dozen or so wounded.

It was dusk when the red field was won and the firing ceased. The joy of the men was beyond words. They walked about, taking each other by the hand, or if a cheer was started anywhere, catching it up and sending it on with a will. In this language, which is beyond *words*, the gratitude of the army found voice. The wounded lifted weak hands and voices to shout for victory, and men whose life-blood was ebbing fast as they lay on the field thanked God that the day was won, and died. Night deepened and the troops prepared to sleep in the camp of the enemy. Thousands of fires were lighted on the hill, groups earnestly discussing the chances and glory of the day and the virtues and valor of the gallant dead, and the tone of thankful joy grew deeper as one after another brought good news of victory. Ten, twenty, thirty, forty-five and at last sixty, pieces of artillery were reported to be captured, and ten thousand prisoners, beside the wounded. Could the enemy ever recover from such a blow? Would they ever again boast over the Chickamauga victory? In the far Northern homes, we knew our friends would gather for the Thanksgiving feast upon the morrow. What a Thanksgiving they would have if they knew how we had swept away Bragg's army!

within the city was being heaped up the wreckage of the great battle. Thousands of stands of arms, some broken, some complete, piled up like cordwood in some convenient place, were being counted over and checked off by the officers and employees of the ordnance corps. Sherman had already hurried up the river to the relief of Burnside. The stars and stripes floated above Lookout, and day by day streams of blue clad onlookers climbed up the laddered palisade, to look over the scene of conflict, and wonder how the result had been attained. River and trains were being crowded to their utmost capacity to bring supplies, not merely for the present needs of the army, but in order to accumulate enough for the campaign which the spring must bring and of which Chattanooga must be the point of supply. For two months the regiment lay in Chattanooga in the very vortex of that wonderful storm of preparation which the amazing, intellectual activity of General Grant had set in motion.

That was a memorable campaign of preparation which intervened between the fall campaign of 1863 and the spring campaign of 1864, in and about Chattanooga. One can hardly realize its character until he comprehends the fact that all the vast resources of the Northwest were concentrated upon the accumulation at that point, of supplies of every sort and character. Arms, ammunition, food, clothing, transportation, horses, mules, cattle, tents,—everything that an army could need—were hurried forward with a profusion and lavishness quite incredible to one who has never witnessed the concentrated abundance which war provides for its great engines of destruction, the armies it employs. The railroads running from Louisville to Nashville, and from Nashville on to Chattanooga, were crowded to their utmost capacity. Almost every hour during the few days he remained at Chattanooga General Grant was demanding and compelling an increase in the number of cars handled by those roads every twenty-four hours. Two great rivers mberland and the Tennessee, were crowded with flotillas, ng forage and stores to Nashville, and establishing ed depots all the way from that point to the Tennessee. meantime an army of civil employees, numbering at one more than 8,000 men, were gathered at Chattanooga, dgeport, in the Trenton Valley, running saw-mills, g charcoal, working forges, building immense machine spanning the river with a permanent bridge, buildew railroads from the Cumberland to the Tennessee, new tracks, putting up telegraph wires, accumulating bridge material and extra engines — doing everything that military skill could suggest and the unbounded resources of a great empire supply, to make the army of Sherman when it should set forth on its spring campaign the most perfect of military engines. So, while the game of war was still, save for a battle Burnside was fighting up the river, the work of preparation went on and the Gibraltar of the Confederacy was transformed into the

ergt. George D. Elder.

perfectly equipped base of operations which ederal army of the West ever had. Chattanooga e a hive of industry, the hum of whose labors ceased by night or day; for war was not only

[illegible] Dwight Elder, Co. E. It has been impossible to get any [illegible] in regard to Sergt. Elder beyond what appears in the tables, the fact that he has for several years been a resident of Mecklen-

preparing for much greater feats of arms, but was also laying the foundation of an industrial empire, which should be the boast of the very people then in arms against the union. A month, two months and order began to evolve itself out of confusion. Abundance reigned where want had been so severe. There was no lack of tents or clothing. The little mud huts of the siege gave way to the most perfect tentage. Horses grew sleek and fat. Defective wagons were discarded. Teamsters began to boast again of their mules and equipments. Sutlers abounded. Substantial luxuries were to be had for a price—the price itself was lavishly abundant. Greenbacks were as water almost. A great army cannot long remain at rest without offering food to the speculator and prey to the gambler. Fortunately for our army, Chattanooga was an empty house. Of the few inhabitants nearly all had departed, and there was not time to establish there the corruption that contaminates an army encamped near a large city.

With the early days of spring, the great leviathan began to show signs of life. Sherman had returned from up the river. The rejuvenated army began to spread its tentacles. The cavalry with fresh horses and abundant forage grew restless and began to feel the enemy in front and on our flanks. There was news of raids and scouts. The army had stretched along the road by which we had fought in the fall, past the old battlefield of Chickamauga and on to Lafayette, which had been Rosecrans' absurd objective. Camps were scattered all up and down the valley of the Tennessee, above and below Chattanooga, and on the slopes of Missionary Ridge. The winter was one of extreme cold and only the quietude which prevailed through the cessation of active operations saved the troops on both sides from most intense suffering. It was still winter, with only a hint of coming spring in the air, when the great army began to unfold itself and develop the plan of its advance.

There were two methods of advance possible to the Federal Army from Chattanooga. One was that favored by Thomas of a main advance upon Rome, Georgia by way of Lafayette and parallel roads with a strong, co-operative movement from the Tennessee about Caperton's and the region below advancing into the valley of the Coosa, leaving a sufficient force at and about Chattanooga to prevent a possible turning of the left flank or interference with the depot of supplies. This force would also demonstrate, in conjunction with the main movement against the enemy, in the direction of Ringgold and along the Chattanooga and Atlanta railway advancing as the enemy retired or falling back to Chattanooga should they be attacked by an overwhelming force. By this plan, the main attack was to be made in the direction of Rome, Ga., while the advance along the railroad toward Ringgold and Resaca was to be in the nature of a feint. The strategy adopted, exactly reversed this, the real movement being by the left flank and the feint upon the right.

Till the last moment of his life, it is well known that the Hero of Chickamauga insisted that the Chattanooga-Atlanta campaign was a costly, hazardous and unnecessarily prolonged method of accomplishing an inevitable result, of reaching an already foregone conclusion. Within five days after the beginning of the forward movement, he insisted that the Army of the Cumberland should have been in Rome, to be joined within three days by the force advancing from Caperton's. During this movement he claimed that General Johnston would have been unable to deliver a hindering, not to say a damaging blow upon the flank of his army, or even to attack it in any force without surrendering the line of railroad from Chattanooga to Kingston; that once established in the valley of the Coosa the enemy would be obliged to surrender without contest the Chattanooga road, which would become at once a line of supply, while our right would rest in the most productive and least depleted region of the South, northern and middle Alabama—threatening Montgomery, Mobile and the one remaining line of railroad that still united Richmond with the southwest.

Instead of making Atlanta the objective of the summer campaign, advancing on it through a region offering unparalleled resources for a defensive campaign, he would have turned it by advancing along good and safe roads, following the natural conformation of the terraine, and either intervened between the enemy and his base or forced him to surrender the line from Ringgold to Kingston, on which depended all hope of an offensive movement against our left or any diversion into East Tennessee

General Thomas' advocacy of this strategic method for the campaign of 1864 was, as he personally informed the writer, based upon the following specific considerations

1 —That the Army of the Cumberland alone was amply capable of maintaining itself against any offensive movement of the Confederate Army in its front.

2 —That two corps might be added to it in the Valley of the Coosa, without exposing Chattanooga or our left to even a possible successful attack

3 —That seven days were sufficient to effect a concentration at Rome and compel the enemy to concentrate at Kingston or fall back on Atlanta

4 —This movement would put our army in position to elect its future course with absolute certainty of taking the enemy at a disadvantage.

5 —That the enemy would have been compelled to abandon Atlanta by the first of June, by the cutting of the southwest lines, rendering it strategically unimportant

6 —That the two months of hard fighting that intervened between Ringgold and the Chattahoochie were due not so much to the skill of the enemy as to fear of a military maxim to the effect that it is perilous to divide an army in the presence of an enemy This maxim, he insisted, had no application when one part of the army so divided was able of itself to cope with the whole force of the enemy, and the other part was able to fall back upon a fortified point which could only be taken by regular siege

This opinion that the right wing should be the flank of serious attack and the left merely feint upon the enemy's works was maintained by General Thomas throughout the whole campaign against Atlanta and is believed by many to have been fully justified by results. It is well known that General Grant favored Mobile as a preferential objective, which implied a similar line of operations. But it is what was done rather than what might have been done which concerns "The Story of a Thousand," though there is, perhaps, not one of them left surviving who does not believe that if their old commander's plan had been pursued the collapse of the Confederacy would have occurred fully six months before it did, simply because the utter hopelessness of further resistance would have been much sooner apparent.

By the first of May the army, stripped of all superfluity, was ready to move. Every defective man and horse had been sent to the rear. Every tent, save one for each Division General and some flies for brigade and regimental commanders, had been added to the immense stores which filled the great warehouses of Chattanooga. No soldier was allowed an ounce of superfluous weight, and the officers' baggage was reduced to the lowest possible amount consistent with the transportation of company and regimental records. The soft southern spring-time, delayed by the unusual winter, had come swift and redolent. The red clay roads were dry and hard.

For two months the "Thousand" had been at the front, near Ringgold. Every fourth day it was upon outpost duty. On the 29th of April the Division, now the third, with General Baird in command, moved forward, driving in the enemy's pickets. Then there came a lull; the 30th we waited in camp, also the first of May. At dawn upon the second we again advanced, and the battle-summer had begun.

The Military Division of the Mississippi embraced the following armies, which constituted the force under General Sherman's command during this campaign

The Army of the Ohio Major-General John M Schofield, consisting of the Ninth and Twenty-third corps. Of these the former returned to the Army of the Potomac and two divisions of the latter took the field with Sherman leaving three to garrison East Tennessee and Kentucky The two divisions that took the field were commanded by Brigadier-General Miles S Hascall and Jacob D Cox.

The army of the Cumberland, Major-General George H Thomas, consisted of the Fourth, Fourteenth and Twentieth corps, commanded respectively by Major-Generals. O O Howard, John M Palmer and Joseph Hooker.

The Army of the Tennessee under Major-General McPherson, comprised the Fifteenth and portions of the Sixteenth and Seventeenth corps, under Major-Generals, John A Logan, George M Dodge, and Frank P Blair.

The Cavalry consisted of McCook's division of the Army of the Ohio, Garrard's division of the Army of the Cumberland and Edward McCook's brigade of the Army of the Tennessee

The Thousand was a part of the Second Brigade of the Third division of the Fourteenth Army corps which was composed of the following organizations

THIRD DIVISION

Brigadier-General Absalom Baird

FIRST BRIGADE.

Brig -Gen John B. Turchin.
Col Moses B Walker
19th Illinois, Lieut -Col. Alexander W. Raffen
24th Illinois, Capt. August Mauff
82d Indiana, Col Morton C Hunter
23d Missouri, Col William P. Robinson
11th Ohio, Lieut -Col Ogden Street.
17th Ohio Col Durbin Ward

31st Ohio { Col. Moses B. Walker
Lieut.-Col. Fredrick W. Lister

89th Ohio { Maj. John H. Jolly
Col. Caleb H. Carlton

92d Ohio, Col. Benjamin D. Fearing

SECOND BRIGADE

Col. Ferdinand Van Derveer,

Col. Newell Gleason

75th Indiana { Lieut.-Col. William O'Brien
Maj. Cyrus J. McCole

87th Indiana { Col. Newell Gleason
Lieut.-Col. Edwin P. Hammond

101st Indiana, Lieut.-Col. Thomas Doan

2d Minnesota { Col. James George
Lieut.-Col. Judson W. Bishop

9th Ohio, Col. Gustave Kammerling

35th Ohio, Maj. Joseph L. Budd

105th Ohio, Lieut.-Col. George T. Perkins

THIRD BRIGADE

Col. George P. Este

10th Indiana, Lieut.-Col. Marsh B. Taylor

74th Indiana { Lieut.-Col. Myron Baker
Maj. Thomas Morgan

10th Kentucky, Col. William H. Hays

18th Kentucky, Lieut.-Col. Hubbard K. Milward

14th Ohio { Maj. John W. Wilson
Capt. George W. Kirk

38th Ohio { Capt. William A. Choate
Capt. Joseph Wagstaff

ARTILLERY

Capt. George Estep

Indiana Light, 7th Battery, Capt. Otho H. Morgan

Indiana Light, 19th Battery, Lieut. Wm. P. Stackhouse

XXIV.

THE BATTLE SUMMER.

THE Confederate General, J. B. Hood, in his book entitled "Advance and Retreat," characterizes the Chattanooga-Atlanta campaign as one conducted by an army of over seventy thousand men, constantly retiring over "a distance of one hundred miles, from Dalton to Atlanta, with a loss of twenty-two thousand five hundred men, which *presents no action* rising to the dignity of a great battle."

This is undoubtedly correct; yet it is also true, that in the whole history of war there is hardly to be found an instance in which two armies so evenly matched, so long confronted each other with constant skirmishes, rising almost every day to the dignity of serious engagement on some part of their lines. Speaking of a part of this period, General Absalom Baird, commanding the Third Division of the Army of the Cumberland, of which the Thousand was a part, said: "My loss during this period (six days) amounted on an average to about twenty men a day." For four months there was hardly a day in which some part of the line was not engaged, and, in summing up his impression of the whole exhausting campaign, General Baird impressively says:

"The quiet and heroic patience with which all has been undergone and duty performed, whilst establishing for them the highest reputation as soldiers, will tend to cause their hardships to be forgotten. Starting without transportation and with only supplies for an expedition of three or six

the Cumberland, the Army of the Tennessee, and the Army of the Ohio in the field, under command of General Sherman, at the same time was 94,131 Both armies were excellently equipped though the Federal forces were often short of rations, by reason of the difficulty of transportation along the rough mountain roads of the region in which their operations were conducted The discrepancy in numbers was fully compensated by the advantages offered to an army acting on the defensive by the transverse ranges of precipitous hills, across which the Federal army was compelled to advance Forced out of one position by day, the enemy had only to retire to a parallel ridge, equally difficult to be carried at night On the 7th day of May the two armies confronted each other at Rocky-faced Ridge, a sheer wall of granite which no army could surmount, and which required for its defense only the holding of two gaps, Mill Creek and Snake Creek By some strange oversight, the latter was unguarded, and Thomas, who desired to take his whole army through it and fall upon the enemy's rear, was denied, and McPherson sent instead, with a force only sufficient to cause the enemy to withdraw. So the Thousand escaped the shock of battle, only waiting under fire their turn to join the strange procession which filed through the mountain passes on the long toilsome way to Atlanta

One cannot but wonder what would have been the outcome of this campaign had Hood's plan rather than that of General Joseph E Johnston been adopted by the Confederate Army of Tennessee It is nowhere elaborated, but from the hints General Hood gives, and which are confirmed by many incidental allusions on the part of others, it seems that President Davis and General Lee were anxious that the Army of Tennessee, with Polk's Army of Mississippi should be united with Longstreet's corps of the Army of Virginia, and make an offensive movement around the Federal left wing, before our advance from Chattanooga. Such movement falling on Burnside in East Tennessee and at the same time coming by the lower gaps of the Cumberland plateau into Central Tennessee and Kentucky would have been a repetition of the strategy of 1862 upon the part of the Confederates with apparently equal prospect of success. That it was contemplated and approved by such generals as Lee and Longstreet, and that the impetuous Hood left the Army of Virginia in the hope of commanding one wing of the Army of Tennessee in such a campaign shows how sound and brilliant was the strategy which General E. Kirby Smith induced Bragg to adopt two years before.

But even if there was no great battle in the campaign from Dalton to Atlanta, it presented perhaps more days of steady continuous fighting than any other campaign of the war. Every day there was fighting, entrenching or change of position in close touch of the enemy. Almost all the way from Dalton to Atlanta both armies were carefully entrenched at the points of immediate contact. These entrenchments were not of a light and superficial character but solid substantial works, often four or five feet high and from six to ten feet in width at the base. The troops acquired great skill in the erection of these works. General O. O. Howard says of the work of Baird's division at Pine Mountain: "Just where the old lines joined the new (for Johnston's right wing was unchanged) I saw a feat the like of which never elsewhere fell under my observation. Baird's Division, in a comparatively open field, put forth a heavy skirmish line, which continued such a rapid fire of rifles as to keep down a corresponding hostile line behind its well-constructed works, while the picks and shovels behind the skirmishers fairly flew, till a good set of works was made four hundred yards off and parallel to the enemy's.

There were some notable days and notable names added to the Roll of Honor of the Thousand during this campaign.

RESACA.—May 14th and 15th. In this battle the Second Brigade of the Third Division under Colonel Van Derveer was on the left, the First under General Turchin on the right, both in two lines. We moved up the steep ridge under a galling artillery fire taking and holding a position which compelled the enemy to fall back during the night.

SERGT. J. A. MCNAUGHTON.

KENESAW MOUNTAIN.—June 10 to 26, inclusive. The Confederates occupied Kenesaw, Lost and Pine Mountains, which formed an irregular triangle in our front. The Burnt Hickory and Marietta Pike was our road to the north end of Kenesaw. On the 10th The Army of the Cumberland was before Pine Mountain; McPherson on our left lay around the foot of Kenesaw, and Schofield on the right, faced Lost Mountain. Our object was to gain the road that ran between these peaks to Marietta. It seemed impossible to dislodge the enemy from the magnificent lines of works which lined the mountain slope. During this time we built three heavy lines of works, each nearer the enemy, and compelling some reformation of his line. There was

JAMES A. MCNAUGHTON was born in Montville, Ohio, Sept. 16th, 1842. Enlisted as a private in Co. E, rose to the grade of Sergeant; was mustered out with the regiment, and died at Chardon, Ohio, Sept. 4, 1894.

balls was not heard on some part of our line. On , the Confederate general, Leonidas Polk, was killed t of our division. He was usually called the Bish eral, being Bishop of Tennessee when the war br

On the 18th we had gained Pine Mountain nced against a new line of works behind Mud Cr he 19th the enemy fell back on Kenesaw Mountain followed in line of battle as on the days previ s' Division of the Confederates, whom we had me ver's Gap and Chickamauga, was in our front. Aft p skirmish we took position at the base of ntain, near Kirk's House. Here we lay for six d r constant fire of the enemy's artillery on the moun e us, and constantly skirmishing with his entrenc ets in our front. The history of the war has noth romantic than this continuous bombardment from tant mountains that lay in our front.

An assault of Little Kenesaw by the troops of y of the Tennessee, and of a point about a mile so t, by the army of the Cumberland, were ordered to e simultaneously on the 27th of June. Newt sion of the Fourth Army Corps, and Davis' of rteenth were chosen by General Thomas to consti column of assault on Kenesaw. The Third Divis d, was ordered to support Davis. In accordance w order we left our position in the line at ten o'clock t of the 26th, Sunday, marched three miles to t and took position in the right rear of Davis' Divis upport it on that flank. The assaults were m ltaneously as had been ordered. Newton's and Da sions moved on the enemy's works over ground so st f itself to constitute an almost impregnable positi ned with works which made the attempt absolut less. Yet some men of both these divisions reac

ır gallant comrades as they charged up the scraggly slope hich no force could successfully assail in the face of the iemy s fiie Fifteen hundred and eighty was the entire ss of Davis' division, nearly one-third the strength of the ssaulting column McPherson's attack also failed but his ss was less, a little more than a thousand The enemy's ss was very trivial, he being protected by elaborate orks. On this day Colonel Van Derveer was relieved from mmand of our brigade, on account of sickness, Colonel ewell Gleason, of the Eighty-Second Indiana succeeding m, who retained command until the close of the war. olonel Van Derveer was an accomplished officer and very pular with the Brigade Colonel Gleason proved a most ficient successor. Because of the unusual length of his ms, he was jocularly known in the brigade as "Old ongarm

After the assault we kept on digging and fighting. here was an armistice from one o'clock until eight o clock, m, on the 29th, for the purpose of burying the dead lled on the 27th Then the fight began again, and we orked our way closer and closer to the Confederate trenchments until, in some places the lines were not more an thirty yards apart. A head or a hand that showed ove the works was sure to bring a shot A hat hung on ramrod and raised over the parapet would always get one id sometimes three or four bullets through it We lived the trenches and were saved from greater loss by the ibstantial character of our works On the night of the l of July, McPherson marched in our rear to the right of hofield s army. By this movement the left wing of ohnston's army was endangered and he withdrew from his osition. On the morning of the 2d of July our division itered the enemy's works in our front capturing a considable number of prisoners. During the day we passed rough Marietta, Georgia, and on the fourth day, our igade was detached and ordered to return and garrison e town It remained here eight days, the only breathing ell it had in all the long and hot campaign

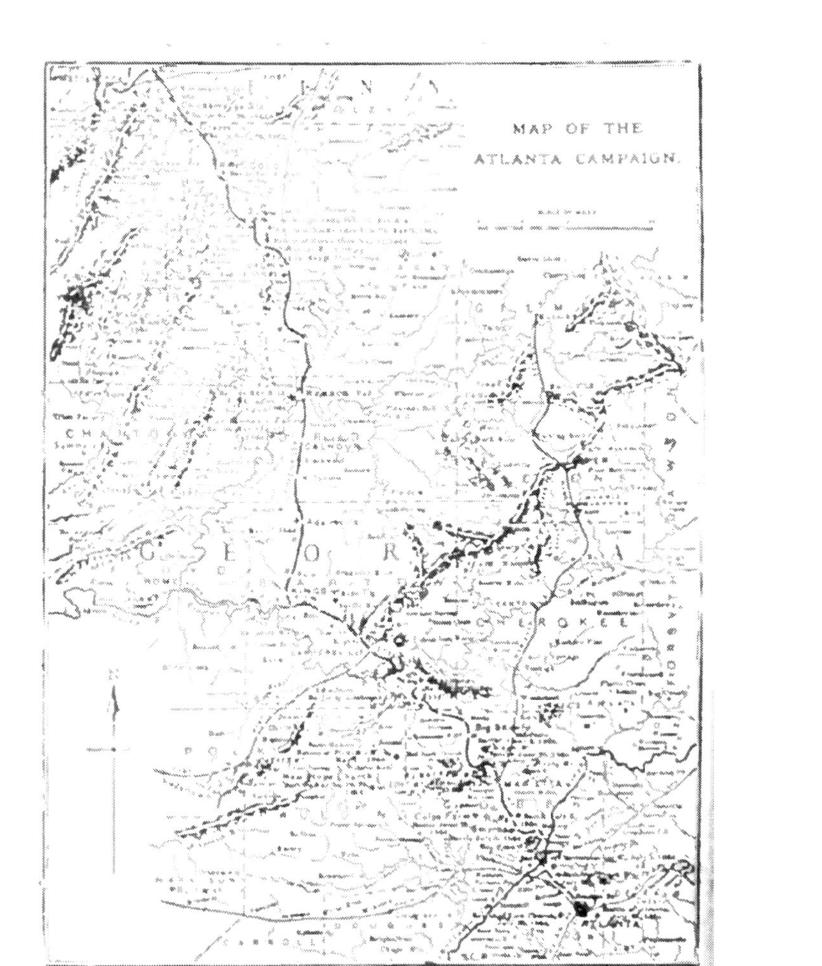

little. It slept tonight where the enemy had camped the

Sometimes it was one flank that advanced, sometimes the other, but it was always a forward movement of the Union Army and a backward movement of the Confederates Much has been written in praise of the Fabian caution of the Confederate commander, but the real reason for this continued and unvarying success is to be found in the amazing alertness and unflagging activity of General William T Sherman No man could have been better fitted for the work he had in hand Whatever error there may have been in the grand strategy of the campaign nothing could have been more perfect than its conduct He seemed to forget nothing, to neglect nothing, to foresee everything. From wing to wing, he was always present in spirit, inspiring watchfulness and permitting his enemy to have no respite An infinitude of detail, instead of wearying, seemed to stimulate him to renewed activity Every department felt his oversight and every detachment was conscious that he had a special oversight of their conduct and effectiveness As evidence of this, the following order addressed to the commanding officer of our brigade while detached at Marietta may be given

"COMMANDING OFFICER, Marietta, Ga

I have ordered three regiments at Marietta and a brigade at Kenesaw This brigade will come to Marietta in case of danger to the depot but Kenesaw is selected on account of its security and proximity, and troops are more easily disciplined in camp than in a town Although you are chiefly needed as a town guard and to handle stores, you should not neglect the military duties Always be prepared for a dash of cavalry Occupy the Court House, and barricade and loophole the doors and windows also make a good ladder to the roof, and make the balustrade bullet-proof so that a party of men on its roof can sweep the streets Other houses should be selected and prepared near the railroad depot A few hours' work will convert any good brick or stone house into a citadel Arms and ammunition should always be kept handy, and pickets kept well out to give notice All citizens of whom you entertain the least suspicion should be sent North, no matter the seeming hardships The safety of our depot must not depend upon the pleasure and convenience of citizens. Should any one be caught molesting our road, telegraph wires or our stores, he should be disposed of finally and summarily, especially if disguised in the garb of a citizen.

W. T. SHERMAN,
Major General Commanding.

That an officer in command of an army of a hundred thousand men should give such attention to minute details is altogether wonderful, but it is only one instance of the all-pervading watchfulness of General Sherman. His antagonist made no successful forward movement simply because, after the first unimproved opportunity at Resaca, he found no chance to strike a blow without exposing himself to a crushing counter-stroke.

THE SIEGE OF ATLANTA began with the crossing of the Chattahoochie River. The city was of importance simply because of the railroads that ran through it. It was the heart of the railway system of the Confederacy since the loss of Chattanooga. Eastward the Georgia Railroad ran through Decatur to Milledgeville, Augusta and Savannah, intersecting on its way the two north and south lines of the Atlantic slope. Southwardly through Jonesborough ran the Macon and Western road, giving an opening to the southeast; and westwardly, at an average distance of five miles south of the Chattahoochie River, ran the Atlanta and West Point road, giving connection with Mobile, Montgomery and the southwest generally.

The city stands on an irregular group of hills, sloping in every direction, cut with numerous waterways and sharp irregular declivities. These were mostly covered with close scrub oak, except where the same had been cut away to give range to the guns mounted in the works erected on every commanding position. Five miles to the northward runs the Chattahoochie, flowing from northeast to southwest, almost perpendicular to our line of approach.

General Sherman's first line of approach was from the north side of the city, being intended to cut the Georgia railroad as well as to prevent irruptions on his line of supply, the railway to Chattanooga. General Thomas was opposed to this method of investment for the very reason which afterwards caused its abandonment. Our army crossed over on pontoons at various points, between the 16th and 20th of July. On the latter day, our division forded Peach Tree Creek and took position on a range of heavy wooded hills to the south of it. Our line extended at that time, to and across the Georgia Railroad. In the afternoon of the 20th, General Hood, who had succeeded Johnston, made a furious attack on the troops at our left, the Fourth and Twentieth corps and the first division of our corps. Failing in this, the enemy fell back to his interior line of works on the hills directly surrounding the city. This was the battle of Peach Tree Creek, perhaps the most important engagement except one, that occurred during the investment of the city.

The position to which the enemy retired was a range of hills about two miles from the city, thoroughly fortified long before, and practically impregnable, covering all the roads entering Atlanta from the North and East. On the 22d we moved to the right and took position at the intersection of the Atlanta and Turner's Ferry road due west of the city. Here we heavily entrenched while the roar of battle came to us from the eastward. On that day was fought what is known as the Battle of Atlanta, in which General McPherson was killed, and the army of the Tennessee lost more than 3,000 men. We held this position until August 3d, being every day subjected to the fiercest cannonading. On the 27th of July the army of the Tennessee moved from the left to our right and were attacked in their new position by Lee's and Hardee's corps of Hood's Army. Though the attack fell mainly on them, the fire along our front was very sharp. This was the battle of Ezra Church. As the battle of Peach Tree Creek had been the hottest just at our left, so that of Ezra Church had its zenith just at our right, both left our division almost unscathed.

On the 3d of August the Fourteenth corps swung over to the extreme right and took position at the mouth of Utoy creek. On the 4th our brigade advanced against the enemy's lines, captured two lines of picket entrenchments, and developed the enemy's position on that part of the field. On the 5th our whole division assaulted the enemy's lines, captured two lines of rifle-pits and threw up entrenchments near the enemy's works. In this assault, the Thousand under Major Edwards constituted the second line of skirmishers. One hundred and sixty prisoners were taken and the loss in the division was about one hundred. "Not being supported on the right or left," says General Thomas in his report, "General Baird withdrew to his former position." From the fifth of August until the twenty-sixth, the Thousand occupied substantially the same position in front of the enemy's works.

The following extracts from the diary of Captain H. H. Cummings give a vivid impression of the daily life of the regiment during the siege:

Friday, August 5, 1864.—This morning we again moved out in the same trim as last night, our regiment detailed to support the skirmish line. After advancing a short distance, perhaps one third of a mile, to the right, we halted and lay down on the rear slope of a low hill 150 yards in rear of the skirmish line, which had crept up to within 150 yards of the rebel skirmish line (an easy matter on account of the thick undergrowth) and had taken such cover as they could. When all was ready a bugle sounded the advance, our skirmishers raised a yell, the enemy let loose a volley cutting the undergrowth wonderfully but otherwise harmless; immediately our men sprang to their feet and rushed forward. In three minutes the rebel rifle-pits were ours and our division was better off by 250 prisoners and with slight loss. In our regimental front alone sixty prisoners were taken in out of the wet. Valle of Co. C, a fine soldier and a reliable, worthy man, rushed up to a pit full of rebels, seized a lieutenant and claimed him as his prisoner. He was immediately shot through the upper portion of the breast by another rebel. He lived but a short time.

We halted near the rebel rifle pits and dug a rifle trench. We had scarcely secured tolerable protection when the enemy opened a very heavy artillery fire upon us from several batteries. The air was full of flying shell and spherical case. I think I have never before experienced so hot a shelling but we lay close and no one was hurt. After the shelling ceased we strengthened our works.

Sunday, August 7, 1864.—To-day our skirmish line was advanced. There was a demonstration along our entire line, for the purpose, I understand, of making a diversion in favor of Schofield who is swinging around to the right.

LIEUT. JAMES CRAYS.

About ten o'clock the line was advanced; at once hot firing, both infantry and artillery opened along the line. We lay down behind our works. The skirmish line in front advanced to within 30 yards of the enemy's rifle pits and halted and shortly fell back.

Sharp firing continued until nearly night; still we had but two men of our detail wounded. This evening there was another spurt of picket firing, which routed us all out, but amounted to nothing. The lines are so close that the

JAMES CRAYS was born in Mahoning Co., O., Oct. 8, 1841, of Scotch-Irish parentage. Lived on a farm until the age of 17, when he entered the drug store of Dr. John Manning in Youngstown, O. Education obtained at district schools,

enemy's balls fly over us constantly, in cases of unusual firing making it decidedly warm, although as the ground descends to the rear from our works they cannot get down very low.

Monday, August 8, 1864.—This morning we moved our line forward about hundred yards to support the 19th Indiana battery which is throwing up a work in front of the left of our regiment and also to conform to the line of the 1st brigade on our right which is also thrown forward. We built very strong works and put up an abattis of sharpened stakes in front. We were now in plain sight and within 700 yards of the enemy's main line. His skirmishers cannot be more than 150 yards distant.

The ground rises from our works to the rear, hence they are no protection to us when a little in rear of our line. I took the precaution in pitching my tent, which is well to the rear and wholly unprotected, to build a pile of logs two feet high in front of my tent.

Tuesday, August 9, 1864.—As I was passing Co. C, going to my breakfast this morning a ball came in striking Larry Kelly of that company as he sat over a fire cooking his breakfast. It entered near his collar bone, passing down, inflicting a mortal wound. Everyone in the regiment knew Larry. His dog, too, had long been a fixture of the regiment. When leaving Louisville, Ky., on the Perryville campaign this dog came bounding to our (Parsons') battery. He immediately enlisted for the war, attaching himself to the battery and to the gun to which Larry belonged. He made it his business to look after the interests of the battery in general and that gun in particular. He distinguished himself by his strict watchfulness over all the property of the battery when strangers were about, and his excellent judgment in determining who were proper characters to have around. At Perryville he shared in the dangers and glory of the occasion and received a wound. When the battery was broken up and Larry returned to the

Hines Academy and Westminster College. He enlisted in the 107th July [illegible], 1862 and was appointed Fifth Sergeant of Co. A when the company was organized, promoted to Orderly Sergeant, commissioned Second Lieutenant but not mustered, commissioned First Lieutenant and mustered, taking old Co. [illegible] He had command of Co. C the last seven months of the war, the only commissioned officer present with the company during that time; was with the regiment in all its engagements and marches; mustered out with the regiment at Washington, D. C. He has been in the [illegible] business ever since, and now resides in Minneapolis, Minn.

regiment, Watch (this dog) accompanied him and has ever since followed this regiment faithfully, always ready "for duty" always in the front, joining in the sports of the regiment with zest knowing, by instinct apparently, when a pig was to be 'foraged' and following on to catch the "game" and receive his share of the prize

Last night, while scouting about our picket line he received a wound which proved mortal Larry was almost inconsolable but he had not long to mourn his constant companion This morning a stray shot, such as killed his dog hit him and gave him a mortal wound

A little later another shot passed through several tents and struck John Fuller of my company in the head, killing him instantly The day passed quietly in every respect except for the balls flying through our camp

Wednesday, August 10, 1864 —On picket This day passed much as picket days in this region do I went on the line at 2 o clock, A M, came off at 10 A M The enemy did not fire much One shot wounded Ed R Cowles of Co G, slightly, grazing his forehead This afternoon we advanced the line considerably, to the edge of the wood in front We found two bodies, one a rebel, the other a Union soldier belonging to the 38th Ohio The whole movement was managed quietly and successfully, relieved about 6 o'clock, P M.

On the 6th of August, General John M Palmer who had commanded the Fourteenth Corps, was relieved at his own request, and succeeded by Brigadier General Richard W. Johnson, who had been in command of the First Division of our corps On the 7th an advance was made of the skirmish line along the whole right wing under cover of heavy cannonading From this time until the 25th the division occupied practically the same position, constantly under fire both of the enemy's skirmishers and artillery

On the 26th of August, General Sherman adopted the course General Thomas had urged immediately after the battle of Peach Tree Creek, a month before Cutting away from his line of supply, the railroad leading north to Chattanooga, he swung his whole army around to the right to destroy the West Point and Macon Railroads, which had already been temporarily cut some distance below by our cavalry, but not to an extent to disable them permanently from use by the enemy. In carrying out this movement we withdrew from our position under a heavy fire on the 26th, moved to the right two or three miles, swung round across the West Point Railroad and took a position facing north. Here we entrenched and destroyed the railroad in the most approved manner. In this work we had already become experts, but were yet to grow more proficient in that long march during which it was to be a chief part of our duty for months. For its most successful performance the force engaged was always divided into three bodies with separate and distinct duties. The first marched in single file along the side of the track to be torn up, until each man stood at the end of a tie. Then, at the word of command, each stooped, took hold of the tie, and, at another word, the whole track was lifted up and overturned. Then this party marched on and renewed the movement. The second party heaped up the ties upon the track, laid the rails across them, leaving the ends extending on each side, and set the ties on fire. The third party, coming up later, took the rails, then red hot in the middle, twisted them about trees or otherwise bent and distorted them so that no rolling-mill could straighten them, wholly destroying the road for use until new ties and new rails should be supplied.

On the 31st of August, our division, advancing in column of attack, seized the Macon and Western Railroad south of Rough and Ready, and on the 1st of September turned south and advanced in line of battle on Jonesborough. On the afternoon of this day, having pressed back the enemy's pickets so as to develop his line of works about Jonesborough, the division was formed in two lines by brigades, and the brigades in two lines by regiments, and advanced to the assault of the enemy's works. Este's and Gleason's brigades composed the left column of assault, Este in front, and our brigade in support. The signal was given at 4:45 P.M. Este's men dashed off with a wild cheer, carrying everything before them. We followed in close supporting distance There was no need They swept the enemy's works, capturing 426 prisoners including 55 officers The brigade numbered 1 139 men and lost in half an hour in killed and wounded 330, or more than 30 per cent of the whole number The Confederates in our front were Lewis' and Govan's brigades of Hardee's Corps The charge was one of the most notable of the war, the bayonet being actually used along the whole front of the brigade The battle of Jonesborough, was the last actual fighting in the siege of Atlanta On the next day the Confederates evacuated the city, and the long and fierce campaign was at an end

The fall of Atlanta was the end of four months of constant struggle Beginning on the 2d of May the campaign closed on the 2d of September During this time, the Union and Confederate armies engaged, suffered the following losses

The losses of General Sherman's army from Chattanooga to Atlanta (May 5th to September 8th, 1864) were, killed, 4,422, wounded, 22,822, captured, 4 422, total, 31,687 The losses of the Confederate army confronting us, under Generals Johnston and Hood were, killed, 3,044, wounded, 18,952, captured, 12 983, total, 34,979.

During these four months, the "Thousand" was in camp, out of the line of fire, *only fifteen days*. Of these, *five days* was the longest period passed in any one camp. They were *eighty-three days* directly under fire, either in battle on the skirmish line, in pursuit of the enemy or engaged in siege operations The other twenty-three days they were on the march. This terrible stretch of continuous duty in the scorching heat of the southern summer is well-nigh unparalleled It was followed by a month of rest, from September 3d until October 2d. One of the men, writing in his journal at the time, declares that no man or officer had "a change of clothing for *fifty-six days*!"

It is no wonder that General Baird in his report of

*See Appendix

Headquarters, City Point, Va.,
September 4, 1864, 9 p. m.

Major-General Sherman:

I have just received your dispatch announcing the capture of Atlanta. In honor of your great victory I have ordered a salute to be fired with shotted guns from every battery bearing upon the enemy. The salute will be fired within an hour, amid great rejoicing.

U. S. Grant,
Lieutenant-General.

2. All the corps, regiments, and batteries composing this Army may, without further orders, inscribe "Atlanta" on their colors. By order of

Major-General W. T. Sherman.
L. M. Dayton, Aide-de-camp.

XXV.

IN PURSUIT OF HOOD.

AFTER the fall of Atlanta came a month of much needed rest. Four months of constant march and battle, from the advance on Resaca on May 2d to the taking of Atlanta on September 2d, had been a severe strain on the physical and mental energies of all. Now, with Hood's army twenty miles away to the southeastward, save a force of observation which touched our pickets on the road to Rough-and-Ready, and relieved of duty save a light picket detail now and then, the men loitered under the groves that crowned the hills about Atlanta; made themselves pleasant quarters; drew fresh clothing and with abundant rations, enjoyed the surcease from war's alarms as only the veteran soldier can. Leaves of absence and furloughs were abundant, but all of very brief duration. The restless Sherman had no thought of wasting time in exulting over his victory. His eye was turned toward the sea, and having expelled the inhabitants of Atlanta from the city, thereby relieving himself of spies upon his movements as well as greatly adding to the embarrassment of his opponent, he set all the forces at his command, at work to prepare for the advance he contemplated.

The railway from Louisville, Kentucky, to Atlanta, Georgia, was run to the utmost limit of its capacity, bringing forward recruits and supplies for the army and taking back the sick, wounded and overworn soldiery, defective horses and equipments. Hartzell of Company H, had been on detached service almost a year, taking recruits from Camp Chase, Ohio, to various parts of the army. Since the army had left Chattanooga his trips had been frequent, bringing on men for the old regiments. Few of them came to the Thousand, but he had been the messenger by whom many remittances were made to those at home. Now, Colonel Perkins and others, who were worn with the long campaign, returned home on furlough. The regiment was left in command of Major Edwards, in what was aptly named "Vacation Camp," with Captain Wilcox second in command.

General Thomas was sent back to Nashville, still retaining command of the Department of the Cumberland, though the greater part of his army remained at the front. To him were sent the halt and maimed, the weak and worn, unattached regiments, commands whose terms of service were soon to expire—in short, all the more undesirable elements of a great army. With these, one division of the Fourteenth Corps, Schofield's Army of the Ohio, and such troops as had been left in garrison in our rear, General Thomas was expected not only to organize an army to hold Tennessee, where Wheeler and Forrest were raiding our communications, but his superior even intimated that he might make an independent movement on Mobile. There was left only the very pick of the Armies of the Military Division of the Mississippi when an event occurred that changed the outlook of affairs with a suddenness altogether remarkable, even in the ever-startling kaleidoscope of war.

The campaign of Hood around the left wing of Sherman's Army, cutting his communications and seeking to prevent a further advance into Georgia by placing himself in the enemy's rear, rather than in his front, was one of the most daring and brilliant movements of the war. For a month, General Hood with an army of forty thousand men had lain, apparently inactive in front of Sherman with his army of ninety thousand men in and about Atlanta, the

CORP. JOSEPH T. TORRENCE.

JOSEPH THATCHER TORRENCE was born in Mercer County, Pa., March 15, 1843. He spent his youth as an iron worker in various furnaces of Western Pennsylvania and Northern Ohio. He enlisted as a private in Company A, 105th O. V. I., and was appointed corporal. He was wounded at the battle of Perryville, October 8, 1862, and discharged for disability January 7, 1865. He was for a time in the personal service of Gov. Tod of Ohio, and was afterwards in the furnaces at New Castle, Pa. In 1860 he went to Chicago, where he has since resided and been engaged in various successful enterprises. He was appointed Colonel of the Second Regiment of Illinois Guards in 1874 and commissioned Brigadier General of the First Brigade Illinois National Guards in 1878. As such he had command of the military force in the city of Chicago during the riots of that year, during which he handled his force of five regiments in a manner to secure the commendation of all. He resigned this position

inhabitants of which had been expelled, being given their option to go North or South, in order that the Army might be unencumbered in its task of making preparations for its future movements. It seemed probable that the purpose of General Sherman was to accumulate there a sufficient supply of rations and forage to enable him to make the movement toward Savannah, even should his opponent adopt the Fabian tactic and destroy all supplies along the route. General Hood, on the other hand, was greatly trammeled as to his movements by the fact that thirty-four thousand Federal prisoners were confined at Andersonville in his rear. If released by Sherman's army they would add greatly to his strength. He was compelled, therefore, to remain on the defensive until arrangements were made for their removal. As soon as this was done he began to cast about for something which he might attempt which offered a reasonable hope of at least deferring the fate impending over the Confederacy. It was evident that if he retained his position Sherman would soon be able to advance on him with a perfectly appointed army of eighty thousand men and send Thomas into Alabama with one of fifty thousand or more. There was no hope of reinforcements or relief from any quarter. The Confederate army would merely have to fall back day by day until it was disintegrated by desertion or compelled to surrender to overwhelming numbers. He therefore conceived the brilliant idea of transferring his army around the right wing of Sherman's forces, crossing the Chattahoochee and falling on the line of supply

1877, and has since been concerned in the establishment and promotion of some of the most important enterprises in the country, such as the Calumet Iron and Steel Company, the Western Indiana Railroad, and the Rolling Mills at Evansville, Ind. He is President of the Chicago and Calumet Terminal Railway, the Calumet Canal and Improvement Company, and the Star [illegible] Steel and Iron Company. His enterprises have yielded him an ample fortune and he is accounted among the most prominent and substantial men of the West. His career has been a most remarkable one, and shows throughout the same enterprise, vigor and attention to details which made him one of the most prominent soldiers of the regiment whose first battle was the last he saw. The story of Gen. Torrence's life reads like a piece torn out of some medieval romance, or a more wonderful than ever the imagination of a Mandeville could trace.

of the Federal Army so as to compel the division of Sherman's army to pursue and head him off from Chattanooga and middle Tennessee

General Hood's preparations for this movement were made with the celerity and subtlety which characterized that commander He knew he could be of no service to the Confederacy if he remained where he was, there was a chance that this bold move might accomplish brilliant results It was a chance worth trying Having determined upon it, he gave his whole soul to its execution, and his movements were so swift that he had gained four days before his alert antagonist could guess out his purpose The order to move was issued on the 28th of September, on the 29th at noon General Hood rode across the pontoon bridge at the head of his infantry and camped that night at Pray's Church Two days afterwards, he was at Lost Mountain, the next day he seized Ackworth and Big Shanty, and the day after the 5th of October, attacked Allatoona

On the day he crossed the Chattahoochee the rumor came that the Confederate Army was moving to our rear It was thought to be a cavalry demonstration The next day the granting of furloughs was stopped and all leaves of absence were suspended On the second of October, Hood's designs had so developed that Sherman determined to pursue with his whole army except one corps left to hold Atlanta Hood had gained a week's start, but Sherman's army was in prime condition elated with victory and accustomed to long and furious marches Probably no army in the world was ever its superior in this respect, and few generals have ever equaled Sherman in capacity to move a large army with extreme rapidity for a long time

On the afternoon of the 3rd of October the Thousand broke camp and started with the army in pursuit On the 4th they recrossed the Chattahoochee, on the 5th reached Marietta on the 8th were at Ackworth, on the 10th at Allatoona, on the 15th crossed the Oostenaula River, on the 16th passed through Snake Creek Gap, which they had passed going the other way on the 12th of May preceding. Then they turned southward, passed a week building a bridge and grinding wheat and corn for supplies at Gaylesville, Alabama, started eastward on the 28th and arrived at Rome, Georgia, on the 31st of October. On the 3rd of November they reached Kingston, Georgia, and remained there in a delightful camp for one week.

On the 11th of November they turned their faces toward Atlanta over the very roads they had already twice traversed since the summer began. This time they destroyed railroad bridges and everything that could be of value to an enemy. Sherman was cutting loose from his base of supplies. They passed through Ackworth, Big Shanty, found Marietta a mass of smoking ruins, and on the 15th reached Atlanta.

In the meantime Hood by the 12th of October had reached Resaca, the point occupied by Johnston five months before when the campaign against Atlanta began, capturing Dalton and all intermediate points except Allatoona and advanced to Tunnell Hill, seven miles from Chattanooga. From this point he turned south and on the 15th was at Cross Roads, nine miles south of LaFayette. Here he determined to halt and deliver battle, but his corps commanders declared that the morale of his army would not justify such a course. The shadow of the end already hung over the Southern soldier. Well would it have been for Hood's renown if he had taken warning from his soldiers' intuitions and spared them farther useless slaughter. His love of battle, sanguine temper, and above all his confidence in the genius of Lee, kept alive in the breast of the shattered veteran a strange, delusive hope that the Confederacy would yet triumph.

Foiled in his plan of engaging Sherman with the concurrence of his superior, General Beauregard, he determined to advance into Tennessee and engage Thomas before the forces of that commander could be concentrated. Overcoming almost incredible obstacles he carried this design into effect, narrowly missing success through the failure of Cheatham to attack Schofield in flank while on the march. One month after leaving his position to the southeast of Atlanta, Hood's army was resting on the banks of the Tennessee waiting to cross while Sherman had turned back to begin the movement which was to end the last act of the great national tragedy

To the men of the Thousand, this month's jaunt despite forced marches, dust and heat, was thoroughly enjoyed Every journal kept during that time is brimful of jollity. The fleeing enemy, the return to scenes of the summer's strife, the fruitful autumn, the attractive scenery and rich harvests of the Coosa Valley, and above all, the universal impression that the end of the war was at hand, tended to make these citizen-soldiers especially gleeful on this vacation trip through the country It is said that even Adjutant Dickerman who had passed unmoved through the fertile fields of Kentucky and the most attractive nooks of the Cumberland Plateau was so impressed by the attractions of Northern Alabama that he proposed to return there and settle, as soon as the war was over. Instead of doing so however, he studied law, became a judge in Michigan, and is now a practitioner in California

Captain Mansfield, too, who had risen from a private in Company H, to be the Chief of Ambulances on the staff of General Baird, of the Third Division of the Fourteenth Corps, records the fascination which this beautiful region had for him, but he also yielded to the attractions of business and politics, and instead of becoming a carpet-bagger in Alabama, he listened to the solicitation of his friends and took a seat in the legislature of Pennsylvania.

One incident of this march illustrates in a curious way the haps of war On the 29th of September, Lieutenant Wm H Castle, then in command of Company E, received a leave of absence for thirty days, from the headquarters of the Army of the Cumberland On the next day the general order announcing a movement of the enemy to the rear, was issued by General Sherman, commanding the

Military Division of the Mississippi. Among other things this order revoked all furloughs of enlisted men still within the limits of the army, and suspended all leaves of absence which had been granted to officers still with their commands. Lieutenant Castle had just received his leave of absence and was still with his command. Throughout the whole march his comrades joked him about his leave of absence, asked him how he was enjoying himself, how the weather was at home, and addressed to him all the good-natured raillery which an unlucky man is the recipient of when his ill-luck happens to have a ludicrous phase.

On the return march the Thousand halted for some days at Kingston, Georgia, went into camp, were paid off, and there was every indication that they would remain there for some time. Other officers who held leaves of absence similar in character to that Lieutenant Castle had, regarding the suspension as at an end, went to the rear. Castle was young, had little experience of the world to begin with, and small inclination to take life seriously. He had risen from the ranks in Company K, was a good-natured fellow, always ready for duty, had never been absent from his command except three days during his term of service, and had only once been under arrest. That once was for not preventing his men from filling their haversacks with ears of corn from an over-turned wagon in a train they were guarding during the starvation days of the Siege of Chattanooga. He was a trim, handsome fellow, and his boyish appearance with some lack of firmness were against him as disciplinarian. Colonel Perkins, who had been absent on leave, rejoined while the regiment was encamped at Kingston.

On the evening of the day the regiment was paid off Lieutenant Castle went to the colonel's tent to inform him that he intended to take advantage of his leave of absence, now almost a month old. Finding several officers there he waited till they should go before mentioning the matter, lest he should awaken their raillery. Presently one of them asked him, jocosely how he enjoyed his "leave of absence." "That is all right," answered the lieutenant, "I am going home on it, now we have driven Hood off the lines and the cars are running again." A shout of laughter greeted this announcement. He was told that his leave was out of date; that he had lost his chance and would have to begin over again. "Well," he replied, "I am going to try it anyhow." Major Edwards said he would be a fool if he did not.

An engine was standing on a siding near the camp with steam up. After leaving the Colonel's tent, he went and asked the engineer when the train would pull out? "I am expecting orders every minute," was the reply. Castle hurried back to his quarters, packed up his traps, turned everything over to First Sergeant George D. Elder, and hurried down to the train. Only box cars were run on these military railroads below Chattanooga, at least. Into one of these he hustled, wrapped himself in his blanket and was soon asleep. Morning came and the train was still on the siding. Several of the officers of the regiment came down and joked with him about his "leave of absence," having stopped the train. About ten o'clock it started. Two days afterwards he reported at the headquarters of the Department of the Cumberland to which the Thousand belonged, in Nashville, presented his leave of absence to the proper staff officer, and had it dated and countersigned, stating the time at which he must report for duty. This was the usual procedure. Furloughs and leaves of absence were granted by the department commander, not by the general commanding the Military Division. So Lieutenant Castle went home on a leave of absence regularly granted and regularly endorsed by the only officer having right to grant such leave. A few days after reaching home he was taken sick; he forwarded a surgeon's certificate to department headquarters, and his leave was extended twenty days. At the end of that time, he reported for duty and was ordered to meet his regiment in Savannah.

that Lieutenant Castle be reported "*as a deserter.*" This was done and for the first time, probably in the history of any war, a man having leave of absence from the general commanding a department, was recommended for dismissal as a deserter When Castle reached Savannah after the expiration of his leave, he was ordered in arrest and soon afterwards dishonorably *dismissed as a deserter*

This is the story as told by Lieutenant Castle thirty years afterwards, confirmed by papers still in his possession, and also, as to its details, by more than thirty members of the regiment who were conversant of the facts in whole or in part It happened just at the close of the war when the country was too much engaged with momentous affairs to have room to right the wrongs of a poor lieutenant Almost every officer in the regiment petitioned for a reversal of this judgment—a judgment rendered without trial or hearing, and without allowing the accused even a copy of the charges preferred against him But the authorities were too busy winding up the multitudinous affairs of a great war when it reached Washington to pay any heed to such a petition So the years went by and a faithful officer still bears the stigma of having been *a deserter*

Worse than that, during all that time, this officer, now a deserving citizen, has been unable to obtain from the War Department *even a copy of the charges against him!* Over and over again he has applied for it, and over and over again, he has been refused

This country is a free country, so we boast but no worse tyranny could be found in autocratic Russia than the action of the War Department in this matter The writer laid a full statement of the case before the present

---

After the war, Lieutenant Castle was for a time a clerk in one of the Departments in Washington studied in the Columbian Law School, graduating in 1869 The mechanical bent was too strong, however and he went back to his business of machinist engaged in manufacturing for a time and is now (1895) in charge of the metal work of the Columbian Novelty Co, of Northeast Pa

Secretary of War (1894-5) pointing out to him the injustice of condemning a man unheard and then refusing him even a copy of the charge against him. It was to no purpose. The only statement ever vouchsafed in regard to the matter, was that "Lieutenant Castle was recommended to be dismissed on account of desertion, by Colonel Perkins, Colonel Gleason and General Baird." It is not believed that Colonel Perkins recommended such dismissal. If he did, it must have been without knowledge of the facts. Such ignorance is not unreasonable considering the fact that he would have had only hearsay knowledge of a matter that happened during his absence from the regiment, and many have judged from the jesting allusions to it that there was something irregular about the leave of absence itself.

However this may be the curious fact is presented of an officer being dismissed the service without trial, without being permitted to see a copy of the charges against him, and branded as a deserter when every moment of his absence was actually covered by a leave of absence from his department commander. In the publication of this incident in periodical form some blame was laid upon Major Edwards. That officer promptly wrote: "If I was the cause of any injustice to Lieutenant Castle no effort of mine shall be lacking to put the matter right." Upon further examination, it was found that Colonel Perkins had returned to the regiment two or three days before this incident happened, so that no responsibility attaches to Major Edwards for the unjust report made of his perfectly legal absence.

It is proper, also to say that the papers in the War Department were shown to Lieut. Castle in 1896 but he was not given a copy nor allowed to make one. Through the influence of Major Edwards, Senator Cushman K. Davis of Minnesota has taken the matter up and it is probable that at some time in the future this curious and no doubt unintended wrong will be righted.

Another incident which occurred on the 11th of October was characteristic of the citizen-soldiery of the war of Rebellion Marching in pursuit of the enemy, the Thousand, after pushing forward from daylight until eleven o clock, halted in a shady grove to hold an election At that time, Ohio voted for state officers, on the second Tuesday of October, and the soldiers of the Thousand were still citizens of the Buckeye State, and entitled by law to vote for governor and state officers Captain Cummings acted as clerk of the polls and Captain Stambaugh, one of the judges of the election, held a haversack, which was used as a ballot box In previous elections a cracker-box served that purpose and in the Presidential election, in November following, it was again restored to duty in that capacity The clerk used a medicine-case, borrowed from the surgeon, for a desk When the halt was over, the polls were closed and re-opened again on reaching the point selected for the camp. The election passed off very quietly The regiment cast 284 votes, all for the "Brough ticket," John Brough being the Union candidate for governor, though one man scratched Brough's name off his ticket So a traveling election for officers of the State of Ohio, was held about five miles beyond Allatoona, and along the road, twelve or fifteen miles toward Kingston in the State of Georgia

a railroad. There was but one question of difficulty connected with this movement which seemed rather a holiday procession than a hostile march through an enemy's country. This was the question of supplies. For these the army depended almost wholly upon the country through which it passed.

The army of General Sherman on the great march from Atlanta, was organized as follows:

The Right Wing, commanded by Major-General O. O. Howard, comprised the Fifteenth Corps, Major-General P. J. Osterhaus, and the Seventeenth Corps, Major-General Frank P. Blair. The Left Wing, commanded by Major-General Henry W. Slocum, comprised the Fourteenth Corps, Major-General Jefferson C. Davis, and the Twentieth Corps, Brigadier-General A. S. Williams. The aggregate force of infantry was sixty thousand men. The cavalry, fifty-five hundred men, was under command of Brigadier-General Judson Kilpatrick.

The Fourteenth Corps was composed of three divisions, the first led by Brigadier-General W. P. Carlin, the second by Brigadier-General James A. Morgan, the third, of which the Thousand was a part, by Brigadier-General Absalom Baird. The Second Brigade of this Division remained the same as in the Atlanta campaign, except the Thirty-fifth Ohio, whose term of service had expired.

For the Thousand and the Division to which it belonged, this march really began at Kingston. The writer, therefore, gives instead of any description he might attempt, a letter-journal of Commissary Sergeant William J. Gibson, extending over this interval, which was written from day to day during the march. In vividness and quaintness, it excels any account of the same that has come under the writer's notice.

The view one gets of the commissary himself is a fine bit of self-revelation. Our army abounded in such scholarly, self-forgetting characters. The chivalry of the North differed from that of the South: it was not self-assertive nor boastful. No finer picture of a volunteer soldier to whom war was an accident not a vocation, could be given than this conscientious commissary-sergeant trudging along with the wagons of the brigade and mixing up in his journal the daily duty of issuing rations and the studies which he had sworn never wholly to abandon during his service. So we see him reading with true student-hunger the strange array of books which the hap of war threw in his way and recording his impressions of them with a *candor* he would hardly exhibit now and with a keenness of which no literary critic need be ashamed.

Kingston Ga., Nov. 12, 1864.

Start about 10 A. M. in the direction of Atlanta: pass the last train of convalescents going North. Set fire to the town and commence destroying the railroad as we go: many conjectures as to our destination all founded on Tecumseh's (Gen. Sherman) remark that he was going to feed his boys on oysters this winter. The romance of seeing "Old Ocean" and picking up shells on the shore makes the trip rather desirable: anything for a change from this wooden country. Pass Cartersville where much Government property is wantonly destroyed and the town burned. Cross the Etowah and camp two miles south: issue rations in the night.

Nov. 13.

In company with Warner (J. R.) and Cowles (E. R.) pass over Allatoona Heights and view the recent battle-field. Day very pleasant and scenery wild. Brigade tears up railroad and burns Ackworth and Big Shanty. Camp a few miles north of Kenesaw Mountain road. Read "Uncollected Writings of Charles Lamb," like them well.

Nov. 14.

Very frosty. The fields are filled with women and children, half-naked refugees from their burning homes. Think of climbing the mountain, but the task is rather too much and I retreat. Pass through Marietta which is in flames, the railroad destroyed by troops in advance of us.

Cross the Chattahoochee at dark and burn the bridge after us. Camp near the river See a great light in front supposed to be Atlanta burning Read "Harper's Monthly" for November

Nov 15

Start at daylight and reach the city by noon. All smoke dust, bustle and confusion Halt on the August Railroad, where the Rebs destroyed eighty cars of ammunition Draw rations and clothing, after night-fall A burning city is a never-to-be-forgotten sight Pick up several abandoned books, but none worth carrying save a Horace I found upon the porch of an empty house

Nov 16

Leave Atlanta (or rather its ashes) at nine A M. Move out through Decatur a distance of nineteen miles, passing over McPherson's battle-field and a wild country ravaged by cavalry Leave Stone Mountain to the left See very few citizens Read ——— "Natural History", quite readable Have sweet potatoes, broiled pork, hard bread and coffee for supper, and cornstalks for bed

Nov 17

Move at seven, pass through Lithonia, destroying the railroad as we go Take dinner in a rustic rusty little village called Congers probably named in honor of Capt Congers of the Revolution, thirty miles from Atlanta The country abounds in sweet potatoes and persimmons. Read Shakespeare's "Sonnets" Read Edward Everett's Introduction to his Greek Grammar, and of course resolve to master Greek some day Halt at eight P M, about thirty-six miles, I should think, from Atlanta. Have sweet potatoes and fresh pork for supper

Nov 18

Reveille at five Have to abandon two fine volumes of Clark's "Commentaries" after reading the Introduction to Joshua Go with foraging detail, become a marvel of mud, burrs, briars, Spanish needles, etc Cross a saffron stream quite hid in tanglewood, called Yellow River, on a broken dam. Pass through Oxford; forage an antiquated quadruped yclept "Rosinante," fair as the driven snow, but by no means "fleet as the wings of the morning." Attacked by guerillas; more scared than hurt. Camp one mile east of Covington, a very pretty village of white mansions with fluted pillars in front; negro women and children crowd around us, and all seem anxious to "go wid yu uns." Forty-five miles from Atlanta. Issue rations of coffee, sugar, salt and sweet potatoes.

Nov. 19.

Start at daybreak, raining. Mount Rosinante; my first day's ride in the army; pass through Sandtown, which I shall always remember for the number of black women there. Read "Medea" of Euripides, translated by Byron; very sentimental it is. Yams abound, a watery sort of sweet potato, the regular sweet potatoes being long and slender, and either white or red, the latter the best. Having marched fifteen miles, we camp in an open field.

Nov. 20.

By a circuitous route pass through Shadyvale, a sort of suburban relic of Southern chivalry, the headquarters of one Whitfield, who *did* own 1500 niggers and 7,000 acres of land; the old nabob is not so rich as he was. The country is rich in forage and beautiful, but the day is too dreary to enjoy traveling. March fourteen miles, eat turnips. Read first chapter Dick's Astronomy.

Nov. 21.

The rain rains cold. Eat fresh pork and sweet potatoes without dishes or seasoning, in the rain and cold and darkness. Ye Gods, what business has a sophomore in the Army? Intensely cold; cross Murderer's Creek. Read second chapter of Dick's Astronomy. Travel about twelve miles without anything of interest.

Nov. 22.

A few drops of snow. See a garden of red, red roses. March six miles and camp on what is said to be Howell Cobb's plantation within eight miles of Milledgeville Find plenty of potatoes, sorghum, salt and peanuts Have fresh pork and chicken for supper Eat some persimmons so rich and sweet, a score quite satisfied my appetite Third chapter of Dick's Astronomy

Nov 23

Start early, did not see General Cobb's mansion, the other buildings are burned The morning is beautiful so is the country Arrive at the Capital about four P M Rather a mean town little better than Ashtabula. State House a great square foundry concern tipsy officers hold a mock legislature and pass some remarkable laws Issue beef Read Plutarch's Agesilaus

Nov 24

Lay in camp Wash and mend a little. Read a chapter in Disraeli's "Curiosities of Literature" Like it well Issue beef, bake peanuts and make a supper of them

Nov 25

March at six across the Oconee on a long, covered bridge, which is soon after burned by the Third Brigade Lend Bucephalus to go foraging Cross Buffalo Creek at a pretty mill-pond with an island in it Country more hilly and pitch-pine larger. Read a review of Grote's "Greece" in the London *Quarterly* Weather pleasant and sky blue Am in good spirits for a lone soldier

Nov 26

Start at daylight, country very swampy mile-posts marked with notches so that niggers can read them Many cotton plantations with their large "Gin-houses" and towering long-armed presses like so many great overgrown cider-mills Cross Town and Gum creeks almost lost in swamps Camp near Sandisville, a very ordinary little town with a Grecian court-house and a monument to Colonel Irwin of the Revolution March fifteen miles Issue potatoes and beef Read about the London police Make a pot of mush

Nov 27

Start at 6 30 Cross Williamson Creek and the Ogeechee River, a slender stream with a monstrous long bridge. Find two bottles of choice wine buried in a garden. See for the first time a live oak (called a water oak by the natives), a majestic looking evergreen, much used in ship building. Pass the Harrison plantation; destroy a vast amount of cotton, wine, Brussels carpets, mahogany furniture, chinaware, silver plate, etc., etc., of untold value. The owner had just sent them from Savannah to his country residence *for safe keeping*. Read some in Story's "Equity Jurisprudence" nearly half a day. March sixteen miles and camp in prairie grass. Issue mutton.

Nov. 28.

Day very pleasant, but road nearly knee deep with sand; marching very laborious. See the first tar pit, a very simple concern; I could make one myself. Rosinante proves to be a very rough trotter. Our division detained a long time in pontooning Rocky Comfort Creek. Passed through Louisville, which is sacked and most of it burned. Read sketches of Hawthorne, Holmes and Emerson in the "Cyclopedia of American Literature," a very neatly gotten up book with portraits, autographs and samples of their writing. March about six miles and camp in corn stubble.

Nov. 29.

Said to be skirmishing nine miles ahead. Examine some queer specimens of hanging moss, silken drapery of nature's own knitting, which drops five and six feet from the boughs on which it grows. It is silver gray, very soft, and much used in making cushions. It gives the oak a very hoary, weird appearance. Feel vexed about my old saddle, which the Colonel has just given to some shoulder straps, and then vexed more to think so small a matter should vex me at all. Read some in "Lalla Rookh," which quite confounds with bombastic names and metaphors, yet has a strange dreaminess about it that is quite enchanting. Issue meal, shorts, coffee, beef, fresh pork and yams. Spend much of the day in culinary operations. Do not march.

Nov 30

Trade Rosinante for a venerable steed whom I shall call Bucephalus, out of respect for his gray hairs. Much noise but little damage on the picket line. Read three chapters in D'Israeli—his prejudices are as offensive as his learning is marvelous, think him a man of more acumen than comprehension. Read five pages of Lalla Rookh. Move one-half mile and issue meal and flour.

Dec 1

So warm, the shade is quite welcome. Start at ten, skirmish with the enemy's cavalry. Pass some pretty little lakes. The woods so full of evergreens we quite forget winter. Can but admire the hanging moss, waving like drapery. Beauregard ordered all forage burned before us, which is not very easy, much of the corn being still on the stalk. March eleven miles and camp "among the pines." Sleep under the wagon on corn stalks, with merely a "sack" and two blankets. Oh winter, blessed be thy sunny side! Read Knickerbocker.

Dec 2

Move at daylight, atmosphere quite heavy, but soon clears up. Pass vast quantities of corn in cribs and cotton in gin-houses. Cross Rock Creek, change our direction southward, march about fifteen miles, issue meal, pork and potatoes. Read some of the "Blue Laws" by which a man is severely punished for kissing his wife on Sunday. Also read Thompson's "Seasons," don't much like it.

Dec 3

Start at seven, take the wrong road and several miles out of the way. Eat black haws and "Buckberries," as the darkies call them, but think they are merely a species of huckleberries. Read "Historical Magazine." One of our regiment finds a reb hid in a cellar with a box of gold coin and watch. Have a good chance to study Kilpatrick's angular features, don't much like them. Pass illimitable fields of unhusked corn. March about ten miles and camp by railroad which is torn up and burned. Issue fresh pork and potatoes. Heavy rain in evening.

Dec. 4.

Air a little chilly. Fight at Waynesboro, four miles to the north. Our division moves around that way, leaving the wagons behind; stay with the latter, and do not move till three o'clock. Read in "Cyclopedia of American Literature;" like it well. Pass through Alexandria *without being [illegible]*. March twelve miles and camp in a cornfield. Issue meal and potatoes. Bake yams by laying them before the fire.

Dec. 5.

Start at daylight. Pine Barrens all the way; scarce another tree to be seen. See some beautiful live oaks and black willows growing in door yards; they look like mammoth apple trees. See for the first time "grass nuts," not unlike wilted beans and tasting like beech nuts; they are sown broadcast and used to feed hogs. See what the Hoosiers called a "wolf den," but did not see its occupant. Read "Titus Andronicus." March eighteen miles and camp in the edge of a wood. Issue potatoes, beef and one box of hard bread, *the first since leaving Atlanta*.

Dec. 6.

Make a breakfast of peanuts. March at eight. Cross a creek that, for aught I could learn, is anonymous. See an old shanty said to have been the headquarters of General Washington at one time; now it is Kilpatrick's. Got quite interested in Spencer's "Faerie Queene," a little obscure on account of its obsolete words and queer orthography. March sixteen miles without seeing anything noteworthy. Camp in a dense forest within two and one-half miles of the Savannah River. Issue potatoes, mutton and beef.

Dec. 7.

March at daybreak. See some strange specimens of giant cactus, called "Spanish daggers" by some, and "palmetto" by others; on top of a knotty stem ten or twelve feet high is a clump of overgrown flag-weed without limb or twig to distinguish it as tree. Also see some wild hollies, a very pretty bush with little clusters of red berries strung like beads along its leafless tendrils. Bucephalus and I came near being run over by a malicious wagon. Read in "Faerie Queen" and "Timon of Athens." March fourteen miles and camp in a thicket. Prepare for bed, and get orders to march immediately. Raining in torrents, road through a dismal swamp, down, down, down among alligators, mules, niggers and inky darkness. Is hell worse? "Neigh," says Bucephalus, as he flounders chin deep in the mire. Toward morning it clears up. We plod on in silence, for such a march makes one sullen. Gaze at the bewildered stars through pines two hundred feet high and wonder why the crazy moon will set in the southeast. Come up with the regiment about daylight. Marched during the night about eight miles. Issue potatoes.

Dec. 8.

Pull out at sunrise, delayed some hours by bad roads, skirmish with rebs in our rear. First Division fortify and set a trap for the "Johnnies." See for the first time a palm-leaf plant, with its stella-form leaves growing just as it is made into fans. Read Cyclopedia of American Literature. Cross Black River near where rebel gun-boat has been shelling during the day. Pass near Washington's Brick Church Hospital built in 1769 and called "Ebenezer," also old Fort Marion on the bank of the Savannah.

Dec. 9.

Move at 8 a. m., go to butcher beef but conclude not to take any, it is so abominably poor. Change to another road farther south. Air quite cool with a strong east wind. Hear heavy cannonading, far to the south east, supposed to be our fleet off Savannah. Country very poor and forage scarce. Found a black child two years old, abandoned in the woods. March eight miles, issue potatoes, hard bread and bacon. Read just enough in "The Joker" to keep from breaking my motto, "Nulla dies sine linea," or several of them.

Dec. 10.

The boys bring in a lot of rice on the stalk to feed their horses. It resembles oats more than any other grain I can think of. Read some in Hamlet with Johnson's notes. Don't think much of the old lexicographer as a judge of poetry. Start at nine; pass rebel "Lunette" (a half a fort) in a dense forest. Much indignation is felt against General Jefferson C. Davis for allowing a host of black women and children to follow us several days and then abandoning them on the north bank of the Black river where many were afterwards killed by inhuman guerillas. Our brigade goes down to destroy the Charleston and Savannah railroad bridge over the Savannah river, two and a half miles from the road. I stay with the wagons, forage some corn and issue some potatoes. Sleep in the rain, the rain, the pleasant rain, with every opportunity for observing its pleasantries, but without admiring one of them; so different is the poetical conception from the practical application of such matters.

Dec. 11.

Said to be Sunday. Build a pine-knot fire to dry the blankets. Read "Faerie Queene," but find nothing of Titania. Spencer's fairies seem to be matters in which Hood or Shakespeare would see no poetry at all. See an orange tree with its thick, double leaves, the first like a heart, the second oblong. Cabbages very large, high as a man's head and four feet across. (The writer evidently refers to the southern vegetable known as "Collards.") Pass through a fine cypress swamp where many Government cattle were mired. The cypress is a beautiful tree with a smooth white shaft, thick at the ground and tapering to a waist, the spray more delicate than the elm which it much resembles, and the limbs all fringed and tasseled with hanging moss. It is quite fairy-like; but what is oddest are the stump-like roots sticking up in all directions, and called "knees;" these, it seems, without bud or sign of life, finally develop into trees. March three miles and camp within ten miles of Savannah. Issue beef.

Dec 12

Go down to see the Savannah river for the first time It is somewhat broader than the Ohio at Cincinnati but not so clear, and is almost on a level with the surrounding country, at this point it rises and falls about five feet with the tide, the banks are lined with the grandest forest trees I ever saw Opposite is a rice plantation of 13,000 acres with its dikes, dams, canals etc, for irrigation (for they say rice has to be kept under water six weeks after planting, and then is cultivated in hills or rows like corn) The canals are filled at the spring-tide The plantation is nearly one hundred years old, and its owner, James Potter is reputed to be worth $3,000,000, there are now acres of rice in stacks which is being used for forage and the mills are run by the soldiers Seven miles down the river are the steeples of Savannah, but alas for my poor sight, I could not see them! In front are the boundless swamps of South Carolina the mother of treason Read Richard III Do not remember reading of that villainous Gloster before Trade Bucephalus for a mule Move half a mile to guard Baird's Headquarters Issue beef and think of old times

Dec 13

Move forward and to the right, about four miles on a line with the other troops, road through a quicksand swamp Country poor no chance to forage, much complaining from hunger which is more imaginary than real, spirits fluctuate, alternately "sailing on high seas" and "sinking in deep waters," a beautiful sight, makes me glad I live to see it, then military annoyances make life burthensome, anon am seated in my library at home teaching Iris to read Read more of the perfidy of Gloster and frailty of Anne they are equally detestable Issue one-fourth rations of hard-bread and one-half sugar and coffee, beef and bacon

Dec 14

Have black peas and biscuit for breakfast. Go back to the rice mills for forage and admire again the grand old live oaks, one of which measures eight feet through the body, forty feet high, and branches extend laterally 120 feet. This vast impenetrable canopy is deep green on the outside, but beneath is gray with clusters of moss hanging everywhere like massive icicles. No wonder the Druids worshiped the oak and peopled it with wood nymphs. There are hundreds of these oaken monarchs in one grove, and by its side is the most beautiful sheet of silvery water I ever beheld, fringed by a thin ribbon of red and yellow willows. Read some of D'Israeli's plausible sophistry. Issue beef.

Dec. 15.

Write a letter home, the first for 37 days; mail a $50 bond; write a letter to Mary. Read D'Israeli's "Philosophy of Proverbs." Like it tip-top. One phrase struck me as fine, if not original: "When our ancestors lived more than ourselves among the works of God and less among those of men." Cowper has nearly the same: "Man made the city, but God made the country." Issue one-fourth rations of hard bread, half of sugar, coffee, pepper, salt and soap, and full rations of beef and bacon.

Dec. 16.

Our Brigade goes foraging with eighty-three wagons. Make a detour to the south and west of Savannah and cross what is called "Big Ogeechee" (probably only the big end of it) at King's Bridge, nine miles above Fort McAllister. See two dispatch-boats laden with mail. Large rice plantation along the river. Country very low and level. Read N. Y. Herald of December 8, the first newspaper for more than a month. Camp two miles south of the river, having marched about twenty miles.

Dec. 17.

Rations "play out" in consequence of having to go farther than we expected. Mule and I start hungry; move south-east about eighteen miles and camp near Station No. 3, on the Savannah and Gulf Railroad. Go two miles for potatoes, coming back with a wagon in the dark, break through a pole-bridge, headlong into the water. Swear a little, to be military. Get a pocketful of hickory-nuts. Read old rebel paper.

Dec. 18.

Move at eight, pass Midway church. Regiment halts. I and a few others go on foraging. We pass three miles south of Riceboro (nearly fifty miles from Savannah) and load up with potatoes. Country so low and near the coast it is nearly all overflowed at high tide. See some very large black willows, thin branches covered with mistletoe; they might easily be mistaken for live oak. Learn the name of an evergreen vine that entwines the bodies and tangles tops of nearly every tree in this country—'muscadine.' Also, see an intensely green tree called wild olive. Read a quaint account of the Katydid illustrated with cuts that would make Katy laugh to behold. Camp on what is called 'Jackson's Breastworks.'

Dec. 19.

Start at sunrise for camp, the train having already loaded and returned. See a black snake six feet long which some of the boys have just killed. Have occasion to notice a specimen of sugar cane which is buried over winter and grows from the joints in the spring and is very large. This country, though now an impenetrable swamp, seems to have been tilled at some time. The woods are full of canals and other signs of rice culture. Recross the Ogeechee and camp in the woods about a mile north of it; at night, build a large fire of yellow pine and read many entertaining things in the "Museum," a very readable book found in Riceboro. Have a social chat with Colonel Perkins for the first time since enlistment.

Dec. 20.

Start at half past five, take the wrong road and countermarch a second time—enough to make Gabriel swear, let alone a tired soldier. Finally run the "blockade" where rebel batteries are in plain sight, but luckily do not molest us. Hear what is said to be the "roar of an alligator, but did not see the beast himself. Arrive in camp about noon. Find two letters from home, the first in forty days. Feel disappointed that there are no more. Draw and issue rations of hard-bread, bacon, rice, coffee and salt. Make a requisition for one pair of pants, one pair shoes, two pairs of socks, two shirts, and one hat. Read Harper.

Dec. 21.

Sweet potatoes, molasses, and rice for breakfast. Draw and issue rations nearly all day long. Every preparation is made to move into the city, but we get no orders. Read one sentence in Museum worth remembering: "He deserves to be beaten who whips nature in a boy for a fault." At night have a small taffy party. Grind some rice on a pair of grist mill burrs turned by hand, and wonder at the stupidity which invented such a negro-killing concern.

Dec. 22.

Pack up again to go to the city, but do not start till noon. Pass five very large cannons which the rebs abandoned in their haste. Camp a mile from town and the boys proceed to build winter quarters. Take a ride through the city. See Pulaski's monument. Am favorably impressed with the city all around. Go to the river and see United States Transport Canonicus and Major-General Osterhaus, commanding the Fifteenth Corps; also a precious little cheese that one of the boys had just bought for $40! Philanthropic gentlemen from New York are retailing apples at *thirty cents a piece!* I can't remember when I saw apples or cheese before. Read four chapters in Vicar of Wakefield. Wish I could write my own experience half as truthfully as this seems to be given.

This wish the writer well fulfilled as this extract from his journal shows.

XXVII.

THE GUIDONS POINT NORTHWARD.

IT WAS, indeed, a merry Christmas for the men of the "Lost Army." The great march was ended. The Army of the West had come down to the sea. Hood, whom Sherman had jocularly offered to "furnish with rations if he would go into Tennessee," had been overwhelmed and destroyed by our old commander, Thomas, since we had heard from the world without. For nearly two months the army of Sherman had been lost. Neither messenger nor dispatch had come through the circling crowd of enemies to tell of their progress or hopes. Only through Confederate newspapers had the world heard of the ninety thousand men who were marching under the soughing pines of Georgia, until Sherman sent his famous dispatch to Lincoln which set the joy-bells of the North ringing again:

"I beg to present you as a Christmas gift the city of Savannah, with one hundred and fifty heavy guns and plenty of ammunition, and also about twenty-five thousand bales of cotton."

To this laconic message, President Lincoln replied:

EXECUTIVE MANSION,
WASHINGTON, D. C., December 26, 1864.

MY DEAR GENERAL SHERMAN:

Many, many thanks for your Christmas gift — the capture of Savannah.

When you were about to leave Atlanta for the Atlantic coast, I was anxious, if not fearful; but feeling you were the better judge, and remembering that "nothing risked, nothing gained," I did not interfere. Now, the undertaking being a success, the honor is all yours; for I believe none of us went farther than to acquiesce. And, taking the work of General Thomas into the count, as it should be taken, it is indeed a great success.

Not only does it afford the obvious and immediate military advantages, but in showing to the world that your army could be divided, putting the stronger part to an important new service, and yet leaving enough to vanquish the old opposing forces of the whole — Hood's army — it brings those who sat in darkness to see a great light.

"But what next?" I suppose it will be safe if I leave General Grant and yourself to decide.

Please make my grateful acknowledgments to your whole army, officers and men.

Yours most truly,
A. LINCOLN.

This graphic summary of the results of the campaign is from the pen of a staff-officer of General Sherman:*

The army marched over three hundred miles in twenty-four days directly through the heart of Georgia, and reached the sea with subsistence trains almost unbroken. In the entire command five officers and and fifty-eight men were killed, thirteen officers and two hundred and thirty-two men wounded, and one officer and two hundred and fifty-eight men missing, making a total list of casualties of but nineteen commissioned officers and five hundred and forty-eight enlisted men, or five hundred and sixty-seven of all ranks. Seventy-seven officers and twelve hundred and sixty-one men of the Confederate army, or thirteen hundred and thirty-eight in all, were made prisoners. Ten thousand negroes left the plantations of their former masters and

---

*Sherman and his Campaigns. By Colonel S. M. Bowman and Lieutenant Colonel R. B. Irwin.

accompanied the column when it reached Savannah, without taking note of thousands more who joined the army, but from various causes had to leave it at different points. Over twenty thousand bales of cotton were burned, besides the twenty-five thousand captured at Savannah. Thirteen

CAPTAIN R. G. MORGARIDGE.

thousand head of beef-cattle, nine million five hundred thousand pounds of corn, and ten million five hundred thousand of fodder, were taken from the country, and issued to the troops and animals. The men lived mostly on

---

REUBEN GEORGE MORGARIDGE was born in Morgan Co., O., May 1, 1838. He was attending school at Conneaut, O., when the war broke out, and on August 2, 1862, he abandoned his books and enlisted as a private in the 105th, being mustered in as a corporal, and was promoted successively to 1st Sergt.,

sheep, hogs, turkeys, geese, chickens, sweet potatoes, and rice gathered by the foragers from the plantations along the route of each day's march. Sixty thousand men taking merely of the surplus which fell in their way as they marched rapidly on the main roads subsisted for three weeks in the very country where the Union prisoners at Andersonville were starved to death or idiocy. Five thousand horses and four thousand mules were impressed for the cavalry and trains. Three hundred and twenty miles of railway were destroyed, and the last remaining links of communication between the Confederate armies in Virginia and the West effectually severed by burning every tie, twisting every rail while heated red hot over the flaming piles of ties, and laying in ruin every depot, engine house, repair shop, water tank and turn table.

From the time that the army left Atlanta until it arrived before Savannah not one word of intelligence was received by the government or people except through the Confederate newspapers, of its whereabouts, movements or fate, and it was not until Sherman had emerged from the region lying between Augusta and Macon, and reached Millen, that the authorities and the press of the Confederacy were able to make up their minds as to the direction of his march.

"Marching in four columns on a front of thirty miles, each column masked in all directions by clouds of skirmishers, Sherman was enabled to continue till the last to menace so many points, each in such force, that it was impossible for the enemy to decide whether Augusta, Macon or Savannah were his immediate objective, the Gulf or the Atlantic his destination, the Flint, the Oconee, the Ogeechee, or the Savannah his route, or what his ulterior design.

This is what Sherman himself says in his report of the army he commanded, of which our Thousand—long since no more a thousand—was a part.

2 [illegible] with the [illegible] of the [illegible] was with it [illegible] term of service. On [illegible] at Eastman Business [illegible] N. Y. the [illegible] excitement he was at [illegible] as Post Master at the latter place [illegible] three years [illegible] where he [illegible] the [illegible]

"As to the rank and file, they seem so full of confidence in themselves, that I doubt if they want a compliment from me; but I must do them the justice to say that, whether called on to fight, to march, to wade streams, to make roads, clear out obstructions, build bridges, make 'corduroy,' or tear up railroads, they have done it with alacrity and a degree of cheerfulness unsurpassed. A little loose in foraging, they 'did some things they ought not to have done,' yet, on the whole, they have supplied the wants of the army with as little violence as could be expected, and as little loss as I calculated. Some of these foraging parties had encounters with the enemy which would in ordinary times rank as respectable battles.

SERGT. M. A. TEACHOUT.

"The behavior of our troops in Savannah has been so manly, so quiet, so perfect, that I take it as the best evidence of discipline and true courage. Never was a hostile city, filled with women and children, occupied by a large army with less disorder, or more system, order, and good government. The same general and generous spirit of confidence and good feeling pervades the army which it has ever afforded me especial pleasure to report on former occasions."

MARSHALL A. TEACHOUT was born in Royalton, Cuyahoga Co., April 12, 1842. When enlisted as private in Co. D, 105th, Aug. 12, 1862, he was employed as clerk in his father's store. He participated in all the campaigns, marches and battles in which the regiment was engaged except the battle of Missionary Ridge, having been wounded in the left thigh at the battle of Chickamauga, was in the hospital at Nashville, Tenn., at that time; was made sergeant of he Company on the 16th day of February, 1864; was taken prisoner with oth-

The halt in Savannah was merely that of a giant waiting to catch his breath between two great efforts. The fleet which lay in waiting brought supplies of all kinds in lavish profusion. The great War Secretary, Stanton, came down to confer with the victorious leader. The new department of the South was created. Sherman was given command from the Gulf to Virginia, from the Mississippi to the sea. He only paused to arrange for its orderly control, to have Schofield's army of the Ohio sent around to New Berne, N. C., and then at the head of his exultant host he turned his course northward to perform the other half of his great undertaking and place his command in touch with the left wing of Grant's army. On the 12th of February the march began. It was the rainy season, and three hundred miles of swamp and lagoon, with a score of swollen rivers, lay between them and their destination. A wary more alert enemy, the army of General Joseph E. Johnston, was again in their front and on their flank. What did these things matter? They were Sherman's soldiers, elated with the memories of victories achieved and obstacles overcome.

---

ers by John Morgan while on a foraging expedition under command of Captain Canfield, Jan. 21, 1863; was paroled at McMinnville and returned at once to the regiment. At close of the war he was employed as clerk in store at Painesville; went to McMinnville, Tenn., in 1873, and remained there and at Chattanooga six years, engaged in the lumber and hardware business most of the time since [illegible]. Present address, Columbus, O.

XXVIII.

OUR FORAGERS.

THE method of collecting supplies on this march has given rise to the most acrimonious discussion connected with the history of the war.

The consideration of this question has been seriously complicated by the personal feeling and bias of those who have written in regard to it. The ex-Confederates have generally pictured "Sherman's bummers" as little less than fiends incarnate, and insisted that the unnecessary and wholly unjustifiable destruction of private property, especially in the State of South Carolina, left an ineffaceable stain upon the Federal soldier as a wilful and reckless violator of the rules of civilized warfare. It must be admitted that the camp-fire tales to which the people of the North have listened for a generation, have very often been of a character to support this view.

To state the matter fairly, the following questions arise:

1. What is the right of an invading force with regard to the private property of the country through which it passes?

2. Did our army overstep the limitations imposed by the rules of civilized warfare and to what extent?

3. If so, where does the responsibility for such excesses rest?

The consideration of this matter cannot be avoided in a work of this character It might be supposed that the writer would simply declare that what was done was either necessary or unavoidable, and, therefore, excusable This is the general course adopted by those who have written from the standpoint of the Northern soldier He is unable to do so Though yielding to none in devotion to the cause for which we fought, and proud of the character of the citizen-soldiery who composed this army, he lived for fifteen years after the close of the war, on the edge of the path it made, was acquainted with hundreds of families whom the "bummers" visited and has heard, beside many a hospitable hearth, the story of their deeds These tales cannot be questioned, indeed, they are irrefutably confirmed by every journal, of that march, now in the writer's possession They made the listener's face grow hot with shame—shame for the very men of whom he was most proud, the very cause in which he most exulted, the very people to whose civilization he looked with highest hope for the future That some of those who suffered became implacable haters of the whole people whose army brought the pillagers to their doors, he cannot wonder, that by far the greater number looked back upon it with quaint forbearance as an inevitable misfortune of warfare, is not easy to explain, while the fact that the Northern soldier has come to regard it and to speak of it at his re-unions, as a jest, rather grim and rough, but more comical than otherwise is to him a matter of great surprise He believes that very little blame attaches to the men of Sherman's army for these excesses There are bad, rough spirits in every army, and these naturally sought the opportunity for license which the forager's duty offered, but if there had been, on the part of the commanding officer, a disposition to prevent such excesses, this class of men would have been prevented from securing place on such details

So far as the Thousand is concerned, the writer is happy to say that its colonel did all in his power to prevent the coarser and ruder spirits in his command from becoming the dominant element in such details, and assigned to the command of the same an officer especially marked for his sense of right, his religious character and obligation. Lieutenant W. H. Forbes was the leader of the regimental prayer-meeting and the chief of our foragers from the third day after we left Atlanta till the army reached Goldsborough, North Carolina, and resumed the normal method of supply by wagon-trains which brought the pungent bacon and luscious hard-tack. Fortunately he is still in the land of the living; the writer asked him to give an account of the foragers under his command, and leaves him to tell his story in his own words:

"At Covington, Georgia, we reached the garden spot of the south, and foraging began by order of Gen. Sherman. The first hundred miles to Milledgeville was a huge picnic, reaching the capital in seven days. Foraging was conducted by details from each company.

"We here learned by the papers that great efforts would be made for our destruction. Our trains being loaded with ammunition, coffee, sugar, and a small supply of crackers, with plenty of forage in sight, we were not dismayed.

"Taking a ten mile gait we easily removed the barricades, substituted pontoons for bridges destroyed, and brushed the cavalry aside. Still the great destruction and concealment of property made the foragers' duty more arduous, and we would have seen harder times but for the colored people in this second stage of the campaign. They hailed our arrival with pleasure and were ever willing to disclose hidden supplies and pilot us to distant swamps that concealed horses, cattle and forage. We appreciated their services. What with rushing off our line of march to support Kilpatrick and subsequent hard marches to regain our place in the advancing column, we would not have had time to ferret out supplies but for their help. In our glorification of this march great honor should be accorded them. The foragers were grateful. The blacks were anxious for freedom, and many followed us. However, we succeeded very well and had abundance until we reached the Millen and Augusta Railroad.

"Here we entered what is known as the pine barrens, about forty miles wide The second day from the railroad we struck this waste It may be described as sandy and often marshy, largely covered with pine and scrub oak Unproductive, and thinly settled by "poor-whites," living in rude tenements, who raised small patches of corn, sweet potatoes and a small black bean called by the natives "peas" Last but not least a species of hog known as "razor-backs," and quite difficult to capture. About the time of entering this territory the enemy changed their mode of operations, Wheeler's command moving to our rear This left the way open to our foragers to cover a wide extent of territory, but their utmost endeavors were poorly rewarded—at times barely getting subsistence for their own needs

"Striking tidewater we entered the ricefields, the crop had been harvested and taken to the high ground The hulling mills were mostly destroyed, and procuring food from this source was similar to taking the hulls from oats Our rations for a week were a sharp reminder of the dark days in Chattanooga During this time we had invested the outer works of Savannah

"From this camp the entire brigade, taking most of the division wagons were out four days on a forage trip across the Ogeechee River and along the Gulf Railroad to Hinesville station Here we found potatoes, beans, meat molasses and corn sufficient to load the train On our return a battery across the flooded fields fired upon us, probably it was amusement for them with no casualties on our part

"Next day a general advance was made, when the enemy, leaving their guns and ammunition, abandoned the city Communication with the fleet ended our work as foragers for the time being

"The halt in Savannah was very pleasant, plenty of rations oysters in the shell, butter and other luxuries were obtained from the city and transports Good quarters and an abundance of dry fuel from adjacent brickyards completed our happiness, until we were ordered out for picket duty, seven miles distant We were still there when the campaign through the Carolinas was inaugurated

"Crossing the Savannah River at Sister's Ferry we first entered South Carolina There was a well-defined opinion among the soldiers—often expressed—that if we ever got into South Carolina we would make them understand what invasion meant 'Torpedoes! be careful!' was the sign that attracted our attention as we left the pontoons. Treading carefully in the beaten path, we soon reached high grounds and found Robertsville reduced to ashes. We thought Bobtown would be a more appropriate name. We camped a short distance beyond. Everything that would readily ignite was fired. Fencing, houses and barns were all consumed, and everything we could use was taken and what we could not use destroyed.

Foraging was conducted while in the swamp-lands by the same methods pursued in Georgia, that is by detailing men each day. Cotton was always destroyed. The writer remembers his first experience with it. Entering a large gin house with much loose cotton ready for the press, the light particles adhering to the timbers and rafters, he struck a match and threw it on the pile. Immediately there was a flash and a roar all over the structure. He bounded out in quick time and thereafter was more cautious.

"At times, splendid mansions were occupied by general officers of our commands and guarded seemingly with a desire to save them. The soldiers believing in justice, details from forage squads lingered near until the guards were withdrawn, when they were fired.

"Tramping through swamps with continuous rains made progress very laborious. Our wing, Slocum's, being the left, had but slight annoyance from the enemy. Successful foraging depended much upon the lay of the land and character of the products. We remember one red letter day. We captured hams, eggs, milk, poultry and other supplies with the largest goobers (peanuts) we ever saw.

The rivers were numerous and the foragers had to be in at the crossings, which were mostly by pontoons. Our foragers being the first into Barnwell had taken a considerable amount of stuff and had it piled in a house on the square. The Twentieth Corps troops coming up, an officer ordered us to clear out, as we had no business there. A refusal brought on a war of words, and for a time it looked as if weapons would be used. General Williams was attracted to the scene and was inclined to side with his men, but we had possession and knew we were in the right. We presume there were five hundred soldiers surrounding the building when General Jefferson C. Davis came up. His decision was that the Fourteenth Corps men had the best claim, having done the collecting of the forage. This was our first unfriendly encounter with that Corps, but not the last one. We were not always victorious After leaving Barnwell we guarded the wagon trains until we reached Lexington, near Columbia

"The foragers were the only representatives of the 105th Ohio, who entered the capital of South Carolina Its destruction by fire was a re-enactment of the tragedy of Atlanta the suffering and wretchedness of the harmless people being very great I will mention one incident Comrade Weldy of Company H, asked a fine-looking gentleman before we entered the burned district, if he had any eggs 'I ll see,' was his reply. Returning he said there were 'two dozen in the house'

"Forgetting our usual mode, Weldy asked the price 'Fifteen dollars per dozen is what I paid for them' 'But how much in silver?' 'Ten cents sir' The trade was soon consummated, this being the only instance of payment for supplies of any sort known to me, while in the state of South Carolina

"Making a brief halt, for the city was well patrolled, we returned across the river and resumed our course toward Alston, reaching there next day The country was more rolling and fertile and the foragers got in some good work while the troops were tearing up the railroad At this point we had an exciting time, and came near being taken in by the enemy's foraging train, guarded by a regiment and two pieces artillery We had passed over a mill-pond and through a cornfield from which the ears had been plucked to the owner's residence on the highway and were helping ourselves, when one of the boys in the second story discovered their skirmish line advancing rapidly He gave the alarm and we hastily got out of sight and took cover in the willows along the side of the mill pond awaiting developments The enemy evidently were pushed themselves and gave us no further trouble This was the first time we had seen the enemy in force since leaving Savannah Being nine miles from camp we took a new route and were soon loaded with plunder

"From Alston via Winnsborough the foragers did well, there being considerable to work upon We had also learned that being wholly or partially clothed in citizens' dress was helpful in our labors Most of the able-bodied colored men had been removed from our line of march, which we regretted

"Just before crossing the Watteree, we were again put on train duty When all but a part of our division and wagons had passed over, the pontoons broke and we were

delayed over two days The rain coming down in torrents made our march to the Pedee River the most disagreeable and exhausting we had ever encountered, for both men and animals We had to make up for lost time, never getting into camp before midnight, and off again by sunrise Getting to camp, huge fires were built, and while waiting for coffee we would wade into a brook wash off the mud, and dry by standing around the fires In the day time we did fairly well, but after dark it was terrible But little foraging was done that week, the troops in advance of us cleaned up and burned most everything of value

"Crossing near Sneedsboro into North Carolina, our division went to the front A new arrangement was made for foraging We were ordered to report at the colonel's quarters about eight o'clock at night He stated that an order was issued increasing the number of foragers, to detail the men permanently and not be changing except for cause, run no unnecessary risks and bring in all the supplies we could obtain He thought we would be more efficient if mounted He also informed us that Gen Johnston was concentrating troops in our front and that great caution would be necessary As we were now out of South Carolina the burning of private buildings should be discontinued Two hours afterward, we moved out of camp, passing the cavalry pickets at midnight By noon next day, we had collected animals for most of the detail At a mill near Rockingham N. C, we procured meal and all we could utilize, feeding our new mount upon corn A squad in gray observed our movements from a hill, we made no unnecessary delay but started home, well loaded Our camp began to assume a sort of cavalry appearance

"Starting a little late next morning, we got into the toils by mixing up with General Baird's staff and attaches A stentorian 'Halt!' huddled us up in some confusion Stating our mission we were allowed to pass with the injunction, 'be out of the way before the troops are in motion hereafter '

"His remark that we were the most unique cavalry outfit in the department, probably was true A few had saddles borrowed from teamsters, others had blankets, and some were bare-back The bridles were of various contrivances We did look odd, but we were good

"This day we entered the belt of timber where turpentine and rosin is made The stills were deserted and near

ate in the evening to a mill gathered corn ground four sacks of meal and returned to camp before daylight

Our brigade having the lead we moved upon Fayetteville, reaching there about noon—the 75th Indiana on the skirmish line, the 105th supporting it only to find the enemy safely over and the bridge on fire The rosin-fire was frequently commented upon as causing us to lose a favorable opportunity to capture or scatter Hardee's forces We were discreetly silent as to its cause

We halted in Fayetteville four days The cessation of rains and the bright shiny weather together with needed rest made this camp the most pleasant I can recall Here we wrote letters home forwarding via Wilmington and Washington the first opportunity since leaving Savannah Capturing a large bundle of woven socks ready to be sewed together we learned the comparative worth of Confederate money and greenbacks The women employed would do the work for $1.00 per pair in their money or fifty pairs for a $1.00 in greenbacks

"Breaking camp the morning of the 15th the most of our corps was pushed forward towards Raleigh while our division was relegated to guard the trains that proceeded upon the direct road to Goldsborough The foragers were not successful in finding much of value, the rebs having made a clean sweep We heard faint echoes of Averysborough and took a hand on the second day at Bentonville Two days thereafter we entered Goldsborough a ragged, motley crew Contrasting our appearance with Schofield's command, before whom we passed in review, it did not seem possible we had ever come out of the same band box

The next day a few of our forage squad went out north of the town We had evidence that the enemy were watchful Two of our soldiers with the usual dark red line around the neck and protruding tongue were left by the roadside We had seen similar ghastly spectacles on three previous occasions since leaving Columbia always accompanied with warnings of like treatment if captured while foraging showing the vital importance the supplies were in carrying on the conflict Without these same supplies we could not have made the campaign

"While returning to camp the first fatality to one of our number occurred Daniel Rush, of Company B, fell out to get some fodder for his mule being in sight of our troops no danger was apprehended the rest going on Shortly afterwards a well-mounted horseman came up behind and shot him through the body, just a few rods inside the Twenty-third Corps' camp lines, and was away before those who witnessed the scene realized what had occurred He was cared for and brought to the hospital next morning but died two days afterwards

"He was of our most fearless and successful foragers It was a sad escort that kept time to the beats of the muffled drum. With victory almost achieved, and a widowed mother eagerly awaiting his return, no wonder the tears were not withheld as our comrade was lowered to his silent resting place

"Receiving an abundance of rations and clothing at Goldsboro, our special avocation ended Most of the Confederacy was depleted true their men were yet in the field, and braver soldiers were never mustered, but they had not the supplies to sustain them, therefore, the collapse, which soon occurred

"Having all my letters written home on file, descriptive of army life and doings I have tried to be accurate in culling the foregoing I have omitted personalities largely practical jokes and laughable incidents, not wishing to ruffle the good nature of participants, and will conclude with an illustration of our efficiency given by a Southern man years after hostilities ceased

"He said that Sherman's foragers, (he called them 'bummers') were so persistent that if he were enclosed in a lane with the foragers at one end and the devil at the other, he would rather try conclusions with the latter, for when the scrimmage was over there would be something left for the family, but with the former, not a thing "

No one can read the account which Lieutenant Forbis gives, or recall the allusions in the account given by Commissary Gibson, without arriving at two conclusions

That pillage was a frequent and unpunished thing upon this march before South Carolina was reached, and after reaching North Carolina

That the burning of dwellings and farm buildings was very frequent along the line of march through South Carolina

By this is not meant that necessaries for the support of the army, or which might prove valuable to the enemy, were taken or destroyed, but that money, valuables and personal property belonging to non-combatants along the route were taken or destroyed not for the public benefit but merely to gratify lawless inclination. There was no show of effort to repress such tendency, from which the soldiers naturally inferred that it was endorsed and approved by the General in command. The remarks of the Colonel to the foragers of the Thousand after leaving South Carolina amply sustain the claim that it was by deliberate purpose that the army was "turned loose" in South Carolina. The orders issued upon the subject by General Sherman were apparently fair enough, but the practice under them was certainly of the very loosest character. In the writer's opinion the conduct of our army in this respect cannot be justified or excused. It was not warfare under the rules which civilization imposes on an invading foe, but such pillaging as characterizes the inroads of undisciplined marauders.

With an army of the character of that which General Sherman led this was wholly unnecessary. The fact that so few crimes of a personal character were committed amply attests this fact.

If the commander of this army had officially assumed responsibility by directing houses and barns to be burned along the line of march through South Carolina and permitting his soldiers to take money, silver, books, furniture and whatever else they desired in Georgia and North Carolina, it would have been a military measure for which he alone would have been responsible. By seeming to forbid and failing to prevent, he left the blame to fall upon the men, who without the encouragement of such tacit approval would never have dreamed of perpetrating such acts. As a consequence the opprobrium falls upon the soldiers instead of resting where it ought, upon the General. It is the only thing in the history of the war for the Union which is really regrettable. It occurred not because the volunteer soldier was a pillager or "bummer" by inclination but because he was made so by a laxity of discipline which whether intentional or unintentional resulted in putting a slur upon the fair fame of this army which it is useless to deny and folly to extenuate The writer has arrived at this conclusion much against his will, but fifteen years' residence in the very region through which the army passed, has so familiarized him with the facts as to make any other course impossible

Carolina Hitherto the fighting had all been on the outer edge of the Confederacy. This produced a false impression of its strength and solidarity Now an army of eighty thousand had swept through its very center and Sherman's Army in North Carolina, became, practically, a prolongation of Grant's left wing Schofield with the Army of the Ohio had come around by sea and joining with the force at New Berne had met Sherman at Goldsborough Two hundred thousand men were ready to fall upon the fragments of Confederate power when Lee broke from the trenches at Petersburg, in the desperate hope of uniting with Johnston at Danville, massing before Sherman and retreating through the Carolinas But that very movement had been foreseen. The fiery Sheridan was on his flank and Appomattox saw the end of the Army of Northern Virginia With it the Confederacy fell The exact extent which the remarkable movement from Atlanta, Georgia, to Raleigh, North Carolina contributed to this result can hardly be overestimated. The army of Sherman had cut a path sixty miles wide through the heart of Georgia to Savannah, destroying all north and south connections, cotton, forage, bacon corn, cattle, hogs, sheep, poultry, meal and in general, all supplies From Savannah to Goldsborough, North Carolina the army occupied an average width of forty miles, and through the State of South Carolina the destruction was even more complete It compelled the surrender of Savannah, Charleston, Wilmington and the abandonment of seven hundred miles of seacoast, thus putting an end to blockade running, on which the Confederacy depended for so large a portion of its military supplies Yet, as General Sherman well stated in his report, after enumerating all these things: "The real object of this march was to place this army in a position easy of supply, whence it could take an appropriate part in the spring and summer campaigns of 1865. This was completely accomplished on the 21st of March by the junction of the three armies and the occupation of Goldsborough, North Carolina"

By the "three armies" in this report General Sherman alluded to the re-organization of his army which was effected with the lightning-like rapidity which characterized all his mental processes, as soon as he reached Goldsborough. The right wing, still under General Slocum, was designated the Army of Georgia; the left wing retained its original designation of the Army of the Tennessee, still commanded by General Howard; while the center, General Schofield's command, composed of the Tenth and Twenty-third Army Corps, was designated the Army of the Ohio. This was the organization adopted for the brief and bloodless campaign which followed. The Thousand retained the same brigade and division relations as heretofore.

In speaking of the difficulties of this great strategic march and the character of the army making it, General Sherman says:

"I beg to express in the most emphatic manner my entire satisfaction with the tone and temper of the whole army. Nothing seems to dampen their energy, zeal or cheerfulness. It is impossible to conceive a march involving more labor and exposure, yet I cannot recall an instance of bad temper by the way or hearing an expression of doubt as to our perfect success in the end. I believe that this cheerfulness and harmony of action reflects upon all concerned quite as much real honor and fame as 'battles gained' or 'cities won,' and I therefore commend all generals, staff, officers and enlisted men, for these high qualities, in addition to the more soldierly ones of obedience to orders and the alacrity they have always maintained when danger summoned them 'to the front.'"

So the three great armies lay about the sleepy little city of Goldsborough, busy with the work of replenishing the clothing and equipment which the toilsome march from Savannah had outworn, while the restless brain of their commander evolved the details of the next swift-coming movement. General Grant once told the writer that in almost every consultation he had with Mr. Lincoln in which maps were referred to, the President's finger would wander down to the region between the Roanoke and Cape Fear rivers, in North Carolina, and he would say: "Somehow I think the matter will be ended about here." And there it was to be ended. The three armies at Goldsborough were in perfect condition. Almost three years of continuous marching, with every now and then a fight, had hardened their muscles and given self-reliance and invincible courage and determination. As an army they could probably endure more hardship, march farther in less time, pursue an enemy more relentlessly and guard against one more cautiously, endure defeat with more patience and improve victory with as much celerity as any army ever assembled. They were the very men to undertake the pursuit which it was expected would have to be made of the disorganized forces of the Confederacy, when Grant should give the word and Sheridan should break the leash, and swing around the left of Lee, cutting off his line of supply and making the fall of Petersburg and Richmond a necessity. It was intended that the two armies should move at the same time, but the contingencies of transportation made it a week later before

CORP. W. K. MEAD.

WILLIAM K. MEAD was born in Mahoning County, September 15, 1835; enlisted August 1, 1862; was captured at the battle of Perryville; was exchanged and joined the regiment at Murfreesborough, Tenn., in the spring of 1863; was continuously with it until mustered out at the close of the war. Lived in Indiana until 1883; then went to Scranton, Miss., and engaged in a lumber business

Sherman's ragged veterans were all shod and clothed and he was ready to take his part in the last play of the great game of war which had begun four years before. He counted on the wonderful marching powers of his men, trained by the long journeys they had made from the banks of the Mississippi and Ohio, to make up for the delay. In the meantime, the spring had come; the orchards were in bloom; the oaks were covered with the tender sheen of young leafage. The weather had been good for some time but at the last moment the late spring rains began to fall and the red-clay roads were soon slippery quagmires. It would not do to delay, however, and as soon as the clothing was distributed and the reorganization complete, we were on the march in the closing campaign.

On the 10th of April, 1865, the movement was begun which was to blot the Southern Confederacy from existence in so short a time and with so little bloodshed, that its importance has been almost lost sight of. Johnston's surrender being ordinarily esteemed an inevitable result of the fall of Richmond and the dispersion of Lee's army. In a sense this is true, but such a result might at least have been long deferred had it not been for the magnificent army which on this day started on the great turning movement its commander had projected, the object of which he had defined in orders to his subordinates, as follows:

"The next grand objective is to place this army (with its full equipment) north of the Roanoke River, facing west, with a base of supplies at Norfolk and at Winton or Murfreesborough, on the Chowan, and in full communication with the Army of the Potomac, about Petersburg; and also to do the enemy as much harm as possible *en route*."

The plan of the movement was briefly stated as follows:

"The left wing, Major-General Slocum commanding, will aim straight for the railway bridge near Smithfield, thence along up the Neuse River to the railway bridge over Neuse River, northeast of Raleigh (Powell's), thence to Warrenton, the general point of concentration. The center, Major-General Schofield commanding, will move to Whitley's Mill, ready to support the left until it is past Smithfield, when it will follow up, substantially, Little River to Rolesville, ready at all times to march to the support of the left, after passing Tar River, *en route* to Warrenton

"The right wing, Major-General Howard commanding, preceded by the cavalry, will move rapidly on Pikeville and Folk's Bridge, ready to make a junction with the other armies in case the enemy offers battle this side of Neuse River about Smithfield, thence, in case of no serious opposition on the left will work up towards Earpsborough, Andrews' Bridge and Warrenton

"Major-General Schofield will hold, as heretofore, Wilmington, with the bridge across North Branch as an outpost, New Bern and Kinston as its outpost, and will be prepared to hold Wynton and Murfreesborough as soon as the time arrives for that move The navy has instructions from Admiral Porter to co-operate, and any commanding officer is authorized to call on the navy for assistance and co-operation, always in writing, setting forth the reasons—of which, of necessity, the naval commander is the judge"

The Thousand was with the left wing, which was ordered to "aim straight for the railroad bridge near Smithfield We reached the point designated on the twelfth The bridge was in flames But even as we halted, the roar of thousands shouting in triumph fell upon our ears, and a staff-officer dashed by us, waving a dispatch, his face aflame with excitement, hoarsely screaming, over and over, the words: "Lee has surrendered!" "Lee has surrendered!" A whirlwind of Yankee cheers followed his course until the pine woods echoed as they had never done before with the glad acclaim of tens of thousands!

Men huzzahed, laughed, and, perhaps wept, in the delirium of that moment From end to end of the blue-clad columns went up waves of exultant shouts, which swelled and died away only to break out afresh far into the murky spring night that followed We knew it was the beginning of the end, and pushed forward lest the enemy in our front should escape without a blow On the next day, Raleigh, the capital of North Carolina, surrendered. The Third Division pressed on to Holly Springs in pursuit of the enemy. On the 15th we were halted by orders from the

ies. It is not strange that the victorious General in his agerness to conclude the struggle exceeded his powers and rovisionally accepted a political convention rather than a ilitary capitulation. On the 18th the woeful news was eceived of the assassination of President Lincoln. It is ardly possible to imagine now what a gloom it cast over he triumphant army. More than any man in our history, e was everybody's ideal neighbor—everyday companion nd friend. To the soldiers he was an especially vivid, unique and kindly personality. No one doubted his patriotism, sincerity, self-devotion or kindliness. Great leaders were admired and loved. Lincoln was regarded with a sort of worship. Everyone felt as if he had lost the dearest of all friends. There was a hush over all the army as the flags were draped, and anger burned hot against the Confederates, whom all

the armistice This awoke deep feeling There was talk of conflict between the soldiers of the two Union armies There need have been no apprehension Those who remembered how Halleck moved when in command of the great army before Corinth should have known that there was no fear of his troubling Johnston's forces until long after the ten days' armistice had expired. But Grant came in a day or two, unconscious as ever, not taking over the command but counselling his lieutenant, keeping himself carefully in the background, so that on the 26th, when the armistice expired, it was General Sherman, and not his superior, who received the surrender of General Johnston and his army

With the shouts of victory were united yearnings for home The citizen soldiers of the Union had done their work—accomplished the task which they went forth to do—and nothing now could restrain their eagerness to return to peaceful life. Their leaders and the government they served were in full accord with their sentiments Almost for the first time in history, an army was ready to disband and its leaders eager to promote its dissolution, in the very moment of victory.

No time was lost The surrender was consummated on the 26th of April, on the 27th it was announced in General Orders, on the same day the order given below was issued, providing for the speedy dispersion of the greater part of the army

"HEADQUARTERS MILITARY DIVISION OF THE SOUTH, NEAR RALEIGH, N C, April 27, 1865

"SPECIAL FIELD ORDERS NO 66

"Hostilities having ceased, the following changes and disposition of the troops in the field will be made with as little delay as practicable ·

---

of typhoid fever at the time his regiment was fighting the battle of Stone River, his health was so impaired that he was obliged to accept his discharge At the re-organization of the Militia when Morgan made his raid into Ohio, he was commissioned a Major by Governor Tod He has filled many town offices with great credit, and was one of the original incorporators of the Sunday School Association which grew into the world-wide Chautauqua Assembly He now resides at Knox, Pa

"I.—The Tenth and Twenty-third Corps will remain in the Department of North Carolina, and Major-General J. M. Schofield will transfer back to Major-General Gillmore, commanding Department of the South, the two brigades formerly belonging to the division of Brevet Major-General Grover at Savannah. The Division Cavalry Corps, Brevet Major-General Kilpatrick commanding, is hereby transferred to the Department of North Carolina, and General Kilpatrick will report in person to Major-General Schofield for orders.

"II.—The cavalry command of Major-General Stoneman will return to East Tennessee, and that of Brevet Major-General J. H. Wilson will be conducted back to the Tennessee River in the neighborhood of Decatur, Alabama.

"III.—Major-General Howard will conduct the Army of the Tennessee to Richmond, Virginia, following roads substantially by Lewisburg, Warrenton, Lawrenceville and Petersburg, or to the right of that line. Major-General Slocum will conduct the Army of Georgia to Richmond, by roads to the left of the one indicated for General Howard, viz: by Oxford, Boydton and Nottoway Courthouse. These armies will turn in at this point the contents of their ordnance trains, and use the wagons for extra forage and provisions. These columns will be conducted *slowly* and in the best of order, and aim to be at Richmond ready to resume the march *by the middle of May*.

"IV.—The Chief Quartermaster and Commissary of the military division, Generals Easton and Beckwith, after making proper disposition of their departments here, will proceed to Richmond and make suitable preparations to receive those columns, and to provide them for the further journey."

It will be observed that the General Commanding did not designate this as a march; it was a "journey"; the Generals were to conduct slowly and leisurely this three-hundred mile march to the capital of the Nation. This was the General's idea; the soldiers had other notions.

XXX.

THE HOMESTRETCH.

HE Thousand lay in camp at Holly Springs, N. C., when the order for the northward march was received on the 28th of April, 1865. Every one was eager for the start. During the day it was learned that the Twentieth Corps, having the roads at our right, would have a little less distance to march, and were expected to reach Richmond in advance of us. This fact at once awakened the old rivalry between the Eastern and Western troops in the Army of the Cumberland. The Twentieth Corps was composed of troops originally from the Army of the Potomac; the Fourteenth Corps had been at the West from the beginning, and were all Western troops. Maps were consulted, and it was found that the roads the two corps were to pursue united in one, about two days' march north of the southern line of Virginia. At once the soldiers of the Fourteenth Corps, who had always boasted of superior marching powers, determined to reach this point in advance of the Twentieth. Inspired by this and the irrepressible desire to reach their homes at the earliest possible moment, they made the march to Richmond one of the most furious in their whole term of service. The weather was hot; the roads in splendid condition. From the very first the men pressed the pace, so that the place for the morning halt was reached long before the time for it. The men were clamorous to go on. "Change horses, and go ahead!" they shouted to their officers. The halt was shortened, and the march resumed in deference to the universal clamor. Those in command thought the eagerness of their men would soon subside. When the column halted, with the sun still an hour high, the Fourteenth Corps had made almost twice the distance designated for the first day's march—nearly thirty miles. The next day they marched twenty-five miles; on the next over twenty, reaching the junction of the roads and getting ahead of the Twentieth Corps. Yet, their ardor did not abate. The heat was very oppressive. Despite the fact that they were veterans, the ambulances were crowded with foot-sore men—yet the others pressed on, up through the fertile regions of Southern Virginia, where tobacco and corn took the place of cotton-fields through which they had marched so long, and great long-armed oaks shaded the road instead of the soughing pines of Georgia and the Carolinas. The sands and the swamps were gone too—rolling hills, sparkling rivers, and smooth red-clay roads, not yet grown very dusty, took their places. How the men laughed and cheered each other on! How the country people stared at the rollicking blue-coats! They crossed the Roanoke River, the forks of the Meherrin, the Nottoway, the Appomattox! On the day they crossed this historic stream the Thousand marched *twenty-seven miles and lost four men from sunstroke!* This, not in obedience to orders, but because the war was over and they were going home! How could they take a funeral gait under such circumstances? All the time the air was full of jests and quips. Years afterwards the people living along the line of march told of the universal jollity. Many a time has the writer listened to the story in the farm-houses of Virginia. The Northern soldier, even in the most serious emergencies, was much given to humor, as a few instances will show.

While in camp at Fayetteville, a detail of the Thousand was ordered out, after dark, one rainy night. One of them remarked with the utmost complacency that he was "glad he had got hold of a bottle a little while before.' He turned it up; there was a gurgling sound It was suggested that he pass it on He did so—and, as it went down the line each in turn sampled the contents The next morning every face, but his, was black and smudged. The bottle had contained ink, and no one had made any exclamation, from fear that the joke upon the next one in the line would be lost

Even better than this was the joke played upon a Fayetteville paper, while Colonel Perkins was Provost-Marshal of the city and the Thousand were detailed as guards. Some printers found a form of the *Eagle* printed on one side The impression was on wall-paper, but its language was fierce and truculent as if Sherman had been a thousand miles away It even suggested that he was "lost in the swamps" The boys turned the sheets over and struck off a thoroughly "loyal" impression, full of fun and reliable news on the other side!

After the battle of Hoover's Gap, the Thousand bivouacked in the woods, where the fight had been going on It rained steadily. One of them in lying down found that the man next him had fallen asleep with no blanket over him After shaking and scolding him, he finally threw a part of his own blanket over him and went to sleep On waking up the next morning he found it was a Confederate who had been killed during the night His comrades were inclined to banter him, but, looking at the dead man, he exclaimed, with perfect seriousness "Well, I'll be blamed, if that isn't *about* the coldest bed-fellow I ever had!"

The irrepressible Eaton, of Company G, was topping out a chimney with a small campkettle, from which the bottom had been removed, at the most pinching time of the siege of Chattanooga, when a general officer rode by and said to him "My man, don't you know that if you put that kettle on the top of your chimney it will not draw?"

"Draw?" said Eaton, as he saluted with his muddy hand. "You don't know that chimney as well as we do,"

General. We boys were just now talking about taking it down to the Commissary to *see if it wouldn't draw rations!*"

The spirit of fun was rampant on this last march—the whole army was like a host of boys just out of school. On the eighth day they were in camp, three miles south of Richmond, Va. In that time they had marched *two hundred and five miles!*

They arrived ten days sooner than was expected. The rations which had been ordered to meet them had not yet arrived. It became necessary to borrow supplies for them from the troops stationed about Richmond. The men were badly used up by this furious march, but they still clamored to go on. On the 11th of May, three days before they were expected to arrive at Richmond, they were on the march for Washington. The first day on this trip they made twenty-two miles. In eight days they had passed over the historic battle-fields; had crossed the Rapidan at Raccoon Ford, and Rappahannock at Kelly's Ford; had passed Manassas Junction, crossed Bull Run, and marched through Centreville to Alexandria. Four years before, lacking a few days, the writer passed over the same road, going the other way to the first great battle of the war.

"The Honorary Secretary."

Three days only they lay in camp. Then came the GRAND REVIEW, the most notable spectacle ever wit-

veterans, fresh from the scenes of strife, went streaming past the reviewing stands, crowded with generals, under whose eyes they had fought, and dignitaries, who wondered at them as they passed They cared little for these. War had dulled their curiosity They knew their generals, and loved them

Grant and Sheridan were as much their own as those who had made the Great March with them. Only one was absent—Thomas, the revered leader of the Fourteenth Corps from its first organization until it was taken from him, when he was sent back after Atlanta had fallen. Yes, there was one other—one whom every soldier had dreamed of seeing in the hour of final victory The thought of the martyred President obtruded itself in every mind. The fact that he would not enjoy their triumph robbed it of no little of its sweetness But their eyes scanned most eagerly the surging crowds upon the sidewalks, seeking ever some familiar face, some loved eye Less than one-fifth of the Thousand had enjoyed respite or furlough during their entire term of service of almost three years No wonder they were homesick Thousands of the best soldiers of the great armies deserted at the last moment, that they might behold their loved ones even a day sooner than they otherwise would. Sherman's army, with its long, swinging stride and curious array of foragers, was certainly a unique element of this wonderful national pageant As it passed the reviewing stand, "Uncle Billy" Sherman himself draped the colors with a wreath of flowers—and there were many bronzed cheeks down which the tears flowed as he bade them good-bye. Great, generous, impulsive, warm-hearted, alert, and restless leader of a great and glorious army! His memory brightens with the years—and theirs were filled with loving admiration as they looked back at what intervened between that final review and the May morning two years before, when, for the first time, they advanced under his command and drove in the pickets before Resaca! Two wonderful years they had been, without a single backward step taken

before an enemy. Only when in pursuit of Hood had they turned back the way they had come, even for a single rod

On the next day came the march across the Long Bridge to a camp on the outskirts of Washington For the first time since it crossed the Ohio, on the day after it was mustered in, the Thousand encamped on ground which had never been in possession of the Confederacy. Seven days more—making out muster-rolls and reports which had been sadly neglected in their long march On the thirtieth of May came the farewell address of General Sherman * On the second of June all was complete, and they were mustered out On the next day they took the cars for home *via* Baltimore and Pittsburg, reached Pittsburg at eleven o'clock at night, but found a bountiful repast awaiting them, arrived in Cleveland at ten o'clock on the fifth, marched to the old barracks, had a grand reception, listened to speeches from Governor David Tod, to whose call they had been the first to respond, and other notables, turned over ordnance, were paid off, and on the eighth of June, 1865, after two years, nine months, and eighteen days of service—after a farewell address from Colonel Perkins, no longer young and shy, but grave and masterful—the Thousand was disbanded, shook hands in farewell, and departed for their several homes—not, indeed, a thousand, but three hundred and fifty-five war-worn veterans

And the others? Two hundred and twenty-seven lay buried, here and there, along the devious tracks they had pursued, from Cincinnati to Washington. Two hundred and twenty-seven more had been lost by resignation or discharge—almost every one for wounds or disability. One hundred and sixty-three had been transferred to other commands Thirty-eight were mustered out elsewhere, being absent from the regiment on detached service or in hospitals. Thirty-six were "absent without leave," mostly deserters.

* See Appendix

Of the whole number, two hundred and fifty-nine had been wounded in action, and one hundred and eighty-two had been prisoners of war. It brought back its colors, shot to shreds, but never once touched by the hands of an enemy, and deposited them in the capital of the State, one of the many monuments there gathered which attest the courage and steadfastness of her sons in the time of the nation's peril.

XXXI.

RELIGIOUS CHARACTER.

F the Thousand, as of a large number of the Federal regiments raised in the country portions of the North, it may be said that it was not only composed of intelligent men, but had a fair proportion of church members among its rank and file. From the best information now available, it is believed that about 28 per cent. of its number were members of some church when they entered the service, and that about 80 per cent. of the survivors have since become such. We had during our term of service two chaplains, who were on duty with the regiment, taking all the time of both, just three months and three weeks; though they held their commissions as such for more than two years' service. One of them was on duty at the hospitals of Chattanooga during a portion of that time. Because of the brief time they spent in actual service with the Thousand, it has not been thought necessary to give any particular account of them or their work. Neither was with the regiment long enough to make any serious impression on its life or the religious character of officers or men.

Temperate, orderly, and well disciplined as it was, the Thousand could lay little claim to being a religious regiment. Of the officers, only three or four, it is believed, were church members; and it must be admitted that even these few were by no means notable for their christian profession. Except Captain Bowers, of Company K, none of the original officers made any special effort to organize, keep alive or improve the religious sentiment of the rank and file. The others were not what would be called irreligious. There was little profanity among them, though most of them were capable of a reasonable amount on an occasion calling for especial vigor of expression. There was very little intoxication, though most of them drank a little now and then. Except on one or two occasions when there was some especially good news and little prospect of active service, there were perhaps but one or two who ever showed signs of intoxication, though it is said that on one occasion there was but one captain and one lieutenant present with the regiment who were quite fit for duty as officer of the day and officer of the guard. But news of Vicksburg and Gettysburg coming on one day was a serious strain on the abstemiousness of any Union soldier! It is but fair to admit, however, that the religious element of the Thousand owed little to its officers, though they offered no hindrance beyond mere indifference.

On the other hand, too much praise cannot be accorded a score or so of enlisted men, mostly non-commissioned officers, who from first to last never failed to bear testimony to the faith they professed. A few of them were to be found in each company, and their influence was in all respects most salutary. A number of them have since become ministers of various denominations. Several of them were killed or died of wounds. The only one available to give a reliable account of their work is Sergeant Forbes, of Company B, afterwards promoted to lieutenant. As in the last chapter he gave an account of the foragers of the regiment, in this we will allow him to tell the story of its praying circle. The writer takes this occasion to express his profound gratitude as a member of the regiment that the commander of its foragers was also the leader of its prayer-meeting.

The religious element of the 105th was not well organized at the formation of the regiment, in consequence of the hasty departure for the front. There were representatives from the Baptist, Presbyterian, Disciple, Methodist, and other churches among its members. The first service held in the regiment was a prayer-meeting at the last camp occupied in Louisville, Ky. (It is probable that there may have been a few Catholics, but Lieut. Forbis makes no mention of the fact, and none of the survivors have reported themselves as such.)

The following Sabbath, the largest delegation of church members ever assembled in the regiment went into Louisville for worship. At this time, but one death had occurred in the regiment.

LIEUT. CHARLES A. BRIGDEN.

The pursuit of Bragg's army began October 1st. On the 8th, the disaster that befell the 105th at Perryville was a severe blow. The fearful loss in the regiment told with especial force in our band of members. The evening after the battle, Captain Bowers, a noble Christian officer, called his company around him, and having explained the object of the meeting, they sang a hymn that attracted the attention and presence of a large part of the regiment. The prayer he offered was fervent and appropriate, with fifty dead lying upon the battlefield and over two hundred wounded, many of them in the agonies of death. The im-

CHARLES A. BRIGDEN was born in New Haven, Conn., February 21, 1817. He helped recruit Company I of the 105th, and was made First Lieutenant of that company. He had at that time three sons in the service, and another one enlisted a few months later. He was wounded at the battle of Perryville and resigned on account of ill health January 1, 1863. He was afterwards elected Auditor of Trumbull County and served two terms. He died at Warren, Ohio, September 29, 1887. He was a member of the Bell-Harmon Post, and was highly esteemed by his comrades and all who were acquainted with his life and character.

pressiveness of that service will not soon be forgotten. If the title of chaplain had been conferred upon the Captain it would have been hailed with delight by all present; he was capable, having been a minister previous to his enlistment, and would have influenced the regiment for good.

Moving over the field the following day, where our dead still lay, was an object sermon indelibly stamped upon our memories. Two miles beyond we halted, when a detail was sent back to bury them.

After fourteen days of severe marching our brigade, which had in the meantime been detached, arrived in Munfordville, Ky., in a snow-storm. A summary of morning reports showed three hundred for duty, one hundred and thirty sick in camp. Since the first of October we had had no tents, some were without blankets, and the most of the overcoats had been discarded on the retreat to Louisville. The exposure was depleting the ranks very rapidly. For two days we had quarters in the depot, when the bell-tents were brought up, and a camp in regulation style established.

The second week here, our Chaplain, Rev. Aaron Van Nostrand, joined the command, and was assigned to a tent with Quartermaster Wright. The following Sabbath the regiment was formed on three sides of a square, and paid marked attention to his discourse. As the Chaplain was past middle life, and not able to withstand the exposure of camp life, we assembled in front of his tent for next Sabbath's service. Preaching at 10 a. m. was announced a week later, but at that hour he was not in condition to officiate. He returned to Ohio, and died at his home in Painesville, February 27th, 1863.

We left this camp November 30th, and were constantly on the move until we joined the Army of the Cumberland in Murfreesboro, Tenn., in January, 1863. March 22d, the brigade turned out for funeral services, by the Chaplain of the 123d Illinois, on account of the killed at Milton. Prayer-meetings were held weekly whenever the members were off duty, Comrade Knight, of Company I, taking a prominent part.

May 10th, a representative of the Christian Commission preached for us in the regiment. After the sermon it was proposed that a Young Men's Christian Association be organized, when forty were enrolled; prayer and praise meetings to be held Wednesday and Saturday evenings, for the greater convenience of members, and preaching on Sunday, when we could get any one to officiate.

When we moved to Boiling Spring, three miles out we prepared a place for meetings in the grove—logs were rolled into convenient shape for seats. In addition to other exercises on Sunday, a large number met at 2 o'clock for Bible study

May was a delightful month and was improved to the utmost, constant drilling and numerous inspections had brought the regiment to the highest perfection yet attained, and this happy feeling was reflected and expressed in our religious association, there was great development in Christian character and influence

The abatement of card-playing and profanity was quite noticeable The ministration of a chaplain, such as the 9th Kentucky had, would have given a wonderful impetus to the moral activity of the regiment We will refer again to the morning reports, showing the status at that time Six hundred present for duty, ten only in camp hospital

On June 24th 1863, we gave up these pleasant surroundings to participate in the Tullahoma campaign Meetings for prayer, by the Association, were held whenever practical When the enemy was driven beyond the Cumberland Mountains, we established a camp soon after crossing Elk River The campaign had not been severely contested but the discomfort from almost constant rains, from the day we started until crossing the river in July was very exhausting Comrade Manasses Miller, of Company H, preached his initial sermon, taking for his text the word "Watch" We were greatly edified and pleased at the ability with which he developed his subject, we anticipated much in the future but our brother's modesty was a bar to his continuance, he has since become a successful minister

July 26th, we advanced to the foothills of the mountains and halted in a beautiful location, and were fitting up in grand shape when ordered to hold ourselves in readiness to march at a moment's notice—we had an exceedingly pleasant and profitable meeting the second evening here. From this time until we crossed the Tennessee at Shell Mound, all services were regular and well attended At University Place, a resident Baptist minister preached for us the first Sabbath Bro Knight on the succeeding one was giving us an excellent exhortation, when a violent storm came on—our temple, a chestnut tree, being no protection against the elements, a sharp run to the tents terminated the exercises The Commission gave us, while here, a supply of hymn books and six hundred papers for distribution that were highly appreciated

attended during this campaign One evening, at Utoy Creek, we met in a little grove about one hundred yards in rear of the works While in session, the enemy began a spirited artillery fire The shots in passing cut branches from the trees, dropping some in our midst As soon as the fearful shriek and missile passed by, the prayer would be continued These meetings were a source of great enjoyment during that arduous campaign—the spirit of the Lord was with us to comfort and sustain

Entering Atlanta September 8th, we camped in a grove, policed and arranged comfortable quarters, then prepared a large, circular space, partially covered with brush, and were ready for services when Chaplain Morton arrived

Under the leadership of Lieutenant Allen and Sergeant Stewart, a choir of sixty had been practicing an hour a day The first sermon in four months was delivered in a drizzling rain, in front of the Colonel s quarters Bible readings and other means of grace were held at the bush tent We expected a good rest; the relief from constant firing and attendant annoyances was greatly appreciated We planned for enjoyment, but Sherman said Hood must be looked after, and we obligingly accompanied him back to Gaylesville, Ala ; then moved on to our railway line of transportation at Kingston, when the sick, our Chaplain being of that number, were sent to Chattanooga

The succeeding thirty-nine days were of ceaseless activity Reaching Savannah, we reorganized our Christian Association by including the workers of the 101st and 87th Indiana Regiments Our temple was a small grove of pines, the evenings being cool, the services were preceded by building a fire The attendance was increased by the colored brethren their quaint ways of illustrating by allusions to Lincoln, Sherman, and his soldiers, as their deliverers, were amusing and instructive Two consecutive Sabbaths we attended services in the city, by resident ministers, the music was grand, they gave us a cordial welcome and an invitation to come again

After leaving the city, the next two months were spent in traversing the swamps of the Carolinas, with the exception of a brief halt at Fayetteville, we had no rest until we entered Goldsborough, N C The eighth day of April, the Chaplain came to us, and next day delivered an excellent discourse to an attentive audience, the prayer meeting in the evening was of great interest On the 10th we began our last campaign against the foe by way of Smithfield to Jones Crossroads fourteen miles from Raleigh The 23d, the Chaplain preached to the brigade his eulogy of the martyred President was very impressive The following Thursday evening prayer and praise meeting was a glad and happy one— Johnston had surrendered the previous day That grand old doxology, "Praise God from whom all blessings flow," gave the most expressive exposition of that occasion This was the last religious meeting of a general character held in the field—three days afterward we were "Homeward Bound"

XXXII.

THIRTY-YEARS AFTER.

CAPT. BRADEN.

THE Thousand has melted back into the life from which it went forth at the bidding of the country. Its record in peace has been as honorable as it was in war. Scarcely a life has been of a character to bring a blush to the cheeks of his comrades. Now, as when it was organized, farmers greatly predominate in the ranks of the survivors. There are mechanics, clerks, business men, a half-dozen lawyers, half a score of clergymen, five physicians, four bank presidents, two publishers, three or four editors; two who have been judges of state circuit courts; two State Senators; one who has been a member of two Constitutional Conventions; two representatives in state legislatures; three have been judges of probate; two have been sheriffs; three county treasurers; two county auditors; three county surveyors; more than one-half the residue, town trustees, school directors or other local offices; and almost all have filled positions of trust and honor, in their respective neighborhoods, in churches, societies and business, which show the esteem in which they are held by their fellows. Nearly all of them are members of the Grand Army of the Republic; and one is the Commander-in-chief of its largest department, Pennsylvania. Most of the officers belong to the different commanderies of the Legion of Honor. They are scattered in twenty-seven states, everywhere attesting by enterprise, probity and character, the great truth that the

ALBION W. TOURGEE.

daughter of the regiment, is counted as a daughter by every one of the lessening company of veterans whom each year she greets with undiminished warmth.

As the years go by and the number of familiar faces grows rapidly less at each reunion those who survive have still the consolation of knowing that in peace as well as in war the Story of the Thousand told in worthy deeds and lives adds a modest but positive something of luster to that noblest of all inheritances, the citizenship of the Great Republic which it is our glory that we helped to give to every person born or naturalized in the United States or subject to its jurisdiction. For the Magna Charta of American liberty was in fact first traced by the swords of her citizen-soldiers before it was written in the constitution.

THE END

ITINERARY

OF THE

105TH REGIMENT,

OHIO VOLUNTEER INFANTRY.

August 21, 1862 to June 8, 1865.

COL. GEO. T. PERKINS.
1863.

Giving the location of the regiment for every day of its service.

Compiled from various sources, chiefly the Journal of Comrade L. Newton Parker of Co. I.

ADJT. ALBERT DICKERMAN.
1862.

AUGUST 1862.

12—21. Camp Taylor, Cleveland, Ohio.
22—24. Covington, Kentucky.
25—29. Lexington, Kentucky.
30— Marched toward Richmond, Kentucky.
31— Returned to Lexington, Kentucky.

SEPTEMBER 1862.

1— 5. On retreat to Louisville, Kentucky.
6—15. In camp, four miles from Louisville, Kentucky.
16— Review in Louisville, Kentucky.

17—21 In camp near Louisville Kentucky
23 Moved beyond railroad, Louisville Kentucky
24—30 In camp, Louisville Kentucky

October 1862

1 Began march on Perryville campaign
2— On march
3 Arrived at Taylorsville Kentucky
4— Arrived at Bloomfield Kentucky
5— In camp (Sunday)
6—7 On march, toward Perryville
8 BATTLE OF PERRYVILLE KENTUCKY
9—10 In camp on battle-field
11—12 On march to Danville, Kentucky
13—19 In camp at Danville, Kentucky
19—20 Forced march to Lebanon Kentucky
21—28 In camp at Lebanon Kentucky
29—31 On march to Munfordville, Kentucky

November 1862

1—29 In camp at Munfordville, Kentucky
30 Began march to Glasgow, Kentucky

December 1862

1 Arrived at Glasgow, Kentucky
2—5 In camp near Glasgow Kentucky
6—9 On march to relieve Hartsville Tennessee
10 Arrived at Hartsville Tennessee
11—25 In camp at Castalian Springs Tennessee
26 On march
27 Passed through Scottsville Kentucky
28— Waded Barren River
29 Arrived at Glasgow, Kentucky
31 On march

January 1863

1 On march
2 Arrived at Cave City Kentucky
4—7 On march to Nashville via Bowling Green Ky
8—10 In camp, three miles out of Nashville, Tennessee, on Murfreesboro Pike
11—12 Train guard, Nashville to Murfreesboro, Tenn
13—18 In camp Murfreesboro Tennessee
19 Captain Ephraim Kee died

20—	In camp Murfreesboro
21—	Forage party captured, near Murfreesboro, Tenn
22—31	In camp and on forage details

FEBRUARY 1863

1— 5	On reconnaissance toward Lebanon, Tennessee
6—	Passed through Lebanon, Tennessee.
7— 8	Crossed Stone River on wagons, used as pontoons
9—	Return to camp in Murfreesboro, Tennessee
10—13	Train guard to Nashville, Tennessee
14—	Return to camp at Murfreesboro, Tennessee
15—18	In camp
19—22	On reconnaissance, two regiments
23—	Return to camp at Murfreesboro
24—	In camp.
25—	First payment since regiment left Covington, Ky
26—28	In camp.

MARCH 1863.

1— 2.	In camp, Murfreesboro, Tennessee
3— 7	On reconnaissance
8—16	In camp.
17—18	On reconnaissance with brigade
19—	Arrive at Auburn, Tennessee
20—	BATTLE OF MILTON, TENNESSEE
21—24	In camp
25—26	Grand Review.
27—31	In camp, Murfreesboro, Tennessee

APRIL 1863

1— 5	In camp
6—	Company B detached as guard at Hospital
7—19.	In camp
20—30.	On reconnaissance, toward Liberty, Tennessee

MAY 1863

1—10	In camp, Murfreesboro, Tennessee
11—	Moved camp to new position
12—29	In camp.
29—	Company B rejoined regiment
30—31.	In camp

JUNE 1863

1—23	In camp.
24—	Started on Tullahoma campaign
25—	BATTLE OF HOOVER S GAP, TENNESSEE

26 In line of battle beyond Hoover's Gap
27 Arrived at Manchester, Tennessee
29–30 Marching and skirmishing

JULY 1863

1 Entered Tullahoma, Tennessee
2— Crossed Elk and Duck Rivers pursuing Bragg
3–6 On march
7–9 In camp
10 COLONEL HALL DIED AT MURFREESBORO, TENNESSEE
11–24 In camp
25 Moved camp beyond Decherd, Tennessee
26–28 In camp
29 March to top of Mountain—Camp University
30–31 In camp University Heights, Tennessee

AUGUST 1863

1–15 In camp University Heights, Tennessee
16–19 On march Battle Creek Valley Road
20–29 In camp near Jasper, Tennessee
30 Crossed Tennessee River at Shell Mound

SEPTEMBER 1863

1–2 In camp at Shell Mound, Tennessee
3–5 On march to Trenton, Georgia
6 In camp near Trenton, Georgia
7 Marched to foot of Lookout Mountain Range
8 In camp
9 Heard of evacuation of Chattanooga by Confederates
10— Began march across Sand Mountains
11 Arrived at top of mountain
12— In camp near Pond Spring, Georgia
13 Marched three miles to Hog Jaw Valley
14 In line of battle near Pond Spring, Georgia
15 Marched 10 a. m., to meet Palmer's Division
16 In camp near Pond Spring, Georgia
17 Skirmishing on the right
18 Marched all night to the left
18–22 Companies C and H detailed with train
19–20 BATTLE OF CHICKAMAUGA
21 Fell back to Chattanooga, Tennessee
22–30 Besieged in Chattanooga, Tennessee. Short rations, heavy duty, frequent skirmishing

October 1863

1—19 Besieged in Chattanooga,
20— Moved camp to right of railroad.
21—31 In camp, heavy duty, light rations

November 1863

1—22 Besieged in Chattanooga
23— Form line of battle left of Fort Negley
24— BATTLE OF LOOKOUT MOUNTAIN.
25— BATTLE OF MISSIONARY RIDGE
26— Thanksgiving Day—Pursuing the enemy
27—28 On march toward Ringgold, Georgia.
29— Return to Chattanooga
30— In camp, Chattanooga

December 1863

1—31. In camp at Chattanooga Tennessee, and vicinity

January 1864

1—24. In camp at Chattanooga and vicinity
25—27 Reconnaissance toward Harrison, Georgia.
28— Return to camp at Chattanooga, Tennessee.
29—31 In camp in Chattanooga

February 1864

1—20 In camp at Chattanooga
21— Advance to Ringgold, Georgia
22—29. In camp near Ringgold, Georgia.

March 1864

1— On outpost, in front of Hooker's Pass, near Ringgold, Georgia
2—31 In camp in front of Ringgold, with outpost duty every fourth day

April 1864.

1—28 Same as March On outpost near Ringgold, Ga.
29— Reconnaissance Drove into enemy's pickets.
30—31 In camp near Ringgold, Georgia

May 1864

1— In camp near Ringgold, Georgia
2— Reconnaissance toward Tunnel Hill, Georgia, and return.
3— 6 In camp Preparing to advance

7 — General advance. Formed line of battle near Tunnel Hill, Georgia.

8 Moved forward cautiously; frequent skirmishes.

9 Pressing the enemy back.

10 Long march to the right.

11 Halted all day.

12 Moved at 3 a. m. through Snake Creek Gap. Enemy falling back to Resaca.

13 Crowded the enemy all day until dark.

14 BATTLE OF RESACA.

15 Fighting to hold works captured the day before, in front of Resaca.

16 — Enemy disappeared from our front.

17 In pursuit. Marched through Calhoun, Georgia.

18 Still pursuing; passed through Adairsville, Georgia.

19 Marched along railroad to Kingston, Georgia.

20–21 On skirmish line at the front.

22 All extra baggage sent to the rear.

23 Marched south by southeast all day; waded Etowah River; bivouacked in woods.

24 Under arms all day.

25–27 On march, guarding trains.

29–31 Train guard.

JUNE, 1864

1 Very hard march to the front; bivouacked in reserve.

2–4 Constant skirmishing day and night.

5 Sharp skirmishing all night. Enemy withdrew.

6–7 Marched half a day; halted and threw up strong works.

8–9 Quiet. No fighting.

10 Moved forward. Skirmishing all day.

11 Still pressing enemy. March all night.

12 Tired out. Slept in line in reserve.

13 Reconnaissance.

14 Moved forward. Hot fighting.

15 Secured good position and threw up works.

16 Attacked; held position.

17 Enemy fell back. Advanced in second line.

18 Moved up on enemy's lines. Hot work.

19 Sharp skirmishing. Enemy withdrew to Kenesaw.

20–25 Constant skirmishing.

26 Moved to right with great caution.

27 BATTLE OF KENESAW MOUNTAIN.

28— Hold position
29— Truce to bury dead
30— Night attack to secure an advance line

JULY 1864

1— 2 Before Kenesaw
3— Enemy withdraw Follow in pursuit
4— Enter Marietta, Georgia
5—10 In camp at Marietta, Georgia
11— Ordered to the front
12—13 On reconnaissance
14—16 In camp, spires of Atlanta visible
17— Crossed Chattahoochee River on pontoons
18— Marched down river two or three miles
19— At the front Sharp fighting
20— BATTLE OF PEACH TREE CREEK
21— Drove enemy at 3 p m Pursued until dark
22— Enemy fell back , following him closely
23— Hot work and hot weather
24— Sunday both sides rest
25—31 In trenches before Atlanta, Georgia

AUGUST 1864

1— 7 Siege of Atlanta continued
8— Regimental dog " Watch " mortally wounded
9— Kelley, owner of Watch " mortally wounded
10—11 Heavy shelling
12—13 Brigade and division extending lines
14—19 Heavy duty Constant skirmishing
20— Companies D H and I sent to the right
21— TWO YEARS SERVICE COMPLETED
22— Usual siege-work.
23—26 BATTLE OF ATLANTA
27— Sharp attack Captain Ambrose E Mason died
28— Moved to right at daylight to Red Oak Station
29— In camp
30— Worked all day destroying railroad
31— Moved to the front

SEPTEMBER 1864

1— BATTLE OF JONESBOROUGH
2— ATLANTA TAKEN
3—12 In camp
14—15 Foraging Crossed Chattahoochee River

16—26 In camp near Atlanta, Georgia, with picket duty now and then. Numerous leaves and furloughs.
27— Colonel Perkins and Lieut. Lockwood start home.
28 Major Edwards detailed on Court Martial. Captain Wilcox in command.
29 Report of enemy in our rear. Lieutenant Castle received leave of absence for thirty days.
30 No more furloughs to be granted. Enemy moving to the rear.

OCTOBER 1864

1—2 Under orders to move in pursuit of Hood.
3 Begin march at 2 p. m.
4 Re-crossed Chattahoochee on R. R. bridge.
5 March through Marietta, Georgia.
6 Passed point of Kenesaw Mountain.
7 On march toward Ackworth, Georgia.
8 On march; halted near Ackworth, Georgia.
10 On march through Allatoona Pass.
11 March toward Kingston, Georgia, till noon. Hold State election in the afternoon.
12 March toward Rome, Georgia.
13— In camp until 4 p. m.; marched until 2 a. m.
14 March at daylight; arrive at Calhoun, Georgia.
15 Cross Oostanaula River on pontoons.
16 March through Snake Creek Gap.
17 General Sherman issues order to prepare for a long and arduous campaign in pursuit of Hood.
18— March south, leaving LaFayette to the right.
19 On the Summerville Road.
20 Pass Logansport Postoffice.
21—28 Regiment running mill, grinding wheat and building bridge at Gaylesville, Alabama.
29 On march toward Rome, Georgia.
30 Arrive at Rome, Georgia.
31 In camp near Rome.

NOVEMBER 1864.

1 Foraging.
2 On march.
3—11 In camp at Kingston, Georgia.
12 March over road we had already twice traveled, toward Ackworth, Georgia.

13— Destroy railroad, pass through Ackworth, arrive at Big Shanty
14— Tear up railroad Marietta burning
15— March to Atlanta Destroy everything that could give aid and comfort to the enemy
16— MARCH TO THE SEA BEGUN Passed Decatur Georgia
17— Standing order to break camp at 7 a m March through Lithonia and Congress, Ga
18— March through Oxford, Ga cross Yellow River
19— March toward Monticello, Georgia
20— Arrive at Shady Dale, Georgia Destroy stores
21— On march toward Milledgeville, Georgia
22— In advance of corps Camp twelve miles from Milledgeville
23— Arrive at Milledgeville Legislature ADJOURNED before we arrived
24— In camp near Milledgeville Georgia
25— March through Milledgeville Camp eight miles beyond
26— Sharp skirmish at Sandersville Georgia
27— Rapid march northwestward Burned large amounts of cotton
28— On march Reached town of Louisville Georgia
29—30 Marching with constant skirmishes

DECEMBER 1864

1— Ordered to the front Drove back enemy
2— 3 Marched and tore up railroad track
4— Sent to support cavalry at Waynesboro, Georgia
5— 7 On march, low swampy region
8— Enemy attack rear guard, in line until midnight
9—10. On march, destroying railroad
11— Nearing Savannah wade very wide stream
12— Capture boat loaded with supplies
13— Moved round to right sharp fighting
14—15 FORT McALLISTER TAKEN COMMUNICATION OPENED WITH THE NORTH
16— On march, crossed Ogeechee River
17— In rear of train, no rations
18— March early
19— On march Cold nights
21— ENEMY EVACUATED SAVANNAH
22— Camped in suburbs of Savannah
23—31 In camp, Savannah, Georgia

January 1865

1—19 In camp, Savannah, Georgia
20— Moved up the river seven miles above city
20—24 In camp seven miles above city
25— Moved to camp fifteen miles from Savannah
26 On march. Roads blocked with felled timber
27 Marched to Springfield, Georgia
28 Marched up Savannah River
29—31 In camp; river too high to cross

February 1865

1—4 In camp waiting for river to fall
5— Crossed Savannah River into South Carolina
6 In camp
7 March eleven and a half miles; pass through Robertsville, South Carolina
8— On march. "MARKING OUR COURSE WITH FIRE"
9 On march, road leading toward Augusta, Georgia
10 Marched to Barnwell C. H., S. C., and camped
11— Started at noon for Williston, South Carolina; camp after dark
12— Hard march of twenty miles; tore up R. R. track; water scarce
13 Reach Edisto river about noon
14— Crossed S. Edisto and N. Edisto; camp 11 p. m.
15 March until 10 p. m.; a tough day
16 March through Lexington C. H., S. C.
17— Start late; crossed river on pontoons
18— Built corduroy roads; marched near Broad River
19 Crossed river; tore up R. R. track; marched to Alston, South Carolina
20— In camp, and on forage expedition
21— Started for Winsborough, South Carolina
22 Tore up R. R. north of Columbia, S. C.
23 Marched to Rocky Mount, S. C., camped
24—28 In camp; streams high; pioneers having trouble with pontoons
28 Move at midnight until daylight crossing river

March 1865

1 March at daylight; our regiment in advance
2 March; our regiment in rear
3 Crossed Lynches Creek near night

4—	CHARLESTON, S. C., OURS! WILMINGTON, N. C., ALSO!
5—	March to Great Pedee River.
6—	In camp; "NO VANDALISM IN THE 'OLD NORTH STATE.'"
7—	March without breakfast, trouble with pontoons.
8—	March twenty-five miles. Left Rockingham, North Carolina on our left.
10—	On march; bad roads, short rations.
11—	March five miles, enemy strong in front.
12—	March toward Fayetteville, North Carolina.
13—	Camp in Fayetteville. Destroy machinery of Arsenal.
14—	Troops on move through town.
15—	Brooks, of Co. D, wounded by citizen.
16—	Marched at 3 a. m.; eight miles and camped.
17—	Only made three miles, built corduroy road.
18—	Only made five miles; built corduroy road.
19—	Heavy firing at front; roads very bad.
20—	Sent to front. BATTLE OF BENTONVILLE.
21—	In camp.
22—	March towards Goldsborough, North Carolina.
23—	March through Goldsborough and camped.
24—	Regiment looks hard, clothes and bodies worn with marching.
25—	Dan Rush killed. No one safe outside camp.
26—	In camp; large mail; first since January 10th.
27—31	In camp, building works, on picket.

APRIL, 1865.

1— 2.	In camp, near Goldsborough, North Carolina.
3—	Review.
4— 7.	In camp. NEWS OF THE FALL OF RICHMOND AND PETERSBURG RECEIVED!
8— 9.	In camp, Goldsborough, North Carolina.
10—	Moved at 8 a. m. Skirmishing at intervals.
11—	On march at daylight; our brigade in advance.
12—	Enemy contesting every inch of ground, took Smithfield, N. C. NEWS OF LEE'S SURRENDER RECEIVED!
12—	March to Clayton, North Carolina.
13—	Mayor and citizens surrender Raleigh, N. C.
14—	Move at 8 a. m. March all day.
15—	On march.

16— Pass through Holly Springs. Clay Eddy, Co. K, shot.

17— In camp; arrest man who shot Eddy.

18— WOEFUL DAY! NEWS OF LINCOLN'S ASSASSINATION RECEIVED!

19–23— In camp.

24–26— NEWS OF JOHNSTON'S SURRENDER.

28— Moved through Holly Springs, N. C., and camped.

29— In camp.

30— Start on home stretch via Richmond, Virginia.

MAY, 1865.

1— On March; made twenty-five miles; halted an hour before sundown.

2— On march; made over twenty miles; got ahead of 20th Corps.

3— On march; made over fifteen miles; crossed Roanoke River.

4— On march; made over twenty miles; crossed South and North Forks of Meherrin River.

5— Crossed Nottaway River.

6— Marched twenty-seven miles; crossed Appomattox River; lost four men with sunstroke.

7— Marched twenty-five miles; camped three miles from Richmond, Virginia. MARCHED 205 MILES IN LAST EIGHT DAYS!

8–10— In camp near Richmond, Va.; men badly used up.

11— Marched twenty-two miles.

12— Marched ten miles; passed Hanover C. H., Va.

13— Marched at 5 a. m.; passed through New Market, Virginia.

14— Marched seventeen miles, marking westward.

15— Marched twenty-one miles; crossed Rapidan River at Raccoon Ford.

16— Marched fourteen miles; crossed Rappahannock River at Kelly's Ford.

17— Marched seventeen miles; crossed Aquia Creek.

18— Marched twenty-one miles; passed Manassas Junction; crossed Bull Run; marched through Centerville.

19— Marched ten miles; camped near Alexandria, Va.

20–21. In camp near Alexandria, Virginia; preparing Muster Rolls.

23— Regimental inspection.

24— Grand review in Washington, color-bearer received bouquet from General Sherman

25— Moved camp, crossed Long Bridge, camped on Union ground

26—31 In camp near Washington, making out Muster Rolls

June 1865

1— Making out Muster-out Rolls, getting ready to go home

2— All over mustered out, start for home tomorrow

3— Homeward bound via Baltimore & Pittsburg

4— Reached Pittsburg 11 p m , left 1 a m for Cleveland Ohio

5— Arrive in Cleveland 10 a m had reception, occupy old barracks

6— 8 Turn over ordnance—addressed by Governor Tod —are paid off and discharged—start for home— CITIZENS AGAIN !

The whole period of service from the date of Muster-in, August 21, 1862, until finally discharged at Cleveland, Ohio, June 8, 1865 was three years nine months and eighteen days. The distance marched in that time was over 3000 miles From the time the regiment left the cars at Lexington, Kentucky on the 25th of August 1862 until it left Washington, D C , June 3d, 1865 neither the regiment, as a body, nor any company of the same was on any train of cars or boat, or had any transportation It marched all the way, passing through seven states The statistics of loss and details of individual service may be found in the tables of the appendix.

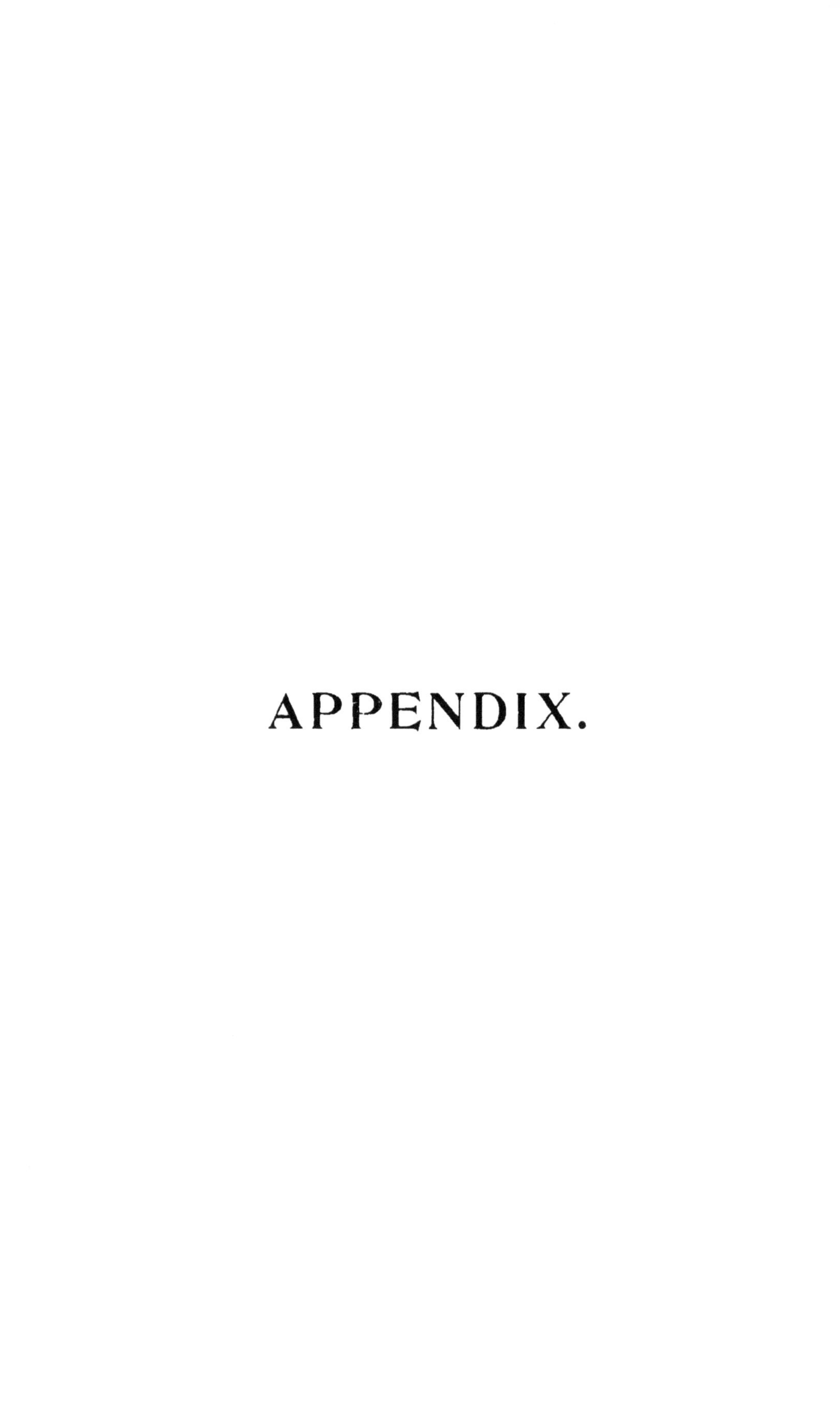

APPENDIX.

APPENDIX.

1

REPORT OF COLONEL ALBERT S. HALL OF THE PART TAKEN BY THE ONE HUNDRED AND FIFTH OHIO INFANTRY IN THE BATTLE OF PERRYVILLE.

Having commanded the One hundred and fifth Regiment Ohio Volunteer Infantry in the engagement of the 8th instant near Perryville, Ky., it becomes my duty, although now commanding the Tenth Division, to report the part taken by said regiment in the battle. The regiment was on the march from Mackville to Perryville as part of the Thirty-third Brigade, commanded by General W. R. Terrill, in the Tenth Division, commanded by Brigadier-General James S. Jackson, in the First Army Corps, commanded by Major-General McCook.

The Thirty-fourth Brigade, commanded by Colonel Webster, of the Ninety-eighth Regiment Ohio Volunteer Infantry, was in the advance, and engaged the enemy at about 2.30 p. m. On hearing the fire of the skirmishers, General Terrill ordered forward the Thirty-third Brigade with all possible dispatch, and reached the field about 3 p. m.

My regiment was marching in rear of Parsons' battery, and at the moment of reaching the field was ordered to form on the left of the road in reserve. This point was occupied but a few moments when the order of General Terrill was given to file to the left through the timber to the extreme left of the Union forces. Upon reaching my position I found the One hundred and twenty-third Regiment Illinois Volunteer Infantry, Colonel Monroe, hotly engaging the enemy to the right and rear of Parsons' battery, then in position.

At the moment of coming into position on the left and rear of Parsons' battery, it was apparent that the enemy were determined to charge through the left of the One hundred and twenty-third Illinois Volunteers and cut off the battery.

This movement was immediately and effectually repulsed by the destructive fire of Parsons' battery and the charge of that wing of my regiment, most gallantly led by Major Perkins, executed by order of General Terrill, who was personally present.

The fire at this moment was terrific beyond description, and the running through my line of a six-horse team drawing a caisson created some disorder in my center. At almost the same moment of this repulse of the enemy, a determined assault was made by them on our left. A battery opened on us from the enemy's right, and from the form of the ground nearly enfiladed my line. Parsons' battery was stationed on a sharp crest of open ground about eighty yards from a wood occupied by the enemy. From this crest the ground descended to the woods and then ascended, so that the enemy [illegible] consecutive battalions in rear of each other. The battery was placed on a crest which abruptly terminated on the left a few yards from the guns, exposing the support to a cross-fire from the enemy's extreme right, of which the enemy was not slow to discern, and promptly availed themselves.

Thus at the distance of only fifty yards the enemy opened fire upon Parsons' battery and the One hundred and Fifth Regiment Ohio Volunteer Infantry, [illegible] to the enemy almost terrible fire, receiving a direct fire and the fire of an [illegible] the woods. The battery becoming disabled and the road battery on our flank making our position untenable, by the order of General Terrill in person I moved my regiment sixty yards to the rear and formed in the edge of a corn field, the corn not broken down. The enemy followed the movement, and when they had reached the crest, our former position, received a fire that opened their ranks with the wildest havoc. But the position of the ground was such that we were still under the fire of their battery, and the quick eye of General Terrill discovering a movement of the enemy in a ravine to turn our left, he ordered the regiment to retire into a cornfield in our rear, which was done in good order and promptly formed. In this cornfield, being much exposed to the artillery and musketry of the enemy and hidden from each other by the corn, some irregularity occurred in the line when a movement by the flank, then ordered by General Terrill, who could not be seen or heard distinctly by the command, tended still more to divide and scatter the regiment. The most of the living, however, followed the movement promptly and formed in the rear of Bush's battery, by General Terrill's order, and there remained in its support until the close of the engagement. At this last position, in the rear of Bush's battery, our brave and beloved Terrill, who had stood by my side and moved with my regiment from the moment it was engaged, fell mortally wounded by the fragment of a shell. At this moment the disability of the General threw the command of the Thirty-third Brigade upon me. I turned over the command of the One hundred and Fifth Regiment Ohio Volunteer Infantry to Lieutenant Colonel Tolles, and proceeded to collect the Brigade.

In the early part of the engagement, and before the Thirty-third Brigade became engaged, Lieutenant Colonel Tolles, with eight companies, by order of General Terrill, was sent to the left of the road in rear of the line of battle to protect the rear. He joined me at Bush's battery, having come forward and joined in the engagement with the Eightieth Illinois Regiment. Of the bravery manifested by the officers and enlisted men of the One hundred and Fifth Regiment Ohio Volunteer Infantry I can speak with the highest satisfaction. Not an officer and but few of the enlisted men flinched from the hail of death or left their positions unless ordered by their proper officers.

In the engagement at Perryville they have covered themselves with imperishable honor. Citizen soldiers, with not twenty days' drill, they have exhibited the coolness and efficiency of veterans. Of the mortality and of our wounded I speak with choking sorrow. Captain L. Dwight Kee, Company I, and Robert Wilson, of Company H, are no more; they fell upon that fatal crest by Parsons' battery, the former dead, the latter mortally wounded. Braver or better men never lived; truer patriots never offered a holier sacrifice to their country's cause. On the same spot twenty-nine enlisted men of my regiment gave their lives to the cause of constitutional liberty, each a precious offering on freedom's altar. God of the true and brave, these are thine; their country calls them no more. There too on that fatal spot were wounded not less than 150 of their gallant comrades. A. S. Hall.

II

Concerning Cannon Captured by the Third Division of the Army of the Cumberland at the Battle of Missionary Ridge

It has not been deemed advisable to cumber the text of this volume with the controversy that has arisen in regard to the capture of cannon and prisoners on Missionary Ridge The truth about the matter is very easy to perceive The division captured the guns in its front and also prisoners who opposed them Being then moved to the left along the crest of the Ridge other forces came up and occupied the ground over which they had passed and claimed to have captured the guns they found abandoned there, in some cases without knowledge of their previous capture also the prisoners who were in our rear, The following extract from Rev David B Floyd's History of the Seventy-fifth Indiana Volunteers' gives a very clear account of the matter, and is supplemented by the reports of Colonel Van Derveer, General Turchin and General Baird in regard to the same

"It was in this struggle of our Division with Cheatham's Division (Third Division Fourteenth Army Corps) that Colonel E H Phelps, the heroic commander of the Third Brigade was killed He was the only commander above a regiment that lost his life in the taking of Missionary Ridge by the Army of the Cumberland

"Cheatham's Confederates were trying to remove from our front a piece of artillery to which two wounded horses—one of them a gray—were attached Some of our boys were struggling to capture it The line of battle of the rear regiments in our brigade at this moment was in a recumbent position On witnessing Cheatham's men and ours grappling for this piece of artillery, Colonel Robinson ordered his regiments to arise, fix bayonets form line of battle facing north with the right wing of the regiment extending down the east slope of the Ridge and to charge along the slope of the Ridge in the direction of this piece of artillery"

Certain parties have been laboring hard for twenty-five years to make it appear that the famous charge of the Army of the Cumberland up the face of Missionary Ridge was made alone by the Divisions of Sheridan and Wood, of the Fourth Corps and that these two divisions captured all the cannon and prisoners Baird's entire Division and two Brigades of Johnson's Division of the Fourteenth Corps who were in the assault and captured their share of prisoners and cannon are overshadowed by these parties The Fourth Corps did not constitute the Army of the Cumberland by any means Even officers of high rank—like Sheridan and Hazen—got into a wrangle over the capture of these cannon One accuses the other of misappropriation of these field-pieces, and hauling them off when they did not capture them Certain it is, that some very shameful and dirty work was done in this regard as the accompanying reports of our Brigade and Division commanders will show In his official report Colonel Van Derveer says

"As my men sprung over these works, the enemy's cannoneers were caught in the act of loading and were bayonetted or driven off before they could fire their pieces Five guns were found here in position and captured by the Brigade, two by the Second Minnesota and three by the Thirty fifth Ohio The larger part of the enemy retired beyond the Ridge toward the left, vigorously pursued and driven near half a mile For thirty minutes a very determined resistance was made by the enemy Many of the troops of my command having in their charge up the Ridge lost their regimental organizations were in some disorder for a short time but all pressed toward the enemy The Ninth Ohio and the Seventy fifth Indiana came up in good order, and were placed in line perpendicular to the Ridge and fronting the Rebels [illegible] upon both sides and my Brigade [illegible] the crest of Missionary Ridge. After the action one other [illegible] artillery [illegible] by the enemy was found by the Seventy-fifth [illegible] and taken charge of [illegible] guns that were captured by my command [illegible] while [illegible] pursued the enemy along the Ridge [illegible]. While they were thus absent the pieces were hauled off [illegible] to Brigadier General Wood's Division which [illegible] *[illegible] taken [illegible] ground [illegible] Division* [illegible] I was informed that they were [illegible] taken [illegible] where they could be used against the enemy. My Brigade at the [illegible] captured [illegible] caisson with six horses attached and a limber with [illegible] of horses. These too were taken to the rear with the guns. *No other troops [illegible] this battery [illegible] taken.* The enemy were driven from it by [illegible] own men and we thus lost possession while [illegible] engaging the retreating Rebel force.

General Turchin commanding the First Brigade of our Division in his report says:

"After leaving the Ridge I do not know what became of the cannon captured by my Brigade, but as Beatty's Brigade, Wood's Division, occupied the [illegible] which we stormed and [illegible] of the ground to the left of [illegible] I presume the guns were taken by the regiments of General Beatty's command and perhaps [illegible] the Second Brigade of our Division.

The fact was that reaching the top of the hill we had more serious work to perform than to count and guard cannon. The enemy was in strong force [illegible] our [illegible] and until the Second and Third Brigades [illegible] to them, all our energies were directed to fighting the enemy, and not to [illegible] displaying systematically the captured cannon."

General Absalom Baird, the commander of the Division, says in his report:

"[illegible] movement from the point where my right gained the top to the extreme left ten or twelve pieces of artillery were captured. My men found them in the possession of the enemy, some with strong infantry supports. They drove [illegible] from them and passed over them in pursuit. One of these batteries was recaptured by a [illegible] of the enemy [illegible]. The credit of capturing seven of these guns is claimed by the First Brigade, and the Second claim to have taken two. It is not impossible that two are the same in the [illegible] of the parties, for the men got much mingled together at the end of the assault, yet they may be distinct. Certain it is that *[illegible] the [illegible] regiment [illegible] of the [illegible] engaged that they [illegible]*.

While thus engaged upon the extreme left the guns which we had captured, and which we had left in the position where we had found them, were carried off to the rear, and we have since been unable to identify them [illegible] to reclaim them. I learn that all the guns turned over to the chief of artillery have been claimed by those presenting them as their capture, leaving none for this Division. I regret for the sake of the brave men who so fearlessly risked their lives in taking them that this is so, but I felt at the time that we [illegible] duty to perform as long as there was an enemy to be encountered, [illegible] that of stopping to secure trophies for exhibition after the battle. In [illegible] I was not quite sure that without strenuous exertion would we be able to [illegible] what we had already gained. In considering the evidence of these captures which I submit [illegible] half of my command, I trust that the General Commanding will remember that the [illegible] of the enemy being widely scattered [illegible] Ridge [illegible] spot [illegible] to have captured an unusual number must not only have taken possession of the works *in its own front*, but must have passed widely to the right and left along the crest, *before the arrival of other troops* The prisoners whom we captured, most of them, like the guns, were sent to the rear to be taken care of by others less occupied Out of more than 300 taken we have receipts for less than 200 "

III

Extract from the Report of Major-General Absalom Baird, Commanding Third Division, Fourteenth Army Corps, on the Atlanta Campaign

" September 3d, it was announced that Atlanta had been evacuated, and our campaign was at an end In this long, remarkable, and glorious campaign the soldiers of this army have endured fatigues, sufferings, and privations which will never be known or related The quiet and heroic patience with which all has been undergone, and duty performed, whilst establishing for them the highest reputation as soldiers will still tend to cause their hardships to be forgotten Starting without transportation and with only the supplies for an expedition of three or six weeks these things have been required to last for four months, so that often our officers, lying in the dirt and rain for days without shelter, have been unable to preserve the ordinary cleanliness which is essential to health, and many have broken down for want of proper food During the greater part of the time our men have lain constantly under the enemy's fire at every moment liable to be picked off, whilst the sound, not of distant artillery and musketry, but of the closely-whistling bullet and bursting shell, has seldom been out of their ears The rest which they have experienced by the simple cessation of these noises has been great Our losses, in the slow operations of the trench on picket, on daily and nightly skirmishes as well as in battle, although distributed over a great length of time, yet equal in the aggregate the casualties of the greatest battles The following report exhibits the total loss of the division in killed and wounded during the campaign from the 7th of May to the 7th of September

	Killed		Wounded		Missing		Total		
	Officers	Men	Officers	Men	Officers	Men	Officers	Men	Aggregate
Division Staff			1		1		2		22
First Brigade	7	55	15	277		2	22	334	356
Second Brigade	3	23	10	179		4	13	206	219
Third Brigade	4	109	31	487		10	35	606	641
Total infantry	14	187	57	943		16	72	1146	1216
Artillery				9				9	9
Total of Division	14	187	57	952	1	16	72	1155	1225

'This loss of 1 225 officers and men is to be compared not with the aggregate effective force of 8 460 men with which we entered upon the campaign but with a much smaller average in the field as the time of many regiments soon expired reducing our strength at the end of the campaign to an aggregate of 4 840 officers and men

The division captured during the four months [illegible] men including 61 officers. One hundred and forty seven of these desired to be sent to the rear and classed as deserters, the rest as prisoners of war. It will be seen by this that while the division has not lost in all [illegible] prisoners, that it has taken from the rebel army independent of those killed and wounded almost as many men as it has lost in battle. Some flags have been captured but not all turned over to me. Of material trophies however we have obtained but little except arms of no great value to our army.

A. BAIRD,
Brigadier General, Commanding Division.

IV

EXTRACT FROM THE REPORT OF COL. GLEASON COMMANDING SECOND BRIGADE ON THE ATLANTA CAMPAIGN

The Brigade Commander reports the following concerning the Second Brigade during this campaign:

During the whole of this laborious and eventful campaign the officers and enlisted men of this brigade have at all times manifested that patience and cheerful attention to duty for which they have heretofore been so signally distinguished. Where all have done so well it would seem unjust to discriminate. I cannot however fail to commend the faithful conduct of Lieutenant Colonel W. O'Brien commanding Seventy fifth Indiana Volunteers, Lieutenant Colonel Thomas Doan One Hundred and First Indiana Volunteers, Lieutenant Colonel J. W. Bishop Second Minnesota Veteran Volunteers, Lieutenant Colonel E. P. Hammond Eighty seventh Indiana Volunteers, Lieutenant Colonel George T. Perkins One Hundred and Fifth Ohio Volunteers and Major Joseph L. Budd Thirty fifth Ohio Volunteers, also Major C. J. McCole commanding Seventy fifth Indiana Volunteers since July [illegible] and Major Charles G. Edwards commanding One Hundred and Fifth Ohio Volunteers in support of the skirmish line during the advance on August 5 and Major R. C. Sabin Eighty seventh Indiana Volunteers commanding skirmish line, all of whom have handled their respective commands with promptness and ability. These officers deserve great credit for their gallant, strict and faithful execution of orders on all occasions. There are many line officers and enlisted men who deserve special mention, but the limits of this report will only allow me to respectfully refer to the reports of the regimental commanders. When the brigade left Ringgold the effective force numbered 25[illegible]. Two regiments, the Ninth Ohio and Thirty fifth Ohio have left the brigade on account of the expiration of their term of service. The Second Minnesota is still absent. Effective force present in four regiments 112[illegible].

Casualties of four regiments:

	Killed		Wounded		Missing		
	Officers	Men	Officers	Men	Officers	Men	Aggregate
87th Indiana Volunteers, Lieut Col. E. P. Hammond		[illegible]	1	[illegible]	1	[illegible]	[illegible]
75th Indiana Volunteers, Major C. J. McCole		[illegible]	1	[illegible]	1	25	[illegible]
101st Indiana Volunteers, Lieut Col. Thomas Doan		2	2	[illegible]	2	[illegible]	[illegible]
105th Ohio Volunteers, Lieut Col. George T. Perkins		1	1	[illegible]	1	33	[illegible]
Total		15	[illegible]	[illegible]	5	114	[illegible]

"The casualties of the Second Minnesota and Thirty-fifth Ohio regiments will bear a proportional average with the above regiments, including one officer in each regiment killed The members of the Brigade Staff—Captain Clinton A Cilley, Acting Assistant Adjutant General, Captain Samuel L' Hommedieu, Assistant Inspector General Captain Sanford Fortner, Provost Marshal, Captain M D Ellis Topographical Engineer Lieutenant C C Colburn Acting Aide-de-Camp, Lieutenant W H Osborn Acting Commissary of Subsistence Lieutenant W H Conner Acting Assistant Quartermaster—have faithfully discharged the duties of their respective departments Captains Cilley and L' Hommedieu having been absent since July 15th, Captains Fortner and Ellis have performed their duties the former that of Acting Assistant Adjutant General, the latter Acting Inspector, in a highly efficient manner

"I am Major very respectfully, your obedient servant

N GLEASON,

Colonel Eighty-seventh Indiana Volunteers Commanding Brigade"

V

COPY OF DISCHARGE FROM NAVAL SERVICE

This is to certify that No 89, HENRY C SWEET, MASTER AT ARMS has this day been honorably discharged from the United States Steamer "General Thomas," and from the Naval service of the United States

Dated this June 24 1865

GEO P RAND,
Acting Paymaster

Approved,
GEO MORTON
Acting Master

REVERSE

(RECORD OF ENLISTMENT)

Henry C Sweet, August 17 1864 occupation mason, eyes blue, hair dark, complexion fair, height 5 feet 7 inches Served on U S S "General Thomas"

VI

FAREWELL ORDER OF GENERAL SHERMAN

HEADQUARTERS MILITARY DIVISION OF THE MISSISSIPPI,
IN THE FIELD, WASHINGTON, D C, May 30 1865

"SPECIAL FIELD ORDERS, No 76

"The General Commanding announces to the Armies of the Tennessee and Georgia that the time has come for us to part Our work is done and armed enemies no longer defy us Some of you will be retained in service until further orders And now that we are about to separate to mingle with the civil world, it becomes a pleasing duty to recall to mind the situation of National affairs when but little more than a year ago, we were gathered about the twining cliffs of Lookout Mountain and all the future was wrapped in doubt and uncertainty Three armies had come together from distant fields with separate histories yet bound by one common cause — the union of our country and the perpetuation of the Government of our inheritance There is no need to recall to your memories Tunnell Hill with its Rocky Face Mountain and Buzzard Roost Gap, with the ugly forts of Dalton behind We were in earnest and paused not for danger and difficulty but dashed through Snake Creek Gap, and fell on Resaca then on to the Etowah, to Dallas Kenesaw, and the heats of summer found us on the banks of the Chattahoochee, far from home and dependent on a single road for supplies. Again we were not to be held back by any obstacle, and crossed over and fought four heavy battles for the possession of the citadel of Atlanta. That was the crisis of our history. A doubt still clouded our future, but we solved the problem and destroyed Atlanta, struck boldly across the State of Georgia, secured all the main arteries of life to our enemy, and Christmas found us at Savannah. Waiting there only long enough to fill our wagons, we again began a march which for peril, labor and results will compare with any ever made by an organized army. The floods of the Savannah, the swamps of the Combahee and Edisto, the high hills and rocks of the Santee, the flat quagmires of the Pedee and Cape Fear Rivers were all passed in midwinter, with its floods and rains, in the face of an accumulating enemy; and after the battles of Averysborough and Bentonsville we once more came out of the wilderness to meet our friends at Goldsborough. Even then we paused only long enough to get clothing, to reload our wagons, and again pushed on to Raleigh and beyond, until we met our enemy, suing for peace instead of war, and offering to submit to the injured laws of his and our country. As long as that enemy was defiant, nor mountains, nor rivers, nor swamps, nor hunger, nor cold had checked us; but when he who had fought us hard and persistently offered submission, your General thought it wrong to pursue him further, and negotiations followed which resulted, as you all know, in his surrender. How far the operations of this army have contributed to the overthrow of the Confederacy, or the peace which now dawns on us, must be judged by others, not by us. But that you have done all that men could do has been admitted by those in authority, and we have a right to join in the universal joy that fills our land because the war is over, and our Government stands vindicated before the world by the joint action of the volunteer armies of the United States.

To such as remain in the military service, your General need only remind you that successes in the past are due to hard work and discipline, and that the same work and discipline are equally important in the future. To such as go home he will only say that our favored country is so grand, so extensive, so diversified in climate, soil and productions, that every man may surely find a home and occupation suited to his tastes, and none should yield to the natural impatience sure to result from our past life of excitement and adventure. You will be invited to seek new adventure abroad, but do not yield to the temptation, for it will lead only to death and disappointment.

Your General now bids you all farewell, with the full belief that as in war you have been good soldiers, so in peace you will make good citizens; and if unfortunately new war should arise in our country, Sherman's Army will be the first to buckle on the old armor and come forth to defend and maintain the Government of our inheritance and choice.

VII

BIOGRAPHICAL SKETCH

When the form was made up containing page 31 it was found not only that the sketch of Corporal William Smith had been omitted but that the sketch itself had been mislaid. A note was therefore inserted referring to the Appendix.

WILLIAM [illegible] SMITH was born December 17, 1842, at Warren, Trumbull County, Ohio, [illegible] New [illegible] parents. His ancestors on both the maternal and paternal [illegible] the Revolutionary War. On the maternal side his [illegible] father and seven sons served in the war for Independence. He enlisted in the 105th, August 13, 1863, with his brother Horatio both as privates, and an hour later left for camp, was appointed corporal of Company K, was wounded on the head at the battle of Perryville, and soon after suffered an attack of fever, from which he recovered, with hearing so much impaired as to be unfit for active service in the ranks. Declining a discharge, however, he was detailed as brigade-wagonmaster, in which capacity he served through the Tullahoma and Chickamauga campaigns, or from Murfreesborough to Chattanooga, was then detailed by General Thomas to duty in the Depot Quartermaster's Department, with his brother Horatio and was mustered out with the regiment. He stuck the first stakes and laid out the first avenues in the National Cemetery, at Chattanooga and was present at the first interment in that beautiful resting place of our patriot dead. He has never married, and lives on the old homestead at Orwell, O.

Comrade Smith was one of the few members of the regiment to encounter personal adventure when isolated from his command. Soon after the battle of Perryville, while he was yet suffering from a wound he was ordered to carry dispatches to Lebanon, Ky. The country was full of Confederate soldiers who had straggled from Bragg's wing or been on leave when he was compelled to retreat. Besides that, Morgan was scouting through the country, and was supposed at that time to be on his way to Lebanon and it became advisable to get dispatches through to the commanding officer.

Smith, with two companions, undertook the task. Having become separated from these, when they had lost their way, he pushed on alone, being fearful of capture, and presently came upon the smoking remnant of a wagon train, which one of Morgan's detachments had captured and burned. Making a wide detour, he again approached the road near nightfall being then very hungry and greatly exhausted. Coming to a house, which gave evidence of plenty, if not welcome, he rode up and found himself in the presence of three men in Confederate uniform. It was too late to retreat, both himself and his horse being utterly done out. So he determined to make the best of the situation, and asked the master of the house, who was sitting on the porch with them, for supper and lodging for himself and his horse. While putting up the horse, a colored man gave him directions as to his route, and advised him to set out as soon as he could. He needed no advice of that sort. Returning to the house, he ate supper with the Confederates, neither asking any questions, and they seeming as uneasy as he felt. After the meal they sat about the fire for a while, as the season was cool, then Smith excused himself, went to the barn, found his horse already equipped, with a luncheon in one of the bags—mounted, rode quietly away, and spent the night in the first big cornfield which he found. In the morning he went on his way, and in the afternoon arrived safely at Lebanon where he found his regiment in camp.

VIII

EXPLANATION OF ROSTER AND TABLES

The 105th Ohio Volunteer Infantry was ordered to rendezvous at Camp Taylor, Cleveland, Ohio, on August 12th, 1862. Companies A, C, G and H were mustered into the United States service on August 20th, Companies B, D, E, F and I on August 21st, Field and Staff August 21st, Captain James R. Paxton, Fifteenth U. S. Infantry, mustering officer. It was mustered out near Washington, D. C., June 3d, 1865, by Captain Jacob Kline, Sixteenth U. S. Infantry. Disbanded at Camp Taylor, Cleveland, Ohio, June 8th, 1865.

The following roster is copied from the original rolls through the kindness of the Adjutant General of the State of Ohio, by Mr Arthur R Warren. A large number of errors in the roster published by the State have been corrected and it has been made possible by reference to the tables annexed to trace with accuracy the military history of every member of the regiment. These tables are designated by Roman numerals as follows:

I Promotions and reductions
II Wounded
III Captured
IV Transferred
V Mustered out absent from regiment
VI Killed and died in service
VII Resigned and discharged
VIII Missing and absent without leave
IX Record of previous service
X Color guard
XI Recapitulation

ABBREVIATIONS

The following abbreviations are used in the Roster and tables:

Apt Appointed
D Died in service
Dis Discharged
K Killed in action
M o Mustered out absent from regiment
Pr Promoted
P Captured or prisoner
Red Reduced
Res Resigned
S Previous service
V R C Veteran Reserve Corps
V V E Veteran Volunteer Engineers

Roman numerals designating tables should be read: See Table I, etc.

The preparation of these tables would have been an impossibility but for the indefatigable exertions of Comrade L Newton Parker assisted by Comrade M L Maynard. It is believed that the system adopted through their exertions gives the most complete and easily accessible military record of all the members of a regiment ever prepared.

ROSTER

105th OHIO VOLUNTEER INFANTRY.

From Original Muster-in-Rolls, with References to Historical Tables.

NAME	RANK	AGE	ENT SERV	REMARKS
		FIELD AND STAFF		
Albert S Hall	Colonel	31	June 3, 1861	Died See note 1
William R Tolles	Lieut Col	37	Aug 20, 1861	Resigned See note 2
George T Perkins	Major	26	Aug 10, 1862	* Pr See note 3
Charles N Fowler	Surgeon	34	Aug 12 1862	* Pr See note 4
Harvey S Taft	Ass Surg	35	Aug 19, 1862	Dismissed Aug 10 1863.
Joseph G Paulding		35	"	Resigned Apr 8 1863
Ambrose M Robbins	Adj t	25	Aug [illegible]1, 1862	Res Mar 28, 1863 See IX
Marshall W Wright	R Q M	43	"	Resigned Apr 13 1864
Aaron Van Nostrand	Chaplain	43	Sep 26, 1862	Died Feb 27, 1863 Painesville O
		SUBSEQUENT STAFF OFFICERS		
Charles G Edwards	Major	26	July 23 1862	* Pr See note 5
John Turnbull	Ast Surg	23	June 29, 1863	* Appt'd from civil life
Albert Dickerman	Adj't	22	July 28 1862	* Appt'd March 29 1863.
Stanley B Lockwood	R Q M	22	Aug 10 1862	* Appt d June 8 1864
Aaron D Morton	Chaplain	41	Sep 13, 1864	*
		ORIGINAL NON-COMMISSIONED STAFF		
Albert Dickerman	Sgt Maj	22	July 28, 1862	Pr See table I Co I.
Horatio M Smith	Q M S	27	Aug 13 1862	Pr See table I Co K.
William J Gibson	Com Serg	24	Aug 7, 1862	* See table I Co G
John Meharg	Hos St'd	22	Aug 11, 1862	* See table I Co H
Horace Rawdon	Prin Mus	37	Aug 9, 1862	See table I Co I
		SUBSEQUENT NON-COMMISSIONED STAFF		
Irwin Butler	Serg Maj	19	Aug 9 1862	* Pr See I Co C
Porter Watson		21	Aug 6 1862	* See I Cos A and D
Lester D Taylor	"	29	Aug 12, 1862	* See I Co E
George W Cheney	Q M S	18	Aug 4, 1862	See I Co G, * See note 6
William Doty	Priv Mus	24	Jan 5, 1864	See I Co F See note 7.

Note 1—Promoted from Lieut-Col 24th Regiment O V I Aug 11 1862; to Brevet Brig'r-Gen'l to date Oct 8, 1862 Died July 10, 1863, at Murfreesboro Tenn, interred at Charleston Portage Co, Ohio

Note 2—Promoted from Captain Co B 41st Regiment O V I, August 9, 1862 promoted to Colonel July 10, 1863, but not mustered Resigned January 29 1864

Note 3—Promoted to Lieut-Col July 10, 1863, to Colonel February 18, 1864, but not mustered to Brevet-Colonel March 13 1865 Wounded September 20 1863, in the battle of Chickamauga, Ga Mustered out in command See IX

Note 4—Captured September 20 1863 while on duty in the hospital at Chickamauga, Ga Mustered out with regiment.

Note 5—Promoted from Captain Co A July 10, 1863 to Lieut-Col February 18, 1864 but not mustered, Brevet Lieut-Col March 13 1865 Wounded at Perryville Ky, October 8, 1862 also at seige of Atlanta, August 25, 1864 Mustered out with regiment

Note 6—Promoted to 1st Lieut October 24, 1864 but not mustered

Note 7—Transferred to the 38th Regiment O V I, as Principal Musician, June 1, 1865

Roster Company A.

NAME	RANK	AGE	DATE OF ENLISTMENT 1862	REMARKS
Charles G Edwards	Captain	26	July 23	Pr W S I II IX *
Richard J See	1st Lieut	23		Pr W S I II IX *
Daniel B Stambaugh	2d Lieut	23	"	Pr W S I II IX *
Patten Himrod	1st Sergt	23	Aug 1	Pr S Res I VII IX
Porter Watson	Sergt	21	Aug 6	Pr S I IX *
Nathan W King		26	July 26	Killed See VI
James Crays		30	"	Pr W See I II *
Lafayette McCoy		30	"	W D See II VI
Joseph T Torrence	Corporal	21	Aug 5	W Dis See II VII
James Brown		21	July 25	Pr W See I II *
James Morris		36	Aug 5	Pr * See I X
Isaiah J Nessle		18	Aug 6	Pr W See I II *
John F McColom		20	July 31	W Tr See II IX
William H Cratz		35	July 26	Pr K See I VI
Joseph H Applegate		22	July 29	Killed See VI
William Phillips		22	Aug 5	W See II *
John [illegible]	Wagoner	24	Aug 1	Dis See VII
Anderson George S	Private	38	Aug 1	Dis See VII
Allen James		18	Aug 6	*
Alexander Samuel L		19		*
Barr Alexander		43	"	P D See III VI
Burns Michael		23	Aug 4	W See II *
Boyle John A		25	"	W P D See II III VI
Bailey Henry B		20	"	W See II *
Bowen Thomas		20	July 26	P See III *
Conklin George		18	July 31	W Dis See II VII
Cook Donald		40	Aug 2	Tr See IX
Cowley Hugh		20	Aug 5	W P See II III *
Coulter James C		26	Aug 1	P D See III VI
Davis William G		28	Aug 6	Pr W * See I II X
Edmonds David		22	Aug 5	P See III VIII
Fair Emanuel		34	Aug 6	P Dis See III VII
Flecker John		42	Aug 3	W Dis See II VII
Fielding Charles		35	July 27	W Dis See II VII
Filer James		28	Aug 7	*
Foster John C		30	Aug 6	P Tr See III IX
George Thomas		22	Aug 2	*
Hanify John J		27	July 28	W Dis See II VII
Helliger Frederick		18	Aug 6	W P See II III *
Hunter James		41	July 26	Dis See VII
Hulburt Frank		21	Aug 5	W P See II III VIII
Halloway Dixon		22	Aug 2	*
Harber Aaron		27	July 28	P Tr See III IX
Jones, William L		34	Aug 5	Tr See IX
Jewell John D		28		Pr Dis See I VII
Jones William		40	Aug 6	*
Jones David D		20	July 31	Dis See VII
Jarra Thomas		22	Aug 11	*
James Frederick		22	Aug 5	W See II *
Kyle Wesley		20	July 31	P See III *
Kelley Mahershalal		24	Aug 1	* See X
Kelley Stephen T		30	Aug 2	Tr See IX
Knox Andrew		27	Aug 5	*
Kay Robert		21	Aug 6	Pr See I *
Lally Thomas		32	July 28	*
Lewis, Benjamin B		22	Aug 6	Died See VI
Moore, Ashley		22	July 31	*
Moore, Francis		18	July 28	*
Malcomson James		35	July 28	P Tr See III IX
Miles John		26	Aug 6	W * See II
Morris Thomas H		38		Dis See VII
Morris Isaac		28	July 26	P D See III VI
Miller, Albert		24	July 21	Killed See VI
McFall Simon P		22	July 28	W * See II
McKibben Robert		30	Aug 3	Tr See IX
McGinty Michael		40	Aug 4	Killed See VI
McKanna Dennis		32	July 27	*
McDonald John B		30	Aug 2	*
Nox, James F		17	July 31	Dis See VII

Roster Company A—Continued.

NAME.	RANK	AGE	DATE OF ENLISTMENT, 1862	REMARKS
Niblack, Henry	Private	19	Aug 5	Killed See VI
O'Harra James	"	18	Aug 4	Dis See VII
Price, William B	"	18	July 26	Died See VI
Porter, Robert C	"	18	Aug 6	Pr P * See I, III,
Patterson James	"	26	July 25	Tr See IV
Phillips, John		20	Aug 5	*
Parker John T	"	32	July 31	*
Reep, Reuben B	"	17	"	P D See III VI
Rees Richard	"	34	July 26	W Dis See II, VII
Robbins, Daniel	"	42	July 24	Dis See VII
Renn John W	"	27	Aug 5	P Dis See III, VII
Smith, Daniel A		26	Aug 1	Tr See IV
Stewart, John Alex r	"	26	Aug 2	Tr See IV
Stewart, John Allen	"	22	July 29	P Tr See III, IV
Stewart, Samuel M	"	20	July 28	P Dis See III VII
Stewart, William W	"	20	July 27	Died See VI
Stein, Jacob	"	27	Aug 5	Tr See IV.
Stambaugh, John E	"	20	July 26	P See III, *
Sparrow, Emmons	"	21	Aug 5	P See III VIII
Smith Benjamin	"	24	Aug 1	P D See III VI
Thomas, John B	"	40	July 26	Died See VI
Tyrell, Thomas	"	19	Aug 9	W Dis See II VII
Walser George W	"	31	Aug 2	Pr W D See I, II, VI
Wise, Jonathan	"	24	"	*
Wetherstay Henry	"	22	"	W D See II, VI
Williams, Richard	"	44	Aug 6	See VIII
Williams, James	"	19	Aug 9	Killed See VI
Williams, Clytus	"	19	Aug 7	W D See II, VI
Webb John H		22	July 21	Died See VI
Young, Lewis	"	26	July 25	*
RECRUITS				
Charles C Stover	Musician	24	Dec 16 1863	Tr See IV
Baker, George	Private	21	Mar 22, 1864	Tr See IV
Bailey, William	"	19	Mar 21, 1864	Tr See IV
Christy, James	"	27	Jan 4, 1864	Tr See IV
Heiliger, Oscar C F	"	18	Mar 31, 1864	Tr See IV
Herrington Frederick	"	38	Dec 12, 1863	Tr See IV
Hotham, Leonard K	"	19	Jan 4, 1864	Tr See IV
Houston, Richard	"	36	Mar 31, 1864	W D See II, VI
Howard, Edward L	"	35	Jan 4, 1864	Tr See IV
Huston Dickson	"	36	Mar 31, 1864	Died See VI
Kaine, Anthony	"	19	Jan 5, 1864	Tr See IV
McCambridge Patr k	"	35	Apr 6, 1864	Tr See IV
McLarin John	"	30	Nov 11, 1863	Died See VI
O'Donal, John	"	23	Dec 31, 1863	Tr See IV
Porter Lewis	"	40	Mar 31, 1864	Tr See IV
Rayen James T	"	31	Sep 19, 1864	Term, one year, *
Reed Eli S	"	36	Feb 2, 1864	Tr See IV
Rowe, James	"	35	Mar 4, 1864	Tr See IV
Russell, Elijah B	"	35	Dec 20 1863	Tr See IV, VI
Shingledecker John	"	**	Mar. 31, 1864	Died See VI
Stambaugh, Sam'l N	"	19	Oct 12 1864	See IV
Stewart, James	"	32	Feb 10 1864	Tr See IV
Stewart, Cyrus	"	37	Mar 31, 1864	Tr See IV
Warner, John W	"	22	Mar 25, 1864	Tr See IV
Whetstone, David C	"	22	Mar 21, 1864	W Tr See II, IV

COMPANY B.

NAME	RANK	AGE	DATE OF ENLISTMENT 1862.	REMARKS
Ephraim Kee	Captain	25	Aug 2	Died See VI
Andrew D Braden	1st Lieut	27	July 19	Pr S See I, IX *
Henry L Niles	2d Lieut	35	July 23	Resigned See VII
Jonas F Wannamaker	1st Sergt	23	Aug 10	Killed See VI
William H Forbis	Sergt	22	Aug 7	Pr S See I, IX, *

Roster Company B.—Continued.

NAME	RANK	AGE	DATE OF ENLISTMENT 1862	REMARKS
Merritt Emerson	Sergt	24	Aug 8	Pr D S See I VI IX
Edward S Palfreeman		30	Aug 10	Died S See VI IX
William Hughes		21	Aug 2	W Tr See II IV
James M Dickerman	Corporal	37	Aug 12	Dis See VII
John B Ramsey		21	Aug 10	*
Michael Hess		30	Aug 12	Dis See VII
George P Center		34		Dis See VII
John A Ewart		19	Aug 11	Died See VI
Norval B Colt		31	Aug 12	Dis See VII
Daniel Fenwick		23	Aug 3	Dis S See VII IX
Henry L Emery		22	Aug 4	Dis See VII
Aaron F Merritt	Musician	22	Aug 8	S See IX *
Ellsby Ballard	Wagoner	22	Aug 12	*
Ballard Jonathan	Private	44		Killed See VI
Beebe Henry L		2?	Aug ?	P See III VIII
Bell Edward M		35	Aug 1?	W Dis See II VII
Bear Enos		21	Aug 7	*
Bear Abner		19	Aug 12	W * See II V
Burlingame Marcus		19	Aug 6	Died See VI
Caldwell Calvin		20		W D See II VI
Card Joseph		34	Aug 1?	Dis See VII
Craver Adam		24		*
Colton Francis		23	Aug 11	P See III *
Crawford James A		23		P D See III VI
Center Henry H		24	Aug 12	Dis See VII
Davis Marshall		1?	Aug 10	Dis See VII
Downs Jasper		19		Dis See VII
Davidson John P		19	Aug 8	*
Dilley Herman		26	July 11	Died See VI
Drennon John		21	Aug 10	Killed See VI
Ensign William		21	Aug 12	*
Faurot James I		20	Aug 10	*
Granger George W		26	Aug 11	Pr Dis See I VII
Grim Albert		18	Aug 10	W D See II VI
Grim Ephraim		21		W See II *
Hillman Hubert L		20	Aug 6	Pr See I *
Hart Seth		21	Aug 11	*
Hart Simeon		18		*
Hart Adelbert		19	Aug 10	P D See III VI
Hathaway James W		20	Aug 11	W D See II VII
Helsley John I		1?	Aug 10	Killed See VI
Hurst Henry		19		Died See VI
Holtz Wilson S		18	Aug 7	Pr See I *
Hadsell Edwin		21	Aug 10	P See III *
Hartman Joseph		19		Died See VI
Kelley Hugh R		35	Aug 11	W P D See II III VI
Kittridge Isaiah S		32		Dis See VII
Kinney Edwin J		19	Aug 11	Dis See VII
Kennedy Benjamin F		20	Aug 11	Killed See VI
Lewis Edwin D		23	Aug 9	W Dis See II VII
Lattin Wright		25	Aug 10	* See V
Lydon John J		28	Aug 8	W D See II VII
Long Lewis		34	Aug 10	Tr See IX
Lowery Hugh		22	Aug 11	*
Mason Charles H		21	Aug ?	P See III *
Mackey Alexander		27	Aug 7	P See III *
Mayhigh Benjamin H		18	Aug 11	*
Mahannah Harvey		21	Aug 10	W Dis See II VII
Mayer William		24	Aug 8	P Tr See III IX
Murphy John A		19	Aug 11	W See II *
Oliver Cyrus		37		Tr See IX
Prentice Albert D		30		P Tr See III IX
Prentice Edward		18		Tr See IX
Phillips Dwight R		19	Aug 10	P See I.I VIII
Percy Lauren A		21	Aug 2	*
Perkins Addison		30	Aug 8	Died See VI
Pound Noah J		22		Pr W See I II *
Pradon Stephen		37		Dis See VII
Ryan Jacob		25	Aug 3	Killed See VI

Roster Company B—Continued.

NAME	RANK	AGE	DATE OF ENLISTMENT 1862	REMARKS
Ragan, Ralph E	Private	22	Aug 10	*
Recker, Christopher F	"	28	"	Killed See VI
Rush, Daniel	"	18	Aug 11	W P D See II, III, VI
Sage, James	"	11	Aug 6	Died See VI
Sager, Edward W	"	21	Aug 8	Dis See VII
Scott, Hiram J	"	27	Aug 7	Pr W D See I, II, VI
Stephenson Homer	"	18	Aug 11	*
Sparks, Lorenzo H	"	19	Aug 10	Tr See IV
Stowe, Harmon W	"	21	Aug 6.	Dis See VII
Shafer, William J	"	19	Aug 7	*
Shafer, Charles	"	21	Aug 11	W P See II, III, *
Shafer, Jacob	"	19	Aug 4	P See III, *
Smith, Benjamin F	"	19	Aug 10	*
Smith John	"	20	"	P See III, *
Snodgrass Hugh J	"	34	Aug 11	*
Stewart, Charles	"	24	Aug 8	Pr W See I, II, *
Thomas George M	"	39	Aug 9	*
True, William C	"	21	Aug 12	Killed See VI
Tait, Samuel K	"	31	Aug 11	W D See II, VI
Tuttle, Albert P	"	20,	Aug 10	*
Tuttle, Osman B	"	22	Aug 12	Pr See I *
Ulrich, Martin W	"	21	Aug 11	P Dis See III, VII
Williams John S	"	20	Aug 3	Pr S See I, IX, *
Welsh, William C	"	19	Aug 10	P D See III, VI
Wildman, John E	"	19	Aug 9	P See III, *
Walcott, Newton L	"	20	Aug 10	Died See VI
RECRUITS				
Dayton, Charles R	"	20	Oct 21, 1863	Tr See IV
Decker, William,	"	23	Feb 13 1864	Tr See IV
Harver William	"	26	Mar 22 1864	Tr See IV
Heath, Henry	"	18	Jan. 5, 1864	Died See VI
Jackson, Hugh W	"	18	Feb 8 1864	Tr See IV
Johnson William H	"	37	Dec 22, 1863	Tr S See IV, IX
Lake Lafayette	"	18	Feb 8, 1864	Tr See IV
Rawdon Calvin L	"	43	Jan 4 1864	Tr S See IV, IX
Rawdon, Martin B	"	41	Jan 2 1864	Tr See IV
Shafer, Morrison P	"	18	Feb 9, 1864	Tr See IV
Weirman, Samuel	"	20	Nov 11, 1863	Tr See IV

COMPANY C.

NAME	RANK	AGE	DATE OF ENLISTMENT 1862	REMARKS
Henry P Gilbert	Captain	44	July 16	Res See VII
Ambrose C Mason	1st Lieut	21	July 23	Pr D S See I VI IX
James H Baird	2d Lieut	38	"	Pr Res See I, VII
Irvin Butler	1st Sergt	19	Aug 9	Pr Res, See I, VII
Austin W Wilson	Sergt	23	Aug 12	Dis See VII
Jacob Turney	"	31	Aug 2	S See IX *
Charles C Fowler	"	35	Aug 12	Red See I, *
John Geddes		25	Aug 11	S See IX, *
Robert D Allen	Corporal	31	Aug 2	Pr See I *
Robert J Stewart	"	25	Aug 11	W Dis See II, VII
Lafayette Seaton	"	27	Aug 2	Red W S I, II IX, *
John B Miller	"	27	July 30	Pr W See I II, *
Evan Lewis	"	30	Aug 2	Red S See I, IX, *
Albert Jastatt	"	28	Aug 9	W See II, *
James G Townsend	"	23	Aug 11	W Dis See II, VII
Clinton F Moore	"	20	Aug 9	Pr See I, *
Christian Hughes	Musician.	21	"	*
Thomas C Hogle	"	19	Aug 8	Tr See IV
Charles E Miller	Wagoner	32	Aug 7	W. P See II, III, *
Adams William F	Private	26	Aug 12	*
Brandt, John B	"	35	Aug 9	Tr See IV
Bartholomew Erastus	"	42	Aug 8	P D See III, VI
Blackmore, Samuel	"	38	Aug 11	Dis See VII

Roster Company C—Continued.

NAME	RANK	AGE	DATE OF ENLISTMENT 1862	REMARKS
Bolter James	Private	32	Aug 7	Dis See VII
Burgess, John		39	Aug 11	Dis See VII
Culver James		21	Aug 12	*
Casper Clarence D		17		*
Davis John W		28	Aug 11	*
Donovan James		26	Aug 6	W See II *
Davis William R		38		W D See II VI
Davis Morgan W	"	22	Aug 7	W Dis See II VII.
Evans William		24		W D See II VI
Evans Lazerah		23	Aug 12	*
Esgar Benjamin		23		Pr Red D s See I VII
Edwards James L		21		*
Edwards John P		19	"	W * See II V
Frazier John H		21	Aug 10	Dis See VII
Frazier, Isaac		21	Aug 8	W Dis See II, VII
Fuller Harvey A		25	Aug 9	Dis See VII
Godshall William H		19	Aug 8	Died See VI
Green George W		23	Aug 12	*
Graham William P		21	Aug 9	Tr See IV
Green John W		24	Aug 11	*
Hinds Reuben L	"	40		W Dis See II, VII
Hull Hiram F	"	33	Aug 9	Tr See IV
Hood Michael J	"	20		*
Hawley Joel		30	Aug 11	Dis See VII
Healy Joseph		29	Aug 7	W See II *
Jack William		31		Dis See VII
Jones, Thomas		21	Aug 9	Dis See VII
Jessop Thomas		23	Aug 11	*
Jones William		23	Aug 6	P See III *
Kingsley Jasper B		28	Aug 11	Dis See VII
Kelly Lawrence		26	Aug 12	W D See II VI
Lewis Caleb		27		W See II *
Lawrence Henry	"	30	Aug 1	Dis See VII
Lewis William		25	Aug 9	P See III, *
McKinley, Theron S		23	Aug 8	*
McLain Richard H		19	Aug 10	P D See III VI
Moser, Philip H		21	Aug 6	W Dis See II VII
McKenzie James R		19	Aug 8	P See III VIII
Miller, Lemuel B		20		W D See II VI
Moser Lemuel	"	32	Aug 9	Died See VI
Mackey John M		31	Aug 15	P See III, *
Morris William		24	Aug 12	*
Manwaring Morgan		28	Aug 9	See VIII
Moser Charles J		36		Dis See VII
Osborn, Alfred	"	28		P See III *
Powers Wilson S		18	Aug 11	P See III *
Price, Lemuel		23	Aug 15	W D See II VI
Phillips Joseph		30	Aug 6	Dis See VII
Powers John		23		W Dis See II VII.
Quigley Thomas		33	Aug 12	W Tr See II IV
Rowlee, Robert A		20	Aug 15	Pr See I *
Rosser, John P		34	Aug 9	P See III *
Ruppert, Samuel		19	Aug 8	Pr See I *
Roberts John		22	Aug 12	P See III *
Reis George L		18	"	*
Robinson, Thomas		23	Aug 4	P See III VIII
Richards David T	"	40	Aug 6	Dis See VII
Rodgers James	"	25	Aug 9	*
Richards, William T	"	32	"	See VIII
Rees, William R	"	33	Aug 6	P See III *
Shook Cornelius	"	22	Aug 8	W D See II, VI
Seachrist Isaiah		21	"	P See III *
Sutton Samuel		19	Aug 9	P See III *
Scoville, Horace H	"	29	Aug 11	Dis See VII
Sinclair, John		24		*
Sheaflor, David J		32		P See III *
Stewart Nelson O		21		P D See III VI
Smith Thomas		41	Aug 12	Dis See VII
Stewart James A		25	Aug 11	Dis See VII

Roster Company C—Continued.

NAME.	RANK	AGE	DATE OF ENLISTMENT 1862	REMARKS
Thomas, Thomas A	Private	19	Aug 12	*
Townsend Charles W		17	Aug 7	W Dis See II, VII
Tibbitts Austin	"	24	Aug 11	Pr See I, *
Vally Adolphus	"	30	Aug 6	W K See II, VI
Whitehouse Edward	"	27	"	Tr See IV
Walker, Homer B		20	Aug 12	*
Walker, Samuel	"	22	Aug 6	*
Wambaugh John	"	20	Aug 11	W Tr See II IV.
White, Andrew N	"	18	Aug 6	Killed See VI
RECRUITS				
Canon, William	Private	26	Feb 16, 1864	Tr See IV
Davis, Gwilym	"	21	Mar 8, 1865	Period Tr See IV
Davis, Morgan	"	21	"	Tr See IV
Dice, George M	"	20	Jan 15 1864	Tr See IV
Heir, George	"	24	Mar 8 1865	Tr See IV
Heir Thomas	"	21	Feb 21, 1865	Tr See IV.
Richards, John B	"	33	Feb 22, 1865	Tr See IV
Thomas, John B	"	23	Feb 21, 1865	Tr See IV
Webster Daniel	"	18	Feb 2, 1864	Tr See IV

COMPANY D.

NAME	RANK	AGE	DATE OF ENLISTMENT 1862	REMARKS
George L Riker	Captain	31	July 24	W R See II, VII
Henry H Cummings	1st Lieut	22	July 25	Pr See I, * Capt
Alonzo Chubb	2d Lieut	23	July 24	W P Res See II, III, VII
Stanley B Lockwood	1st Sergt	22	Aug 10	Pr W See I II * R Q M
Edward P Young	Sergt	25	Aug 8	Dis See VII
Solomon D Williams	"	43	Aug 10	W D See II, VI.
William D Curtis	"	37	Aug 6	Tr See IV
Warren Jennings	"	35	Aug 10	* S See V IX
Edwin N Durton	Corporal	21	July 28	See VIII
Robert N Shepherd	"	22	"	Pr See I *
Seth Weeks	"	37	Aug 6	Pr * See I V
Clinton A Nolan	"	33	Aug 12	Dis See VII
Harvey E Clark	"	30	Aug 7	W Dis See II, VII
George W Jewell	"	29	Aug 10.	Dis See VII
Harlan P Hall	"	20	Aug 8	Tr See IV
Francis M Judd	"	28	Aug 6	W Tr See II, IV
Hendrick E Paine	Musician	18	July 31	Dis See VII
William E Stickney	"	28	Aug 9	*
Michael Ward	Wagoner	19	"	W Dis See II, VII.
Allen, Nathan W	Private	47	Aug 13	Dis See VII
Ayers Hamilton	"	27	Aug 12	*
Ackley, Amiel J	"	37	Aug 11	W * See II, V.
Allen Minor A	"	21	"	*
Alderman, Victor	"	24	Aug 12	See VIII
Allen, Henry D	"	20	Aug 11.	Dis See VII
Barker, Frank M	"	23	Aug 10	Dis See VII
Back Ferdinando C	"	25	July 22.	Tr. See IV
Baker Edwin N	"	20	Aug 10	W Dis See II, VII
Blakely Harlow	"	18	Aug 5	W Dis See II, VII
Brooks, Eugene	"	26	Aug 12	Killed See VI
Brookins, Norman L	"	19	Aug 7	*
Brooks, Samuel	"	20	Aug 6	W P Dis See II III, VII
Bentley Murray J	"	21	Aug 7.	Dis See VII
Barnes, Calvin	"	19	Aug 12	*
Belden, Francis E	"	22	Aug 13	P D See III, VI
Britton John C	"	20	Aug 3.	Pr K See I, VI
Callender John E		21	Aug 5	S See IX *
Carpenter, Thomas W	"	21	"	Dis See VII
Cady Fordyce W	"	18	"	Tr See IV
Canfield Henry F	"	19	Aug 8	Pr W See I II *
Chesney, Samuel P	"	21	July 28	W Dis See II VII

Roster Company D—Continued

NAME	RANK	AGE	DATE OF ENLISTMENT 1862	REMARKS
Crandall Charles	Private	28	Aug 12	Died See VI
Doolittle Charles L		30		Pr * See I V
Doty David		18	Aug 8	*
Dart William H		19	Aug 5	Dis See VII
Elwell Isaac		27	Aug 9	Dis See VII
Fergus Melancthon L		28	Aug 10	See VIII
Grover Alonzo		35	Aug 4	P Tr See III IV
Grover Almon		2[illegible]	Aug 12	*
Gates Levi H		26	Aug 6	Dis See VII
Garner Frederick R	"	18	Aug 12	Killed See VI
Giddings Anson I		19	Aug 9	P Tr See III IV
Hall Albert	"	30	Aug 8	Died See VI
Hall Henry		2[illegible]		P Tr See III IV.
Hall James E		25	Aug 12	Tr See IV
Hall Edwin		21	Aug 13	Dis See VII
Hickson George		36	Aug 10	Dis See VII
Hopkins Floyd		21		See VIII
Jackson Stewart D		22	Aug 9	P See III *
Johnson William W	"	25	Aug 1	Killed See VI
Kerr Moses		21	Aug 10	Killed See VI
Knowles Alfred A		18	Aug 8	*
Lamport Benjamin G		25	Aug 13	Died See VI
Lewis George I		18		W D See II VI
Martin John		20	Aug 10	W D See II VI
Morse Bliss		25		Pr P See I III *
Morrison John		22		See VIII
Mayhew Edwin H		2[illegible]	Aug 5	Died See VI
McVitty Joseph		18	Aug 9	W Dis See II VII
Nash Harrison		21	Aug 13	W Dis See II VII
Nash Aver W		26	Aug 8	Died See VI
Nash Daniel P		27	Aug 13	Killed See VI
Pelton Watson		25	Aug 10	W Dis See II VII
Philbrook Charles H		38	Aug 6	Dis See VII
Pierce George L		21	Aug 11	W See II VIII
Potts Samuel J		23		W See II *
Place Ira	"	45		W See II *
Price Walter		2[illegible]		Died See VI
Palmer Edwin		22		Died See VI
Prouty Lucius A		21	Aug 9	W D See II VI
Raymond Alfred		21	Aug 1	See VIII
Randall Walter	"	18	Aug 5	W See II VIII
Rockafellow Oscar H		30		Dis See VII
Reynolds, George W	"	37	Aug 8	Tr See IV
Sager Harvey C		18	Aug 1	Dis See VII
Spring Charles B		25	Aug 5	W Dis See II VII
Sills Joshua H		18	Aug 1	P See III *
Turner Charles	"	33	Aug 6	Dis See VII
Tinan Orlando W		21	Aug 10	*
Taylor, James H		18	Aug 12	Pr See I *
Teachout Marshall A		30		Pr W P See I II III *
Tanner Harvey		25	Aug 10	Dis See VII
Upton William R	"	21	"	Dis See VII
Vickers Frederick	"	19	Aug 9	W * See II V
Warren Albert		19		Dis See VII
Webster Francis		19	Aug 12	W See II *
Wells Walter C		31	Aug 6	Tr See IV
Wakelee Oscar R		23	Aug 9	W * S See II V IX
Wellman Alonzo		4[illegible]	Aug 10	Tr See IV
Wakelee Arthur H		1[illegible]	Aug 8	W * See II V
Ward Elmer H		19	Aug 9	Died See VI

RECRUITS

NAME	RANK	AGE	DATE OF ENLISTMENT	REMARKS
Buck Fernando C		13	Dec 28 1863	Tr See IV
Barnard Philo		18	Mar 28 1864	Dis See VII
Lockwood Pulaski		36	Dec 11 1863	Tr See IV
Payne Alvin H		18	Mar 2[illegible] 1864	Died See VI
Swayne John		18	Dec 2[illegible] 1863	Tr See IV
Wakelee Byron		18	Dec 2[illegible] 1864	Tr See IV

Roster Company E.

NAME	RANK	AGE	DATE OF ENLISTMENT 1862	REMARKS
Byron W Canfield	Captain	26	July 24	W P Res See II, III, VII
William R Tuttle	1st Lieut	25	July 9	Pr See I, *, Capt Co H
John A Osborn	2d Lieut	26	Aug 6	Res See VII
John C Hathaway	1st Sergt	31	Aug 6	Dis See VII
La Royal Taylor	Sergt	35	"	Pr Dis See I VII
Julius A Moffatt	"	31	"	Pr Res See I, VII
Edward Patchin	"	29	Aug 8	W Dis S See II, VII, IX
James A Mowrey	"	29	Aug 9	Red See I III, *
Dean D Tucker	Corporal	22	Aug 8	Pr See I, IX *
George D Elder	"	21	Aug 11	Pr See I, *
Charles C Hitchcock	"	18	"	Killed See VI
Jonas Alshouse	"	41	Aug 5	Red Tr See I IV.
Stephen Patchin		24	Aug 11	Pr See I *
Miles J Whitney	"	19	Aug 4	S Dis See IX VII
Fernando C Conley	"	35	Aug 7	Red Tr See I, IV
Philo Boughton		31	Aug 12	Discharged See VII
Milton L Maynard	Musician	28	Aug 11	*
Albert Dickerman	"	22	July 28	Pr, See I, *, Adjnt
Albert A Champlin	Wagoner	22	Aug 11	P See III *
Ayers Josiah	Private	21	Aug 5	W D See II VI
Alexander Festus	"	18	Aug 2	Died See VI
Alberts, Washington	"	18	Aug 3	W D See II VI
Alshouse, William	"	32	Aug 6	*
Bowers, David C	"	21	July 24	Killed See VI
Brewer, Justin	"	21	July 30	Tr See IV
Bagg, Wilford A	"	24	"	D S See VI IX
Button Justin	"	21	Aug 5	W Dis See II, VII
Bond, Joel D	"	35	Aug 6	Died See VI
Bridgeman, Ansel O	"	23	Aug 7	P D See III, VI
Beckwith, James	"	27	Aug 11	Died See VI
Bridgeman, Edward S	"	26	Aug 12	Died See VI
Case, Gideon	"	18	Aug 5	W D See II, VII
Cutts, Jesse	"	30	Aug 11	*
Dickerson, Alonzo L	"	23	Aug 4	*
Dixon, Madison	"	20	Aug 7	Died See VI
Dusenbury Oscar	"	19	Aug 11	Pr See I, *
Dayton, William	"	21	Aug 12	P D See III, VI
Eggleston, Wellington	"	21	"	P * See III, V
Fowler, Justin	"	23	Aug 5	Dis See VII
Frazier, Calvin	"	21	"	Dis See VII
Fleming, James H		28	Aug 11	*
Fisher, Omi L	"	33	"	Died See VI
Grant, Preserved H	"	20	July 26	*
Griste, Luman	"	18	Aug 7	Pr W Dis See I, II VII
Hayden, Eugene	"	20	Aug 8	W Dis See II, VII
Hathaway Gilbert B	"	25	Aug 1	Dis See VII
Hale, William H		22	Aug 4	S K See IX, VI
Hitt, Oliver	"	22	Aug 7	W Dis See II VII
Hill, Almon	"	19	Aug 8	P See III *
Hill, Elisha	"	23	Aug 11	*
Humiston, John F	"	23		Pr W S See I II, IX, *
Hilbert Percival	"	18	Aug 12	Dis See VII
Hayes, Elisha W	"	23	"	P Tr See III IV
Jones Delavan	"	26	Aug 7	W * See II, V
Johnson Austin		20	Aug 6	Died See VI
Knox, Dexter	"	18	Aug 8	W D See II, VI
King, John Harvey	"	18	July 28	Dis See VII
King, Eleazar A		28	Aug 4	W * See II, V
Logan, Henry	"	19	Aug 5	Tr See IV
Ladow Sylvester		22	"	W * See II V
Ladow Henry		19	"	W Dis See II, VII
Langston, Henry	"	19	Aug 11	W See II, *
Latimer, Olney P		26	Aug 12	W Dis See II, VII
McFarland, McKendree	"	20	Aug 5	P See III, *
McNaughton, John	"	18	Aug 12	Pr W See I, II, *
McNaughton James A	"	20	"	Pr See I, *
Mack, Charles B	"	18		*
Norton, James H		30.	Aug 1	Tr See IV

Roster Company E—Continued.

NAME	RANK	AGE	DATE OF ENLISTMENT 1862	REMARKS
Osborn David		22	Aug 9	Killed See VI
Potter Edward		41	Aug 5	P See III *
Pugsley John		25		Dis See VII
Phillips George W		19		Died See VI
Porter Tilden W		24	Aug 6	*
Phillips Robert		19		W Dis See II VII
Pease Sherman		34	Aug 8	Pr See I *
Potter Elwood		16	Aug 11	*
Pease Byron A		21	Aug 8	Pr P K See I III VI
Quiggle Oscar P		21	July 30	*
Richards Evan		21	Aug 5	Pr See I *
Russell Elmer		21	Aug 8	W * See II X
Reed Daniel J	"	29	Aug 11	P See III *
Slade, Sherman C		19		Dis See VII
Silvernail Amos H		23		Died See VI
Strickland Walter		22	Aug 1	P D See III VI
Stellwell William		21	Aug 5	P See III *
St John George		24		Killed See VI
Smith Nathan M		21	Aug 7	W See II *
Sanborn Homer I		20	Aug 8	Died See VI
Strong Elmer	"	18	Aug 9	Dis See VII
Stocking John K	"	23	Aug 11	W See II *
Stocking Charles H		30		W Dis See II VII
Taylor Lester D		29	Aug 12	Pr See I *
Townsley Philetus		19	Aug 7	W See II *
Turner William		30	Aug 11	Dis See VII
Tucker, John T	"	19	"	W D See II VI
Way Merill	"	25		Died See VI
Watts Alonzo S	"	30	Aug 6	P See III *
Webb Ezra		34		W Dis See II VII
Webb Sylvester		35	"	W See II VIII
Watrous Samuel N		45	Aug 9	W Dis See II VII
Whiting John J		18	Aug 12	Killed See VI

RECRUITS

NAME	RANK	AGE	DATE OF ENLISTMENT	REMARKS
Pease Abner J		18	Dec 28 1863	Tr See IV
Patchin David		18	Dec 1 1863	Tr See IX

COMPANY F.

NAME	RANK	AGE	DATE OF ENLISTMENT 1862	REMARKS
Sherburn H Williams	Captain	35	Aug 1	Resigned See VII
Alfred G Wilcox	1st Lieut	21	Aug 8	Pr See I * Capt
Lester D Burbank	2d Lieut	35	July 25	Resigned See VII
Norman D Smith	1st Sergt	34	Aug 5	Pr See I * 1st Lieut
Charles R Brown	Sergt	26	July 29	Pr P See I III *
David C Beardsley		26	Aug 5	W * See II X
Harrison J Fuller		21	Aug 11	W D See II VI
Frederick T Cook		23	Aug 7	*
James W Allen	Corporal	30	Aug 5	Pr W See I II *
Michael Cooney		41	"	Dis See VII
George I Squier		21	Aug 12	Dis See VII
Lathrop A Johnson	"	27	Aug 7	Pr See I *
Dwight H Woodard	"	4[illegible]		Red W P See I II III *
Edwin R More		[illegible]	Aug 13	Died See VI
Henry B Potter	"	19	Aug 7	Pr See I *
Isaac D L Schram		27	Aug 4	*
Daniel F Hopkins	Musician	29	Aug 8	Dis See VII
Charles Sheldon		27	Aug 15	*
Ara H Drake	Wagoner	27		Dis See VII
Axer John H	Private	1[illegible]	Aug 7	W Tr See II IX
Axer Stephen D		2[illegible]		Dis See VII
Barnes James		[illegible]	Aug [illegible]	P D See III VI
Bisby George W		[illegible]	Aug 7	Died See VI

Roster Company F—Continued

NAME	RANK	AGE	DATE OF ENLISTMENT, 1862	REMARKS
Bailass, Robert B	Private	21	July 26	W D See II, VI
Brindle, James M	"	21	July 28	*
Brown, Arthur L	"	32	Aug 7	Dis See VII
Ball, Joseph	"	21	July 26	Killed See VI
Bottin, Elias T	"	18	Aug 2	Killed See VI
Burnett, Isaac	"	18	Aug 4	P D See III, VI
Ball, Thomas	"	34	Aug 5	Died See VI
Branch, Edward P		18	Aug 11	Dis See VII
Brewster, Oliver R	"	21	"	W D See II, VI
Button, Jared		19	Aug 2	Dis See VII
Clark, Nathan T		19	July 25	W P See II, III, *
Call, Francis M		18	July 30	Tr See IV
Cassidy, John	"	36	Aug 5	Tr See IV
Crawford Emery		18	Aug 6	W P Dis See II, III, VII
Crofford Stephen H		30	Aug 7	*
Caley, Charles	"	23	Aug 6	W P See II, III, *
Childs, Jarius	"	30	"	Pr K See I, VI
Colgrove, Melvin J	"	18	"	Dis See VII
Cooley, Levi	"	30	Aug 10	Dis See VII
Downing, John D	"	24	Aug 15	W P See II III *
Doolittle, Charles F	"	19	"	P K See III, VI
Davidson, Erastus	"	24	July 25	P See III *
Dimmick, Orlando	"	25	Aug 14	W P Tr See II III IV
Ely, Ira	"	39	Aug 6	Pr W P See I, II, III, *
Foote, Loami M	"	19	Aug 7	Tr See IV
Fales, Frank		19	"	Tr See IV
Greenfield, Judson	"	19	Aug 6	P See III, *
Gardner James W	"	32	Aug 11	*
Green Horace	"	26	July 30	P See III, *
Granger, Franklin	"	22	Aug 7	See VIII
Hale Elias B	"	42	Aug 11	Killed See VI
Hausch John	"	28	Aug 9	Dis See VII
Haver, Thomas T	"	28	July 25	Killed See VI
Holmes Hiram A	"	22	July 30	Dis See VII
Huston, Emmet C	"	31	Aug 4	Killed See VI
Keyes, Anson	"	35	Aug 11	Dis See VII
Kelsey Arthur	"	19	July 25	P Dis See III, VII
King, Nelson	"	21	Aug 1	*
King Josiah		23	Aug 6	See I, II III, VI
Lester David		30	Aug 5	Pr W See I, II *
Lemunyan Smith H		22	Aug 7	*
McClintock, Charles W		18	Aug 5	W D See II, VI
Morton, Henry	"	17	Aug 7	Dis See VII
McElwain, Edwin W		24	Aug 7	W Dis See II VII
Marsh, Henry		19	Aug 6	W P See II, III, VIII
Morse John H		21	Aug 5	Dis See VII
Martin George		24	Aug 8	W P D See II, III, VI
Malone Sydney D		33	July 30	See VIII
Newcomb, Frank E	"	21	Aug 4	Tr See IV
Newcomb, Selah W	"	19	"	W D See II VI
Nye, Ira		20	Aug 12	Killed See VI
Odell David W		21	Aug 1	W See II, *
Payne Wallace B	"	18	Aug 4	P See III *
Phelps Franklin W	"	19	Aug 7	Dis See VII
Phillips Albert		21	July 25	W Dis See II, VII
Parks, John		23	Aug 6	Dis See VII
Prouty, Royal	"	19	"	Dis See VII
Richmond, William		25	Aug 11	W Dis See II, VII
Randall James G		21	Aug 6	W Dis See II, VII.
Radcliff, Charles		18	July 30	W * See II, V
Schram Watson S		19	July 25	P See III, *
Sharpe George H		21	July 26	*
Smith, Frederick	"	35	July 31	Killed See VI
Smith Marsh, Jr		18	Aug 5	Dis See VII
Sweet, Benjamin F		22	Aug 6	Dis See VII
Slayton William T		21	"	Dis See VII
Simmons Reuben M	"	28	Aug 7	*
Snediker, Orrin	"	26	Aug 8	*

Roster Company F—Continued

NAME	RANK	AGE	DATE OF ENLISTMENT 1862	REMARKS
Sober Austin	Private	18	Aug 12	Dis See VII
Sober, Henry M		19	Aug 8	Dis See VII
Sober, Spencer		21	Aug 14	Died See VI
Strong Orestes L		21	Aug 12	Dis See VII
Tanner Henry H		21	Aug 7	See VIII
Tuily William		18		Dis See VII
Waller Harrison		19	Aug 5	W D See II VI
Waters Rollin A		21	Aug 4	Tr See IX
Young Benjamin		31	Aug 4	Dis See VII

RECRUITS

NAME	AGE	DATE OF ENLISTMENT	REMARKS
Blood Adomo	18	Feb 2 1864	Tr See IX
Cousins Levi B	19	Jan 5 1864	Tr See IV
Doty William	24	Jan 5 1864	P Tr See I IX
Ferry William	18	Jan 2 1864	Tr See IV
Gray Charles	19	Jan 5 1864	Tr See IV
Hobert Marcene	18	Jan 26 1864	Tr See IV
Kelsey Arthur	21	Jan 10 1864	Tr See II IX, IX
Ketchum Daniel	18	Jan 12 1864	Tr See IX
Manchester Lyman	18	Jan 13 1864	Tr See IV
Pierce Alson I	19	Jan 20 1864	Tr See IV
Rand Cassius M	18	Dec 28 1863	Tr See IV
Riley Charles H	18	Jan 26 1864	Tr See IX
Sadler John	20	Jan 20 1864	Tr See IV
Saxton Seymour	24	Feb 21 1864	Tr See IX
Scott Chauncey B	19	Jan 5 1864	Tr See IV

COMPANY G.

NAME	RANK	AGE	DATE OF ENLISTMENT 1862	REMARKS
William S Crowell	Captain	20	June 27	Res S See VII, IX
Albion W Tourgee	1st Lieut	21	July 11	See II III VII IX
E Abbott Spaulding	2d Lieut	21		See I II VI Co E
Weber F Thompson	1st Sergt	22	July 23	Red Pr S See I IX •
Joseph R Warner	Sergt	24	July 15	See I •
William B Braman		23		W Dis See II VII
Benjamin F Cushing		22		W Dis See II VII
Joseph George		25	July 26	Killed See VI
William H Barnes	Corporal	19	July 21	Red Tr See I IX
Orson L Marsh		21	July 23	P Dis See III VII
George L Felch		23	Aug 7	Pr Dis See I VII
Luke Northway		2[illegible]	July 26	Died See VI
Norris L Gage		22	Aug [illegible]	W Dis See II VII
Orlando G Clark		21	Aug 2	Dis See VII
Daniel H H Wheaton		20	July 20	W Dis See II VII
Charles W Baxter		2[illegible]	July 21	Dis See VII
Leander A Oliver	Musician	18	Aug 9	•
Jerome B Hawkins		19	Aug 8	S See IX VIII
Benjamin F Hewitt	Wagoner	20	July 25	Died See VI
Anderson Charles W	Private	22	Aug [illegible]	Dis See VII
Abbott Simon M		23	July 1[illegible]	P See III VIII
Barker Edwin I I		27	Aug 7	W Tr See II IX
Bachelor John W		2[illegible]	Aug [illegible]	Dis See VII
Brooks L I [illegible]		18	Aug [illegible]	•
Batt Jerry		1[illegible]		Pr Red See I •
Benjamin Lovestue I		20	July 2[illegible]	P See III •
Blood John C		18	Aug [illegible]	Dis See VII
Blood Fayette		21	Aug 4	Pr Tr See I IX
Baldwin Franklin		32	Aug 2	See II III VI
Benton Joel S		2[illegible]	Aug [illegible]	Died See VI
Cook Lowe		[illegible]	July [illegible]	P Tr See III IX
Christie James T		19	Aug [illegible]	W D See II VI
Chapin Stephen W		18	Aug [illegible]	P D See III VI
Caulkell Burroughs		2[illegible]	Aug 5	Dis See VII

Roster Company G—Continued.

NAME	RANK	AGE	DATE OF ENLISTMENT 1862	REMARKS
Crater, Oscar F	Private	39	"	Pr See I *
Cowles, Zeri	"	22	July 22	Died See VI
Cowles, Edwin R	"	24	July 24	W See II, *
Chapman, Zephaniah	"	21	July 17	Died See VI
Cheney, George W		18	Aug 4	Pr See I * Q M S
Compton, John D	"	19	Aug 2	W P D See II, III, VI
Drake, William		30	July 15	Tr See IV
Devoe, William P	"	26	July 24	P See III, VIII
De Wolf, William		21	Aug 6	*
De Wolf, John W	"	23	Aug 2	Tr See IV
Eaton, Irvin		18	"	P See III *
Felch, Franklin	"	21	Aug 4	W D See II, VI
Fox, Daniel M	"	20	Aug 2	*
Gant, William H	"	21	Aug 7	W D See II, VI
Gibson, William J	"	24		Pr See I * Com Sgt
Galbraith, Elbert P	"	18	"	W Dis See II, VII
Gifford, Harley N	"	22	Aug 5	Dis See VII
Greenough, John R	"	25	Aug 2	Pr See I *
Gould, Daniel C	"	19	July 20	W D See II, VI
Gillett, Leonard	"	19	Aug 6	*
Giddings, Francis W	"	19	July 24	W Tr See II, IV
Glancy, Charles A	"	21,	Aug 5	Pr See I *
Heath, Luther F		22	Aug 1	Dis See VII
Heath, Adoniram J		24	Aug 6	W See II *
Hall, Aaron		33	"	Dis See VII
Jones, James L	"	21	Aug 1	P D S See III, VI, IX
Kirby, George		36	Aug 5	Tr See IV
Kenney, Snel		18	"	W D See II, VI
Leavitt, Edwin R		21	July 16	Killed See VI
Lobdell, Dudley		18	Aug 5	W Dis See II, VII
Merritt, Eliphalet		30	Aug 6	Dis See VII
Morgaridge, Reuben		23	"	Pr See I * Capt Co D
Metcalf, George L	"	22	Aug 5	Tr See IV
McCreary, Harrison	.	18	"	W Dis See II, VII
Mills, Allison W	"	20	July 24	Pr See I *
Nichols, Hezekiah		39	July 30	Died See VI
Northway, Sherman		20	Aug 1	Dis See VII
Noyes, John P		27	Aug 7	Dis See VII
Newboe, Edgar		30	Aug 6	Dis See VII
Olds, William C	"	19	"	Pr See I *
Piper, Delos S		19	Aug 7	Killed See VI
Phelps, George K		19	Aug 6	Died See VI
Peck, Jasper	"	18	Aug 7	*
Pease, John D	"	31	Aug 5	* See V
Parker, Seth	"	23	"	P D See III, VI
Pettibone, Francis A	"	18	"	*
Reeves, Edwin		20	"	Pr See I *
Richmond, Sherman S	"	21	Aug 6	* See V
Rogers, William		18	July 26	Dis See VII
Rood, Orville A		20	July 31	P See III *
Rowe, Francis A		29	Aug 6	Dis See VII
Spencer, John C		32	Aug 7	P Tr See III, IV
Shipman, Wilson D	"	18	Aug 6	Died See VI
Smith, Jerome L	"	39	"	W D See II, VI
Shepherd, Horace		26	"	Dis See VII
Stevens, John E		18	"	*
Sill, John S	"	23	Aug 7	Dis See VII
Sill, Theodore		19	Aug 5	Tr See IV
Spaulding, Asa B	"	19	July 16	Killed See VI
Shultz, Jacob	"	19	July 25	*
Swartout, Lacy	"	34	Aug 5	Tr See IV
Stoll, Henry C	"	19	Aug 7	W P * See II, III, V
Turney, Albert A	"	37	July 23	Died See VI
Thompson, Lamonzo	"	25	Aug 4	Pr See I *
Waterman, William A	"	20	Aug 7	W D See II, VII
Waterman, Adna	"	18	"	W D See II, VI
Whipple, Perry M.........	"	26.	Aug 6	W D See II, VII

Roster Company G—Continued.

RECRUITS

Henry Adams	2d Lieut		Oct [illegible] 1862	[illegible] appt D See VI
Faller George A	Private	18	Jan 2 1864	W D See II VI
Faller, Martin H	"	21	Jan 2 1864	Tr See IV
Mann, Herman D		32	Jan 5 1864	Tr See IV
Parker William H		44	Jan 5 1863	Dis See VII
Richardson George A		20	Dec 22 1863	Died See VI
Sweet Jesse M		27	Jan 5 1864	W Tr S See II IV, IX
Torry Seneca D		31	Jan 5 1864	Tr See IV
Whitmore Chauncey		18	Jan 4 1864	Died See VI
Williams Milton	"	19	Dec 22 1863	Tr See IV

COMPANY H.

NAME	RANK	AGE	DATE OF ENLISTMENT 1862	REMARKS
Robert Wilson	Captain	40	Aug 9	Killed See VI
William H Clark	1st Lieut	27	July 23	Res See VII Co F
John C Hartzell	2d Lieut	21	Aug 5	Pr * See I X
Ira P Mansfield	1st Sergt	20	Aug 9	Pr W See I II *
Florentine M Simon	Sergt	19	July 21	W Dis See II VII
John McHarg		22	Aug 11	Pr See I *
Amos Cobbs		31	Aug 8	Red See I *
Abram S McCurley		24	Aug 9	W See II *
James S Caldwell	Corporal	30	Aug 5	Pr See I *
Joseph Carbaugh		23	Aug 11	Pr See I *
Horace G Ruggles		30	"	Dis See VII
William K Mead		27	Aug 1	P See III *
Manassas Miller		21	Aug 9	W See II *
Andrew Geddes		21	Aug 5	W See II *
Almon Eastman		28	Aug 11	Tr See IV
Henry R Myer		23		Dis See VII
Samuel Bright	Musician	19		*
William M Taylor		23		*
David Bricker	Wagoner	44	July 28	Dis See VII
Armstrong, William T	Private	20	Aug 8	Killed See VI
Allen, Joseph S		21	Aug 11	*
Allen Jesse F		40		*
Bennett, Thomas		25	July 30	Dis See VII
Boyle George A		1[illegible]	Aug [illegible]	Pr Red Dis See I VII
Brown Frederick		23	Aug 9	*
Bollard John H		[illegible]	Aug 11	Pr See I *
Boughton Horace		18		Killed See VI
Bachecker Jacob		24		*
Brenaman Constantine		1[illegible]	Aug [illegible]	W See II *
Baker Sylvester		1[illegible]	Aug 1	*
Baker William H		1[illegible]		W D See II VI
Cessna, John W		22	Aug 5	*
Cobbs Eli		1[illegible]	Aug [illegible]	*
Courtney Frederick		26	Aug [illegible]	Tr See IV
Dean Benjamin		31	Aug 11	Died See VI
Dull George M	"	32		Pr See I *
Ellenger John I	"	18		P See III *
[illegible] Zimri	"	21		W See II *
Flaugher, Joseph H	"	22	Aug 5	* See X
Fishel Eben B	"	1[illegible]	Aug 11	Died See VI
Fishel Solomon	"	18	Aug 30	*
Grossman John		18		P See III *
Hartman Nathan	"	1[illegible]	Aug 5	Killed See VI
Harrison, Jeremiah	"	2[illegible]	Aug [illegible]	P See III *
Hartzell Joshua	"	18	Aug [illegible]	P See III *
Hayes David		21	Aug 11	P See III *
[illegible]	"	18		W K See II VI
Hart Alfred		23	Aug 2	W Tr See II IV
H[illegible], Chauncey M	"	[illegible]	Aug 11	Tr See IV
H[illegible], Henry		[illegible]	Aug [illegible]	P See III VIII
[illegible] William D		[illegible]	Aug [illegible]	W D See II VI

Roster Company H – Continued

NAME	RANK	AGE	DATE OF ENLISTMENT 1862	REMARKS
Kaiser Frank	Private	21	Aug 11	P See III, *
Kirkbride James		25	"	W P Tr See II, III IV
Kirkbride, Joseph		23	"	Dis See VII
Kirkbride Asher		18	"	W P D See II III VI
Kirk Robert A		24	"	W See II *
Marlow William T		19	Aug 9	*
Myers, Jonathan		25	Aug 6	W Dis See II VII
Miller Addison		21	Aug 9	W Dis See II, VII
Mathias Edmund H		27	Aug 7	*
Middleton, William H		21	Aug 11	P See III, *
McCurley James		21		*
Musser, Hazard	"	18	"	See VIII
McCurley John C		19		Died See VI
Mathers, James T	"	19		Dis See VII
Nesbitt, John W		22	"	Pr W See I, II, *
Naylor, James B		20	Aug 6	P See III, *
Naylor, William H		22	Aug 8	W D See II VI
Noble, Homer		20	Aug 9	Died See VI
Ovington John R		22	Aug 1	*
Owen, Eli J	"	22	"	P D See III VI
Park James	"	20	Aug 11	P See III *
Price, Charles D		18	Aug 6	P See III *
Rummel Joseph		21	Aug 9	P K See III VI
Raub, Samuel K		18		P See III, *
Roahr, Charles	"	20	Aug 11	Died See VI
Raub, Isaac C F		20		Died See VI
Sherman Albert A	"	18	July 23	Died See VI
Shuick, George W		22	Aug 6	P See III *
Stratton Eli		21	Aug 8	Killed See VI
Shields, Homer J		20	Aug 11	*
Strawn Charles D		24	"	*
Stewart, Royal M	"	21	Aug 9	P Tr See III, IV
Stutler, Jesse		23		P See III, *
Silver, Allen	"	35	Aug 11	*
Silver, Jason W	"	24		Pr P See I, III, *
Smith, George J		25	"	Pr See I *
Spitler, George J	"	31	Aug 9	P See III, *
Spitler, Peter		24	Aug 9	*
Umstead Daniel W		18	Aug 1	Died See VI
Van Norden Charles A	"	18		P See III *
Venable, Peter	"	22	Aug 11	*
White, Francis		27	Aug 1	*
Weldy, Samuel		19	Aug 5	*
Weldy, Moses	"	28	Aug 11	W P See II, III, *
Wilson David A		21	"	*
Whetstone Jeremiah	"	27	"	*
Watson Alexander T		47	"	Dis See VII
Wire, Samuel.	"	21	"	P See III
Yoder, Ezra	"	21	Aug 6.	Dis See VII
Young, John	"	23	Aug 11	Tr See IV
		RECRUITS		
Shaffer, James	"	19	Feb 15 1864	Tr See IV
Whetstone, Isaac B	"	19	Mar 24 1864	Tr See IV
Witmer Lewis		18	Feb 24 1864	Tr See IV
Witzeman Benjamin	"	20	Mar 28 1864	Tr See IV

COMPANY I.

NAME	RANK	AGE	DATE OF ENLISTMENT 1862	REMARKS
L Dwight Kee	Captain	33	Aug 2	Killed See VI
Charles A Brigden	1st Lieu	45	July 23	W Res See II, VII
William H Osborn	2d Lieut	24		Pr See I * 1st Lieut
L Newton Parker	1st Sergt	20	Aug 8	Pr W See I II *
Albert H Smith	Sergt	19	July 28	Dis See VII
Solomon Ball		41	Aug 9	*

Roster Company G—Continued.

RECRUITS

Henry Adams	2d Lieut		Oct [illegible] 1862	[illegible] D Sec VI
[illegible] George A	Private	1[illegible]	Jan 2 1864	W D Sec II VI
[illegible] Martin H		2[illegible]	Jan 2 1864	Tr Sec IX
Mann Herman D		[illegible]	Jan 5 1864	Tr Sec IX
Parker William H		1[illegible]	Jan 5 1864	D S Sec VII
Richardson George S		[illegible]	Dec 22 1863	Died Sec VI
Sweet Jesse M		27	Jan 5 1864	W Tr S Sec II IX IX
Torry Seneca D		31	Jan 5 1864	Tr Sec IX
Whitmore Chauncey		1[illegible]	Jan [illegible] 1864	Died Sec VI
Williams Milton		1[illegible]	Dec 22 1863	Tr Sec IX

COMPANY H.

NAME	RANK	AGE	DATE OF ENLISTMENT 1862	REMARKS
Robert Wilson	Captain	[illegible]	Aug 9	Killed Sec VI
William H Clark	1st Lieut	27	July 23	Res Sec VII Co E
John C Hartzell	2d Lieut	21	Aug 5	Pr [illegible] Sec I X
Ira P Mansfield	1st Sergt	2[illegible]	Aug 9	Pr W Sec I II *
Florentine M Simon	Sergt	1[illegible]	July 21	W D S Sec II VII
John McHarg		22	Aug 11	Pr Sec I *
Amos Cobbs		31	Aug [illegible]	[illegible] Sec I *
Abram S McCurley		21	Aug [illegible]	W Sec II *
James S Caldwell	Corporal	2[illegible]	Aug [illegible]	Pr Sec I *
Joseph Carbaugh		23	Aug 1[illegible]	Pr Sec I *
Horace G Ruggles		2[illegible]		D S Sec VII
William K Mead		27	Aug 1[illegible]	P Sec III *
Manassas Miller		21	Aug [illegible]	W Sec II *
Andrew Geddes		21	Aug 5	W Sec II *
Simon Eastman		28	Aug 11	Tr Sec IX
Henry R Myer		23		D S Sec VII
Samuel Bright	Musician	1[illegible]		*
William M Taylor		23		*
David Bricker	Wagoner	[illegible]	July 2[illegible]	D S Sec VII
Armstrong William T	Private	2[illegible]	Aug [illegible]	Killed Sec X
Allen Joseph S		21	Aug 11	*
Allen Jesse F		[illegible]		*
Bennett Thomas		25	July [illegible]	D S Sec VII
Boyd George A		1[illegible]	Aug [illegible]	Pr [illegible] D S Sec I VII
Brown Frederick		23	Aug [illegible]	*
[illegible] John H		2[illegible]	Aug [illegible]	Pr Sec I *
Boughton Horace		1[illegible]		K[illegible] Sec VI
Bachecker Jacob		23		*
Brenaman Constantine		[illegible]	Aug [illegible]	A Sec II *
Baker Sylvester		1[illegible]	Aug [illegible]	*
Baker William H		1[illegible]		W D Sec II VI
Cessna, John W		22	Aug 5	*
[illegible]		1[illegible]	Aug [illegible]	*
Courtney Frederick		2[illegible]	Aug [illegible]	Tr Sec IX
Dean Benjamin		[illegible]	Aug [illegible]	Died Sec VI
D[illegible] George M	"	22		Pr Sec I *
E[illegible] John I	"	1[illegible]		P Sec III *
[illegible] Zimri	"	21		W Sec II *
[illegible] Joseph H	"	[illegible]	Aug	* Sec X
Fisher Eben B		[illegible]	Aug [illegible]	Died Sec VI
Fisher Solomon		1[illegible]	Aug [illegible]	*
Grossman John	"	[illegible]		P Sec III *
Hartman Nathan		[illegible]	Aug [illegible]	Killed Sec VI
Harrison Jeremiah	"	[illegible]	Aug [illegible]	P Sec II *
Hartzell Joshua	"	1[illegible]	Aug [illegible]	P Sec III *
Hayes David		[illegible]	Aug 1[illegible]	P Sec III *
[illegible]		1[illegible]		W K Sec II VI
H[illegible] Alfred	"	21	Aug [illegible]	W Tr Sec II IX
H[illegible], Chauncey M	"	1[illegible]	Aug	Tr Sec IX
H[illegible], Henry		[illegible]	Aug [illegible]	P Sec III VIII
[illegible] Willard D		[illegible]	Aug [illegible]	W D Sec II VI

Roster Company H—Continued

NAME	RANK	AGE	DATE OF ENLISTMENT 1862	REMARKS
Kaiser, Frank	Private	21	Aug 11	P See III *
Kirkbride, James		25	"	W P Tr See II III IV
Kirkbride Joseph	"	23	"	Dis See VII
Kirkbride Asher		18	"	W P D See II III VI
Kirk, Robert A		24	"	W See II *
Marlow, William T		1[illegible]	Aug 9	*
Myers, Jonathan		25	Aug 6	W Dis See II VII
Miller, Addison		21	Aug 9	W Dis See II VII
Mathias Edmund H		27	Aug 7	*
Middleton, William H		21	Aug 11	P See III *
McCurley James		21		*
Musser, Hazard		18	"	See VIII
McCurley John C		19		Died See VI
Mathers James T		19		Dis See VII
Nesbitt, John W		22	"	Pr W See I, II *
Naylor, James B		20	Aug 6	P See III *
Naylor William H		22	Aug 8	W D See II VI
Noble Homer		20	Aug 9	Died See VI
Ovington, John R		22	Aug 1	*
Owen, Eli J		22	"	P D See III, VI
Park, James		20	Aug 11	P See III *
Price, Charles D		18	Aug 6	P See III *
Rummel, Joseph		21	Aug 9	P K See III VI
Raub, Samuel K		18		P See III *
Roahr Charles	"	20	Aug 11	Died See VI
Raub Isaac C P		20		Died See VI
Sherman, Albert A	"	18	July 23	Died See VI
Shuick George W	"	22	Aug 6	P See III *
Stratton, Evi		21	Aug 8	Killed See VI
Shields, Homer J	"	20	Aug 11	*
Strawn Charles D	"	24	"	*
Stewart, Royal M	"	21	Aug 9	P Tr See III, IV
Stutler, Jesse		23	"	P See III *
Silver, Allen	"	35	Aug 11	*
Silver, Jason W	"	24		Pr P See I III, *
Smith, George J	"	25		Pr See I *
Spitler, George J		31	Aug 9	P See III, *
Spitler Peter	"	24	Aug 9	*
Umstead Daniel W	"	18	Aug 1	Died See VI
Van Norden Charles A	"	18		P See III *
Venable, Peter	"	22	Aug 11	*
White, Francis	"	27	Aug 1	*
Weldy, Samuel	"	19	Aug 5	*
Weldy, Moses	"	28	Aug 11	W P See II, III *
Wilson, David A		21		*
Whetstone Jeremiah	"	27		*
Watson, Alexander T	"	47	"	Dis See VII
Wire, Samuel	"	21	"	P See III
Yoder, Ezra		21	Aug 6	Dis See VII
Young, John		23	Aug 11	Tr See IV
RECRUITS				
Shafter, James	"	19	Feb 15 1864	Tr See IV
Whetstone Isaac B	"	19	Mar 24 1864	Tr See IV
Witmer Lewis	"	18	Feb 24 1864	Tr See IV
Witzeman Benjamin		2[illegible]	Mar 28 1864	Tr See IV

COMPANY I.

NAME	RANK	AGE	DATE OF ENLISTMENT 1862	REMARKS
L Dwight Kee	Captain	33	Aug 2	Killed See VI
Charles A Brigden	1st Lieu	45	July 23	W Res See II, VII
William H Osborn	2d Lieut	24		Pr See I * 1st Lieut
L Newton Parker	1st Sergt	20	Aug 8	Pr W See I II *
Albert H Smith	Sergt	19	July 28	Dis See VII
Solomon Ball		41	Aug 9	*

Roster Company I—Continued.

NAME.	RANK.	AGE	DATE OF ENLISTMENT 1862	REMARKS.
William Wallace	"	21	"	Pr See I * Captain
William Enos	"	21		W See II *
Collins E Bushnell	Corporal	22		P Dis See I VII
Alden J Brooks		22	Aug 13	Pr W See I II *1st Lieut
Robert N Holcomb	"	18	Aug 5	W Dis See II, VII
Charles B Hayes	"	26	Aug 8	Pr See I *
Robert S [illegible]	"	[illegible]	Aug 7	Tr See IV
Cyrus Crippen		28	Aug 11	Died See VI
Hugh M Boys	"	25	"	W * See II V
Dallen J Turner	"	21	Aug 8	W P * See II III, V.
Horace Rawdon	Musician	37	Aug 9	Pr Red. See I, *
William L Guild	"	41	Aug 13	Dis. See VII
Joseph B Ashley	Wagoner	[illegible]	"	P. See III, *
Anderson Thomas	Private	23	Aug 8	* See V
Andrews Elmer H		22	Aug 9	W. D S See II, VI, IX
Butler Frank A		23	"	W. * See II V
Butler, Lucius C	"	[illegible]	"	Killed See VI
Bridgeman Thomas		30	Aug 11	Dis See VII.
Barb Gabriel P		18	Aug 5	*
Bower, John M	"	[illegible]	Aug 11.	*
[illegible] Ambrose J		22	Aug 9	Pr W D See I, II, VI
Bunting, Robert L		[illegible]	Aug 7	Tr See IV.
Beckwith Ira W	"	[illegible]	Aug 5	See VIII
Bower, David	"	[illegible]	Aug 11	*
Caldwell, William S	"	[illegible]	Aug 1	Dis See VII
Cook John S	"	[illegible]	Aug 7	Killed See VI
Collver George I		[illegible]	Aug 11	W See II *
Cox, Seymour A	"	[illegible]	Aug 8	Killed. See VI
Creighton, William	"	19	Aug 9	W D See II VI
Collar, Henry	"	19	Aug 7	Killed See VI
Delano, Horace		35	Aug 9	W See II. *
Fobes, Ferdinand F	"	20	Aug 11	Died See VI
Frisby Augustus F	"	18	Aug 9	W Dis See II VII
Giddings Frederick M		27	Aug 8	Pr W. D. See I, II, VI.
Grim Jacob		[illegible]	Aug 6	*
Haddock John		[illegible]	"	Dis See VII
Harrison, M[illegible] J	"	23	Aug 9	P D See III, VI
Hiscock, Hezekiah H		18	Aug 5	*
Harrison, [illegible]	"	19	Aug 8	P * See III V
Hazeltine John G		[illegible]	Aug 9	W. Tr See II IV.
Hanson [illegible]	"	18	Aug 12	*
Heath, M[illegible]	"	18	Aug 8	Dis See VII
Hubbart, Homer	"	21	Aug 9	*
Holcomb M[illegible] H	"	[illegible]	Aug 12	Dis See VII
H[illegible], William J	"	[illegible]	Aug 7	W Dis See II VII
Haines, George	"	[illegible]	Aug 8	Tr See IV
H[illegible] Samuel		18	Aug 9	W P Dis See II III VII
Josl[illegible], [illegible]	"	[illegible]	Aug 5	P See III *
[illegible] M		[illegible]	Aug 8	P See III *
Kellogg John	"	[illegible]	Aug 9	P Tr See III IV
K[illegible] A		[illegible]	"	P See III *
K[illegible] Newt[illegible]		[illegible]	Aug 7	P See III *
K[illegible]		[illegible]	Aug 9	W D See II VI
K[illegible] Thomas J		[illegible]	Aug 7	Tr See IV
L[illegible]		[illegible]	Aug 9	Tr See IV
Leonard Horace A		[illegible]	"	Dis See VII
Lyman, G[illegible] W		[illegible]	"	W P Dis See II III VII
Lyman [illegible] W		[illegible]	Aug 2	W See II VIII
[illegible] M		[illegible]	Aug 9	Dis See VII
M[illegible]		[illegible]	Aug 12	See VIII.
M[illegible] H		18	Aug 5	See VIII.
M[illegible] Marvin		[illegible]	Aug 13	W P See I III *
M[illegible]		[illegible]	Aug 12	Killed, See VI
M[illegible]				W P See II [illegible] *
N[illegible]			Aug [illegible]	P See III *
P[illegible] W			Aug 12	Tr See IV
Perry W[illegible]		[illegible]	Aug [illegible]	W Tr See II [illegible]
P[illegible]			"	W P See II III *
P[illegible]		[illegible]	"	Pr W D See I [illegible] VI.

Roster Company I—Continued.

NAME	RANK	AGE	DATE OF ENLISTMENT 1862	REMARKS
Reynolds, Philip	Private.	31	"	Pr. W P Dis See I, II III, VI
Rulapaugh, John	"	40	Aug 5	Tr. See IV
Rowe, Albert G		22	Aug 8	W. P D See II, III, VI.
Smith, Cyrus T	"	25	Aug 12	P See III *
Sperry, Henry H		21	Aug 9	Dis See VII
Steele, Calvin F	"	20	"	P Dis See III VII
Sealy, Esau A	"	28.	Aug 6	W D. See II, VI
Storier, John T	"	19	Aug 9	*
Triloff, William F	"	18	Aug 11.	W * See II, V.
Thompson, John		29	Aug 7	*
Tuttle, Hartson	"	18	Aug 8	Dis See VII
Thurbur, Silas		29	Aug 9	Died See VI
Thomas, George	"	22	Aug 8	Died See VI
Tidd, Jeremiah M		24	Aug 9	*
Talcott, Whitman B	"	20	Aug 8	W D See II, VI
Udall, Orrin		20	Aug 5	Pr. See I, *
Wilcox, William R	"	19	Aug 9	* See V
Windram, Robert	"	35	Aug 5	Dis See VII
Whitcomb, Ervin A		24	Aug 9	Pr W K See I, II, VI.
Webb, Darwin	"	20	Aug 13	W Tr See II IV
Webb, Henry	"	18	"	W. Dis. See II, VII
Webb, Albert		20	"	*
Wilcox Daniel E		35	"	Dis See VII
Wildman, Ira	"	42	Aug 8	Tr See IV
Young, George W	"	20	Aug 9	Pr See I *
Yokes, Ezra	"	19	"	*
RECRUITS				
Lane, George	"	27.	Dec 23, 1863	Tr See IV

COMPANY K.

NAME	RANK	AGE.	DATE OF ENLISTMENT 1862.	REMARKS.
Edward V Bowers	Captain	19	July 28	Res See VII
Henry C Sweet	1st Lieut	21	July 16	See I IX VII, Co I
Leverett A Barnard	2d Lieut	29	Aug 7	Pr D See I VI Co F
William H Castle	1st Sergt.	22	Aug 12	Pr Dis See I VII, Co F
George L Mason	Sergt	28	Aug 11	Pr See I, *
Nelson H Smith	"	25	Aug 13	*
Austin Adams	"	26.	Aug 11	Dis See VII
Charles H Harris	"	23.	Aug. 4	Dis. See VII
Alanson Gary	Corporal	20	"	Dis See VII
Alba B Martin	"	21	Aug 11	Dis See VII
Howard S Stephens	"	24	Aug 7	Died See VI
John Mann		22	Aug 6	Red Tr See I, IV
Wesley L Jarvis	"	19	Aug 4	*
William O Smith	"	19	Aug 13	W * See II, V
Andrew Perkins	"	19	Aug. 9	Red S See I, IX *
Lewis Price	Musician	21	July 27	S Dis See IX, VII
John Price	"	27	"	S Dis See IX, VII
Lewis H Roberts	Wagoner	23	Aug 8	Dis See VII
Atkins, Levi	Private	40	Aug 11	Died See VI
Arnold, Orrin		27		Pr W D See I, II, VI.
Alfred, Aldrich	"	30	Aug 9	*
Alderman, Ellsworth A	"	18	Aug 12	P See III, *
Alderman Cassius M		18	"	P See III *
Amidon, Edmund S	"	30	Aug 13	Dis. See VII
Burgett, Harrison	"	20	Aug 4	Tr See IV
Burgett, Harrison H	"	21	Aug 9	Tr See IV
Bishop, John H		18	Aug 6	Died See VI
Brett, Thomas	"	23	Aug 9	Dis See VII
Burlingame Edwin R	"	40	Aug 11	W Dis See II, VII.
Bates Charles F	"	25	Aug 12	W Dis See II VI
Bates, Charles H	"	18	Aug 13	Died See VI
Babcock, Benjamin N		36	Aug 2	W See II, *

Roster Company K—Continued.

NAME.	RANK	AGE	DATE OF ENLISTMENT 1862	REMARKS
Bliss Charles H	Private	[illegible]	Aug 11	Dis. See VII
Blakeslee F[illegible]		[illegible]	"	*
Barnard Francis N		[illegible]	Aug [illegible]	W. Dis. See II, VII
Bigelow William I		[illegible]		W. P. See II, III *
Blakeslee James E		27	Aug 6	Dis. See VII
Ch[illegible] J[illegible]			Aug 5	Pr. D. See I, VI
Colb David G.		[illegible]	July 9	Dis. See VII
Clapp Elverton J		2[illegible]	Aug 11	Pr. See I *
Darrow Alfred		2[illegible]	Aug [illegible]	P. S. See III, IX *
D[illegible] J[illegible]		1[illegible]	Aug 11	Dis. See VII
E[illegible] Clayborne A		1[illegible]		See I, II, III, VI
Early Eldridge F		1[illegible]	Aug 13	W. Dis. See II, VII
Fowler Ezra		[illegible]	Aug 5	Dis. See VII
Ferguson Charles A		[illegible]	Aug 6	Dis. See VII
Fobes Henry H			Aug 9	Killed. See VI
Fuller John		1[illegible]	Aug 11	Killed. See VI
Earl William		1[illegible]	Aug 9	Tr. See IX
F[illegible] Lewis [illegible]		[illegible]	Aug 13	Dis. See VII
Garry David		2[illegible]	Aug 4	P. Dis. See III, VII
Getty Frederick [illegible]		2[illegible]	Aug 13	Killed. See VI
Hicock Clay		1[illegible]	Aug [illegible]	W. Dis. See II, VII
Holden William D		[illegible]	Aug 12	Died. See VI
Humphrey Marcus W		[illegible]	Aug 13	Dis. See VII
Hutchinson Stephen [illegible]		[illegible]	"	W. * See II, V
Hires Isaac		[illegible]	Aug 4	P. See III *
Hall Frederick W		1[illegible]	Aug 11	See VIII
Hanna Lyman P		20	Aug 7	W. Dis. See II, VII
Howard William		[illegible]	Aug 6	Killed. See VI
Hutchinson David		31	Aug 12	P. D. See III, VI
Hutchinson Arthur G		1[illegible]	Aug 13	P. Dis. See III, VII
Hill Cleney L		1[illegible]	Aug 12	Dis. See VII
Harback Ira W		1[illegible]	[illegible] 11	Dis. See VII
Johnson George W		20	Aug 11	Dis. See VIII
Jenkins Aaron		1[illegible]	Aug 12	W. P. See II, III *
Jordan Lysander P		2[illegible]		Pr. See I *
Kinney Albert H		1[illegible]	July 30	Pr. See I *
King George		25	Aug 11	Died. See VI
King Amos H		[illegible]	"	P. * See III, X
Laskey, Matthew		25	Aug 5	See VIII
Morgan Seymour L.		21	Aug [illegible]	*
Olmstead Selden		22	Aug 13	Dis. See VII
Parker Albertus W		[illegible]	Aug 8	Tr. See IX
Powers William H		2[illegible]	Aug 13	Dis. See VII
Pangburn Horace W		1[illegible]		*
Pratt Charles		1[illegible]	"	P. See III *
Rasey, Chester		1[illegible]	Aug 9	Dis. See VII
Rasey Charles		21	"	Dis. See VII
Roberts James F		1[illegible]		*
Smith Alexander		1[illegible]	Aug 6	Killed. See VI
Smith Wilson W		[illegible]	Aug 13	Dis. See VII
Smith, Horatio M		27	"	Pr. Tr. See I, IX
Shepherd Lorin		1[illegible]	July 2[illegible]	See VIII
Shaw Henry		[illegible]	Aug 5	Dis. See VII
Scoville Henry		17	Aug 11	*
Stow, Egbert		22	Aug 12	*
Seymour George		23	Aug 4	P. See III *
Sweet Elliott S		21	Aug 12	Tr. See IX
Slater, Albert A		22	Aug 13	P. See III, *
Taylor Francis A		21	Aug 5	See VIII
Williams Thales P		27	Aug 9	Dis. See VII
Wright William W		2[illegible]	Aug 13	W. Dis. See II, VII
Williams Joel		21	Aug 4	W. P. See II, III *
Warren Francis		18	Aug 12	P. See III *
Watrous John I		2[illegible]	Aug 9	P. See I, *
Wilson Frederick W		[illegible]	Aug 11	* See X
Webb Andrew W		31	Aug 12	W. D. See II, VI.
RECRUITS				
Enos Andrew	Private	1[illegible]	Jan. 1 1864	Tr. See IX
Tower Herbert	"	1[illegible]	"	Tr. See IX

TABLE I.

Promotions and Reductions.

COMPANY A.

NAME	RANK	FROM	TO	REMARKS
Charles G Edwards,	Captain	July 23 1862	July 10, 1863	Pr to Major.
Henry H Cumings,		Feb 18, 1864	Mar 20, 1864	Tr to Co K
Richard J See	"	Mar 20, 1864	Sept 20, 1864	Tr to Co G
Daniel B Stambaugh,	"	Mar 21 1864	Muster out	
Richard J See	1st Lieut	July 23, 1862	Dec 22, 1862	Pr to Capt Co K
Daniel B Stambaugh,	"	Dec 22, 1862	Mar 21, 1864	Pr to Captain
Norman D Smith,	"	May 25, 1864	Muster out	
Daniel B Stambaugh,	2d Lieut	July 23, 1862	Dec 22, 1862	Pr to 1st Lieut
Patten Himrod	"	Jan. 15, 1863	Mar 28 1863	Pr 1st Lieut CoC
Norman D Smith	"	May 12, 1863	Not mustered	
William H Castle,	"	Feb 20, 1863	Feb 18, 1864	Pr 1st Lieut Co E
Patten Himrod,	1st Sergt	Muster in	Jan 15, 1863	Pr 2d Lieut
James Crays,	"	Jan 15, 1863	Feb 18, 1864	Pr 1st Lieut CoK
Robert Kay	"	Feb 18 1864	Muster out	
Porter Watson,	Sergt	Muster in	Feb 27, 1863	Pr to Sergt Maj
Nathan W King	"	"	Sept 19, 1863	Killed, VI
James Crays	"	"	Jan 15, 1863	Pr to 1st Sergt
Lafayette McCoy,	"	"	Mar. 7, 1863.	Died VI
Robert Kay,	"	Not given	Feb 18, 1864	Pr to 1st Sergt
James Brown	"	"	Muster out	Pr from Corp
John D Jewell,	"	"	Not given	Discharged VII.
William H Craig	"	"	Sept 20, 1863	Killed, VI
Isaiah J Nessle,	"	"	Muster out	Pr from Corp
James Morris,	"	"	June 10, 1865	Table V
Robert C Porter,	"	"	Muster out	Pr from Corp
Joseph T Torrence,	Corp	Muster in.	Jan 7, 1863.	Discharged VII
John F McCollom,	"	"	Nov. 21, 1864	Tr IV, Color g'd
Joseph Applegate,	"	"	Oct 8, 1862	Killed VI
William Phillips	"	"	Muster out	
William G Davis,	"	Not given	May 3, 1865	Table V
George W Walsen,	"	"	June 28, 1863	Died VI

COMPANY B.

NAME	RANK.	FROM.	TO	REMARKS
Ephraim Kee,	Capt	Aug 20 1862.	Jan 19, 1863.	Died, VI.
Andrew D Braden,	"	Jan 18 1863	Muster out	
Andrew D Braden,	1st Lieut.	July 19, 1862	Jan 18, 1863	Pr Captain
Albert Dickerman,	"	Jan 21, 1863	Mar 29, 1863	Apt'd Adjutant
Ira F Mansfield,	"	May 15, 1863	Muster out	Detached duty.
Henry D Niles	2d Lieut	July 23, 1862	Feb 12 1863	Resigned, VII
Merritt Emerson	"	Mar 28, 1863	June 13, 1863	Died, VI
Jonas F Wannamaker,	1st Sergt	Muster in	Oct 8 1862	Killed, VI
William H Forbis	"	Not given.	Oct 24, 1864	Pr 1st Lieut Co E
John G Williams	"	"	Muster out	
William H Forbis,	Sergt	Muster in	Not given	Pr to 1st Sergt
Merritt Emerson	"	"	Mar 28, 1863	Pr to 2d Lieut
Edward G Palfreeman,	"	"	June 18, 1864	Died VI
William Hughes,	"	"	Oct 23, 1863.	Tr IV
John S Williams,	"	Not given.	Not given	Pr to 1st Sergt
Noah J Pound,	"	"	Muster out	
Wilson G Hultz	"	"	"	
Charles Stewart	"	"	"	
Osman B Tuttle,	"	"	"	
James M Dickerman,	Corp	Muster in.	Oct 14, 1862	Dis See I VII
John B Ramsdell,	"	"	Muster out	Color guard
Michael E Hess,	"	"	Feb 27, 1863	Dis See I VII
George F Center,	"	"	Oct 16, 1862.	Dis See I, VII
John A Ewalt	"	"	July 8, 1863	Died VI

Table I—Company B—Continued.

Name	Rank	From	To	Remarks
[illegible] Cox	"		Oct 14, 1862	Dis. Sec. I, VII
[illegible]			Oct 4, 1862	Dis. Sec. I, VII
[illegible]	"		June [illegible]	Dis. Sec. I, VII
George W. [illegible]		Not given.	Sep 11, 1863	Dis. Sec. I, VII
[illegible] J. Scott			Sep 25, 1863	Died VI
[illegible]	"		Muster out	

COMPANY C.

NAME	RANK	FROM	TO	REMARKS
Henry P. [illegible]	Capt	July 23 1862	Jan 17 1863	Resigned, VII
Ambrose C. Mason		Jan 17 1863	Aug 27 1864	Died VI
Ambrose C. Mason	1st Lieut	July 23 1862	Jan 17 1863	Pr. to Captain
James H. Laird		Jan 17 1863	Mar 12 1864	Resigned VII
[illegible]		Mar 2?, 1863	July 10 1863	Pr to Capt Co F
Reuben J. Mo[illegible]		July 10, 1863	Nov 3 1864	Pr to Capt Co D
William C. Olds,		Sept [illegible] 1864	Muster out	
James H. Laird	2d Lieut	July 23 1862	Jan 17 1863	Pr to 1st Lieut
William C. Olds,		May 12 1863	Not mustered	
Irvin [illegible]	"	Jan 1? 1863	May [illegible] 1863	Resigned VII
Irvin [illegible]	1st Sergt	Muster in	Dec 1? 1862	Pr to Sergt Ma
Clinton I. Moore,		Dec 1? 1862	Muster out	
Clinton I. Moore	1st Lieut	Oct 21 1864	Not mustered	
Austin W. [illegible]	Sergt	Muster in	Oct 2? 1862	Discharged VII
Jacob Turney,	"	"	Muster out	
John Geddes		"		Color Sergt
John L. Miller		Dec 1? 1862		Pr from Corp
Robert D. Allen	"	Not given		Pr from Corp
Clinton I. Moore	Corp	Muster in	Dec 1? 1862	Pr to 1st Sergt
Robert J. Stewart,	"		Oct 22 1862	Discharged VII
Albert Jastatt	"	"	Muster out	
James G. Townsend,	"	"	Mar 27 1863	Discharged VII
Samuel R[illegible]		Not given	Muster out	Pr from private
Robert A. [illegible]	"			Pr from private
Austin [illegible]	"	"		Pr from private
[illegible]	"	"	Not given	Pr from private

REDUCED

NAME	RANK	FROM	TO	REMARKS
[illegible]	Sergt	Muster	Not given	Reduced to ranks
Lafayette [illegible]	Corp			Reduced to ranks
[illegible]		"		Reduced to ranks
[illegible]	"	Not given		Reduced to ranks.

COMPANY D.

NAME	RANK	FROM	TO	REMARKS
[illegible]	Capt	[illegible]	[illegible]	[illegible]
[illegible]	Major	[illegible]	Not mustered	
Reuben J. Mo[illegible]		Nov [illegible]	Muster out	[illegible]
[illegible]	1st Lieut.	[illegible]	[illegible]	Pr to Capt Co [illegible]
[illegible]		May [illegible] 1863	[illegible]	[illegible]
[illegible]		May 2? 1864	Muster out	Pr from [illegible]
[illegible]	[illegible]	[illegible]	Oct 1? 1863	[illegible]
Stanley [illegible]	1st Sergt	Muster in	Jan 15 1864	[illegible]
[illegible]		Not given	Muster out	Pr from [illegible]
[illegible]	Sergt	Muster	[illegible]	Dis. Sec. [illegible]
[illegible]			[illegible]	Dis. Sec. [illegible]
[illegible]	"		[illegible]	Tr. Sec. IV
[illegible]	"		Muster out	[illegible]
[illegible]		Not given		Pr from [illegible]
[illegible]				Pr from [illegible]
James H. [illegible]	"	"	"	Pr Sergt Maj.
[illegible]	Corp	Muster	Not given	Sec. VIII
[illegible]			[illegible] 1862	Dis. Sec. [illegible]
[illegible]	"	"	May [illegible]	Dis. Sec. [illegible]
[illegible]			Sep 11 1864	Dis. Sec. [illegible]
[illegible]	"		[illegible]	Tr. Sec. IV
[illegible]			July 27 1864	Tr. Sec. IV
[illegible]		Not given	Nov [illegible]	Killed Sec. VI.
[illegible]			Muster out	[illegible] Sec. II
[illegible]			May [illegible] 1865	M. O. Sec. [illegible]
[illegible]		"	Muster out	

Table I—Continued, Company E.

NAME	RANK	FROM	TO	REMARKS
Byron W Canfield	Capt	July 24, 1862	Jan 29, 1863,	Resigned VII
E Abbott Spaulding,	"	Jan 29, 1863	Sep 26, 1863	Died, II VI
Patten Himrod,	"	July 10, 1863	May 5, 1865	Resigned VII
William R Tuttle	1st Lieut.	July 9, 1862	Oct 8 1862	Pr to Capt Co H
Albion W Tourgee	1st Lieut	Sept 21, 1863	Dec 6, 1863	See II III VII
E Abbott Spaulding	"	Oct 8, 1862	Jan 29, 1863	Pr to Captain
William H Clark,	"	Mar 2 1863.	May 15 1863	Resigned, VII
William H Castle,	"	Feb 18, 1864	Jan 10 1865	Dis See VII
William H Forbis,	"	Oct. 24, 1864	Muster out	
John A Osborn,	2d Lieut	Aug 6, 1862	Jan 19 1863	Resigned VII
James W Allen,	"	Jan 29, 1863	Apr 19 1863	Tr to Co F
William H Forbes,	"	May 12, 1863	Not mustered	
Julius A Moffett,	"	Feb 20, 1863	Aug 13 1863	Resigned VII
John C Hathaway	1st Sergt	Muster in	Jan 11, 1863	Discharged, VII
Julius A Moffett,	"	Jan 11, 1863	Feb 20, 1863	Pr 2d Lieut
LaRoyal Taylor,	"	Feb 20, 1863	May 16, 1883	Discharged, VII
George D Elder,	"	May 16, 1863	Muster out	Sergeant
Edward Patchin,	Sergt	Muster in	Dec 29, 1862	Discharged VII
John F Humiston	"	Not given	Muster out	Pr from Corp
James A McNaughton,	"	Sept 1, 1864	"	Pr Corp, April 10, 1863
Lester D Taylor,	"	Jan 11, 1863	June 20 1864	Pr to Sergt Maj
Dean D Tucker,	"	Jan 11 1863	Muster out	Pr from Corp
Stephen Patchin,	"	Apr 17, 1863	"	Pr. from Corp
Charles C Hitchcock,	Corp	Muster in	Oct 8, 1862	Killed, VI.
Miles J Whitney,	"	Jan 11, 1863	Muster in	To Sergeant
George D Elder,	"	"	Mar 11, 1863	Discharged VII
Philo Boughton,	"	"	Mar 27, 1863	Discharged, VII
Sherman Pease,	"	Oct 31, 1862	Muster out	Pr from private.
Luman Griste,	"	Dec 31, 1862	Feb 24, 1864	Discharged, VII
Oscar Duzenbury,	"	Jan 11, 1863	Muster out	Pr from private
Evan Richards,	"	Jan 11 1863	"	Color guard
Byron A Pease,	"	Aug 31, 1863	Aug 4, 1864	Killed VI
John McNaughton,	"	Sept 4, 1864	Muster out	Pr from private
Albert Dickerman,	Musician	Aug 21, 1862		Pr to Serg-Maj

REDUCED

NAME	RANK	FROM	TO	REMARKS
James A Mowrey,	Sergt	Muster in	Not given	Reduced to ranks
Jonas Alshouse,	Corp	"	"	Reduced to ranks
Fernando C Conley		"	"	Reduced to ranks

COMPANY F.

NAME	RANK	FROM	TO	REMARKS
Sherburn H Williams	Capt	Aug 1 1862.	Jan 13 1863	Resigned, VII
Alfred G Wilcox,		Jan 13, 1863	Muster out	
Alfred G Wilcox,	1st Lieut	Aug 8 1862	Jan 13, 1863	Pr to Captain
Leverett A Barnard,		Jan 29 1863	Feb 17 1864	Died, VI
James W Allen	"	Feb 18, 1864	Muster out	
Lester D Burbank,	2d Lieut	July 25, 1862	Feb 20 1863	Resigned VII
James W Allen		Apr 19 1863	Feb 18 1864	Pr to 1st Lieut
Norman D Smith,	1st Sergt	Muster in	May 25, 1864	Pr to 1st Lieut
Charles R Brown,	"	Aug 3, 1864	Muster out	Pr from Sergt
David C Beardsley,	Sergt	Muster in	June 2, 1865	Table V
Harrison J Fuller,		"	Oct 26, 1862	Died, VI
Frederick T Cook,	"	"	Muster out	
James W Allen		Not given	Jan 29 1863.	Pr 2d Lieut Co E
Lathrop A Johnson,		Feb 24 1863	Muster out	Pr from Corp
Henry B Pitner,	"	Aug 3 1863	"	Color guard
Michael Cooney,	Corp	Muster in	Mar 7 1863	Discharged VII
James W Allen,	"	"	Not given.	Pr to Sergeant
George I Squeir,	"	"	Oct 28 1862	Discharged, VII
Edwin R More,	"	"	Mar 1, 1894	Died VII
Isaac D L Schram,	"	"	Muster out	
Josiah King	"	Not given	Oct 25, 1863	Died VI
David Lester,	"	Dec 31, 1862	Muster out	
Darius Childs,	"	Feb 29, 1862	June 18 1864	Killed VI
Ira Ely	"	Feb 21, 1864	Muster out	
Doty William,	"	Jan 5, 1864	Dec 23 1864	Pr to Prin Mus

REDUCED

NAME	RANK	FROM	TO	REMARKS
Dwight H Woodard,	Corp	Muster in	Not given	Reduced to ranks

Table I—Continued, Company G

NAME	RANK	FROM	TO	REMARKS
William G. Crowell	Capt	Aug 6, 1862	Aug 22 1864	Resigned See VII
Robert J. S[illegible]		Sept 20 1864	Muster out	
Albion W. Tourgee,	1st Lieut	July 11, 1862	Sep 25 1863	Tr Co E II III VII
Albert F. Brooks	"	Feb 18, 1864	Muster out	On duty at Dept H Q rs
[illegible] Spaulding	2d Lieut	July 11, 1862	Oct 8 1862	Pr 1st Lieut Co E
Henry Adams		Oct 8, 1862	Feb 20 1863	Appt from Civil life See VI
Albert F. Brooks		May 8 1863	Not mustered	
Reuben G. Morgard		Jan 13 1863	Feb 10 1863	Pr 1st Lieut Co [illegible]
Wilbur F. Thompson	1st Sergt	Muster in	Not given	Reduced
Reuben G. Morgar[illegible]		Not given	Jan 13 1863	Pr 2d Lieut
William C. Olds		Jan 13 1863	Sep 8 1864	Pr 1st Lieut Co [illegible]
Lamonzo Thompson		Dec 30 1864	Muster out	Pr to Corp Sergt
William B. Braman	Sergt	Muster in	Nov 20 1862	Dis See VII
Benjamin F. Cushing			June 25 1864	Dis See VII
Joseph George,			Oct 8 1862	Killed See VI
George L. Leach			Sep 18 1863	Dis See VII
John K. Greenough			Muster out	Pr from private
Anson W. Miles		Jan 23 1864		
Wilbur F. Thompson,	"	Not given		
Charles A. Graves,	"	Dec 30, 1864		Pr from Corp
Orson L. Marsh	Corp	Muster in	June 22 1863	Dis See VII
Luke Northway			May 8 1863	Died See VI
Norris L. Gaze	"		Feb 18 1863	Dis See VII
Orlando G. Clark	"		Oct 3 1863	Dis See VII
Daniel H. H. Wheaton			Dec 18 1862	Dis See VII
Charles W. Butler,		"	May 14 1863	Dis See VII
Fayette Rood		Not given	Apr 1864	Tr See IV
Oscar F. Crater			Muster out	
Wilbur F. Thompson		Feb 11 1864	Not given	Pr to Sergt
Edwin Reeves		Not given	Muster out	
Jerry Butt		"	Not given	Reduced
George W. Cheney	Priv	Muster in	Feb 1863	Pr Q M S
William J. Gibson,	"	"	Aug 30 1862	Pr Com Sergt

REDUCED

NAME	RANK	FROM	TO	REMARKS
Wilbur F. Thompson	1st Sergt	Muster in	Not given	To the ranks Pr
Joseph K. Warner	Sergt			His own request
William H. Barnes,	Corp	"	"	To the ranks
Jerry Butt	"	Not given	"	To the ranks

COMPANY H.

NAME	RANK	FROM	TO	REMARKS
Robert Wilson	Captain	Aug 9 1862	Oct 8, 1862	Killed VI
William R. Tuttle		Oct 8 1862	Muster out	Asst Prov Mar on Gen Sherman's Staff
John C. Hartzel		Sept 8 1864	Muster out	Detach service
William H. Clark	1st Lieut	July 23 1862	Mar 2 1863	Tr to Co L.
John C. Hartzell		Jan 13 1863	Sep 8 1864	On detached service after Feb 15 1864 See V
John C. Hartzell	2d Lieut	Aug 9 1862	Jan 13 1863	Pr to 1st Lieut
Ira F. Mansfield		Feb 12 1863	May 15 1863	Pr to 1st Lieut
Ira F. Mansfield	1st Sergt	Muster in	Feb 12 1863	Pr to 2d Lieut
George M. Dull		July 27 1863	Muster out	Pr from private
Florentine M. Simons	Sergt	Muster in	Jan 1 1863	Discharged VII
John McHarg			May 1 1863	Pr to Hos Std
Abram S. McCurdy			Muster out	
John W. Nesbitt		Not given		Pr from Corp
James S. Cadwell				Pr from Corp
George J. Smith				Pr to Corp

Table I—Company H—Continued.

NAME	RANK	FROM.	TO	REMARKS
Horace G Ruggles	Corporal	Muster in	Oct 25 1862	Discharged VII.
William K Mead		"	Muster out	
Manassas Miller	"	"	"	
Andrew Geddes	"	"	"	
Almon Eastman	"	"	Nov 13, 1863	Tr, IV
Henry R Meyer	"		May 28, 1863,	Discharged VII
Jason W Silver		Not given	Muster out	
John H Bellard				
George V Boyle	"	"	Not given	
		REDUCED		
Amos Cobbs	Sergt	Muster in	Not given	His own request
Joseph Carbaugh	Corp		"	Reduc'd to ranks
George V Boyle	"	Not given	"	Reduc d to ranks

COMPANY I.

NAME	RANK	FROM	TO	REMARKS
L Dwight Kee	Captain	Aug 2, 1862	Oct 8, 1862	Killed See VI
Henry C Sweet	"	Oct 8, 1862	May 12, 1863	Dis See VII
William Wallace		May 12 1863	Muster out	
Charles A Brigden	1st Lieut	July 23 1862	Jan 21, 1863	Resig d See VI
William H Osborn		Feb 27, 1863	Muster out	Detached duty
William H Osborn	2d Lieut	July 23, 1862	Oct 8, 1862	Pr 1st Lieut Co K
Albert Dickerman		Oct 8, 1862	Jan 21, 1863	Pr 1st Lieut Co B
William Wallace	"	Jan 21, 1863	May 12, 1863	Pr to Captain,
L Newton Parker	1st Sergt	Muster in	Jan 1 1863	Reduced to Serg
William Wallace	"	Jan 1 1863	Jan 21, 1863	Pr to 2d Lieut
Collins E Bushnell	"	Jan 21 1863	May 9, 1863	Dis See VII
Harvey W Partridge,	"	May 9 1863	Nov 11, 1863	Died See VI
L Newton Parker	"	Nov 11, 1863	Muster out	
Albert H Smith	Sergt	Muster in	Nov 1, 1862	Dis See VII
Solomon Ball	"	"	Muster out	
William Wallace	"	"	Jan 1 1863	Pr to 1st Sergt
William Enos	"	"	Muster out	
Charles B Hayes	"	Nov 11 1863		Color Guard
Edwin A Whitcomb,	"	Nov 1, 1862	Sep 20, 1863	Killed VI
George W Young	"	Sep 20 1863	Muster out	Pr from Corp
Alden F Brooks	Corporal	Muster in	Feb 18, 1864	Pr 1st Lieut Co G
Robert N Holcomb	"	"	Mar 5, 1863	Dis See VII
Robert S Abell	"	"	Mar 31, 1864	Tr See IV
Cyrus Crippen	"	"	Oct 28 1862	Died See VI
Hugh M Boys	"	"	Muster out	
Dillen J Turner	"	"	"	
Philip Reynolds	"	Not given	May 30, 1864	Dis See VII
Orrin Udall	"	"	Muster out	
Ambrose J Bailey	"	Nov 11 1863	Feb 18, 1864	Died See VI
Fred k M Giddings	"	Jan 21, 1863	Apr 21, 1863	Died See VI
Horace Rawdon	Musician	Aug 9 1862	Aug 31, 1863	Pr to Prin Mus
		REDUCED		
L Newton Parker.	Sergt	Jan 1, 1863	Nov 11, 1863	Pr to 1st Sergt
Horace Rawdon	Musician	Sep 12, 1864	Muster out	His own request

COMPANY K.

NAME	RANK	FROM	TO	REMARKS
Edward V Bowers	Captain	Aug 10, 1862	Dec 22, 1862	Res See VII
Richard J See	"	Dec 22 1862	Mar 20 1864	Tr to Co A
Henry H Cummings	"	Mar 20 1864	Muster out	Tr from Co A
Henry C Sweet	1st Lieut	July 16, 1862	Oct 8 1862	See II VII Co I
William H Osborn		Oct 8, 1862	Feb 27, 1863	Tr to Co I
Horatio M Smith	"	Jan 18, 1863	Jan 16, 1864	Pr Tr See IV
James Crays		Feb 18, 1864	Muster out	
Leverett A Barnard	2d Lieut	Aug 10, 1862	Jan 29, 1863	Pr 1st Lieut Co F
Horatio M Smith		Dec 22 1862	Jan 18 1863	Pr 1st Lieut
Stanley B Lockwood	"	Jan 15, 1863	May 12, 1863	Pr 1st Lieut Co D

Table I—Company K—Continued

NAME	RANK	FROM	TO	REMARKS
William H Castle	1st Sergt	Muster in	Feb 20, 1863	Pr 2d Lieut Co A
George L Mason		Feb 20 1863	Muster out	Pr from Sergt
Nelson H Smith	Sergt	Muster in		
Austin Adams			Oct 14, 1862	Dis See VII
Charles H Harris			Nov 24 1863	Dis See VII
Elverton J Clapp		Not given	Muster out	Pr from Corp
Lysander P Jordan				Pr from private
Clayborne A Eddy			May 15 1865	Dis See VI
Alanson Gary	Corporal	Muster in	Oct 13 1862	Dis See VII
Albee B Martin			Nov 19 1863	Dis See VII
Howard S Stephens			Oct 5 1864	Died See VI
Wesley L Jarvis			Muster out	
William O Smith				Detached See V
Julius C Cheney		Not given	Sep 17 1863	Pr D See VI
Orrin Arnold			Oct 19 1863	Pr D See VI
John L Watrous			Muster out	Pr Color guard
Albert H Kinney				
Horatio M Smith	Private	Muster in	Aug 25 1862	Pr to Q M S
		REDUCED		
Andrew Perkins	Corporal	Muster in	Not given	Reduced to ranks

TABLE II.
Wounded.

COMPANY A.

NAME	RANK	WHEN	REMARKS
Charles G Edwards	Captain	Oct 8, 1862	Perryville, three times
Richard J See	1st Lieut		Perryville Ky
Daniel B Stambaugh	2d Lieut	Sep 20, 1863	Chickamauga Ga
James Crays	Sergt	Oct 8, 1862	Perryville Ky
Lafayette McCoy	"	"	Perryville, Ky
James Brown	"	Nov 25, 1863	Mission Ridge Tenn
Isaiah J Nessie	"	Sep 20, 1883	Chickamauga Ga
Joseph T Torrence	Corporal	Oct 8, 1862	Perryville, Ky
John F McCollom		"	Perryville Ky
John F McCollom	"	Sep 20, 1863	Chickamauga Ga
William Phillips		Oct 6, 1862	Perryville Ky
William Phillips		Sep 20, 1863	Chickamauga, Ga
William G Davis	"		Chickamauga Ga
Bailey, Henry B	Private	Oct 8, 1862	Perryville Ky
Bailey, Henry B		June 20, 1864,	Kenesaw Mt, Ga
Boyle, John A		Sep 20, 1863	Chickamauga See VI
Burns, Michael		"	Chickamauga, Ga
Cowley, Hugh		Nov 25, 1863	Mission Ridge Tenn
Conklin, George	"	Oct 8, 1862	Perryville Ky
Fielding, Charles	"	"	Perryville Ky
Flecker John		"	Perryville, Ky
Hanify John J.	"	"	Perryville, Ky
Heiliger, Frederick		"	Perryville, Ky.
Hulburt Frank	"	"	Perryville Ky
Houston Richard	"	July 2, 1864	Kenesaw Mt See VI
James, Frederick		Oct 8, 1862	Perryville, Ky
Miles, John		"	Perryville Ky
McFall Simon P		Sep 20 1863	Chickamauga, Ga
Rees, Richard		Oct. 8, 1862	Perryville Ky twice,
Tyrrell, Thomas	"	"	Perryville, Ky
Wetherstay, Henry			Perryville Ky
Wetherstay, Henry	"	Sep 19 1863	Chickamauga See VI
Walser George W	"	Oct 8, 1862	Perryville, Ky
Williams Clytus	"		Perryville, Ky
Whetstone, David C		July, 1864	Kenesaw Mt, Ga

COMPANY B.

NAME	RANK	WHEN	REMARKS
William Hughes	Sergt	1862	Munfordville, Ky
Noah J Pound		Sep 20, 1863	Chickamauga Ga
Charles Stewart		"	Chickamauga, Ga
Hiram J Scott	Corporal	"	Chickamauga See VI
Bear, Abner	Private	Oct 8, 1862	Perryville, Ky, twice
Bell, Edward M	"	"	Perryville, Ky
Caldwell, Calvin	"	Sep 20 1863	Chickamauga See VI
Grim, Albert		Oct 8, 1862	Perryville Ky See VI
Grim, Ephraim	"	"	Perryville, Ky
Hathaway, James W	"	"	Perryville, Ky
Kelly, Hugh R		Sept 1, 1864	Jonesboro Ga See VI
Lewis, Edwin D		Aug 5, 1864	Near Atlanta Ga
Landon, John J		Oct 8, 1862	Perryville Ky
Mahannah, Harvey		"	Perryville, Ky
Murphy, John A		"	Perryville Ky
Murphy, John A	"	Sep 20, 1863	Chickamauga, Ga
Rush Daniel		Mar 24, 1865	Goldsboro N C See VI
Shafer, Charles		Sep 20 1863	Chickamauga Ga
Tatt, Samuel K		Oct 8, 1862	Perryville See VI

Table II—Continued, Company C

NAME	RANK	WHEN	REMARKS
John B Miller	Corporal	Oct 8 1862	Perryville Ky
Robert J Stewart			Perryville Ky
James G Townsend			Perryville Ky
Lafayette Seaton			Perryville Ky twice
Charles E Miller	Wagoner.		Perryville, Ky, twice
Hayes William R	Private		Perryville, See VI
Donovan James			Perryville Ky
Hayes Morgan W			Perryville Ky
Edwards John I			Perryville Ky
Evans William		June 3 1864	Pumpkinvine Creek Ga See VI
Frazer Isaac		Oct 8 1862	Perryville, Ky
Holmes Reuben B			Perryville Ky
Healy Joseph		Mar 20 1863	Milton Tenn
Kealy Lawrence		Aug 9 1864	Atlanta Ga See VI
Lewis Caleb		Oct 8 1862	Perryville Ky
Miller Lemuel B			Perryville Ky
Moser Philip H			Perryville Ky
Powers John			Perryville Ky.
Price Lemuel			Perryville, Ky
Quigley Thomas		Mar 20 1863	Milton Tenn
Shook Cornelius		Oct 8 1862	Perryville Ky
Townsend Charles W			Perryville, Ky
Vay Adolphus			Perryville Ky
Wambaugh John			Perryville Ky

Two were wounded June 11 1864 and two August 7 1864 whose names have been forgotten

COMPANY D.

NAME	RANK	WHEN	REMARKS
George L Riker	Captain	Oct 8 1862	Perryville Ky
George L Riker		July 28 1864	Atlanta Ga
Alonzo Chubb	2d Lieut	Oct 8 1862	Perryville Ky
Alonzo Chubb		Sep 19 1863	Chickamauga Ga
Stanley B Lockwood	1st Sergt	Oct 8 1862	Perryville Ky
Solomon D Williams	Sergt		Perryville See VI
Marshall A Teachout		Sep 19 1863	Chickamauga Ga
Harvey L Clark	Corporal	Oct 8 1862	Perryville Ky
Francis M Judd			Perryville Ky twice
Henry I Canfield		Sep 19 1863	Chickamauga Ga
Michael Ward	Wagoner	Mar 3 1865	Lynch's Creek S C
Alsey Amiel J	Private	Oct 8 1862	Perryville Ky
Bayer Edwin N			Perryville Ky
Blakey Harlow		Sep 19 1863	Chickamauga Ga
Brooks Samuel		Mar 15 1865	Fayetteville N C
Chesney Samuel P		Oct 8 1862	Perryville Ky
Lewis George L			Perryville Ky See V
McAtty Joseph			Perryville Ky
Martin John			Perryville See VI
Nash Harrison			Perryville Ky
Peyton Watson			Perryville Ky
Pease George E			Perryville See VIII
Place Ira			Perryville Ky
Potts Samuel J			Perryville Ky twice
Prouty Lucius A			Perryville See VI
Ruble Walter			Perryville See VIII
Spott Charles B			Perryville Ky
Vickers Frederick		Sep 20 1863	Chickamauga Ga
Vickers Frederick		June 22 1864	Kenesaw Mt Ga twice
Wallace Oscar R		Oct 8 1862	Perryville Ky
Wallace Oscar R		July 28 1864	Atlanta Ga
Webster Francis		June 24 1863	Hoover's Gap Tenn
Webster Francis		Nov 25 1863	Mission Ridge Tenn

Table II—Continued, Company E.

NAME	RANK	WHEN	REMARKS
Byron W Canfield	Captain	Oct 8 1862	Perryville Ky
E Abbott Spaulding,	"	Sep 20 1863	Chickamauga See VI
Edward Patchin	Sergt	Oct 8, 1862	Perryville Ky
Luman T Griste	Corporal	Sep 19, 1863	Chickamauga Ga
John McNaugnton		Nov 25 1863	Mission Ridge, Tenn
Ayers, Josiah	Private	Oct 8, 1862	Perryville See VI
Alberts, Washington	"	"	Perryville, Ky
Button, Justin	"		Perryville, Ky.
Case, Gideon			Perryville, Ky.
Humiston, John F		"	Perryville, Ky.
Hilt, Oliver	"		Perryville, Ky
Hayden Eugene	"		Perryville, Ky
Jones, Delavan	"		Perryville Ky
Knox, Dexter	"		Perryville See VI
King, Eleazar A		June 18 1864	Kenesaw Mt Ga
Ladow, Sylvester	"	Oct 8, 1862	Perryville Ky
Ladow, Sylvester	"	June 18, 1864	Kenesaw Mt Ga
Latimer, Olney P	"	Oct 8, 1862	Perryville, Ky
Latimer, Olney P	"	Sep 1, 1864	Jonesboro, Ga
Langston Henry	"	Oct 8, 1862	Perryville, Ky
Ladow, Henry			Perryville, Ky
Phillips Robert			Perryville Ky
Russell Elmer		June 25, 1863	Hoover's Gap, Tenn
Smith, Nathan M		Oct 8 1862	Perryville, Ky
Stocking John K		"	Perryville, Ky, twice
Stocking Charles H		"	Perryville Ky
Tucker John T			Perryville See VI
Townsley, Philetus		"	Perryville Ky
Webb Sylvester		Nov 29, 1862	Munfordville Ky
Watrous Samuel N	"	Oct 8, 1862	Perryville, Ky
Webb, Ezra ..	"	"	Perryville, Ky

COMPANY F.

NAME	RANK	WHEN	REMARKS
Harrison J Fuller	Sergt	Oct 8, 1862	Perryville See VI
David C Beardsley		Nov 25, 1863	Mission Ridge, Tenn
Josiah King	Corporal	Sep 19, 1863	Chickamauga See VI
James W Allen		Oct 8, 1862	Perryville, Ky, twice
Dwight H Woodard		"	Perryville, Ky
David Lester		June 18, 1864	Kenesaw Mt, Ga
Auxer, John H	Private	Oct 8, 1862	Perryville Ky
Auxer, John H		Sep 20, 1863	Chickamauga, Ga
Barlass, Robert B		Sep 19 1863	Chickamauga See VI
Brewster, Oliver R		Oct 8, 1862	Perryville See VI
Crawford, Emery		"	Perryville, Ky
Crawford, Emery	"	Sep 19, 1863	Chickamauga Ga
Clark, Nathan T	"	Oct 8, 1862	Perryville, Ky
Caley, Charles			Perryville, Ky
Dimmick, Orlando		Sep 20, 1863	Chickamauga Ga
Downing, John D	"	Sep 19, 1863	Chickamauga Ga
Ely, Ira		Nov 25, 1863	Mission Ridge Tenn
Kelsey Arthur		June 18, 1864	Kenesaw Mt Ga
McClintock, Charles W		Oct 8, 1862	Perryville, Ky See VI
Martin George			Perryville Ky
McElwain, Edwin W			Perryville, Ky.
Marsh, Henry			Perryville Ky
Newcomb, Selah W	"	"	Perryville See VI
Odell, David W	"	Nov 25, 1863	Mission Ridge, Tenn
Phillips, Albert .	"	Oct 8, 1862	Perryville Ky
Radcliffe, Charles	"	"	Perryville Ky
Randall, James G	"	"	Perryville Ky
Richmond, William		"	Perryville, Ky, twice
Waller, Harrison		"	Perryville See VI

COMPANY G.

NAME	RANK	WHEN	REMARKS
Albion W Tourgee	1st Lieut.	Oct 8, 1862	Perryville, Ky
E Abbott Spaulding	2d Lieut	"	Perryville See II F

Table II—Company G—Continued.

NAME	RANK	WHEN	REMARKS
William B Braman	Sergt	Oct 8 1862	Perryville Ky See VI
Benjamin F Cushing		Sep 20 1863	Chickamauga Ga
[illegible] L [illegible]	Corporal	Oct 8 1862	Perryville, Ky twice
[illegible] H H Wheaton			Perryville Ky
[illegible] Frank [illegible]	Private		Perryville Ky
[illegible] Edmund J			Perryville Ky
Chris[illegible] James J			Perryville Ky
Cowles Edwin R		Aug 10 1864	Atlanta Ga
Compton John D		July 22 1864	Peach tree Creek Ga See VI
Felch Francis [illegible]		Nov 25 1863	Mission Ridge See VI
[illegible] George A		May 13 1864	Resaca See VI
Gant William H		Oct 8 1862	Perryville Ky See VI
[illegible] Daniel C			Perryville Ky, See VI
Galbraith [illegible] P			Perryville Ky
Giddings Francis W			Perryville Ky
Heath Adoniram J		Nov 25 1863	Mission Ridge Tenn
Kenny [illegible]		Oct 8 1862	Perryville Ky
Lobdell [illegible]			Perryville Ky twice
McCreary Harrison			Perryville Ky
Stoll Henry C			Perryville Ky
Smith Jerome L			Perryville See VI
Sweet Jesse M		Aug 5 1864	Atlanta Ga
Waterman William A		Oct 8 1862	Perryville Ky
Waterman Adna			Perryville See VI
Whipple, Perry M			Perryville Ky

COMPANY H.

NAME	RANK	WHEN	REMARKS
Ira F Mansfield	1st Sergt	Oct 8 1862	Perryville, Ky
Florentine M Simon	Sergt		Perryville Ky
Abram S McCurley			Perryville Ky
John W Nesbit		June 18 1864	Kenesaw Mt Ga
Manassas Miller	Corporal		Kenesaw Mt Ga
Andrew Geddes			Kenesaw Mt Ga
Baker William H	Private	Oct 8 1862	Perryville See VI
Brenaman Constantine		May 14 1864	Resaca Ga
Engle Zimri	"	Oct 8 1862	Perryville Ky
Engle Zimri		June 11 1864	Kenesaw Mt Ga
Homstine, B[illegible]	"	Oct 8 1862	Perryville Ky
Hunt Alfred	"		Perryville Ky
Ingling William D	"		Perryville See VI
Kirk Robert A			Perryville Ky
Kirkbride Asher		Nov 25 1863	Mission Ridge See VI
Kirkbride James		Oct 8 1862	Perryville Ky
Miller Addison		"	Perryville, Ky
Myers Jonathan			Perryville Ky
Naylor, William H	"	"	Perryville See VI
Weldy Moses		Aug [illegible] 1864	Atlanta Ga

COMPANY I.

NAME	RANK	WHEN	REMARKS
Charles H Brigden	1st Lieut	Oct 8 1862	Perryville Ky
L Newton Parker	1st Sergt		Perryville Ky
Harvey W Partridge		Sep 20 1863	Chickamauga See VI
William Enos	Sergt	Oct 8 1862	Perryville, Ky
Alden F Brooks	Corporal		Perryville Ky
Hugh M Boys		Sep 20 1863	Chickamauga Ga
Robert N Holcomb		Oct 8 1862	Perryville Ky
Dillen J Turner			Perryville Ky
Philip Reynolds		Sep 19 1863	Chickamauga Ga
Ambrose J Bailey		Nov 25 1863	Mission Ridge See VI
Andrews Elmer H	Private	Oct 8 1862	Perryville See VI
Butler Frank A		Aug 30 1864	Near Atlanta Ga
Collver George L		Dec 30 1862	Near Glasgow Ky
Creighton William		Oct 8 1862	Perryville See VI

Table II—Company I—Continued.

NAME.	RANK	WHEN	REMARKS
Delano, Horace	Private	"	Perryville, Ky
Frisby Augustus B.			Perryville, Ky
Gidelings, Frederick M	"	"	Perryville Ky
Hake Samuel		Sep 20, 1863	Chickamauga, Ga
Hazletine, John G	"	"	Chickamauga Ga
Haine William J	"	Oct 8, 1862	Perryville, Ky
Knight, Hiram T	"	Sep 19, 1863	Chickamauga See VI
Lyman, John W	"	Oct 8 1862	Perryville, Ky
Lyman, George W .	"	"	Perryville, Ky
Morris, Thomas G .		"	Perryville, Ky
Morse, Marvin .	"	Aug 4 1864	Atlanta, Ga
Perry, Worthy	"	Oct 8, 1862	Perryville Ky.
Perkins, Lucius .	"	Aug 13 1864	Altanta Ga
Rowe, Albert G . . .	"	June 14, 1864	Kenesaw Mt See VI
Sealy, Esau A .	"	Nov 25, 1863	Mission Ridge Tenn
Sealy, Esau A	"	Aug 3, 1864	Atlanta See VI
Talcott, Whitman B	"	Oct 8 1862	Perryville See VI
Tiloff, William F.		Feb 18, 1865	Broad River, S C
Whitcomb, Edwin A .	"	Oct 8, 1862	Perryville, Ky
Webb, Darwin	"	"	Perryville, Ky

COMPANY K.

NAME	RANK	WHEN	REMARKS
Clayborne A Eddy	Sergt	Apr 16, 1865	Near Holly Springs N C See VI
William O Smith	Corporal	Oct 8, 1862	Perryville, Ky
Orrin Arnold		Sep 19, 1863	Chickamauga See VI
Babcock, Benjamin N	Private	Sep 23, 1863	Chickamauga, Ga
Bates, Charles F.		Oct 8, 1862	Perryville See VI
Burlingame, Edwin R	"	"	Perryville, Ky.
Barnard, Francis N. .	"	"	Perryville Ky
Bigelow, William E	"	June 18 1864	Kenesaw Mt, Ga
Early, Elbridge F		Oct 8, 1862	Perryville, Ky
Hicock, Clay		"	Perryville, Ky.
Hanna, Lyman P		"	Perryville, Ky
Hutchinson, Stephen J		Nov 25, 1863	Mission Ridge, Tenn
Jenkins, Aaron		Oct 8, 1862	Perryville, Ky
Webb Andrew W .	"	"	Perryville See VI
Williams, Joel	"	"	Perryville, Ky
Wright, William W	"	"	Perryville, Ky

TABLE III.
Captured.

COMPANY A.

NAME	RANK	WHEN	REMARKS
Robert C Porter	Sergt	Jan 21 1863	Near Murfreesboro Paroled.
Barr Alexander	Private		Near Murfreesboro Paroled
Bowen Thomas			Near Murfreesboro Paroled
Boyle John A			Near Murfreesboro Paroled
Coulter James C			Near Murfreesboro Paroled
Cowley Hugh			Near Murfreesboro Paroled
Edmonds, David		"	Near Murfreesboro Paroled See VIII
Fair Emanuel			Near Murfreesboro Paroled
Foster John C		"	Near Murfreesboro Paroled
Hulburt Frank			Near Murfreesboro Paroled See VIII
Harber, Aaron		"	Near Murfreesboro Paroled
Hollgen Frederick	"	Sep 20 1863	Chickamauga Exchanged
Kyle Wesley		Jan 21 1863	Near Murfreesboro Paroled
Morris Isaac		Sep 20, 1863	Chickamauga Died See VI
Malcomson James		Jan 21 1863	Near Murfreesboro Paroled.
Rup Reuben B			Near Murfreesboro Paroled
Renn John W			Near Murfreesboro Paroled
Smith Benjamin		Sep 20 1863	Chickamauga Died See VI.
Sparrow Emmons			Chickamauga See VIII
Stambaugh John		Jan 21 1863	Near Murfreesboro Paroled
Stewart John Allen		"	Near Murfreesboro Paroled
Stewart, Samuel M		"	Near Murfreesboro Paroled

COMPANY B

NAME	RANK	WHEN	REMARKS
Beele Henry I	Private	Oct 8 1862	Perryville Paroled See VIII
Colton Francis		Sep 20 1863	Chickamauga Escaped from Andersonville
Crawford James A			Chickamauga Exchanged D See VI
Hart Adelbert		Jan 21 1863	Near Murfreesboro Paroled
Hart Adelbert		Sep 20 1863	Chickamauga Exchanged D See VI
Hadsell Edward		Jan 21 1863	Near Murfreesboro Paroled
Kerr Hugh K			Near Murfreesboro Paroled
Mayer William	"		Near Murfreesboro Escaped
Mason Charles H			Near Murfreesboro Escaped
Phillips Dwight B		Sep 20 1863	Chickamauga Ga See VIII
Prentice Albert D		Jan 21, 1863	Near Murfreesboro Paroled
Rush Daniel			Near Murfreesboro Paroled
Shafer Jacob			Near Murfreesboro Paroled
Shafer Charles			Near Murfreesboro Paroled.
Smith John			Near Murfreesboro Paroled
Urich Martin W			Near Murfreesboro Paroled
Wildman John I			Near Murfreesboro Paroled
Welsh William C		Sep 20 1863,	Chickamauga, Died See VI

COMPANY C.

NAME	RANK	WHEN	REMARKS
Bartholomew Erastus	Private	Sep 20 1863	Chickamauga Died See VI
Jones William		Jan 21 1863	Near Murfreesboro Paroled
Lewis William			Near Murfreesboro Paroled

Table III—Company C—Continued.

NAME	RANK	WHEN	REMARKS
Mackey, John M	Private	Jan 21, 1863	Near Murfreesboro Escaped
McLain, Richard H		"	Near Murfreesboro Paroled
McKenzie, James R			Near Murfreesboro Paroled See VIII
Miller, Charles E	Wagoner	"	Near Murfreesboro Paroled.
Osborn, Alfred	Private	"	Near Murfreesboro Paroled
Powers, Wilson S	"	"	Near Murfreesboro Paroled
Rosser John P	"	"	Near Murfreesboro Paroled
Robinson, Thomas	"	"	Near Murfreesboro Paroled See VIII
Rees William R	"	"	Near Murfreesboro Paroled
Roberts, John		"	Near Murfreesboro Paroled
Sutton, Samuel		"	Near Murfreesboro Paroled
Shealon David J	"	"	Near Murfreesboro Paroled
Seachrist, Isaiah		"	Near Murfreesboro Paroled
Stewart, Nelson O ..	"	"	Near Murfreesboro Paroled

COMPANY D.

NAME	RANK	WHEN	REMARKS
Alonzo Chubb .	2d Lieut	Jan 21, 1863	Near Murfreesboro Exchanged May 8, 1863
Marshall A Teachout	Corporal	"	Near Murfreesboro Paroled
Brooks, Samuel	Private	"	Near Murfreesboro Paroled
Belden, Francis E	"	Sep 20, 1863	Chickamauga D See VI
Giddings, Anson E .	"	Jan. 21, 1863	Near Murfreesboro Paroled
Grover Alonzo	"	"	Near Murfreesboro Paroled
Hall, Henry	"	"	Near Murfreesboro Paroled
Jackson Stewart D .	"	"	Near Murfreesboro Paroled
Morse, Bliss	"	"	Near Murfreesboro Paroled
Sill, Joshua H .	"	"	Near Murfreesboro Paroled

COMPANY E

NAME	RANK	WHEN	REMARKS.
Byron W Canfield	Captain	Jan 21, 1863	Near Murfreesboro Exchanged May 8, 1863
Albert A Champlin	Wagoner	"	Near Murfreesboro Paroled
Bridgeman, Ansel O	Private	"	Near Murfreesboro Paroled
Dayton, William ..	"	Sep 19, 1863	Chickamauga D See VI.
Eggleston, Wellington	"	Feb 1, 1865	Sister's Ferry, Ga Paroled See V
Hayes, Elisha W		Jan 21, 1863	Near Murfreesboro Paroled
Hill, Almon	"	"	Near Murfreesboro Paroled
Mowrey, James A .		Sep 20, 1863	Chickamauga Exchanged
McFarland, McKendrie		Jan 21, 1863.	Near Murfreesboro Escaped
Pease, Byron A .		"	Near Murfreesboro Paroled
Potter, Edward	"	"	Near Murfreesboro Escaped
Reed, Daniel J .. .	"	"	Near Murfreesboro Paroled
Strickland Walter	"		Near Murfreesboro, Paroled
Stillwell, William ..	"	"	Near Murfreesboro, Paroled
Watts, Alonzo S	"	"	Near Murfreesboro. Escaped

COMPANY F.

NAME	RANK	WHEN	REMARKS
Charles R Brown .	Sergt	Sep 20, 1863.	Chickamauga Escaped from rebel prison, Danville, Va
Josiah King	Corporal	Sep 19, 1863	Chickamauga Died See VI
Burnett, Isaac .	Private	Jan 21, 1863	Near Murfreesboro Paroled
Burnett Isaac		Mar 19, 1863	Near Milton, Tenn Exchanged D See VI
Barnes, James . . .	"	Jan. 21, 1863	Near Murfreesboro Paroled
Caley, Charles	"	"	Near Murfreesboro Paroled

Table III Company F Continued

NAME	RANK	WHEN	REMARKS.
Clark Nathan T			Near Murfreesboro Paroled
Crawford Emery			Near Murfreesboro Paroled
Davidson Erastus	"		Near Murfreesboro Paroled
Dimmick Orlando			Near Murfreesboro Paroled
Doolittle Charles J			Near Murfreesboro Paroled
Downer John D			Near Murfreesboro Escaped
Fay Ira			Near Murfreesboro Paroled
Green Horace			Near Murfreesboro Paroled
Greenleaf [illegible]			Near Murfreesboro Paroled
Kelsey Arthur			Near Murfreesboro Paroled
Marsh Henry		Sep 19 1863	Chickamauga Ga Escaped See VIII
Martin George			Chickamauga Ga Died See VI
Payne William B		Jan 21 1863	Near Murfreesboro Escaped
Schram Watson S			Near Murfreesboro Paroled
Woodard Dwight H		Sep 19 1863	Chickamauga Ga Paroled

COMPANY G

NAME	RANK	WHEN	REMARKS
[illegible] W T[illegible]r	1st Lieut	Jan 21 1863	Near Murfreesboro Tenn Exchanged May 5 186[illegible]
Orson L Marsh	Corporal		Near Murfreesboro Paroled
Abbott Simeon M	Private	Oct 8 1862	Perryville Paroled See VIII
Benjamin Livingstone J		Jan 21 1863	Near Murfreesboro Tenn Paroled See VIII
Baldwin Franklin	"		Near Murfreesboro Paroled
Chapin Stephen W			Near Murfreesboro Paroled
Compton John D			Near Murfreesboro Paroled
Cook Luke			Near Murfreesboro Paroled
Dever William P		Sep 1 1862	Near Frankfort Ky Paroled See VIII
Eaton Irwin		Jan 21 1863	Near Murfreesboro Paroled
Jones James I			Near Murfreesboro Paroled
Jones James L	"	Sep 20 1863	Chickamauga Ga D See VI
Parker Seth		Jan 21 1863	Near Murfreesboro Paroled
Rood Orville A			Near Murfreesboro Paroled
Spencer John C			Near Murfreesboro Paroled
Stoll Henry C		Feb 1 1865	Near Sister's Ferry Ga Paroled See V

COMPANY H.

NAME	RANK	WHEN	REMARKS
William K Mead	Corp	Jan 21 1863	Near Murfreesboro Paroled
Jason W Silver			Near Murfreesboro Paroled
Ellinger John F	Private		Near Murfreesboro Paroled
Grossman John			Near Murfreesboro Paroled
Hartzell Joshua			Near Murfreesboro Paroled
Harrison Jeremiah			Near Murfreesboro Paroled
Hayes David			Near Murfreesboro Paroled
Hutton Henry		Oct 8 1862	Perryville Paroled See VIII
Kirkbride James		Jan 21, 1863	Near Murfreesboro Paroled
Kirkbride Asher			Near Murfreesboro Paroled
Keiser Frank		"	Near Murfreesboro Paroled
Middleton William H			Near Murfreesboro Paroled
Naylor James E			Near Murfreesboro Paroled
Owen [illegible]			Near Murfreesboro Paroled
Peck James			Near Murfreesboro Paroled
Pierce Charles D			Near Murfreesboro Paroled
Rapp Samuel K			Near Murfreesboro Paroled
Rammel Joseph			Near Murfreesboro Paroled.
Stewart Royal M			Near Murfreesboro Paroled
Shock George			Near Murfreesboro Paroled
Spitler George J	"		Near Murfreesboro Paroled
Stauffer Jesse			Near Murfreesboro Paroled
Van Norden Charles A.		"	Near Murfreesboro Paroled
Wire, Samuel	"	"	Near Murfreesboro Paroled.
Weldy, Moses	"	"	Near Murfreesboro Paroled.

Table III—Continued, Company I.

NAME.	RANK	WHEN.	REMARKS
Dillen J Turner......	Corp	Sep 20, 1863	Chickamauga Paroled See V
Philip Reynolds	"	Sep, 19, 1863	Chickamauga Paroled See II
Joseph B Ashley	Wagon'r	Jan 21 1863	Near Murfreesboro Escaped
Harrison, Manuel J	Private	Sep 20, 1863	Chickamauga D See VI.
Harrison Salathiel	"	"	Chickamauga Paroled See V
Hake, Samuel	"		Chickamauga Paroled See II
Jones, Roderick M	"	Sep 2 1862	Lexington, Ky Paroled
Jones, Roderick M	"	Jan 21, 1863	Near Murfreesboro Escaped
Joslin, Benjamin	"		Near Murfreesboro Paroled.
Kellogg, John		"	Near Murfreesboro Paroled.
Kelly, Edgar A		"	Near Murfreesboro Paroled
Knowlton Newton	"		Near Murfreesboro Escaped
Lyman George W		"	Near Murfreesboro Paroled
Morse, Marvin		Sep 2, 1862	Lexington, Ky Paroled
Morse, Marvin	"	Jan 21, 1863	Near Murfreesboro Paroled
Morris, Thomas S	"	"	Near Murfreesboro Paroled.
Northway, Henry D	"	"	Near Murfreesboro Paroled
Perkins, Lucius	"	"	Near Murfreesboro Paroled
Rowe, Albert G	"	"	Near Murfreesboro Paroled
Steele Calvin F	"		Near Murfreesboro Escaped
Smith, Cyrus T....	"	"	Near Murfreesboro. Paroled

COMPANY K.

NAME.	RANK	WHEN	REMARKS
Alderman, Ellsworth A.	Private	Jan 21, 1863	Near Murfreesboro Paroled
Alderman Cassius M	"	"	Near Murfreesboro Paroled
Bigelow, William E	"	"	Near Murfreesboro Paroled
Darrow Alfred	"		Near Murfreesboro Paroled
Eddy, Clayborne A	"		Near Murfreesboro Escaped
Gary, David	"	"	Near Murfreesboro Paroled.
Hutchinson, Arthur G	"	"	Near Murfreesboro Paroled
Hutchinson, David	"	"	Near Murfreesboro Tenn Paroled D See VI
Hines, Isaac		"	Near Murfreesboro Paroled
Hines, Isaac		Sep 19, 1863	Chickamauga, Ga Paroled
Jenkins, Aaron	"	Jan 21, 1863	Near Murfreesboro Paroled.
King, Amos H	"	Mar 1, 1865	Lancaster S C Paroled
Pratt, Charles	"	Jan 21, 1863.	Near Murfreesboro Escaped
Slater Albert A	"	"	Near Murfreesboro Paroled
Seymour George	"	"	Near Murfreesboro Paroled
Warren Francis	"	"	Near Murfreesboro Paroled
Williams, Joel..	"	Oct 8, 1862	Perryville, Ky Exchanged

TABLE IV.

Transferred.

Abbreviations

V R C —Veteran Reserve Corps
V V E —Veteran Volunteer Engineers

COMPANY A.

NAME	RANK	WHEN	REMARKS
John F McCollom	Corporal	Nov 21 1864	To V R C Dis Dec 5 1864 for disability
Charles C Stover	Musician	June 1 1865	To Co B 38th O V I • July 12 1865
Baker George	Private		To Co B 38th O V I • July 12 1865
Bailey William			To Co F 38th O V I • July 12 1865
Christy James			To Co K 38th O V I • July 12 1865
Cook Dugald		July 20 1863	To Co E 1st Regt V V E • June 21 1865
Foster John C		July 27 1863	To Co I 18th Regt V R C • July 1 1865
Harber Aaron		Jan [illegible] 1865	To Co F 7th Regt V R C • June 28 1865
Helliger, Oscar C F		June 1 1865	To Co K 38th O V I • July 12 1865
Herrington Frederick		"	To Co A 38th O V I • June 19 1865
Hotham Leonard K			To Co A 38th O V I • July 12 1865
Howard Edward L		"	To Co K 38th O V I • July 12 1865
Jones William L		"	To Co A 38th O V I
Kaine Anthony			To Co K 38th O V I • July 12 1865
Kelly Stephen T		Feb 15 1864	To V R C
McCambridge, Patrick		June 1 1865	To Co K 38th O V I • July 12 1865
McKibben, Robert		Oct [illegible] 1863	To 121 Co 2d Battalion V R C • June 29 1865
Malcomson James		Dec 28 1864	To Co H 5th Regt V R C • July 5 1865
O Donal John		June 1 1865	To Co K 38th O V I • July 12 1865
Patterson James		"	To Co D 38th O V I
Porter Lewis		Feb 7 1865	To Co A 15th Regt V R C • July 22 1865
Reed Ell S		June 1 1865	To Co K 38th O V I • July 12 1865
Rowe James		"	To Co K 38th O V I • July 12, 1865
Russell Elijah B		"	To Co K 38th O V I • July 12 1865
Smith, Daniel A		Sep 12 1863	To V R C
Stambaugh Samuel S		June 1 1865	To Co F 38th O V I • July 12 1865
Stein Jacob		Mar 17, 1864	To V R C
Stewart, James		June 1 1865	To Co K 38th O V I • July 12 1865
Stewart John Alexander		July 29 1863	To Co B 1st Regt V V E • Sep 28 1865
Stewart John Allen		Mar 11, 1864	To V R C

Table IV—Company A—Continued.

NAME	RANK	WHEN	REMARKS
Stewart, Cyrus	Private	June 1, 1865	To Co K 38th O V I * July 12 1866
Warner, John W	"	"	To Co A 38th O V I * July 12 1865
Whetstone, David C		"	To Co A 38th O V I * July 12 1865

COMPANY B.

NAME	RANK	WHEN	REMARKS
William Hughes	Sergt	Oct 23, 1863	To 87th Co 2d Battalion V R C as Sergt * June 28, 1865
Dayton, Charles R	Private	June 1, 1865	To Co C 38th O V I * July 12 1865
Decker, William			To Co B 38th O V I * July 12, 1865
Harven, William		"	To Co B 38th O V I as Wm Harbor * July 12, 1865
Jackson, Hugh W		"	To Co C 38th O V I * June 7, 1865
Johnson William H	"	"	To Co D 38th O V I * July 12 1865
Lake, Lafayette		"	To Co B 38th O V I * July 12 1865
Long Lewis	"	Mar. 16, 1864	To V R C
Moyer, William	"	July 20 1864	To Co C 1st Regt V. V. E Sep 26 1865
Oliver, Cyrus	"	Aug, 1, 1863	To Co K 12th Regt V R C Dis June 1 1865
Prentice, Albert D	"	Apr 30, 1864	To 154th Co 2d Battalion V R C Dis for disability May 26, 1865,
Prentice, Edward	"	Sep. 23, 1863	To V R C
Rawdon, Calvin L	"	June 1, 1865	To Co K 38th O V I * July 12 1865
Rawdon, Martin B	"	"	To Co B 38th O V I * July 12 1865
Shafer, Morrison P	"	"	To Co B 38th O V I * July 12, 1865
Sparks, Lorenz H	"	May 31, 1864	To V R C
Weirman Samuel	"	June 1 1865	To Co B 38th O V I * July 12, 1865

COMPANY C.

NAMES.	RANK	WHEN.	REMARKS
Thomas C, Hogle.	Musician	Dec 22, 1864	To Co I 15th Regt V R C * July 1, 1865
Brandt, John B.	Private	Apr. 11 1864	To Co H 12th Regt V R C * June 29 1865
Carron, William	"	Dec 21 1864	To Co A 15th Regt V R C. * July 22 1865
Davis, Gwilym		June 1, 1865	To Co D 38th O V I * July 12, 1865
Davis, Morgan		"	To Co D 38th O. V I * July 12 1865
Dice George M	"	"	To Co D 38th O V I * July 12, 1865
Graham, William P		July 18, 1864	To Co A 1st Regt V V E * Sep. 26, 1865
Heir, George	"	June 1 1865	To Co C 38th O V I * July 12, 1865
Heir, Thomas	"	"	To Co C 38th O V I * July 12, 1865
Hull, Hiram F	"	July 18, 1864	To Co A 1st Regt V V E * Sep 26, 1865
Quigley, Thomas	"	Sep, 1, 1863	To V R C

Table IV—Company C—Continued.

NAME	RANK	WHEN	REMARKS
[illegible]		June 1, 186[illegible]	To Co [illegible] 8th O V I [illegible] July 12 1865
Thomas J[illegible] B			To Co [illegible] 8th O V I [illegible] July 12 [illegible]65
W[illegible]		Sep [illegible] 1 18[illegible]3	To V R C
W[illegible]ster D[illegible]		June 1 18[illegible]	To Co D 8th O V I [illegible] July 12 18[illegible]
Whit[illegible]			To Co F [illegible]8th O V

COMPANY D.

NAME	RANK	WHEN	REMARKS
W[illegible] D[illegible]	Sergt	Se[illegible] 15 1863	To V R C
Harlan P H[illegible]	Corporal	J[illegible] 1 18[illegible]	To Co I [illegible]8th O V I [illegible] July 12 1865
Francis M [illegible]		[illegible] 27 18[illegible]3	To V R C
[illegible]	Private	Apr 2[illegible] 18[illegible]	To Gunboat service
[illegible]		J[illegible] 1 1865	To Co I [illegible]8th Reg[illegible] O V I [illegible] July 12 1865
[illegible]		[illegible] 18[illegible]3	To Co I [illegible]8th Regt V [illegible] July 1 1865
[illegible]		Mar 7 18[illegible]	To V R C
[illegible]		J[illegible] 2[illegible] 18[illegible]	To Co I [illegible]8th Regt V R C [illegible] July 1 18[illegible]
H[illegible]		Mar [illegible] 18[illegible]	To Co K 5th Regt V R C [illegible] July 2[illegible] 1865
H[illegible] James L		Oct [illegible], 18[illegible]	To 17th [illegible] Cav [illegible] 11 186[illegible]
L[illegible]		J[illegible] 1 1865	To Co C 8th O [illegible] June 21 1865
[illegible] W		Apr [illegible] 18[illegible]	To Co G [illegible]th Regt V R C [illegible] July [illegible] 1865
[illegible]		June 1 1865	To Co I [illegible]8th O V I [illegible] July 12 1865
Wak[illegible] B[illegible]			To Co I 8th O V I [illegible] July 12 1865
W[illegible]		Mar 1[illegible] 18[illegible]	To V R C
W[illegible]		Apr 2[illegible] 18[illegible]	To Gunboat service

COMPANY E.

NAME	RANK	WHEN	REMARKS
[illegible]	Private		To Co G 15th Regt V R C [illegible] July [illegible] 1865
[illegible]		Mar 15 18[illegible]	To Co K 5th Regt V R C [illegible] July [illegible] 18[illegible]
[illegible] Fernando C			To V R C
H[illegible] W		July 18 1864	To V V I
[illegible] Henry		Mar 1[illegible] 1864	To V R C
[illegible]		Mar 15 1865	To 15th Co 2d Battalion V R C [illegible] June [illegible] 1865
P[illegible]		Ju[illegible] 1 1865	To Co [illegible] 8th O V I [illegible] July 12 186[illegible]
P[illegible]			To Co I [illegible]8th O V I [illegible] July 12 1865

COMPANY F.

NAME	RANK	WHEN	REMARKS
W[illegible]	P[illegible]	June 1 18[illegible]	To 8th O V I [illegible] June [illegible] 186[illegible]
[illegible] J[illegible] H	Private	Apr 22 18[illegible]	To 15th Co 2d Battalion V R C [illegible] July 12 1865
[illegible]		J[illegible] 1 1865	To Co I [illegible]8th O V I [illegible] July 12 1865

Table IV--Company F—Continued.

NAME	RANK	WHEN	REMARKS
Call, Francis M	Private	May 31, 1864	To 151st Co 2d Battalion V R C * June 30, 1865
Cassidy John	"	Jan 22, 1863	To V R C
Cousins, Levi B	"	June 1 1865	To Co E 38th O V I * July 12, 1865
Dimmick, Orlando	"	Mar 7, 1864	To 2d Battalion V R C * June 17, 1865
Fales, Frank	"	May 6, 1863	To Co F 1st Regt V V E * June 27, 1865
Perry William		June 1, 1865	To Co E 38th O V I * July 12, 1865
Foote Lormi M	"	Feb 11 1864	To V R C
Gray Charles		June 1, 1865	To Co E 38th O V I * July 12, 1865
Hobert, Marcene	"	Sep 20 1864	To 23d Regt V R C
Kelsey, Arthur		June 1, 1865	To Co F 38th O V I * July 12 1865
Ketchum, Daniel			To Co F 38th O V I * June 13, 1865
Manchester, Lyman	"		To Co E 38th O V I * July 12 1865
Newcomb Frank E	"	Dec 12, 1863	To V R C
Pierce, Alson I	"	June 1 1865	To Co G 38th O V I * July 12, 1865
Riley, Charles H	"	"	To Co E 38th O V I * July 12 1865
Rand, Cassius M	"	"	To Co G 38th O V I Absent sick * June 10 1865
Saddler John	"	"	To Co E 38th O V I * July 12, 1865
Saxton Seymour		"	To Co I 38th O V I * July 12, 1865
Scott, Chauncey B	"	"	To Co I 38th O V I Dis for dis May 20, 1865
Waters, Rollin A	"	April 6, 1864	To 149th Co 2d Battalion V R C * June 30 1865

COMPANY G.

NAME	RANK	WHEN	REMARKS
Fayette, Blood	Corporal	Apr 18 1864	To U S Navy
Barker, Edmond J	Private	Mar 13, 1865	To 155th Co 2d Battalion V R C * July 26, 1865
Barnes, William H	"	July 29, 1864	To Co B 1st Regt V V E * June 30, 1865
Cook Luke		Mar 15, 1864	To V R C
De Wolf John W		Apr 1864	To U S Navy
Drake William	"	Dec 12 1863	To V R C
Fuller, Martin H	"	June 1, 1865	To Co K 38th O V I * June 2, 1865
Giddings, Francis W	"	Dec 15 1863	To 120th Co 2d Batln V R C
Kirby George	"	July 20, 1864	To Co E 1st Regt V V E * Sep 26, 1865
Metcalf, George L	"	July 27, 1863,	To Co H 8th Regt V R C * July 2, 1865
Munn Herman D	"	Jan 28, 1864	To V R C
Sill, Theodore	"		To Co E 17th Regt V R C. * June 29, 1865
Spencer, John C	"	Mar 16 1864	To Co H 8th Regt. V R C. * July 2 1865
Swartout Lacy	"	July 27, 1863	To Co I 8th Regt V R C * July 1 1865
Sweet, Jesse M	"	June 1, 1865	To Co F 38th Regt O V I * July 12, 1865
Torry, Seneca D	"	"	To Co G 38th Regt O V I * July 12 1865
Williams Milton	"	"	To Co G 38th Regt O V I * July 12 1865

Table IV Continued, Company H.

NAME	RANK	WHEN	REMARKS
Amon, Eastman	Corporal	Nov 13 1863	To Co A 8th Regt V R C * June 17 1865
Courtney, Frederick	Private	July 27 1863	To Co I 18th Regt V R C * July 1 1865
Hornstine Bacila		Feb 23 1863	To Miss Marine Corps
Hunt Chauncey M		Nov 6 1863	To V R C
Kirkhofe James		July 18 1864	To Co A 1st Regt V V E * Sep 26 1865
Shafer, James		June 1, 1865	To Co A 38th Regt O V I * July 12 1865
Stewart Royal M		Nov 28 1863	To V R C
Whetstone Isaac B		June 1 1865	To Co A 38th Regt O V I * July 12 1865
Witmer Lewis			To Co G 38th Regt O V I * July 12 1865
Witzeman Benjamin		"	To Co G 38th Regt O V I * July 12 1865
Young, John	"	Mar 1, 1864	To V R C

COMPANY I.

NAME	RANK	WHEN	REMARKS
Robert S Abell	Corporal	Mar 31 1864	To V R C * June 13, 1865
Bunting Robert L	Private	July 29 1864	To Co B 1st Regt V V L * Sep 26, 1865
Hune George		Jan 14 1864	To V R C
Hazeltine John G		Mar 20 1864	To Co H 19th Regt V R C. * July 13 1865
Kellogg John		Sep 21 1864	To 187th Co 1st Battalion V R C
Knowles Thomas J		July 18 1864	To Co A 1st Regt V V E * Sep 26 1865
Lane, George		June 1 1865	To Co B 38th O V I * July 12 1865
Lockwood Edgar	"	Nov 28 1863	To V R C
Patchin James W	"	Mar 15, 1865	To 35th Co 2d Battalion V R C * July 17 1865
Perry Worthy		Jan 5 1864	To Co C 23d Regt V R C * July 13 1865
Rulapaugh John		Sep 26 1863	To V R C
Webb Darwin		Oct 29 1863	To Co C 15th Regt V R C * July 13 1865
Wildman Ira	"	May 18 1863	To Miss Marine Brigade

COMPANY K.

NAME	RANK	WHEN	REMARKS
Horatio M Smith ..	1st Lieut	Jan 16, 1861	Pr Capt Post Q M Chattanooga * Brevt-Maj U S V
Burgett, Harrison	Private	Oct 29 1863	To V R C
Burgett Harrison H	"	July 18, 1864	To V V E.
Enos Andrew		June 1 1865	To Co G 38th O V I * July 12 1865
Earl William	"	Aug 3 1863	To V R C
Mann John		July 27 1863	To Co E 17th Regt V R C * June 17, 1865
Parker Albertus W			To Co I 8th Regt V R C * July 1 1865
Sweet Jillitt S		Aug 19 1863	To Co D 2d Regt V R C * July 5 1865
Towen Herbert	"	June 1 1865	To Co G 38th O V I * July 12, 1865

TABLE V.
Mustered Out at Close of War,

ABSENT FROM REGIMENT FOR CAUSE.

COMPANY A.

NAME	RANK	WHEN	WHERE	REMARKS
James Morris	Sergt	June 10 1865	Cleveland, O	Det service
William G Davis	Corp.	May 3, 1865	Cleveland, O	Ab Wounded.
Kelley, Mahershalal	Private	"	Cp Dennison, O	Ab Sick

COMPANY B.

NAME	RANK	WHEN	WHERE	REMARKS
Bear Abner	Private	June 9 1865.	Cleveland O	Det service
Lattin, Wright	"	May 30, 1865	Madison Ind	Ab Sick

COMPANY C.

NAME	RANK	WHEN	WHERE	REMARKS
Culver, James	Private	July 14 1865	Cleveland O	Ab Sick
Edwards John F	"	June 10 1865	Cleveland, O	Det service
Evans Ezeriah	"	July 17, 1865	Cleveland, O	Ab Sick

COMPANY D.

NAME	RANK	WHEN	WHERE	REMARKS
Warren Jennings	Sergt	June 10, 1865	Cleveland, O	Det service.
Seth Weeks	"	June 2, 1865	Nashville, Tenn	Det service
Charles E Doolittle	Corp	May 31, 1865	Nashville, Tenn	Det duty
Ackley Amiel J	Private	June 27 1865	Columbus O	Det duty
Vickers Frederick	"	June 1, 1865	Cleveland, O	Ab Wounded
Wakelee, Oscar R	"	June 16, 1865	Cleveland, O	Det service
Wakelee, Arthur B	"	"	Cleveland, O	Det service

COMPANY E.

NAME	RANK	WHEN	WHERE	REMARKS
Eggleston Wellington	Private	June 16 1865	Camp Chase, O	Ab Prisoner
Jones Delavan		June 15 1865.	Nashville, Tenn	Det in hos
King, Eleazar A	"	June 26 1865	Cleveland O	Wounded & det.
Ladow Sylvester	"	June 9 1865	Nashville, Tenn.	Ab Wounded
Russell, Elmer	"	May 30 1865	Nashville, Tenn	Det Hos duty

COMPANY F.

NAME	RANK	WHEN	WHERE	REMARKS
David C Beardsley	Sergt	June 2 1865	Camp Dennison	Det duty
Radcliff Charles	Private	May 17, 1865	Nashville, Tenn	Ab Sick

COMPANY G.

NAME	RANK	WHEN	WHERE	REMARKS
Pease John D	Private	June 2, 1865	Cp Dennison, O	Ab Sick
Richmond Sherman S	"	June 3 1865	Nashville, Tenn	Det duty
Stoil, Henry C	"	June 16, 1865	Camp Chase, O	Ab Prisoner.

COMPANY H.

NAME	RANK	WHEN	WHERE	REMARKS
John C Hartzell	Captain	June 7, 1865	Columbus, O	Det service.
Flaugher, Joseph H	Private	May 29, 1865	New York City.	Ab Sick

COMPANY I.

NAME	RANK	WHEN	WHERE	REMARKS
Hugh M Boys	Corp	May 11, 1865	Nashville, Tenn	Ab Wounded.
Dillen J Turner	"	June 26 1865	Camp Chase, O	Ab Prisoner.
Anderson Thomas	Private.	May 30, 1865	Cleveland O	Det service
Butler, Frank A	"	June 7, 1865	Cleveland, O	Ab Wounded
Harrison, Salathiel	"	June 16 1865	Camp Chase O	Ab. Prisoner
Tiloff William F	"	June 9 1865	Cp Dennison, O	Ab Wounded
Wilcox, William R	"	May 26, 1865	Louisville, Ky	With Hos Corps

COMPANY K.

NAME	RANK	WHEN	WHERE	REMARKS
William O Smith	Corp	June 3 1865	Nashville, Tenn	Det service
Hutchinson Stephen J	Private	June 2 1865	Chattan'ga Tenn	Det service
King Amos H	"	June 24 1865	Camp Chase O	Ab Prisoner.
Wilson, Frederick W	"	July 13 1865	Columbus, O	Det service

TABLE VI.

Killed and Died in Service.

COMPANY A

NAME	RANK	DATE	WHERE	WHERE INTERRED
Nathan W K[illegible]	Sergt	Sep 1[illegible] 186[illegible]	Killed Chickamauga	
Lafayette McCoy		Mar 7 1863	Murfr'sboro Tenn	Stone River Cemetery
William H Craig		Sep 20 1863	Killed Chickamauga	
Joseph Applegate	Corp	Oct 8 1862	Killed Perryv'e	Cp Nelson Ky
George W Welser		June 28 1863	Nashville Tenn	Sec E gr 437
Barr Alexander	Private	Oct 8 186[illegible]	Chattanooga Tenn	Chattanooga Tenn
Boyle John A		Oct 19 1863	Nashville Tenn	Sec 1 gr 116
Coulter James C		July 21 1863	Nashville Tenn	Nashville, Tenn
Houston Richard		Aug 16 1864	Atlanta Ga	Sec J gr 26
Huston Dickson	"			Marietta Ga
Lewis Benjamin B		Mar 21 1863	Murfr'sboro Tenn	Sec N gr 22 Stone R Cemry
McGinty, Michael		Oct 8 1862	Killed Perryv'e	Cp Nelson Ky
McLaren John		July 25 1864	Louisville Ky	Sec B Row 9 gr 71 C H Cem
Miller Albert		Oct 8 1862	Killed Perryv'e	Cp Nelson Ky
Morris Isaac	"	Sep 5 1864	Andersonv'e Ga	Andersonville Ga gr 7[illegible]
N[illegible]bach Henry		Oct 8 1862	Killed Perryv'e	Cp Nelson Ky
Price William B		Oct 29 1862	Louisville Ky	Cave Hill Cemry
Reep Reuben B		Aug 26 1863	Cowan Tenn	Stone R Cemry
Shingledecker John	"	Mar 3 1865	Poland O	Poland O
Smith Benjamin		Sep 18 1864	Andersonv'e Ga	Andersonville Ga
Stewart William W.		Aug 12 1863	University Tenn	
Thomas John B		Nov 19 1863	Munfordv'e Ky	Cave Hill Cemry
Webb John H		Oct 8 1862	Danville Ky	Sec 2 gr 20
Wetherstay Henry	"	Oct 18 1863	Chattanooga Tenn	Sec C gr 376
Williams Clytus		April 3 1863	Murfr'sboro Tenn	Stone R Cemry
Williams James	"	Oct 8 1862	Killed Perryv'e	Cp Nelson Ky

COMPANY B

NAME	RANK	DATE	WHERE	WHERE INTERRED
Ephraim Key	Capt	Jan 19 1863	Murfr'sboro Tenn	Greene O
Merrit Emerson	2d Lieut	June 13 1863	Murfr'sboro Tenn	Vienna O
Jonas E Wannemaker	1st Sergt	Oct 8 1862	Killed Perryv'e	Cp Nelson Ky
Edward S Palfreeman	Sergt	Jan 18 1863	Murfr'sboro Tenn	Sec N gr 16[illegible] Stone R Cemry
John A Ewalt	Corp	July 8 1863	Louisville Ky	Cave H Cemry
Hiram J Scott		Sep 25 1863	Chickamauga Ga	
Ballard Jonathan	Private	Oct 8 1862	Killed Perryv'e	Cp Nelson Ky
Burlingame Marcus		Nov 21 1862	Munfordv'e Ky	Louisville Ky C Hill Cem'ry
Caldwell Calvin		Sep 25 1863	Chickamauga Ga	
Crawford, James A		Feb 1 1865	Annapolis, Md	Annapolis Md
Dilley Herman		Jan 1[illegible] 1863	Gallatin Tenn	Nashville Tenn Sec P gr 34
Drennon John		Oct 8 1862	Killed Perryv'e	Cp Nelson Ky
Grim Albert		Oct 14 1862	Perryville Ky	Cp Nelson Ky
Hartman Joseph		Sep 14 1862	Louisville Ky	Sec A row 2 grave 14 Cave Hill Cemry
Hart Adelbert		Dec 11 1864	New York Har	Buried at sea
Heath Henry		July 9 1864	Nashville Tenn	Sec J gr [illegible]
Helsley John I		Oct 8 1862	Killed Perryv'e	Cp Nelson Ky
Hurst Henry		Dec 11 1862	Munfordv'e Ky	Louisville Ky Cave Hill Cemy
Kelly Hugh R		Sep 8 1864	Jonesboro Ga	Marietta Ga Sec G gr 3[illegible]

Table VI—Company B—Continued.

Name	Rank	Date	Where	Where Interred
Kennedy Benjamin F	Private	Oct 8, 1862	Killed, Perryv'e	Cp Nelson Ky
Perkins, Addison		Oct , 1862	Louisville, Ky	Cave H Cem'ry
Recker, Christopher F	"	Oct 8, 1862	Killed Perryv'e	Cp Nelson Ky.
Rush, Daniel		Mar 24, 1865	Goldsboro, N C.	Raleigh, N C Sec 4 grave 3
Ryan Jacob		Oct 8 1862	Killed Perryv'e	Cp Nelson Ky
Sage, James	"	Dec 21, 1862	Louisville, Ky	Sec B row 6 gr 19, Cave Hill Cemetery
Taft, Samuel K	"	Oct 14, 1862	Perryville, Ky	Cp Nelson, Ky
True, William C	"	Oct 8 1862	Killed Perryv'e,	Cp Nelson Ky
Walcott, Newton L	"	Dec 18, 1862	Munfordv'e, Ky	Louisville, Ky. Cave H Cem'y
Welsh William C	"	Feb 26, 1864	Danville, Va	Danville, Va gr

COMPANY C.

NAME	RANK	DATE	WHERE	WHERE INTERRED
Ambrose C. Mason	Capt	Aug 27, 1864	East Point, Ga	Chatta'ga, Tenn Sec G, gr B
Bartholomew Erastus	Private	June 18 1864	Andersonv'e Ga	Andersville, Ga grave 1995
Davis, William R	"	Oct 30, 1862	Perrville, Ky	Cp Nelson Ky Sec E, gr 117
Evans William	"	June 22, 1864	In field hosp	
Godshall, William H	"	Dec 2, 1862	Munfordv'e, Ky.	Louisvlle Ky Cave H Cem'y
Kelly, Lawrence ..	"	Aug 12, 1864	In field hosp	Marietta, Ga See J, grave 2
McLain, Richard H	"	June 6, 1864	In field hosp	Chatta'ga Tenn Sec C gr 375
Miller, Lemuel B	"	Feb 5 1863	Louisville, Ky	See B row 8 gr 18, Cave Hill Cemetery
Moser Lemuel	"	Dec 24, 1862	Gallatin, Tenn	Nashville, Tenn
Price Lemuel	"	Oct 4 1863	Nashville, Tenn	Sec E, grave 233
Shook, Cornelius	"	Jan 6, 1864	Cowan, Tenn	Murfs'bro Tenn Stone R Cem'y.
Stewart, Nelson O	"	May 29, 1863	Niles, O	Died at home
Vally, Adolphus	"	Aug 5, 1864	Killed Utoy Creek, Ga	Marietta, Ga
White, Andrew N.	"	Sep 19, 1863	Killed Chickamauga, G	

COMPANY D.

NAME	RANK	DATE	WHERE	WHERE INTERRED
Solomon D Williams	Sergt	Oct 28 1862	Perryville, Ky	Cp Nelson, Ky.
John C Britton	Corp	Nov 25, 1863	Killed Mission Ridge	Chatta'ga, Tenn Sec C, gr 290
Belden, Francis E	Private	June 16, 1864	Andersv'e Ga	Andersonville, Ga, gr 2065
Brooks, Eugene	"	Oct 8 1862	Killed Perryv'e	Cp Nelson Ky
Crandall, Charles	"	June 12 1863	Nashville Tenn	Nashv'e, Tenn
Gamer, Frederick R	"	Oct 8, 1862	Killed Perryv'e	Cp Nelson, Ky
Hall, Albert	"	Nov. 9, 1863	Chatta'ga Tenn.	Sec C, grave 289
Johnson William W	"	Oct 8, 1862	Killed Perryv'e	Cp Nelson, Ky
Kerr, Moses	"	"	"	Cp Nelson, Ky
Lamport, Benjamin G	"	Sep 22 1863	Chatta'ga Tenn	Sec C grave 288
Lewis, George E	"	Apr 4, 1863	Danville Ky	Andover, O
Martin, John	"	Nov 19 1862	Perryville Ky	Cp Nelson Ky.
Mayhew, Edwin H	"	Nov 28, 1862	BowlingGr'n, Ky	Nashv'e, Tenn, Sec N, gr 705
Nash, Ayer W	"	Apr. 9, 1863	Murfr'bro, Tenn	Sec E gr 448 Stone R Cem'y
Nash, Daniel P	"	Oct 8, 1862	Killed Perryv'e	Cp Nelson, Ky
Paine, Alvin B		Aug 20, 1864	Chatta'ga, Tenn	Sec C, grave 374
Palmer, Edwin	"	Dec 18, 1862	Bledsoe's Creek, Tenn	Concord, O
Price Walter	"	Aug , 1864	Perry, O	
Prouty Lucius A	"	Oct 12, 1862	Perryville, Ky	Cp Nelson, Ky
Ward, Elmer H	"	Mar 1, 1863	Murfrs'bro, Tenn	Sec D, grave 226 Stone R Cem'y

Table VI—Continued, Company E.

NAME	RANK	DATE	WHERE	WHERE INTERRED
[illegible] Albott Spaulding	Capt	Sep 2[illegible] 1863	Chatta'ga Tenn	Sec [illegible] grave 381
Charles C Hitchcock	Corp	Oct 8 1862	Killed Perryv'e	Burton O
Byron A Pease		A[illegible] 4 1864	Killed Near Atlanta Ga	Marietta Ga Sec J grave 25
A[illegible]rts Washington	Private	Mar 18 1863	Fort Donelson Tenn	
Alexander Festus		Feb 24 1863	Murfr'sboro Tenn	Sec I grave 180 Stone R Cem'y
Ayers Josiah		Oct 14 1862	Perryville Ky	Cp Nelson Ky
Ba[illegible] Wilford A		Dec 7 1863	Murfr'sboro Tenn	Stone R Cem'y
Beckwith James		Oct 9 1863	Louisville Ky	Sec A row 33 grave 2 Cave Hill Cemetry
Bond Joel D		Jan 8 1863	Gallatin Tenn	Nashville Tenn
Bowers David	"	Sep 19 1863	Killed Chickamauga Ga	
Bridgeman Anson O		Apr 8 1863	Murfr'sboro Tenn	Sec I grave 485 Stone R Cemry
Bridgeman Edward S		Jan 18 1863	Louisville Ky	Sec B row 2 grave 49 Cave Hill Cemetry
Dayton William		Oct 18 1864	Andersonville Ga	Andersonville Ga
Dixon Madison		Nov 22 1862	Gallatin Tenn	Nashville Tenn
Fisher Omer L	"	Mar 16 1863	Murfr'sboro Tenn	Sec G gr 382 Stone R Cem'y
Hale William H	"	Oct 8 1862	Killed Perryv'e	Hampden O
Johnson Austin		Sep 14 1863	Nashville Tenn	Sec E grave 838
Knox Dexter	"	Nov 28 1862	Louisville Ky.	Sec B row 3 grave 47 Cave Hill Cemetery
Osborn David	"	Oct 8, 1862	Killed Perryv'e	Cp Nelson Ky
Phillips George W		Dec 10 1862	Louisville, Ky	Cave H Cem'ry
Sanborn Homer L		Oct 6, 1862	Louisville Ky	Cave H Cem'ry
Sivernail Amos H		Oct 9 1862	Louisville Ky	Sec A row 34 grave 3 Cave Hill Cemetery
St John George		Oct 8 1862	Killed Perryv'e	Cp Nelson Ky
Strickland Walter		Apr 23 1865	Cp Dennison O	Grave 328
Tucker John F		Oct 13 1862	Antioch Ch, Ky	Cp Nelson Ky
Way Merrill		Mar 19 1864	Ringgold Ga	Chatta'ga Tenn Sec K gr 500
Whiting John Jr		Oct 8 1862	Killed Perryv'e	Cp Nelson Ky

COMPANY F.

NAME	RANK	DATE	WHERE	WHERE INTERRED
Leverett A Barnard	1st Lt	Feb 17 1864	Windsor O	
Harrison J [illegible]	Sergt	Oct 26 1862	Perryville Ky	
Edw'r R Mer[illegible]	Corp	Mar 1 1864	Parkman O	
Josiah K[illegible]	"	Oct 25, 1863	Atlanta Ga	Marietta Ga Sec A gr 169
Ja[illegible]s Ch[illegible]es	"	June 18 1864	Killed Kenesaw Mt	Marietta Ga
[illegible] Joseph	Private	Oct 8 1862	Killed Perryv'e	Cp Nelson Ky
B[illegible] Isaac		Unknow	Killed	See footnote
[illegible] Th[illegible]		Jan 21 1865	Savannah Ga	Savannah Ga
Barrass Robert B	"	Feb 20, 1864	Willoughby O	
Barnes James		J[illegible] 30 1864	Drowned while returning to the company	
[illegible]sey, Ge[illegible] W		Nov 2[illegible], 1862	M[illegible] Ky	Cave Hill Cem'ry Louisville Ky
Bott[illegible] T		Oct 8 1862	Killed Perryv'e	Cp Nelson Ky
Brewster Oliver R	"	Oct 18 1862	Perryville Ky	
[illegible] Clar[illegible] F	"	June 23 1864	Killed Kenesaw Mt	Sec H grave 8 Marietta, Ga
Ha[illegible]	"	A[illegible] 27 1864	Killed Atlanta	Marietta Ga
Hayer, Thomas I		Oct 8 1862	Killed Perryv'e	Cp Nelson Ky
Heston Emmett [illegible]	"			Cp Nelson, Ky
Mc[illegible] Chas W	"	"	Perryville, Ky	Cp Nelson Ky.

Table VI—Company F—Continued.

NAME	RANK	DATE	WHERE	WHERE INTFRRED
Martin, George .	Private	June 14, 1864	Andersonv'e, Ga	Grave 1930 Andersonville, Ga
Newcomb Selah W	"	Oct 31 1862	Perryville Ky	Cp Nelson Ky
Nye Ira	"	Oct 8, 1862	Killed Perryv'e	Montville O
Smith, Frederick	"	"	"	Cp Nelson Ky
Sober, Spencer	"	Feb 25, 1863	Murfr'sbro, Tenn	Sec 1, grave 125 Stone R Cem'y
Waller, Harrison	"	Dec 15, 1862	Perryville, Ky	

NOTE—Killed, by explosion of steamboat boiler, on Mississippi River while he was returning from Confederate prison

COMPANY G.

NAME.	RANK	DATE	WHERE	WHERE INTERRED
Henry Adams	2d Lieut	Feb 20 1863	Murfr'sbro, Tenn	
Joseph George	Sergt	Oct 8, 1862	Killed Perryv'e	Cp Nelson Ky
Luke Northway	Corp	May 8 1863	Murfr'sbro Tenn	Stone R Cem'ry
Benjamin F Hewitt	Wagon r	Feb 1863	Munfordv'e Ky	
Baldwin, Franklin	Private	May 14 1863	Nashville Tenn	Nashv'e Tenn
Benton Joel S	"	Jan 12, 1863	Munfordve, Ky	Louisville Ky Cave H Cem'y
Chapin, Stephen W	"	Apr 17 1863	Murfr'sbro, Tenn	Sec N, gr 508
Chapman Zephaniah	"	Apr 1, 1863	Murfr'sbro Tenn	
Christie James T		Apr 10, 1865	Goldsboro N C	Sec 4 gr 27
Compton John D	"	July 21, 1864	Peachtree C k Ga	Marrietta Ga Sec 1, gr 331
Cowles Zeri	"	June 19 1863	Murfr'sbro Tenn	Sec N, gr 136
Felch, Franklin	"	Nov 27, 1863	Chatta'ga Tenn	Sec C gr 378
Fuller George V	"	June 10, 1864	Nashville Tenn	Nashville, Tenn
Gant William H	"	Oct 29, 1862	Perryville, Ky	Cp Nelson Ky
Gould Daniel L	"	Oct 10 1862	Perryville Ky	Cp Nelson Ky
Jones, James L	"	Aug 9, 1864	Andersonv'e Ga	Grave 11942
Kenny, Snel	"	Dec 7, 1862	Glasgow, Ky	Tompkinsville, Ky
Leavitt Edwin R	"	Oct 8 1862	Killed Perryv'e	Cp Nelson Ky
Nichols, Hezekiah	"	Jan 2, 1863	Perryville, Ky.	Cp Nelson Ky
Parker Seth	"	Apr 21 1863	Murfr'sbro, Tenn	Stone R Cem'y
Phelps George K	"	Nov 22, 1862	Munfordv'e, Ky	Louisville, Ky Cave H Cem'y
Piper Delos S	"	Oct 8 1862	Killed Perryv'e	Cp, Nelson, Ky
Richardson George N	"	Sep 30, 1864	Atlanta, Ga	Marietta, Ga Sec G, gr 972
Shipman Wilson D	"	Oct 10, 1862	Louisville, Ky	Cave H Cem'y
Smith Jerome L	"	Oct 8 1862	Perryville, Ky	Cp Nelson Ky
Spaulding Asa B	"	"	Killed Perryv'e	Cp Nelson Ky.
Turney Albert A	"	June 7, 1863	Murfr'sbro, Tenn	Stone R Cem'y
Witerman Adna .	"	Oct 21, 1862	Perryville Ky	Cp Nelson, Ky
Whitmore, Chauncey .	"	May 1, 1864	Chatta'ga, Tenn	Sec C, grave 377

COMPANY H.

NAME	RANK	DATE	WHERE	WHERE INTERRED.
Robert Wilson .	Capt	Oct 8, 1862	Killed Perryv'e	Cp Nelson, Ky.
Armstrong Wm T	Private		"	Cp Nelson, Ky
Baker, William H	"	Nov 11, 1862	Bardstown, Ky	Lebanon, Ky
Boughton Horace	"	Oct 8 1862	Killed Perryv'e	Cp Nelson Ky
Dean, Benjamin	"	May 13, 1863	Murfr'sbro, Tenn	Stone R Cem'y.
Fishel, Eben B	"	May 1, 1863	Louisville, Ky	Sec B, row 11, grave 35, Cave Hill Cem'ry
Hartman Nathan	"	Oct 8, 1862	Killed Perryv'e	Cp Nelson Ky
Hunt Alfred	"	Aug 5, 1864	Killed Atlanta	Marietta, Ga
Ingling William D .	"	June 30 1863	Goshen O	.
Kirkbride Asher	"	Nov 27, 1863	Chatta'ga, Tenn	Chatta'ga, Tenn Sec C, gr 286.
McCurley John C		Jan 9, 1863	Nashville, Tenn	Nashville, Tenn
Naylor, William H	"	Oct 8, 1862	Perryville, Ky	Cp Nelson, Ky

Table VI Company H—Continued.

NAME	RANK	DATE	WHERE	WHERE INTERRED
Noble, Homer	Private	Jan [illegible] 186[illegible]	Murfr'sbro Tenn	Sec I gr 136, Stone R Cem'y
Owen [illegible] J	"	Feb 4 1864	Chatta'ga Tenn	Sec C gr 379
Raib Isaac [illegible] P	"	Dec 25, 186[illegible]	Chatta'ga Tenn	Sec C gr 287
Roahr Charles		Sep 1 1863	Nashville Tenn	Sec B gr [illegible]
R[illegible] Joseph		Sep 1, 1864	Killed at Jonesboro, Ga	Marietta, Ga Sec L gr 59
Sherman Albert A	"	Apr [illegible] 186[illegible]	Murfr'sbro Tenn	Sec G gr 379 Stone R Cem'y
Stratton [illegible]	"	Oct 8, 1862	Killed Perryville	Cp Nelson Ky
Umstead Daniel W	"	Mar 22 186[illegible]	Murfr'sbro Tenn	Stone R Cem'ry

COMPANY I.

NAME	RANK	DATE	WHERE	WHERE INTERRED
L. Dwight Kee	Capt	Oct 8 1862	Killed Perryville	Greene O
Harvey W Partridge	1st Sergt	Nov 11 186[illegible]	Chatta'ga Tenn	Sec C gr [illegible] Chatta'ga Tenn
Edwin A Whitcomb	Sergt	Sep 20 186[illegible]	Killed Chickamauga Ga	
Cyrus Cripple	Corp	Oct 28 1862	Louisville Ky	Cave H Cem'y
Ambrose [illegible] B[illegible]		Feb 18 186[illegible]	Nashville Tenn	Nashville Tenn
Frederick M Giddings		Apr 21 186[illegible]	Murfr'sbro Tenn	Sec M grave 25 Stone R Cem'y
Andrews Elmer H	Private	Nov 12 1862	Perryville Ky	Cp Nelson Ky
Butler, Lucius C		Oct 8 1862	Killed Perryville	Cp Nelson Ky
Collar Henry			"	Cp Nelson Ky
Cook John S				Cp Nelson Ky
Cox Seymour A			"	Cp Nelson Ky
Creighton William		Jan 7 1863	Perryville Ky	Cp Nelson Ky
Fobes Ferdinand P	"	Sep 3 1863	Murfr'sbro Tenn	Stone R Cem'y
Harrison Manuel J	"	Aug 3, 1864	Andersonville Ga	Andersonville Grave 4[illegible]
Knight Hiram T		Oct 22, 1863	Chatta'ga Tenn	Sec C gr 25 Chattanooga
Montgomery David R		Oct 8 1862	Killed Perryville	Cp Nelson Ky
Rowe Albert G		June 16 1864	Near Kenesaw Mt Ga	Grave 782 Marietta Ga
Sealy Esau A		Sept 1 1864	Near Atlanta Ga	"
Talcott Whitman B	"	Dec 18 1862	Perryville Ky	Cp Nelson Ga
Thomas, George	"	Apr 10 1863		Sec G grave 71 Stone R Cem'y
Thurbur Silas	"	Aug 8 1863	Nashville Tenn	Sec D grave [illegible] Nashville Tenn

COMPANY K.

NAME	RANK	DATE	WHERE	WHERE INTERRED
Claybourne, A Eddy	Sergt	May 15 186[illegible]	Philadelphia Pa	Philadelphia Pa
Howard, S Stephens	Corp	Oct 5 1864	Atlanta, Ga	Marietta Ga Sec G gr [illegible]
Julius C Cheney		Sep 17 1863	Nashville Tenn	Nashville Tenn
Orrin Arnold	"	Oct 19 1863	Stevenson, Ala	Chatta'ga Tenn
Atkins Levi	Private	Dec 2[illegible] 1862	Glasgow Ky	Glasgow Ky
Bates Charles [illegible]		Dec 15 1862	Louisville Ky	Cave H Cem'y
Bishop John H		Apr 17 1863	Murfr'sbro Tenn	Sec G grave [illegible] Stone R Cem'y
B[illegible] Charles H		Jan 12 1863	Gallatin Tenn	Nashville Tenn
Fobes Henry H		Oct 8 186[illegible]	Killed Perryville	Cp Nelson Ky
F[illegible], John		[illegible] [illegible] 1864	Killed S[illegible] of Atlanta	Marietta Ga Sec J gr [illegible]
Getty Frederick [illegible]		Oct 8 1862	Killed Perryville	Geneva O
H[illegible] William D		Nov 2[illegible] 1862	M[illegible]fordville Ky	Cave H Cem'y Louisville Ky
Howe [illegible] W[illegible]		O[illegible] 8 1862	Killed Perryville	Cp Nelson Ky
H[illegible] [illegible] David		Feb [illegible] 18[illegible]	W[illegible] O	
King G[illegible]	"	May [illegible] 1863	Murfr'sbro Tenn	Sec N gr [illegible] Stone R Cem'y
S[illegible] A [illegible]		O[illegible] 8 1862	Killed Perryville	Cp Nelson Ky
W[illegible] A [illegible]		[illegible] 17 18[illegible]	D[illegible] Ky	S[illegible] D[illegible]

TABLE VII.

Resigned and Discharged.

COMPANY A.

NAME	RANK	DATE	REMARKS
John D Jewell	Sergt		Discharged Pr 1st Lieut 27th Regt U S C T
Joseph Torrence	Corp	Jan 7, 1863	At Louisville, Ky, for disability, wound
John Clingensmith	Wagoner	Feb 2, 1863	Disability
Anderson, George S	Private	Mar 20, 1863	"
Conklin, George	"	May 14, 1863	Disability, from wound
Fair, Emanuel	"	Sep 30, 1864	Disability
Fielding, Charles	"	Sep 30, 1863	Disability, from wound
Flecker, John	"	Feb 8, 1863	Disability
Hanify, John J	"	Apr 17, 1863	"
Hunter, James	"	Jan 9, 1864	"
Jones, David D	"	Feb 28 1863	"
Morris, Thomas H	"	Oct 30, 1863	"
Nox, James P	"	Apr 8, 1863	"
O'Harra, James	"	Oct 28, 1862	"
Renn, John W	"	May 9, 1865	"
Rees, Richard		Jan 7, 1863	Disability, from wound
Robbins, Daniel	"	Apr 30, 1863	Disability
Stewart, Samuel M	"	Sep 10, 1863	"
Tyrrell, Thomas	"	Feb 20, 1863	Disability, from wound

COMPANY B.

NAME	RANK	DATE	REMARKS
Henry D Niles	2d Lieut	Feb 12, 1863	Res on account of ill health
James M Dickerman	Corp	Oct 14, 1862	Louisville, Ky, for disability
Michael E Hess	"	Feb 27, 1863	Gallatin, Tenn, for disability
George F Center	"	Oct 16, 1862	Louisville, Ky, for disability
Norval B Cobb	"	Oct 14, 1862	" "
Daniel Ludwick	"	Oct 4, 1862	Columbus, O, for disability
Henry E Finney	"	June 30, 1865	Cleveland, O, for disability
George W Granger	"	Sep 14, 1863	Louisville, Ky, for disability
Bell, Edward M	Private	Jan 24, 1865	Disability
Card, Joseph	"	Jan 31, 1863.	"
Center, Henry H	"	Oct 14, 1862	"
Davis, Marshall	"	Oct 8, 1862	Louisville, Ky, for disability
Downs, Jasper C		May 7, 1863,	Disability
Hathaway, James W	"	Mar 12, 1863	Columbus, O, for disability
Kinney, Edwin J	"	Oct 30 1862	Louisville, Ky, for disability
Kittridge, Isaiah S	"	Jan 6, 1863.	Gallatin, Tenn, for disabilty
Landon, John J		Nov 13, 1862	Columbus, O, for disability
Lewis, Edwin D	"	Jan 3, 1865	Disability, from wound
Mahannah, Harvey	"	Jan 15, 1863	Columbus, O for disability
Pruden, Stephen	"	Feb 18 1863	Disability
Sager, Edward W	"	Oct 8, 1862	Louisville Ky for disability
Stowe, Harmon W	"	Oct 8, 1862	"
Ulrich, Martin W	"	Mar 10, 1863	Columbus, O, for disability

COMPANY C.

NAME	RANK	DATE	REMARKS
Henry P Gilbert	Capt	Jan 17 1863	Resigned
James H Bard	1st Lieut	Mar 12, 1863	Resigned
Irvin Butler	2d Lieut	May 8, 1863	Res on account of ill health
Austin W Wilson	Sergt	Oct 24 1862	Louisville, Ky for disability
Robert J Stewart	Corp	Oct 22 1862	"

Table VII—Company C—Continued

NAME.	RANK.	DATE.	REMARKS.
James G Townsend	Corp	Mar 27, 1863	Columbus, O for disability.
Blackmore, Samuel	Private.	Oct 18 1862.	Louisville Ky for disability
Bolter James		Feb 24 1863	Gallatin Tenn for disability
Burgess John		Apr 3, 1863.	Murfreesboro, Tenn, disability
Davis, Morgan W		Oct 29 1862	Louisville Ky, for disability
[illegible] Benjamin	"	Oct 17 1864	Disability
Frazier Isaac		Feb 2 1863	Louisville Ky for disability
Frazier John H		Nov 28 1862	Columbus O, for disability
Fuller Harvey A		Oct 18 1862	Louisville Ky for disability
Hawley Joe		Nov 1, 1863	Chattanooga Tenn disability
H[illegible] Reuben F		Jan 11 1863	Columbus O, for disability
Jack William	"	Oct 15 1862	Louisville Ky, for disability
Jones Thomas		Jan 29 1863	Nashville, Tenn disability
Kingsley Jasper B		Nov 1 1862	Columbus O for disability
Lawrence Henry		Mar 11 1863	Murfreesboro Tenn disability
Moser Charles [illegible]	"	Nov [illegible] 1862.	Columbus O, for disability.
Moser Philip H		Feb 10 1863	Perryville Ky for disability
Phillips Joseph		Apr 8 1863	Murfreesboro Tenn disability
Powers John		Jan 29 1863	Louisville Ky for disability
Richards David T		Oct 1 1863	Nashville Tenn disability
Scov[illegible] Horace B		Oct 10 1862	Louisville Ky for disability
Smith Thomas		Feb 27, 1863	Gallatin Tenn, for disability
Stewart James A		Dec 29 1862	
Townsend Charles W		Jan 11 1863	Camp Dennison O disability

COMPANY D

NAME	RANK	DATE	REMARKS
George L Riker	Capt	Sep 23, 1864	Res on account of wound and ill health
Alonzo Chubb	2d Lieut	Oct 14 1863	
Edward P Young	Sergt	July 1 1864	Dis to accept promotion
C[illegible] A N[illegible]	Corp	Oct 11 1862	Louisville Ky for disability
Harvey L Clark	"	May 28 1863	Murfreesboro, Tenn, disability
George W [illegible]well		Sep 11 1863	Disability
Hendrick C Paine	Musician	Feb 26 1863	Gallatin Tenn disability
Michael Ward	Wagoner	June 26 1865	Camp Dennison O disability from wound
Allen Henry D	Private	Oct 21 1862	Louisville Ky, for disability
Allen Nathan W	"	May 12 1863	
Baker Edwin N		Jan 30 1863	Louisville Ky for disability from wound
Barker Frank M		Oct 21 1862	Louisville Ky for disability
Barnard Philo		Mar 29 186[illegible]	Dis by order of War Depart
Bently Murray J		Oct 21 1862	Louisville Ky for disability
Blakely, Harlow		Mar 10, 1864	Dis for disability from wound
Brooks Samuel		May 16 1865	"
Carpenter Thomas W		Mar 12, 1863	Columbus O for disability
Chesney Samuel P		Apr 23 1863	Dis for disability from wound
Dart William H	"	Oct 21 1862	Louisville, Ky, for disability
[illegible]ell Isaac		Oct 13 1862	
Gates Levi H	"	Oct 24 1862	" "
Hall Edwin	"	Oct 18 1862	"
Hickson, George	"	Jan 10 1863	Columbus, O for disability
McVitty, Joseph		Dec 26 1862	Dis for disability from wound
Nash, Harrison		Dec 2 1862	Louisville Ky for disability from wound
Pelton Watson	"	Dec 9 1862	"
Philbrook Charles H	"	Apr 6 1863	Columbus O for disability
Rockafellow Oscar H	"	Jan 6 1863	Gallatin Tenn, for disability
S[illegible]r Harvey C		Sep 2 1863	Louisville, Ky for disability
Spring Charles H		Mar 11 1864	Columbus O for disability, from wound
Turner Charles		Nov. 17 1862	Louisville Ky for disability
Tanner Harvey	"	Mar 29 1863	Disability
Upton William R	"	July 29, 1863	Nashville Tenn for disability.
Warren, Albert C		Oct 17 1862	Louisville, Ky, for disability

Table VII—Continued, Company E

NAME.	RANK	DATE	REMARKS
Byron W Canfield	Capt	Jan 29, 1863	Resigned
Patten, Himiou		May 5, 1863	"
William H Clark	1st Lieut	May 15, 1863	"
William H Castle	"	Jan 10, 1865	Dismissed
John A Osborn	2d Lieut	Jan 19, 1863	Res on account of ill health
Julius A Moffatt	"	Aug 13, 1863	"
John C Hathaway	1st Serg	Jan 11, 1863	Nashv'e, Tenn, for disability
La Royal Taylor		May 16, 1863	Murfr'sbro, Tenn, disability
Edward Patchin	Sergt	Dec 29, 1862	Cincinnati, O, disability from wound
Miles J Whitney	Corp	Mar 11, 1863	Dis to enlist in Mississippi Marine Brigade
Philo Boughton	"	Mar 27 1863	Cincinnati, O, for disability
Luman Griste	"	Feb 24, 1864	Dis for disability from wound
Button Justin	Private	Jan 29, 1863	Louisville, Ky, for disability
Case, Gideon		Jan 1, 1863	Dis to enlist in Mississippi Marine Brigade
Fowler, Justin	"	Oct 10, 1862	Louisville, Ky, for disability
Frazier Calvin		May 18, 1863	" "
Hathaway, Gilbert B		Oct 25 1862	" "
Hayden, Eugene		Jan 13, 1863	Dis to enlist in Mississippi Marine Brigade
Hilbert Percival		Mar 6 1865	Cleveland O for disability
Hitt Oliver		Dec 19, 1862	Louisville, Ky, for disability from wound
King, John Harvey	"	"	Louisville, Ky, for disability
Ladow, Henry	"	Mar. 2, 1863	Murfr'sbro, Tenn, disability.
Latimer, Olney P	"	Mar 7, 1865	Dis for disability from wound
Phillips, Robert.	"	Dec 29, 1862	Cincinnati, O, for disability
Pugsley John	"	Mar 2, 1863	Murfr'sbro, Tenn, disability
Slade, Sherman C	"	Sep 10, 1862	Louisville, Ky for disability
Stocking, Charles H	"	Jan 31, 1863	Cincinnati, O, for disability
Strong, Elmer	"	Feb 15, 1863	Perryville, Ky, disability
Turner, William		Apr 26, 1863	Quincy, Ill for disability
Watrous Samuel N	"	Jan 14 1863	Louisville, Ky, for disability
Webb, Ezra	"	Nov 24, 1862	" "

COMPANY F.

NAME	RANK.	DATE	REMARKS
Sherburn H Williams	Capt	Jan 13, 1863	Resigned
Lester D Burbank	2d Lieut	Feb 20, 1863	Res on acccount of ill health
Michael Cooney	Corp	Mar. 7, 1863	Disability,
George I Squeir	"	Oct 28, 1862	"
Daniel F Hopkins	Musician	Oct 27, 1862	"
Ara B Drake	Wagoner	Oct 20, 1862	Louisville, Ky, for disability
Auxer, Stephen D	Private	Mar 17, 1863	" "
Branch, Edward P	"	Dec 13, 1862	Disability
Brown, Arthur L	"	Oct 18, 1862	"
Button, Jared..	"	Oct 21, 1862	"
Colgrove, Melvin J	"	Oct 4, 1862	"
Cooley, Levi	"	Oct 28, 1862	"
Crawford, Emery.	"	Mar 18, 1865	"
Hausch, John	"	Jan 27, 1863	Gallatin, Tenn, for disability
Holmes, Hiram A ...	"	Oct 11, 1862	Disability
Kelsey, Arthur	"	Apr 20, 1863	Columbus, O, for disability
Keyes, Anson	"	Sep 26, 1862	Disability
McFlwain, Edwin W	"	Jan 31, 1863	"
Morton, Henry	"	Nov 30, 1863	Louisville, Ky, for disability.
Morse, John H.	"	July 20, 1863	" "
Parks, John	"	Oct. 8, 1862	Disability
Phelps, Franklin W	"	May 18, 1863	"
Phillips, Albert	"	Feb 3, 1863.	"
Prouty, Royal	"	June 29, 1863	"
Randall James G	"	May 24, 1865	Louisville, Ky, for disability.
Richmond, William.	"	Jan, 31, 1863	Disability.
Slayton, William T	"	Oct 8, 1862	"
Smith, Marsh, Jr	"	Oct 24, 1862	"

Table VII Company F Continued

NAME	RANK	DATE	REMARKS
[illegible] A [illegible]	Private	[illegible] 31 [illegible]	[illegible] Ky [illegible] disability
[illegible] H[illegible] M		Oct 28 1862	Disa[illegible]
[illegible]		Oct [illegible]	
[illegible] B[illegible]		Apr [illegible]	[illegible] O [illegible]
[illegible] W[illegible]		[illegible] 11 186[illegible]	
[illegible] B[illegible]		May 2[illegible] 18[illegible]	W[illegible]etts Point N Y Harbor

COMPANY G

NAME	RANK	DATE	REMARKS
W[illegible] Crowell	Capt	[illegible]	R[illegible]
A[illegible] W [illegible]	1st L[illegible]	Dec [illegible] 1863	Dis[illegible]
W[illegible] B [illegible]	Sergt	Nov [illegible] 62	
[illegible]		[illegible] 1864	
[illegible] P [illegible]		Sep [illegible] 1863	Dis[illegible]
[illegible] L M[illegible]	Corp	[illegible] 63	Nashv[illegible] T[illegible]
Norris [illegible]		[illegible]	[illegible] O for w[illegible]
[illegible]		Oct 3 1863	[illegible] Ky [illegible]
Daniel H H W[illegible]		Dec 1[illegible] 62	Lo[illegible] Ky [illegible]
Charles W B[illegible]		May 11, [illegible]	M[illegible]rfr[illegible] Te[illegible]
Anderson [illegible] W	Private	Apr 2[illegible]	[illegible] Ky [illegible]
[illegible], John W		Oct [illegible]	
[illegible] John [illegible]		M[illegible] 3 18[illegible]	C[illegible]
C[illegible]		Oct 21 62	L[illegible] Ky [illegible]
G[illegible] P		Oct 13 62	
G[illegible] Harley N		Sep 1[illegible] 1862	
H[illegible] Aaron		Apr 1[illegible] 1863	M[illegible] Ky [illegible]
He[illegible] Luther I		Apr 23 18[illegible]	C[illegible] O [illegible]
[illegible] D [illegible]		18[illegible]	[illegible] Ky [illegible]
McCleary H[illegible]		Apr 21 18[illegible]	C[illegible] O [illegible]
Merritt [illegible]		Apr 2[illegible]	
Newbo[illegible]		Oct 2[illegible] 1862	L[illegible] Ky [illegible]
Northway [illegible]rman		De[illegible] 2[illegible] 1862	
Noyes John P		Oct 2[illegible] 186[illegible]	
Parker W[illegible] H		May 2 18[illegible]	[illegible] O [illegible] War Department
Rogers W[illegible]		[illegible] 18[illegible]	Ga[illegible] Tenn [illegible]
Rowe Francis A	"	Oct [illegible]	Co[illegible] O [illegible]
Shepherd Horace		O[illegible] 2[illegible] 186[illegible]	L[illegible] Ky [illegible]
S[illegible] John S		[illegible] 7 [illegible]63	
Waterman William A	"	M[illegible] 13 18[illegible]	M[illegible]fr[illegible] Tenn [illegible]
Whipple Perry M		O[illegible]	Lou[illegible] Ky [illegible]

COMPANY H

NAME	RANK	DATE	REMARKS
Florent[illegible] M S[illegible]	S[illegible]	[illegible]	Lo[illegible] Ky f[illegible] w[illegible]ds
Horace G R[illegible]	Corp	Oct 2[illegible] 1862	Lo[illegible] Ky f[illegible] d[illegible]
Henry R M[illegible]		May [illegible] 1863	M[illegible]fr[illegible]sboro Tenn d[illegible]
[illegible]	W[illegible]	Feb 2[illegible] 1863	Nashv[illegible]e Tenn by order War Department
B[illegible] Thomas	Private	Sep 20 1863	Lo[illegible] Ky for disab[illegible]
Boy[illegible] George A		Oct [illegible], 1863	"
K[illegible]brid[illegible] Joseph		Oct 16 1862	" "
Mathe[illegible] James T		J[illegible] 12 [illegible]63	Gallatin Tenn, for disab[illegible]
M[illegible] Addison		Jan 23, 1863	Goshen O for wounds
Myers Jonathan		Jan 14, 1863	Louisville Ky, for wounds
Watson A[illegible]xander T		Sep 22 1863	Camp Dennison O disabil[illegible]
Yo[illegible] Ezra		Oct 2[illegible] 1862	Louisville Ky for disability

Table VII—Continued, Company I.

NAME	RANK	DATE	REMARKS.
Henry C Sweet	Capt	May 12, 1863	Dismissed Re-enlis d in Navy
Charles A Brigden	1st Lieut	Jan 21, 1863	Res on account of ill health
Collins E Bushnell	1st Serg	May 9 1863	Murfr'sboro Tenn disability
Albert H Smith	Serg	Nov 1, 1862	Louisville Ky for disability
Robert N Holcomb	Corp	Mar 5, 1862	Bardstown, Ky disability
Philip Reynolds		May 30, 1864	Dis for wound
William E Guild	Music'n	Mar 25, 1863	Murfr sboro Tenn, disability
Bridgman Thomas	Private	Jan 9 1863	Camp Dennison, O, disability.
Caldwell William S	"	Jan 27, 1863	Gallatin Tenn, for disability
Frisby, Augustus B	"	Feb 25 1863	Perryville, Ky, for wound
Haddock, John	"	Feb 20 1863	New Albany, Ind disability
Hame, William J		Nov 5, 1864	Pr U S C T Dis as 1st Lieut, Mar 2, 1865
Hake Samuel	"	Dec 28, 1863	Camp Dennison, O wound
Heath, Milo G	"	May 1 1863	Camp Dennison, O, disability
Holcomb Mark H	"	Oct 9, 1862	Louisville, Ky, for disability
Lattimer, Chauncey M		Oct 15 1862	" "
Leonard Horace A	"	Jan 6 1863	Murfr'sboro Tenn disability
Lyman, George W		July 15, 1863	Louisville, Ky for disability
Steele Calvin F	"	July 14 1864	Order Sec of War
Sperry, Henry H	"	July 20, 1863	Louisville, Ky, for disability
Tuttle, Harrison	"	Oct 15, 1862	" "
Webb Henry	"	Feb 9 1863	" wound
Wilcox Daniel E	"	Dec 30 1862	" disability
Windham, Robert	"	May 26, 1865	Cleveland, O, for disability

COMPANY K.

NAME	RANK	DATE	REMARKS
Edward V Bowers	Capt	Dec 22 1862	Resigned
Austin Adams	Sergt	Oct 14 1862	Louisville, Ky, disability
Charles H Harris		Nov 21 1863	Dis to accept promo ion
Alanson Gary	Corp	Oct 13 1862	Louisville, Ky disability
Alba B Martin	"	Nov 19, 1863	" "
Lewis Price	Musician	May 3, 1863	Murfr sboro, Tenn, disability
John Price	"	Oct 24 1862	Columbus, O, disability
Lewis H Roberts	Wagoner	Nov 10 1862	Louisville, Ky, disability
Amidon Edmund S	Private	Jan 17 1863	Gallatin Tenn, disability.
Barnard Francis N	"	Mar 27, 1863	Cincinnati, O, disability
Blakeslee, James L	"	Oct 9, 1862	Louisville, Ky, disability.
Bliss, Charles H	"	June 29, 1863	Nashville, Tenn, disability.
Brett Thomas	"	Jan 3, 1863	Columbus, O disability
Burlingame, Edwin R	"	Jan 14, 1863	Louisville, Ky, disability.
Cobb David G		Mar 29 1863	Cincinnati, O disability
Dutell, Julius	"	Jan 27, 1863	Gallatin Tenn, disability.
Early, Elbridge F	"	Apr 1, 1863	Columbus, O disability
Fales, Lewis C	"	Sep 14, 1863	Louisville, Ky, disability.
Ferguson Charles A		Dec 17 1862	Columbus, O, disability
Fowler, Ezra	"	Jan 13, 1863	Louisville, Ky, disability.
Gary David	"	May 26, 1865,	" "
Hanna Lyman P		Dec 2 1862	" "
Harback Ira	"	Oct 28 1862	" "
Hicock, Clay	"	Dec 28 1862	Gallatin Tenn, disability.
Hill, Clency E	"	Dec 13 1862	Louisville, Ky disability.
Humphrey, Marcus W	"	Sep 16, 1863	Nashville, Tenn, disability
Hutchinson Arthur G	"	May 30, 1863	Murfr'sboro, Tenn disability
Johnson George W	"	Mar 25 1863	Columbus O, disability
Olmstead Selden	"	Oct 16, 1862	Louisville Ky, disability
Powers William H	"	Oct 20 1862	" "
Rasey, Charles	"	Nov 19, 1862	" "
Rasey Chester	"	Feb 8, 1863	Murfr'sboro, Tenn disability
Shaw Henry	"	May 17 1863	" "
Smith Wilson W	"	Jan 27 1863	Gallatin Tenn disability
Williams Thales F		Nov 14, 1863	Chattanooga Tenn disability
Wright William W	"	Aug 12 1863	Cp Dennison O Order War Department

TABLE VIII.

Missing and Absent Without Leave.

COMPANY A.

NAME	RANK	REMARKS
Edmonds David	Private	See III
Hulburt Frank		See III
Sparrow, Emmons	"	See III "Missing"
Williams Richard		

COMPANY B.

NAME	RANK	REMARKS
Beebe Henry I	Private	See III
Phillips Dwight B		See III "Missing"

COMPANY C.

NAME	RANK	REMARKS
McKenzie James R	Private	See III
Mainwaring Morgan		
Richards, William J	"	
Robinson Thomas		See III

COMPANY D.

NAME	RANK	REMARKS
Edwin N Dunto	Corporal	
Alderman, Victor	Private	
Forges Melancthon L		
Hopkins Floyd		
Morrison John		
Pierce George I		See II "Missing"
Randall Walter		See II "Missing"
Raymond Alfred	"	

COMPANY E.

NAME	RANK	REMARKS
Webb Sylvester	Private	See II

COMPANY F.

NAME.	RANK	REMARKS.
Grater Franklin	Private	
Malone, Sydney D		
Marsh, Henry		See III "Missing"
Tanner, Henry H		

Table VIII—Continued, Company G.

NAME	RANK	REMARKS
Jerome B Hawkins	Musician	
Abbott, Solon M	Private	See III
Devoe, William P	"	See III

COMPANY H.

NAME	RANK	REMARKS
Hutton, Henry	Private	See III
Musser, Hazard	"	"Missing" Perryville Ky

COMPANY I.

NAME	RANK	REMARKS
Beckwith Ira W	Private	
Lyman, John W	"	
McIntyre John F		Sent to hospital. "Sick" Apr 10 1863
Merritt Milan H		

COMPANY K.

NAME	RANK	REMARKS
Hall, Frederick W	Private	
Laskey, Matthew		
Shepherd, Lorin	"	
Taylor, Francis A	"	

TABLE IX.

Previous Service.

NAME	RANK	WHERE	SERVED	REMARKS
[illegible]	Private	Co C [illegible] O V I	3 months	*
[illegible] Andrew D				*
[illegible]		Co F 14th O V I		*
[illegible]		Co D 14th O V I		*
do do	1st Lieut	Co A 24th O V I	[illegible] months	Dis [illegible] 13 '62
[illegible]	Private	Co D 7th O V I	3 months	*
[illegible] Alfred		Co I 14th O V I		*
Edwards Charles [illegible]		Co B 14th O V I		*
[illegible]	1st Lieut	Co G 24th O V I	7 months	Dis Ja[illegible] '62
[illegible] William H	Private	Co [illegible] th O V I	3 months	*
[illegible]		Co E 19th O V I		*
[illegible] John [illegible]	Musician	Band 7th O V I	12 mos	M O Spl Ord
Hawkins Jerome B	Private	Co C 14th O V I	3 months	*
[illegible] William H		Co I 14th O V I		*
[illegible]	Lieut Col	24th O V I	11 mos	Pr to 105th
[illegible]	Private	Co A 2d U S I	2 years	Pr to 105th
[illegible] Walter		3d U S A	[illegible] years	18[illegible] to 18[illegible]
[illegible]		Co D 14th O V I	3 months	*
[illegible] William H		P[illegible] Vols		
Kelsey Arthur		Co F 15th O V I	[illegible] months	Dis Ap[illegible] 20 '63
Lewis Evan		Co C 14th O V I	3 months	*
[illegible]		Co H 7th O V I		*
[illegible]		Co B 14th O V I		*
Merritt [illegible]		Co C 19th O V I		*
[illegible] Edward S		Co C 14th O V I		*
Patchin Edward	Corporal	Co F 19th O V I		*
Perkins Andrew	Private	Co I 14th O V I		*
Price John	Musician	Band 29th O V I	11 mos	M O Spl Ord
Price Lewis	Musician	Band 29th O V I	11 mos	M O Spl Ord
Perkins George [illegible]	2d Lieut	Co B 19th O V I	3 months	*
Rawdon Calvin	Private	1st Pa Vols	2 years	Mexican War
Robbins Ambrose M		Co B 19th O V I	2[illegible] months	Dis July 5 '62
[illegible] Richard J		Co B 19th O V I	3 months	*
[illegible] Daniel B		Co B 14th O V I		*
[illegible] Lafayette		Co C 14th O V I		*
Sweet Henry C		2d Ohio Ind Art'y	12 mos	Dis July [illegible] '62
Sweet Jesse M		Co I 19th O V I	3 months	*
[illegible] Jacob		Co C 14th O V I		*
Thompson Wilb[illegible]		Co D 14th O V I		*
T[illegible]		Co I 14th O V I		*
[illegible] John	Hos Std	17th O V I		*
[illegible] Alton W	Sergeant	Co I 27th N Y I	[illegible] months	Dis for wound Aug 26 18[illegible]
Tolles William R	Captain	Co B 41st O V I	1 year	Pr Lt Col 10[illegible]
Wakelee Oscar K	Private	Co D 7th O V I	3 months	*
Whitney Miles [illegible]		Co I 19th O V I		*
Williams John S		Co H 7th O V I	2[illegible] months	Discharged
do do		Co H 7th O V I	11 mos	Dis O W D[illegible]
Watson Porter		Co I 7th O V I		

* Mustered out with Regiment

TABLE X.

Color Guard---Imperfect.

105th Color Sergeant and Guards.

JOHN GEDDES, Sergeant, Company C.
JOHN B. RAMSDELL, Corporal, Company B.
CHARLES. B. HAYES, Corporal, Company I.
EVAN RICHARDS, Corporal, Company E.
JOHN E. WATROUS, Corporal, Company K.

TABLE XI.

Summary and Recapitulation of the 105th Ohio Volunteer Infantry.

	Original Muster			Recruits							Table VI								
	Commissioned	Enlisted	Total	Commissioned	Enlisted	Aggregate	Table II	Table III	Table IV	Table V	Killed	Died of Wounds	Died of Disease	Died Prisoners	Drowned	Aggregate	Table VII	Table VIII	Mus'd out with Regt
	9		9	2		11	2	1					2			2	5		4
Co A	3	96	99		25	124	31	22	33	3	7	3	14	2		26	19	4	[illegible]
Co B	3	97	100		11	111	19	17	17	2	8	6	14	1		29	23	2	[illegible]
Co C	3	98	101		9	110	21	17	16	3	2	3	8	1		14	26	4	[illegible]
Co D	3	98	101		6	107	20	10	16	7	6	1	9	1		20	31	8	[illegible]
Co E	3	98	101		2	103	20	15	8	5	7	4	15	1		27	31	1	31
Co F	3	97	100		15	115	27	20	23	2	9	7	4	2	2	24	34	4	[illegible]
Co G	3	98	101	1	9	111	27	15	17	3	4	7	17	1		29	31	3	[illegible]
Co H	3	98	101		4	105	19	25	11	2	7	4	9			20	12	2	[illegible]
Co I	3	98	101		1	102	35	19	13	7	7	8	5	1		21	24	4	33
Co K	3	95	98		2	100	16	16	9	4	5	4	8			17	36	4	40
	30	973	1012	3	84	1099	258	177	163	38	62	50	105	10	2	229	378	36	355

Original enlistment		1012	Transferred	163
Recruits....		87	Absent sick, etc	38
		1099	Killed and died	229
			Resign'd and Dis'd	278
Wounded	258		Missing	36
Captured	177		Must'd out with Rgt 355 { Original 352; Recruits 3 }	355
				1099

CPSIA information can be obtained
at www.ICGtesting.com
Printed in the USA
LVHW051421300623
751257LV00015B/186